Unemployment, Hysteresis and the Natural Rate Hypothesis

To My Mother; and Titch

The assistance of Juliet Shaughnessy, Serena Yeoward, Antoni Chawluk and Mo Malek is gratefully acknowledged.

Unemployment, Hysteresis and the Natural Rate Hypothesis

Edited by

ROD CROSS

Basil Blackwell

British Library Cataloguing in Publication Data
Unemployment, hysteresis and the natural rate hypothesis : proceedings of a conference held at the University of St. Andrews, Scotland, July 1986.
1. Unemployment
I. Cross, Rod
331.13'7   HD5707.5

ISBN 0–631–15688–7

Library of Congress Cataloging in Publication Data
Unemployment, hysteresis, and the natural rate hypothesis.

Bibliography: p.
Includes index.
1. Unemployment.   2. Unemployment History.   3. Employment (Economic Theory) I.   Cross, Rod.   II. Chawluk, A.   II. Malek, M. III. Title.
HD5707.5.U555 1987   331.13'7   87–14071
ISBN 0–631–15688–7

Typeset in 10 on 11½ pt Times
by Qualitext Typesetting, Abingdon
Printed in Great Britain by TJ Press Ltd Padstow

Contents

IV ANALYSIS OF HYSTERESIS EFFECTS

V HYSTERESIS EFFECTS AND THE EXPLANATION OF AGGREGATE UNEMPLOYMENT

VI PANEL DISCUSSION: THE IMPLICATIONS OF HYSTERESIS EFFECTS FOR UNEMPLOYMENT POLICY

Contents

Foreword

Hysteresis and Unemployment

JOHN FLEMMING

The view that the natural rate of unemployment is a known constant has never been tenable and has probably never been entertained.

If it is not a constant, on what does it depend? The original formulation laid stress on three sets of factors: technology, social institutions and the type of shock to which the economy is subject. The chapters in this book address the role of a fourth factor – the history of unemployment itself.

Past unemployment might enter the process in two different ways; its effects might be either temporary or permanent. Despite the attempts of the editor to clarify this issue I am not sure whether a temporary effect as well as a permanent effect qualifies as hysteresis.

My own position is that I find it useful to think in terms of an underlying natural rate dependent only on the traditional determinants while allowing considerable scope for the critical level of unemployment which divides regions in which inflation tends respectively to accelerate and decelerate to be influenced by the history of unemployment.

This view precludes two cases which have been advanced: it is inconsistent with the suggestion that the natural rate of unemployment (or more plausibly the logistic transform $\ln[u/(1-u)]$) follows a random walk (unless its basic determinants do – which is unlikely). It is also, and relatedly, inconsistent with the view that unemployment, or its natural rate, is essentially indeterminate.

It is, however, quite consistent with either, or both, of the views advanced in this book: namely that the speed with which unemployment might tend to revert to the natural rate is a function of its distance from it – in particular an inverse function (which makes recessions lengthy if they occur).

Similarly it is consistent with the view that there is a limit to the rate at which unemployment can be reduced without accelerating inflation even if unemployment is initially above both the underlying natural and momentarily critical rates.

The ways in which the history of unemployment affect the natural rate are fairly well established.

1 The possibility that the duration of a person's unemployment affects an individual's effectiveness in acting as a restraint on the wage increases granted to those who remain in employment. Thus the duration composition of the stock of unemployed is relevant as well as its size. Given systematic relationships between duration and relative re-employment probabilities the duration composition can be represented by the history of unemployment.
2 The possibility that those in employment are concerned largely with the probability distribution of the growth rate of employment from the current (historically given) level (though employers may be concerned also about the number of applicants they get for a vacancy which in turn depends on the level of unemployment).
3 The probability that a higher level of unemployment is associated with a lower level of capital formation and a lower rate of growth of the warranted real wage. It may take additional man-years of unemployment to bring expected real wages back into line.

Of these I have made greatest use of the third, though in slightly different terms. It has often been suggested that a productivity growth term belongs in the Phillips curve – typically seen as representing the employees' demand for their share of a growing cake. An alternative view is that expected productivity growth belongs there for the same reason that expected inflation does. Namely that a change in the (perfectly anticipated) rate of productivity growth (e.g. Harrod-neutral technical progress) should no more affect the (quasi-) equilibrium rate of unemployment than should a change in the (perfectly anticipated) rate of inflation.

In the absence of the expected productivity (or expected real wage) term real wages can only be raised without falsifying inflation expectations by having unemployment below the 'natural rate' to the appropriate extent. In this case the equilibrium rate of unemployment varies inversely with the rate of productivity growth and productivity growth should be related to capital deepening, which is likely to vary with changes in the level of unemployment.

Thus the exact role of the history of unemployment may depend on the specification of the Phillips curve and particularly the extent to which other variables are included which might capture the divergence between actual and expected underlying productivity change.

These are all important issues which are illuminated by the contributions to this book.

Preface

This volume contains the papers presented at a conference held at the University of St Andrews, Scotland in July 1986. The idea of organizing a conference grew out of a research project undertaken with Mo Malek, who jointly organized the conference along with my other colleagues, Andrew Allan, Antoni Chawluk and Harold Hutchinson. The secretarial work relating to the conference was done most efficiently by Joan Reed, Helen Bremner, Gladys MacArthur and Mary Rodger. That the conference ran smoothly was due to exertions beyond duty of the conference assistants, Juliet Shaughnessy, Serena Yeoward and John Rendall.

The conference was financed by the Employment Market Research Unit of the Department of Employment; the Economic and Social Research Council; Shell International; the May Wong Smith Trust; the Department of Economics, and the Research Fund of the Faculties of Arts and Divinity, University of St Andrews. Without the good offices of the above organizations the conference would not have been possible.

Ultimately it is the contributions of the participants which make or break a conference. Here the occasion was made special by the participants, many of whom arrived in the middle of hectic schedules from far flung places, who not only contributed papers of high quality but also worked hard to produce an atmosphere of creative discussion. If the conference did something to clarify the nature of the problem of unemployment, this was down to the participants: it would be invidious to single out individuals. Amongst those who were not able to be present at the conference, Charles Feinstein, Richard Layard and Romesh Vaitilingam of Basil Blackwell deserve special thanks for their efforts in helping to set up the conference programme, and in seeing this conference volume to press.

Acknowledgements

I am most grateful to the following publishers for their kind cooperation in allowing the following papers to be reprinted in this volume:

North-Holland Publishing Company for Assar Lindbeck and Dennis J. Snower, 'Union activity, unemployment persistence and wage-employment ratchets', *European Economic Review* (1987);

The Society for Economic Analysis Limited for Kim B. Clark and Lawrence H. Summers, 'Labour force participation: Timing and persistence', *Review of Economic Studies*, XLIX (1982), pp. 825–44;

Oxford University Press for H. Dixon, 'A simple model of imperfect competition with Walrasian features', *Oxford Economic Papers* (1987);

The Institute of Economics and Statistics, University of Oxford for Stephen Nickell, 'Why is wage inflation in Britain so high?', *Oxford Bulletin of Economics and Statistics*, 49(1) (1987), pp. 103–28;

MIT Press and the National Bureau of Economic Research for Olivier J Blanchard and Lawrence H. Summers, 'Hysteresis and the European unemployment problem', in S. Fischer (ed.), *National Bureau of Economic Research Macroeconomics Annual* (1986).

The Contributors

Charles Adams	International Monetary Fund
Andrew Allan	University of St Andrews
Oliver J. Blanchard	Massachusetts Institute of Technology
Alan Budd	Centre for Economic Forecasting, London Business School
Alan A. Carruth	University of Kent
Kim B. Clark	Harvard University
David T. Coe	OECD
Stephen W. Creigh	Department of Employment
Rod Cross	University of St Andrews
Huw Dixon	Birkbeck College, London
John Flemming	Bank of England
Peter R. Hughes	Department of Employment
Gillian Hutchinson	Queen Mary College, London
Harold Hutchinson	University of St Andrews
Tim J. Jenkinson	Merton College, Oxford
Paul Levine	Centre for Economic Forecasting, London Business School
Assar Lindbeck	Institute for International Studies, University of Stockholm
Peter G. McGregor	Fraser of Allander Institute, University of Strathclyde
Marcus H. Miller	University of Warwick
Stephen Nickell	University of Oxford
Andrew J. Oswald	Centre for Labour Economics, London School of Economics
Simon Price	University of Bristol
Peter Smith	Centre for Economic Forecasting, London Business School
Dennis J. Snower	Birkbeck College, London

Contributors

David Stanton   Employment Market Research Unit,
                                   Department of Employment
Lawrence H. Summers   Harvard University
Inge Tötsch   University of Bonn and London School
                                   of Economics

Part I
Introduction

1
Hysteresis Effects and Unemployment: An Outline

ROD CROSS and HAROLD HUTCHINSON

Hysteresis effects on unemployment are 'those which come after' the removal or reversal of the impulses which initially give rise to a change in unemployment: the implication is that once the impulses disappear unemployment will tend to persist in the form acquired during the operation of the impulses. This can be interpreted as implying that shocks to the actual rate of unemployment are propagated in the form of sympathetic changes in the equilibrium rate of unemployment; or, more generally, that the states of rest of economic systems are characterized by unemployment equilibria which, if they exist, depend on the history of the shocks to actual employment.

Joseph Schumpeter's conception of economic 'dynamics' or change attached great significance to such hysteresis effects:

> economic life changes . . . partly because of changes in the data, to which it tends to adapt itself . . . but . . . there is another . . . [source of] . . . change . . . which arises from within the system, and this kind of change is the cause of so many important phenomena that it seems worthwhile to build a theory for it . . . [this] kind of change . . . so displaces its equilibrium point that the new one cannot be reached from the old one by infinitesimal steps. (Schumpeter, 1934, p. 64)

Mainstream, neoclassical theory, however, excluded such effects. Paul Samuelson recalls his 1932–7 days as a classical theorist thus:

> as an equilibrium theorist [I] naturally tended to think of models in which things settle down to a unique position independently of initial conditions . . . technically speaking, we theorists hoped not to introduce hysteresis phenomena into our model, as the Bible does when it says 'we pass this way only once' and, in so saying, takes the subject out of the realm of science into the realm of genuine history . . . in our more realistic moods,

we tacitly used models involving hysteresis: Spain would never be the
same after Colombus: Scarlett O'Hara would be permanently affected by
the Confederate inflation, just as Hugo Stinnes was by the 1920–23
German inflation . . . obviously, in such models all real variables do not
end up unchanged as a result of certain unbalanced introductions of new
M into the system. (Samuelson, 1972, pp. 540–1)

The subsequent evolution of mainstream, neoclassical theory has
tended to exclude hysteresis effects, at least at the formal level of
analysis. The influential manifestation of this exclusion of hysteresis in
the context of the theory of unemployment is to be found in Milton
Friedman's ahysteretic concept of the natural rate of unemployment:

the 'natural rate of unemployment', is the level that would be ground out
by the Walrasian system of general equilibrium equations, provided there
is imbedded in them the actual structural characteristics of the labour and
commodity markets, including market imperfections, stochastic variability in demands and supplies, the cost of gathering information about job
vacancies and labour availabilities, the costs of mobility, and so on.
(Friedman, 1968, p. 8)

In the various alternatives to mainstream, neoclassical theory there
are, of course, certain theoretical systems where initial conditions affect
real variables outside of full equilibrium. In the disequilibrium trading,
or 'reconstituted reductionist', account of Keynesian economics, for
example, temporary equilibria depend on initial stocks, the state of
expectations and so on. Such theoretical systems, however, tend to
retain the concept of a full equilibrium in which hysteresis effects are
absent:

. . . the prevailing view is also that, if exogenous conditions remained
invariable for a long period, prices would progressively shift in such a way
that equality between supply and demand would eventually be achieved
. . . in other words, the Walrasian equilibrium is appropriate for long-run
economic analysis, because in the long run prices are actually flexible and
play the role that was traditionally given to them. (Malinvaud, 1977,
p. 34)

This Keynesian approach

. . . addresses itself not to the state of equilibrium but to the problem of
attaining equilibrium . . . [involving] . . . a construction in which prices
adjust less than instantaneously to economic circumstances, so that at any
point in time the prices may be effectively providing incentives to act, but
the information they reflect will not be appropriate for the equilibrium
that is being approached. (Coddington, 1983, p. 110)

Thus the focus of attention is on how coordination failures may arise from the actual system of prices rather than on how the full equilibrium would be affected by the path of adjustment to equilibrium, as hysteresis would imply.

In a sense, the introduction of hysteresis effects into economic analysis offers a means of resolving some of the incongruities that exist between neoclassical and Keynesian theories: the neoclassical concept of general equilibrium can possibly be retained, though in the form of a continuum of equilibria in which neutrality does not hold; and the Keynesian property of non-neutrality can be retained, though without the property of failure or extreme sluggishness in convergence to equilibrium. The contributions to this volume could be seen as investigating the insights that can be gained from applying the more footloose notion of equilibrium which arises when hysteresis effects are present to the explanation of unemployment.

The fact that the chapters in this volume focus on unemployment rather than on the myriad other economic phenomena to which hysteresis effects are as equally relevant (or irrelevant) requires little explanation. Theories of unemployment of a classical or Keynesian persuasion can explain some of the dramatic increase in unemployment experienced in most Organisation for Economic Cooperation and Development (OECD) countries since the mid 1960s or early 1970s by invoking changes in the supply- and demand-side variables to which their heuristics draw attention (see Bean et al., 1986 for an impressive array of such studies). The theories in question, however, tend to fail to explain why unemployment has remained high into the late 1980s in the face of reversals, or abatements, in the changes in the explanatory variables invoked.

In terms of formal time-series analysis, it has been pointed out that it is difficult to reject the hypothesis that time series for unemployment follow a random walk (see chapters 15 and 16 for evidence – though see also the somewhat contrasting evidence in Nelson and Plosser, 1982). A random walk, such as $U_t = U_{t-1} + E_t$ where U is unemployment and E is a zero-mean white noise process, is an example of a non-stationary process which can be made stationary, so implying the existence of linear properties such as a mean and variance which are invariant over time, only by the application of a time-invariant filter (see Hendry, 1986 for a discussion of this and the related topic of cointegrated variables). Without the application of such a filter, time series which follow a random walk will wander widely: the time expected for the process to return to any given value is in fact infinite. The autocorrelation between the value of the variable at time t and that at $t-1$ is approximately unity for a random walk, implying that a given disturbance to the process will affect all future values, and that the random walk has an indefinitely long memory. Given the nature of statistical inference, however, it will usually not be possible to reject alternative hypotheses, such as that the autocorrelation coefficient is 0.9, in which case the properties of the process will be substantially different.

If it is accepted, as a 'stylized fact', that time series for unemployment do follow a random walk, the challenge for theories of unemployment is to provide a coherent explanation of this phenomenon: at least one hysteresis-based theory (see chapter 15, in the case where insiders immediately lose insider status when they lose their jobs) displays this ability. On the other hand it is worth stressing that a random walk, as an explanandum, should not be conflated with hysteresis, when invoked as part of an explanans: if hysteresis effects are conjoined with other sets of auxiliary hypotheses, random walks are not necessarily implied (for example in chapter 15 this is the case when insiders retain insider status for some time after losing their jobs).

The chapters in this volume fall, without too much forcing, into four parts. The chapters in part II were given as informal pre-dinner addresses. Chapter 2 assesses the plausibility of the received concept of the natural rate of unemployment. Chapter 3 looks at the history of the hysteresis concept since the term was coined by the physicist James Alfred Ewing in 1881.

Part III deals with the individual characteristics of the unemployed. Chapter 4 analyses the way changes in the proportion of long-term unemployed in the labour force affect the unemployment–vacancies relationship. Chapter 5 reviews the UK data sources and summarizes the information which can be gleaned from the UK Labour Force Survey. Chapter 6 assesses the implications of data on inflows and outflows for the unemployed.

Part IV deals with models of markets with hysteresis effects present. Chapter 7 outlines an insider–outsider model of labour markets. Chapter 8 analyses the implications of imperfectly competitive goods markets and union behaviour. Chapter 9 considers the effects of allowing worker effort or quality to vary with unemployment and wages. Chapter 10 analyses the implications of employers using the length of spell of unemployment as a screening device when hiring workers.

The contributions to part V deal with the explanation of aggregate unemployment. Chapter 11 reprints the seminal contribution of Kim Clark and Lawrence Summers to the empirical study of hysteresis effects in labour markets, testing the 'timing' explanation of labour force participation against the hysteresis alternative. Chapter 12 tests for the existence of multiple natural rates of unemployment in Britain. Chapter 13 puts forward an explanation as to why wage inflation has not fallen more rapidly in the face of the unprecendeted levels of unemployment in Britain. Chapter 14 tests for the existence of hysteresis effects in wage equations for OECD countries. Olivier Blanchard and Lawrence Summers in chapter 15 put forward a hysteresis explanation for the persistence of high unemployment in European countries, and check the ability of their model to explain the contrasting US experience, and the experience of earlier epochs. Chapter 16 employs the econometric concepts of encompassing and cointegration to critically appraise empirical work which suggests that the natural rate of unemployment is independent of demand factors. Stephen Nickell in chapter 17 responds to this critical evaluation of his work with Richard Layard.

Finally, part VI contains reflections on the implications of hysteresis effects for unemployment policy. Olivier Blanchard chaired the panel discussion sessions at the conference. The appointed panel discussants, David Stanton, Charles Adams, Marcus Miller and Peter McGregor, in chapters 18 to 21, consider the plausibility of the different approaches to incorporating hysteresis into the analysis of unemployment, and elucidate the policy implications which might be drawn.

REFERENCES

Bean, C., Layard, R. and Nickell, S. (eds) 1986: Unemployment: Proceedings of the Chelwood Gate Conference. *Economica*, supplement, 53, 210(s).

Coddington, A. 1983: *Keynesian Economics: The Search for First Principles*. London: Allen and Unwin.

Friedman, M. 1968: The role of monetary policy. *American Economic Review*, 58 (1), March, 1–17.

Hendry, D. F. (ed.) 1986: Econometric modelling with cointegrated variables. *Oxford Bulletin of Economics and Statistics*, Special Issue, 48 (3), August, 201–307.

Malinvaud, E. 1977: *The Theory of Unemployment Reconsidered*. Oxford: Blackwell.

Nelson, C. R. and Plosser, C. 1982: Trends and random walks in macroeconomic time series. *Journal of Monetary Economics*, 10, 139–62.

Samuelson, P. A. 1972: *The Collected Scientific Papers of Paul A. Samuelson*, Vol. III. Cambridge, MA: MIT Press.

Schumpeter, J. A. 1934: *The Theory of Economic Development*. Harvard: Harvard University Press.

Part II

Part II

Reflections on Hysteresis and the Natural Rate Hypothesis

2
Should Keynesian Economics Dispense with the Phillips Curve?

LAWRENCE H. SUMMERS

My title should surprise the reader. That is certainly its intent.[1] The presence of some sort of Phillips curve describing a process of sluggish price adjustment is often regarded as a defining characteristic of Keynesian models. Leading Keynesian macroeconomics textbooks all assign a central role to wage and price rigidity and to 'natural rate' Phillips curves describing the adjustment of wages and prices. On both sides of the Atlantic, discussions of macroeconomic policy tend to assign a prime role to the concept of the NAIRU (non-accelerating inflation rate of unemployment), the controversial issue being its level. Keynesian economists in the United States point to the stability of the Phillips curve in recent years as decisive evidence upholding their position and refuting the views of New Classical economists. In Britain, Keynesians dolefully track the NAIRU as it continues its upward march into double digits, while remaining resolute in their devotion to the Keynesian paradigm.

Nonetheless, in these remarks I shall try to make the case that models containing standard Phillips curves depicting the sluggish adjustment of prices are fatally flawed as depictions of Keynes' vision of the economy or of reality. More fundamentally, I will argue that the premise common to both Keynesian and Classical macroeconomic models, that a downward sloping aggregate demand schedule and an upward sloping aggregate supply schedule intersect to determine uniquely the level of output and prices, is untenable. Instead, I believe that models allowing for hysteresis effects – models in which equilibria are fragile and history dependent – offer the best prospect for redeeming the promise of Keynesian macroeconomics.

I believe that accounting for hysteresis effects will require revolutionary and not merely evolutionary changes in the way Keynesian (and

Classical) macroeconomists view the world. If this judgment is correct, there is nothing to be gained from my pretending that only minor modifications in textbook treatments are necessary, or that the points made here are already widely appreciated. On the other hand, if my judgments are wrong, there is little cost to my stating them in as vivid and bold a way as I can. These remarks, therefore, highlight the flaws in conventional models and the promise of new approaches, but do not provide balance by stressing the scientific successes that have led sticky price models to become enshrined in textbooks.

Before proceeding further I want to stress a set of considerations that greatly reinforces my convictions. Even its friends must acknowledge that the textbook Keynesian view of aggregate supply possesses many of the attributes that Thomas Kuhn ascribed to dying scientific paradigms: two aspects stand out – its proponents maintain a wholly defensive posture, and the paradigm is subject to regular and substantial amendment. I comment on these two points in turn.

Empirical work within successful scientific paradigms is outward looking. It articulates the paradigm by resolving anomalies, or by demonstrating the paradigm's application to new phenomena. Keynesian empirical work on issues relating to wages and prices is usually inward if not backward looking. Many studies have been directed at defending the fundamental premise that wages and prices are rigid; at demonstrating the continuing validity of an equation estimated several years earlier; or, as often as not, at finding out why an equation estimated several years earlier went off track. While words like menu costs, and overlapping contracts are often heard, little if any empirical work has demonstrated connection between the extent of these phenomena and the pattern of cyclical fluctuations. It is difficult to think of any anomalies that Keynesian research in the 'nominal rigidities' tradition has resolved, or of any new phenomena that it has rendered comprehensible.

More striking evidence of the barrenness of contemporary Keynesian thought comes from statesmanlike overviews of the state of the science. It is difficult to find an overview of the Keynesian tradition that is constructive in charting past triumphs and pointing towards future challenges. Rather, prominent Keynesian evaluations of the state of the field are destructive – being comprised primarily of attacks on the doctrines of the New Classical or Monetarist schools. I think of the major lectures delivered by James Tobin, Franco Modigliani and Robert Solow or of Alan Blinder's recent evaluation of Keynes' contributions. Similar overviews by economists of the New Classical school, notably by Robert Lucas and Thomas Sargent, have a much more constructive and confident tone. This does not guarantee that New Classical economists are right, and indeed they are not. But Keynesian economics should aspire to more than Churchill's defence of democracy as the best of bad alternatives.

Frequent ad hoc adjustments to account for embarrassing realities were a hallmark of Ptolemaic astronomy. It is sad but true that the half life of various Keynesian views about the aggregate supply curve has been little more than a decade. Keynes, in the *General Theory*, proposed that the aggregate supply curve drawn in unemployment-price space was L-shaped. This view was falsified by the coincidence of inflation and less than full employment in the late 1940s and 1950s. By the early 1960s, a derivative was slipped and Keynes' view had given way to the Phillips curve vision of a stable downward sloping relationship between unemployment and the rate of inflation. This view remained popular for not much more than a decade. The stagflation of the 1970s led to the slipping of another derivative and the widespread acceptance of the view that there existed a natural rate of unemployment, which was the only rate at which inflation could remain stable. On this 'expectations augmented' Phillips curve view, there is a trade-off not between current inflation and current unemployment but between permanent inflation and current unemployment.

A decade has now passed since the natural rate hypothesis came to be widely accepted. In what follows, I will argue that it is again time for a major change in Keynesian conceptions. Section I lays out the arguments on normative, logical and empirical grounds against the sticky price Phillips Curve approach to economic fluctuations. Section II explains briefly why New Classical theories are hopeless as descriptions of real world economic fluctuations, especially in Europe. It then demonstrates how hysteresis models can resolve the problems with sticky price formulations and at the same time account for the empirical observations that motivate the Keynesian approach to macroeconomics. Section III concludes by discussing some policy implications of hysteresis models.

The Keynesian Orthodoxy

The orthodox Keynesian view of economic fluctuations goes something like this. Real factors determine uniquely an equilibrium level of output and employment in an economy. Wages and prices, however, are sticky because of long term contracts and sluggish expectations, and so can diverge temporarily from their equilibrium values. As a consequence of price stickiness changes in aggregate demand, typified by an increase in the money stock, affect the quantity of output and employment in the short run. In the long run, purely nominal changes do not have real effects.

The proposition that changes in nominal magnitudes do not have real effects in the long run implies that the long run Phillips curve trade-off is vertical. Increases in the permanent anticipated rate of inflation do not affect the level of unemployment or output. In the short run, however, because wages and prices are inertial, there is a trade-off between inflation and unemployment represented by the short run Phillips curve. This view implies that when disinflationary policies are pursued, as they were at the beginning of this decade in both the United States and Britain, output falls and the rate of inflation declines slowly. Conversely, expansionary policies can temporarily but not permanently increase output. The extent and magnitude of nominal effects on output and employment will depend on the importance of the factors leading wages and prices to be rigid.

These orthodox views are flawed in three important respects. First, they are dispiriting and discouraging: if they were valid, there would be very little scope for macroeconomic policy to increase (or reduce) economic welfare. Second, they are logically deficient in failing to consider seriously the implications of wage and price rigidities for choices about quantities. Third, they are refuted empirically by the great persistence of unemployment and output fluctuations, and by the very substantial variability of output even in settings where wages and prices are highly flexible. Let me develop each of these points.

The Natural Rate Hypothesis is Dispiriting

Contemporary Keynesian views about the inflation-output trade-off are well captured by the slightly stylized Phillips curve relation:

$$\dot{P}_t = b \ \text{GAP} + \dot{P}_{t-1} \qquad (2.1)$$

where GAP represents the difference between output or employment and some natural or equilibrium value consistent with steady inflation. This equation holds that the rate of change of inflation depends on the output gap. Similar expressions may be found in leading Keynesian textbooks like those of Dornbusch and Fischer, Gordon, and Hall and Taylor. Its striking implication for the efficacy of stabilization policies may be seen by summing it over time and rearranging:

$$\overline{\text{GAP}} = (\dot{P}_t - \dot{P}_o)/bT \qquad (2.2)$$

Equation (2.2) holds that over any interval the average value of GAP is proportional to the change from beginning to end in the rate of inflation. Over any period when the rate of inflation does not change, the average value of the output gap must equal zero. Macroeconomic policies which do not raise the long run inflation rate cannot affect the average level of output and employment in the economy. Put differently, stabilization policies can only mitigate recessions to the same extent that they can also limit expansions. Perhaps more strikingly, bad macroeconomic policies cannot reduce the average level of unemployment in an economy over any interval as long as the rate of inflation at the end of the interval is no less than the rate of inflation at the beginning.

This result is very general. It should be obvious that adding lagged values of GAP in order to capture persistence or rate of change effects, or allowing for a more elaborate lag structure on inflation, would not change the result. Some economists prefer to replace lagged inflation in (2.1) by expected inflation, or by a lag distribution of expected inflation at various points in time. In these cases, it is easy to demonstrate that policy cannot affect the average level of the output gap as long as surprises average zero over an interval of sufficient length. While I cannot prove this, my guess is that the conclusion that policy cannot affect average output is likely to be a feature of any model that postulates a unique equilibrium level of output and attributes fluctuations to disequilibrium situations.

If the natural rate Phillips curve (2.1) is accepted as a description of reality, it seems as if Keynesians are fighting for the low ground in their running battles with Classical economists. If increasing output in one period requires accepting an equal output reduction in another, it is hard to see why it matters very much whether policy can increase output for one period, as in the Classical model, or for several periods, as in the Keynesian model, especially since no one really knows how much calendar time corresponds to a model's time periods. The natural rate Phillips curve hypothesis also implies that the social gains from macroeconomic stabilization policies are not very large. Even assuming that the marginal utility of income diminishes very rapidly, Robert Lucas has shown that the social gains from stabilizing consumption around a fixed mean are likely to be very small. Thinking about aspects of fluctuations, it is far from obvious, however, that having 8 million workers unemployed for one year is worse than having 4 million workers unemployed for two years. Certainly, the burden of unemployment is likely to be borne more broadly in the first case than in the second. Stabilization policies also have costs. If they really could do nothing to increase the average level of output, it is doubtful that they could make much contribution to social welfare.

While many Keynesian economists accept equation (2.1), at least as a first approximation, they shrink from its normative implication that policy cannot affect the average level of output over long periods of time. Instead they write and speak as if it were possible to fill in troughs without shaving peaks or accepting ever accelerating inflation. Certainly this was how Keynes saw the proper objective of macroeconomic policy.

Since Keynes wrote, criticism of avoidable recessions has been far more common than criticism of inappropriate expansions. Indeed, while American Keynesians condemn the 'three Eisenhower recessions', and the recessions of 1975 and 1982, as the result of excessively contractionary policies, there is no peacetime period when any consensus regarded policy as too expansionary. Keynesian, and for that matter monetarist, tracts invariably leave the impression that the Depression was avoidable, and that avoiding it would not have saddled current generations with a higher permanent rate of inflation. As I discuss below, I think these convictions are correct. But they cannot be defended within the context of the current mainstream Keynesian model.[2] Justifying activist policy will involve looking elsewhere.

The Logic of Wage and Price Rigidity

Keynesian discussions of the Phillips curve assign a pivotal role to the sluggish adjustment of wages and prices. The idea is that because of wage contracts, menu costs or slowly adapting expectations, wages and prices remain stuck for a time at disequilibrium levels. As a consequence, the argument goes, employment and output are determined not by the intersection of demand and supply curves but by demand alone along the predetermined level of wages and prices. This story makes sense as a depiction of contractions caused by unexpected decreases in demand. In the short run output falls as suppliers of labour are constrained by the sticky downwards wage.

But the mainstream Keynesian model has no coherent explanation at all for booms. Suppose an economy is initially in equilibrium with rigid nominal wages but flexible prices, and the money supply increases unexpectedly.[3] Then the notional demand for labour will exceed the notional supply. Economists concerned with rationing in markets that do not clear worked out the solution to this problem long ago. One would expect to observe the level of employment generated by the supply curve and the realized real wage – a level that must be below the equilibrium level. This, of course, is not what we observe: instead monetary expansions raise employment, contradicting the prediction of the standard analysis of markets in which prices are rigid. The mainstream Keynesian model passes over this difficult observation by assuming simply that output is always demand determined.

The rationale for this assumption is rarely made explicit. Sometimes vague reference is made to contracts entitling employers to force their workers to work overtime. This cannot be important. Apart from the difficulty of enforcing contracts that call for people to work against their will, there is the prominent fact that most cyclical employment gains take the form of more people working, not people working more hours. Another suggestion is that employment gains arise because workers are somehow fooled and do not realize that real wages are lower. This suggestion has more of a Classical than a Keynesian flavour. More importantly, observation suggests that booms cause few regrets. Somehow there are few complaints after cyclical expansions by people who wish that they had not been tricked into working. Perhaps the Keynesian position can be defended by some sort of argument suggesting that demand expansions reduce frictional unemployment – a type of unemployment that is notably absent from the aggregate supply-demand diagrams found in the textbooks.

I am not aware of any convincing answer that those who ascribe cycles to nominal rigidities can give to the problem of explaining booms. This difficulty is really symptomatic of a general problem plaguing all attempts to explain fluctuations in terms of wage and price rigidities. Any serious thought about the rigidities leads one to despair of using standard supply and demand curves along with disequilibrium prices to determine the level of output. Suppose for example that firms and workers agree to long term contracts which fix nominal wages, and that there is no possibility of renegotiating the contracts while they are in force. Is there any reason to expect firms to operate along their labour demand curves? If agreements about employment can be negotiated, than one certainly would not expect the contracts simply to allow firms to move regularly along its demand curve. Even if contracts cannot be negotiated, firms are likely to set employment recognizing that their choices will affect subsequent wage bargains in a variety of ways.

Take another example. It is often noted that firms raise prices infrequently for fear of alienating customers and that this makes the price level more sticky. Grant for a moment that this is an important aspect of the pricing policies of firms. Does it make sense to suppose that their customers always operate along a Walrasian demand curve which makes no allowance for the alienating effect of price changes?

These examples could be multiplied. I think it will usually be found that whatever logic explains wage or price rigidity also undercuts the use of standard supply and demand curves to determine quantities. In every other part of Economics price rigidities lead too little to be bought or sold. Only in Keynesian macroeconomics do wage and price rigidities lead, half of the time, to quantities in excess of their equilibrium level.

Nominal Rigidities and the Real World

In addition to the logical arguments, there are important empirical problems with the nominal rigidities model as an explanation for economic fluctuations. First, this explanation is less plausible in the current era of secular inflation than it might have been at an earlier time. The original Phillips curve could be thought of as capturing tâtonnement effects – more demand pressure meant more rapidly rising prices. The pattern of high unemployment and high inflation observed during the 1970s made it clear that prices could rise rapidly even in the absence of abnormally strong demand conditions. This renders the whole idea of sluggish price adjustment to demand conditions rather less plausible, and suggests instead that inflation is better thought of as generating a sequence of equilibrium price levels.

Second, there is even at this late date no concrete empirical evidence linking the extent of nominal rigidities and the extent of cyclical fluctuations. A number of less than satisfactorily controlled comparisons point in the opposite direction. High inflation countries where wages and prices change extremely frequently have especially volatile economies. The decline in cyclical variability in the United States after World War II coincided with the introduction of three year union contracts, and other institutional relationships often thought to generate nominal rigidities. Employment is most variable among secondary workers: their wages are not set by contract, and are subject to wide variation. Across a sample of OECD countries, Sushil Wadwhani and I recently found a positive association between wage flexibility and output variability.

Third, an essential feature of the mainstream view is the idea that economic fluctuations represent transitory movements away from equilibrium. This idea receives little empirical support. While the evidence of very substantial persistence in output can be explained by arguing that technical progress today suggests greater growth in the future, it is much more difficult for the mainstream view to account for the great persistence in unemployment. Yet in our paper in this volume, Olivier Blanchard and I find that in recent years unemployment in a number of European countries has followed a process very close to a random walk. Over the past century, the first order autocorrelation of unemployment for both the United States and United Kingdom is over 0.9. I am aware of no other evidence suggesting a tendency for output or employment in any country to demonstrate a strong equilibrium reverting tendency.

These empirical considerations, as well as the logical difficulties with nominal rigidity theories, and their disquieting normative implications, lead me to conclude that macroeconomists should look elsewhere in trying to account for economic fluctuations. A fortiori, Classical approaches are not the way to go. This point, as well as the profound problems with the mainstream Keynesian model, is driven home by recent British experience.

The most resolute and right-wing government in Britain since the War has been in power for eight years during which time it has launched major attacks on trades unions and on market imperfections generally. Its commitment to disinflation is not in doubt. Yet more person years of unemployment have been experienced in Britain since 1979 than in the entire period between World War II and Mrs Thatcher's entry into office. In Britain today, about 60 per cent of all unemployment is due to persons in the midst of spells lasting two years or more. Can anyone seriously maintain that this outcome is the result of intertemporal substitution, misperceptions, or efficient search? For that matter, what factor or factors could have doubled that NAIRU over the last seven years? And, continuing wage inflation belies the idea that nominal wage rigidity is responsible for high unemployment.

These phenomena suggest a need to look beyond the mainstream Keynesian or Classical models. I take up this challenge in the next section.

Fragile Equilibria and Hysteresis

One of Keynes' distinctive contributions to the study of economic fluctuations was his stress on the possibility that they were caused by 'animal spirits' – fluctuations in the expectations of businessmen and financiers about future prosperity which are unrelated to real events. His suggestion was that exogenous conditions determine the level of output with a degree of arbitrariness. As a result, there was scope for the expectations about future output to be self-fulfilling. More recent discussions have regarded the question of whether anticipated purely nominal changes have real effects as a litmus test for determining whether a model is 'Keynesian'. And Keynesian economists have produced evidence demonstrating that anticipated nominal changes matter empirically. In a sense these two ideas are closely related. The relevance of animal spirits and of purely nominal changes for the determination of output is difficult to understand in an environment where exogenous conditions sharply determine equilibrium. Were multiple equilibria to be possible, so making the level of output in some sense arbitrary, it would be much easier to understand how extrinsic variables like the money stock or animal spirits could affect the level of output.

My point is well made by example. Consider the problem of the way in which we measure time. Any competent economics graduate student would have no difficulty in proving the following proposition: *the numbers attached by convention to moments when the sun is at different levels in the sky have no effect on an economy's real allocations.* More informally, the time standard is a purely nominal variable that should have no effect on real outcomes. The proof mimics the standard demonstration that doubling the stock of nominal money should have no effect on the level of real output. A unique equilibrium may not exist. But to each equilibrium under time standard A, there will correspond an equilibrium under time standard B, in which all real variables (like the time at which things open relative to the time when the sun is highest in the sky) take on the same values. In the language of the theorist, altering the units in which we measure time does not change the set of equilibrium allocations that the price system can support.

There is one important thing to understand about this proposition: it is false as an empirical statement. Every spring we see daylight saving time imposed, and then observe people getting an extra hour of sunlight after they get home from work. Is there anyone who believes that if daylight saving time did not exist, somehow all opening and closing times in the economy would be altered simultaneously? Over the years, thousands of pages of Congressional testimony have been taken arguing the merits of daylight saving time. Considerations relating to energy conservation, school buses, and the safety and convenience of farm workers have all played a prominent role in these debates. I doubt very much that it has ever been argued that the choice of a time standard is of no consequence because it is a purely nominal variable.

The reasons why the choice of a time standard has real effects are instructive. Imagine a store in a shopping center. Its owner may care about how much time in the sun can be enjoyed after work. But he or she cares far more about opening and closing his shop at the same time that the other stores do. As a consequence many real equilibria in which all firms open and close at the same time are possible. While all storeowners might prefer to open and close an hour earlier in the summer, it would be very difficult to coordinate this outcome in the absence of a change in the time standard. Any one store that changed its hours of operation would regret it, even though all would be better off if all changed. In this setting, daylight saving time is a constructive innovation that yields benefits by shifting the economy from less to more favourable equilibria.

Note several features of this argument. First, the efficacy of daylight saving time depends on people caring more about their relative time of opening than about their absolute time of opening. In a community of hermits, there would be a unique equilibrium in which everyone woke up at the time he or she preferred most, and daylight savings time would have no real effects. The impact of a purely nominal variable – the time standard – is dependent on the fact that multiple real equilibria are possible. Second, sufficiently large changes in the time standard would cause firms to alter their stated opening and closing times. If the US were put on Greenwich mean time, people would not persist in leaving work before the sun had reached its highest point in the sky. Opening and closing times would adjust, and it is impossible to predict just which real equilibrium would be selected. Third, the efficacy of daylight saving time is related to the coordination problem arising because people care about relative rather than absolute time, not about any nominal rigidity in opening and closing times. Stores open and close at different times on different days of the week and in different parts of the year. The costs of posting a sign with opening and closing times have nothing to do with the efficacy of daylight saving time.

What does all this have to do with economic fluctuations generally or hysteresis specifically? I believe there is a very close analogy. In developing it, I will focus on the labour market and on the determination of wages and unemployment. Parallel arguments stressing product market considerations could probably be developed. Figure 2.1 provides a plausible description of the way a given firm sets wages. Concerned about turnover, the problem of motivating its workers, the need to fill vacancies and so forth it uses the wages paid by other firms as a benchmark in setting its own wage. If unemployment is low, the firm is likely to decide to pay higher than prevailing wages. If unemployment is high it will decide to pay lower than prevailing wages. As long as the typical firm would prefer to pay supra-normal wages in a hypothetical zero unemployment situation, unemployment will be observed in equilibrium. If all firms are symmetric, equilibrium is determined at point A, where each firm is happy to pay the average wage.

The slope of the WW schedule in figure 2.1(a) will depend on the relative importance firms attach to other firms' wages and unemployment in setting their own wages. If, as is plausible, other firms' wages have the dominant influence, the WW schedule will be very flat, as in figure 2.1(a). While in this case there is a unique equilibrium unemployment rate, it will be extremely sensitive to anything that moves the WW schedule. Moreover, it should be clear there will be a large number of 'near equilibrium' unemployment rates where the wages firms pay differ only trivially from the optimal wage. In such a setting very small expectational errors are likely to have large effects. In the limit, where firms always want to pay the same wage as other firms over some range of unemployment rates, things become more interesting. A multiplicity of equilibria are possible, as in figure 2.1(b), and so the equilibrium rate of unemployment is arbitrary. As was the case with the time standard, when firms care about conformity above all else it will be possible for extrinsic variables to have important real effects.

It is probably a mistake to distinguish too sharply between the cases depicted in figures 2.1(a) and 2.1(b). Situations with multiple equilibria, and with very weakly determined but unique equilibria, are not likely to be observationally very different. Think about hem lengths. Their determination could be analysed using figure 2.1, replacing unemployment by the average hem length and representing the average woman's desired relative hem length on the vertical axis. Whether there are literarally multiple equilibria or not is unclear. It is obvious that extrinsic variables matter, and that instability is present, as models of multiple equilibria would suggest.

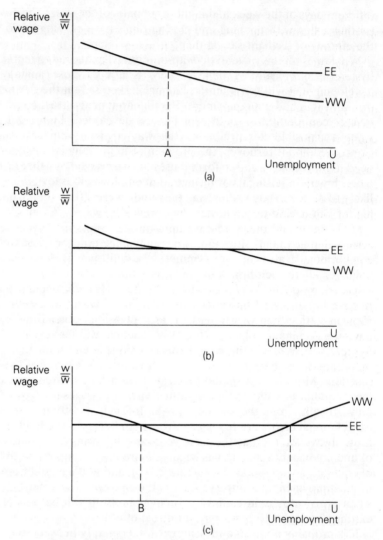

Figure 2.1 *Relative wage setting and unemployment*

There are other possibilities besides those depicted in figures 2.1(a) and 2.1(b). Suppose that increases in unemployment are associated with more generous unemployment benefits; or that the stigma associated with losing a job is reduced; or that, as Blanchard and I argue elsewhere in this volume, increases in unemployment lead insiders to set a lower employment target when they bargain over wages. In any of these cases, the WW schedule might look like that depicted in figure 2.1(c). There will be two equilibrium unemployment rates, B and C. Extrinsic variables can move the economy between the two equilibria.

So far my argument has been that if firms care a great deal about their relative wage, an economy's equilibrium unemployment rate may be very sensitive to small changes in the factors determining unemployment, or that an economy may actually possess many equilibrium unemployment rates. In such settings, it is natural to expect that extrinsic variables could have real effects in moving the economy between equilibria. It is also plausible that unemployment would be unstable because of the possibility of movement between different equilibrium values, as well as movements in equilibrium values. Finally, small changes in the determinants of unemployment may lead to very large movements in equilibrium values. Think of a change in union power that lifted the WW schedule slightly in figure 2.1.

Although I have been brief, I am confident that it is possible to provide detailed microeconomic justifications for the variety of shapes of the WW locus used in figure 2.1. The real challenge at this point is to provide some indication of how an equilibrium is selected, and of how changes in extrinsic variables alter real equilibria. This is where the idea of hysteresis comes in. Surely it is history that determines the equilibrium an economy selects. It is history that conditions the wages that firms expect other firms to pay, and expect workers to expect other firms to pay. Once an economy is in an equilibrium state, it may be reasonable for agents to form expectations that it will remain there. These expectations may prove to be self-fulfilling. Alternatively, as in the time example, it may be reasonable to suppose that agents are myopic in forming expectations about their strategy variable (nominal wages in this case) so that policy can have beneficial effects. Unfortunately, there is only one conclusion of which I am confident at this stage: there is no reason to expect market forces to select automatically the best of many equilibria. Saying more will require our developing a deeper understanding of hysteresis effects than we have at present.

Let me conclude this section by making it clear how models of multiple equilibria and hysteresis can resolve the problems with the mainstream Keynesian model stressed in the first part of these remarks. From the perspective of these multiple equilibria and hysteresis models, the economy does not fluctuate around a unique equilibrium. Instead, it is capable of settling at many different equilibria, one of which is best. Policies that improve today's outcome need not compel the selection of an inferior equilibrium tomorrow. We do not talk about cycles around a fixed mean in people's health. Instead, we talk about their being healthy or getting sick. The multiple equilibrium approach to fluctuations takes a similar view of periods of high and low employment.

It should be obvious that booms are no mystery from the perspective advocated here. They represent simply the attainment of desirable equilibria. Since there is chronic involuntary unemployment in the model sketched here, no one regrets the extra work done in a boom. Since the perspective taken here is that the economy is always in equilibrium, no problems arise of describing quantity choices in the presence of disequilibrium prices.

Finally, models of multiple equilibria do not suffer from the empirical defects of models which emphasize nominal rigidities. They do not predict that systematic inflation should have systematic real effects, or that there should be a relationship between the costs of changing wages and prices and the extent of output variability. Most importantly, they do not carry any implication that economies should exhibit equilibrium reverting behaviour. As in any other social situation where individuals value conformity highly, the model sketched here suggests that outcomes should be both volatile and persistent.

Continuing inflation, rapid GNP growth, the fact that redundancy and short time rates are low by historical standards, and the fact that overtime work is abnormally common, all suggest that it is not fruitful to think of the contemporary British economy as being far out of equilibrium. It is neither plausible nor bearable to think of this equilibrium as being unique. This compels consideration of models with many equilibria.

Conclusions

Robert Lucas, in his celebrated critique of econometric policy evaluation, refers to the false inference that because: 'nominal prices and wages tend to rise more rapidly at the peak of the business cycle than they do in the trough . . . permanent inflation will therefore induce a permanent economic high . . . it is only recently that this notion has undergone the mysterious transformation from obvious fallacy to cornerstone of the theory of economic policy' (Lucas 1976, p. 19). He was right. It is, however, equally fallacious to suppose, as do Lucas and mainstream Keynesians, that because steady inflation does not affect the average level of unemployment nothing else can either. Purging this fallacy will require us to eliminate the natural rate Phillips curve from our models.

My daylight saving time example supports these conclusions. It is easy to imagine time policies that would be undone by the private sector, and so have no real effects. Think of a policy of changing the clocks by three hours every week. Under such a regime, presumably people would find ways of setting opening and closing times which did not lead to stores being open just before dawn. This proves only that there are limits to the equilibria which policy can impose on the economy, not that all policy is ineffective. And it shows that no simple equation can explain the process by which opening and closing hours are determined.

The challenge is to design policies that can work. This will require more detailed hysteresis theories describing how history determines an economy's equilibrium. But a little can be said at a high level of generality. From the perspective of the view of cyclical fluctuations presented here, the problem of economic policy is very much like that of winning at poker. To succeed, one has to guess the endowments, intentions and guesses of others. A poker player can ensure an average outcome by following a simple policy rule – not betting. Many poker players do much better than this. So can shrewd policymakers who, like successful poker players, make case by case judgments and do not shrink from bold actions. Better theories of economic hysteresis can help them out.

NOTES

1 These remarks were presented as a before dinner speech at the Conference on Hysteresis Effects and Unemployment held in St. Andrews, Scotland in July 1986. The freewheeling and unqualified character of my oral presentation has been maintained.

2 One possible defence would stress non-linearities in the relation between GAP and changes in inflation. I am not aware of strong evidence demonstrating the existence of such non-linearities. While an asymmetry between upward and downward adjustment of prices is plausible, the idea of an asymmetry between upward and downward adjustments in the rate of inflation seems less compelling.

3 Similar arguments can be carried out assuming that prices are less than fully flexible and allowing for some flexibility in wages.

REFERENCE

Lucas R. E. Jr. (1976), 'Econometric Policy Evaluation: a Critique', in Brunner, K., and Meltzer, A. H. (eds), *The Phillips Curve and Labour Markets.* Amsterdam: North Holland Publishing Company.

3

On the History of Hysteresis

ROD CROSS and ANDREW ALLAN

The term hysteresis means that which comes after, or is behind. It is derived from the Greek υστερέω, to be behind, and was coined for application to phenomena of scientific interest in 1881 by the Dundonian physicist–engineer James Alfred Ewing: 'these curves exhibit, in a striking manner, a persistence of previous state . . . to this action . . . the author now gives the name Hysteresis (υστέρησις from υστερέω, to be behind) . . . ' (Ewing, 1881b). The distinguishing feature of a system in which hysteresis is postulated to be present is that the behaviour of the system cannot, ex hypothesi, be explained by reference to state variables alone: instead the past history of the system has to be invoked, as well as state variables, in order to explain the behaviour of the system. In economics the focus of attention is often on explaining some type of equilibrium behaviour of economic systems: partial, general, local, temporary, stationary, dynamic and spatial equilibrium concepts are amongst the better known. If the behaviour of economic systems in such equilibrium positions can be explained by reference to present state variables alone the systems can be said to be ahysteretic; if reference to the history of the relevant explanatory variables is required as well, the systems are hysteretic.

Leibniz

Leibniz seems to have been one of the first to have been aware of the epistemological difference between explanations of phenomena which rely on hysteresis and those which do not (see Elster, 1976, which is the source for the following expostion), though Leibniz, writing two centuries before Ewing, did not of course use the term hysteresis. Leibniz objected to the notion of action at a temporal distance, proposed by Descartes, as well as to the notion of action at a spatial distance (e.g. gravitational attraction), proposed by Newton:

For since this command in the past no longer exists at present, it can accomplish nothing unless it has left some subsistent effect behind which has lasted and operated until now, and whoever thinks otherwise renounces any distinct explanation of things, if I am any judge, for if that which is remote in time and space can operate here and now without any intermediary, anything can be said to follow from anything else with equal right. (Leibniz, from the translation of Loemker, 1969, p. 500)

Newtonian theory emerged to dominate the explanation of physical phenomena over the next two centuries or so, despite the objections of Leibniz; or as Elster puts it, 'in an abstract sense Leibniz is certainly right, even if the history of science proved him wrong' (Elster, 1976, p. 373).

Leibniz also discussed what has proved to be the standard example of how to rid explanations which seemingly require hysteresis of their hysteresis. In the case of a swinging pendulum it appears to be necessary to invoke knowledge of the past position of the pendulum as well as the current position in order to explain its future motion. In this case the introduction of the present instantaneous velocity of the pendulum as an additional state variable allows the future motion to be explained, thus removing what seems to be a need to invoke hysteresis in order to explain the motion. Given the nature of the derivative calculus and integration, it can be argued that hysteresis can be removed, epistemologically speaking, by introducing higher order time derivatives as explanatory state variables: 'if we know the present value of all the temporal derivatives, this is equivalent (for analytic functions) to full knowledge about the past' (Elster, 1976, p. 376). As Elster himself points out, however, 'there does not seem to be any gain . . . if hysteresis is eliminated by the introduction of infinitely many state variables' (Elster, 1976, p. 376).

Ewing

Ewing was not the first to discover – here the ontological sense of hysteresis is being employed – the existence of the effects of some force persisting after the force has been removed: this was known in Germany before Ewing's experiments, and had been described as elastische Nachwirkung by Kohlrausch in 1866 (see Glazebrook, 1935, p. 485). Ewing's role in speculating that such effects would be present in a wider set of instances than those covered by his experimental studies, however, and his insistence on using the term hysteresis rather than the phrase 'effects of retentiveness' preferred by his Royal Society assessor Sir William Thompson, suggests that it is not improper to associate the discovery with him: 'he became soaked in it, and was led to invent that name . . . feeling the need of a word that should be sufficiently wide to include not only the phenomenon of magnetic retentiveness but other manifestations of what seemed to be essentially the same thing' (Ewing, 1939, p. 62).

Ewing first applied the concept to his discovery that when iron and steel are stressed the thermoelectric effects on the properties of the metals lag behind the stress applied (Ewing, 1881a), and he coined the term hysteresis in a paper describing a similar lag which was noticed when investigating the transient currents produced by twisting magnetized wires (Ewing, 1881b). Ewing's most celebrated application of the hysteresis effect came in his experimental researches on the behaviour of magnetic fields in ferric metals. The background here was the dramatic change in the view of the nature of physical reality being wrought by Thomson (Kelvin), Maxwell and others, in which field continua replaced the Newtonian notion of motions of material bodies in space. Maxwell's equations do not fit well the behaviour of electromagnetic fields in ferric metals. Ewing explained this anomaly by invoking hysteresis, noting 'the tendency on the part of the metal to persist in any magnetic state it might have acquired' (Ewing, 1893, p. 93). Or, more formally:

> when there are two qualities M and N such that the cyclic variations of N cause cyclic variations of M, then if the changes of M lag behind those of N, we may say that there is hysteresis in the relation of M to N . . . the value of M at any point of the operation depends not only on the actual value of N, but on all the preceding changes (and particularly on the immediately preceding changes) of N, and by properly manipulating those changes, any value of M within more or less wide limits may be found associated with a given value of N. (Ewing, 1885, p. 524)

The famous visual representation of this effect in ferromagnetic fields is the hysteresis loop drawn by Ewing, which still occupies a prominent position in modern texts on electromagnetism (see Duffin, 1980, for example). The hysteresis loop, illustrated in figure 3.1, describes how the electromagnetic characteristics of ferric metals change during a complete cycle of magnetization and demagnetization. Starting from an original state *A* the application of a positive magnetizing force to the field changes the field characteristics to those indicated by coordinate *B*. In the absence of hysteresis the system would return to *A* on removal of the positive magnetizing force. Instead the presence of hysteresis implies that the field characteristics revert to *C* on removal of the positive magnetizing force, the distance *AC* being termed the 'remanence' of the electromagnetic field, a measure of the persistence of induced changes in field characteristics. To regain the original field characteristics a negative magnetizing force *AD* is required, *AD* being termed 'coercivity', a measure of the extra force required to restore the original characteristics. Over a complete cycle of magnetization and demagnetization the system describes the loop *BCDEFG* shown in figure 3.1. The integral $\int MF.\mathrm{d}FC$ measures the work done during the magnetization cycle, and can be regarded as a measure of energy loss, dissipated in the form of heat, due to the presence of hysteresis.

If a complete magnetization cycle is repeated there is no necessary reason why the original loop should be repeated. Different ferric metals also have different hysteresis loops, soft iron having a narrow hysteresis loop with little hysteresis loss, iron–nickel alloy having a wider loop, for example (see Page and Adams, 1969, pp. 349–50). Further complications arise if the magnetizing cycle is aborted or reversed: this generates a species of sub-loops around the loop relevant to a complete magnetization cycle (see Ewing, 1893, p. 95). These complications seem to be highly relevant to the interpretation of economic phenomena in terms of hysteresis, given the differences between economic systems and the tendency of the disturbances affecting the systems to be irregular rather than of a regular cyclical nature.

Ewing left his own hysteresis effects behind in the form of engineering as an academic discipline at Cambridge University, at which he was Professor of Mechanism and Applied Mechanics; in the form of US policy during the 1914–18 war, for Ewing was in charge of the Room 40 decipher group that intercepted the telegram from the German Foreign Secretary, Dr Zimmerman, suggesting an alliance of Mexico with Germany and Japan, which, if successful, would have placed Texas,

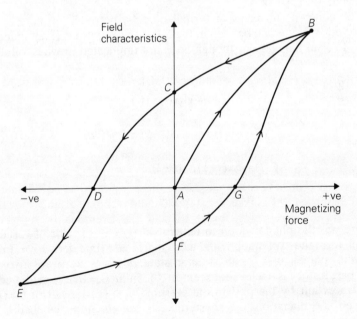

Figure 3.1 *Hysteresis loop diagram*

New Mexico and Arizona in Mexican hands; and in the form of the King's Buildings erected at the University of Edinburgh during his term as Principal (see Glazebrook, 1935).

Hysteresis Elsewhere

Other instances where the invocation of past history, rather than state variables alone, appears to be necessary to explain the relevant phenomena are stress in metals and ferroelectric effects in physics (see Pippard, 1985 for a discussion of the implications for system stability); the Lotka–Volterra model of predator–prey interaction in macrobiology (see Lotka, 1925, for example); Markov chain models of social class mobility (see Coleman, 1973, for example); and location theory (see Goodwin, 1977, for example). More controversially, in the physics of subatomic particles 'according to a recent idea of David Bohm, shared also by Louis de Broglie, the Heisenberg indeterminacy may be the result of the fact that the past history of the elementary particle is not taken into account in predicting its behaviour' (see Georgescu-Roegen, 1971, p. 124); and it has been argued that virtually the whole of biological and social behaviour cannot be satisfactorily explained without hysteresis – 'in the macrobiological and social world getting at the zero level of hysteresis seems utterly impossible' (Georgescu-Roegen, 1971, p. 125).

The contrast, in terms of formal models, between ahysteretic and hysteretic systems can be seen in the following equations (I am indebted here to Paul Samuelson, though he is not implicated in what follows):

$$y\ (t)=f\ [x(t)] \tag{A1}$$

$$\ddot{y}\ (t)=g[t\dot{x}(t),\ x(t)] \tag{A2}$$

$$y\ (t)=\mathrm{b}(t)+\int_{-\infty}^{t} \mathrm{H}(t-s)\ x\ (s)e^{-s}ds \tag{H1}$$

$$\ddot{y}\ (t)=k[\dot{x}(t-1),\ \dot{x}(t-2),\ ------\ ;$$

$$x(t-1),\ x(t-2),\ ------\ ] \tag{H2}$$

where y is the phenomenon to be explained, x is a vector of variables which form the explanation, and a dot indicates a time derivative. In the equations labelled A for ahysteretic, state variables alone are invoked, and past history is irrelevant except in 'the influence that is mediated by the traces left by the past in the present . . . ' (Elster, 1976, p. 373): hence the explanations are ahysteretic. In the equations labelled H for hysteretic, however, state variables alone are not seen to be sufficient to explain the phenomena in question, history being invoked over and above the traces left in the present: hence the explanations are hysteretic. To the economist who is used to specifying time lags in economic relationships the contrast between the A, ahysteretic, and H, hysteretic, equations can be seen most clearly if the equations are seen as relating some notion of the equilibrium value of the y variable to commensurately equilibrium values of the x variables: with the H equations we pass that way only once, other than by coincidence; with the A equations we pass that way again and again and again, in the lack of exogenous disturbances.

The Equilibrium Debate of the 1930s

Interest in the formal issue of whether explanations of the behaviour of economic systems require hysteresis can be traced back at least as far as the 1930s. Interestingly enough, in view of the reactions to Milton Friedman's concept of the natural rate of unemployment which pervade the rest of this volume, the immediate context in which the equilibrium debate arose was Knut Wicksell's concept of the natural rate of interest, which Friedman used as an analogy for the case of unemployment.

> At the Namur meeting of the Econometric Society, September 1935, a discussion arose regarding Wicksell's concept of the 'natural' interest rate . . . the discussion subsequently extended to the question of what in general was to be understood by a 'natural' or 'equilibrium' position of a certain set of economic variables. (Frisch, 1936, p. 100)

Frisch's famous article served to define what proved to be the standard account of an ahysteretic equilibrium for economic systems. During this debate, however, an awareness was expressed of an alternative hysteretic form of equilibrium. The recently deceased Nicholas Kaldor, who reluctantly had to decline an invitation to speak at the conference from which the present volume arises, defined an 'indeterminate' equilibrium as an alternative to the ahysteretic concept of 'determinate' equilibrium:

> Equilbrium will be determinate . . . even if it is only gradually established, so long as the posisition of equilibrium is independent of the actual path followed . . . indeterminateness can only arise through the disturbing influence of intermediary situations . . . . (Kaldor, 1933, pp. 126–7)

Schumpeter

On the other side of the Atlantic during this period, it was Joseph Schumpeter who actively proposed hysteresis as a means of explaining the 'dynamics' of economic systems:

This kind of change . . . arises from within the system . . . and is the cause of so many important phenomena that it seems worthwhile to build a theory for it . . . [this] kind of change . . . so displaces its equilibrium point that the new one cannot be reached from the old one by infinitesimal steps. (Schumpeter, 1934, p. 64)

Even if Schumpeter did not use the term hysteresis in print – this may have been lost in translation or missed by himself – he certainly used the term orally, as James Tobin's account indicates:

The date is 1946 or 1947 . . . the Graduate Economics Club . . . at Harvard . . . the students like to have Schumpeter introduce the visitor because he always puts on a good show . . . this time the visitor was Roy Harrod . . . Schumpeter gave Harrod one of his typical flowery but slightly tongue-in-cheek introductions, ending with 'Ladies and Gentlemen, I give you now . . . Roy Harrod, who is going to tell us about the very important phenomenon of hysteresis' . . . Harrod looked puzzled and flustered, having of course no intention of doing any such thing . . . . (James Tobin, letter to the author 27 May 1986)

Apart from being the source of Tobin's first exposure to hysteresis, Schumpeter's influence left its own hysteresis mark on Nicholas Georgescu-Roegen, who took up a scholarship at Harvard in 1934 before returning to Romania before the 1939–45 war. Georgescu-Roegen, from his early studies of consumer behaviour (reprinted in Georgescu-Roegen, 1966), has consistently argued that hysteresis is necessary in the explanation of the behaviour of economic systems (see above). In relation to the Walrasian general equilibrium system, for example, he argues that the Laplacean demon, or auctioneer, within the system will be frustrated by hysteresis:

An individual who comes to experience a new economic situation may alter his preferences . . . ex post he may discover that the answer he gave to our demon was not right . . . the equilbrium computed by our demon is thus immediately defeated not by the intervention of exogenous factors but by endogenous causes . . . consequently our demon will have to keep on recomputing running-away equilibria, unless by chance he possesses a divine mind capable of writing the whole history of the world before it actually happens. (Georgescu-Roegen, 1971, p. 335)

Georgescu-Roegen is perhaps most famous for his application of the second law of thermodynamics, or the entropy law, to the energy resources of economic systems. Central to this law is the notion of irreversibility over time, which is sometimes confused with hysteresis, and so is worth mentioning here.

Hysteresis implies that phenomena depend on time, or history, in a manner that cannot be reduced solely to the influence of state variables bearing the marks of time, or history, but does not necessarily imply that the processes determining phenomena are irreversible: in electromagnetic fields in ferric metals, for example, changes in the field characteristics can be reversed, but only at the cost of the energy loss indicated by the area of the hysteresis loop (see figure 3.1). With entropy this is not the case:

> A given lump of coal, for example, can be burned only once . . . there is of course the same amount of energy in the heat, smoke and ashes as there was in the lump of coal (. . . stipulated by the first law of thermodynamics governing the conservation of matter-energy), but the energy bound up in the combustion products is so dissipated that it is unavailable for use, unlike the 'free' energy in the coal, and the process cannot be reversed . . . entropy is a measure of this bound or dissipated energy . . . the entropy law says that the entropy of a closed system always increases, the change being from free energy to bound, not the other way about. (Unsigned article in *Science*, 190, 31 October 1975, p. 448)

Samuelson

Paul Samuelson, a graduate student at Harvard at the time of Schumpeter and Georgescu-Roegen, seems to have been a principal source of exposure to hysteresis in the subsequent generation of economists. Edmund Phelps, for example, who was the first to suggest that the 'natural' rate of unemployment could well be haunted by hysteresis, recalls that he 'first heard the term from Paul Samuelson when visiting MIT in 1962–63' (letter to the author, 10 June 1986). Samuelson was aware of hysteresis effects from his studies in electrical engineering: 'I knew that magnets in motors and dynamos tend after use to become "contaminated" by their past . . . my . . . understanding is that the technical word "hysteresis" arose in connection with such phenomena. ' (Samuelson, letter to the author 25 June 1986).

A rising young star of economic theory in the mid-1930s, Samuelson describes how he tended to avoid introducing hysteresis into the explanation of economic phenomena at a formal level: 'technically speaking, we theorists hoped not to introduce hysteresis phenomena into our model . . . ' (Samuelson, 1972, p. 540, from his 1968 book). This reluctance seems to be based on the fact that hysteresis can involve the whole of history:

> for, if we . . . go back to a detailed picturing of the colliding billiard balls, we realise that at best all we can observe is that the present position of the system is in a determinate relationship to all of its past behaviour . . . the behaviour of an effect Y at time t depends upon the whole shape of behaviour at all previous times of its cause X . . . when the equilibrium of

a system depends on (and is dictated by) its path towards equilibrium, the scientist has an uncomfortable feeling. (Samuelson, 1972, pp. 440–1, from his 1965 book)

The irony is that this 'uncomfortable feeling' at taking hysteresis on board at the formal level of analysis, which would take 'the subject out of the realm of science into the realm of genuine history . . . ', has been accompanied by a tendency to take hysteresis seriously: 'in our more realistic moods, we tacitly used models involving hysteresis' (Samuelson, 1972, p. 541, from his 1968 book).

Hysteresis and Preferences

As far as the explanation of specific economic phenomena is concerned, the longest standing invocation of hysteresis seems to be in the context of the theory of choice. Georgescu-Roegen has consistently argued that the preferences of individuals do not change solely because of innovations which are exogenous to economic systems and the individuals involved; rather an important source of change arises endogenously, the preferences of individuals changing in response to their experience of the objects of their preferences, such as consumption:

> the fact that the individual's continuous adjustment to changing price and income conditions changes his tastes seems so obvious that in the past economists mentioned it in passing, if at all . . . in order to determine the equilibrium of the consumer . . . we need to know . . . this particular hysteresis law. (Georgescu-Roegen, 1971, p. 126)

Although not employing the term hysteresis, a famous paper by Haavelmo argued that current utility is not a function purely of current consumption, as the standard ahysteretic analysis would imply, but also a function of past consumption, and the consumption of others (Haavelmo, 1944). The implication is that preferences are not state variables, but rather depend on the history of consumption experience. This means that the experience of the journey changes the objectives that individuals pursue:

> To the extent that my own past consumption makes me into a different kind of person, by inducing a change in my preference structure, hysteresis literally is an externality, because my utility is then influenced by the consumption of other persons, viz. my own past selves. (Elster, 1976, p. 375)

This problem of hysteresis in preferences arises spontaneously in many contexts: one example is the time consistency of optimal plans. The problem can be stated as follows:

An individual is imagined to choose a plan of consumption for a future period of time so as to maximise the utility of the plan as evaluated at the present moment . . . .[o]ur problem arises when we ask . . . if he is free to reconsider his plan at later dates, will he abide by it or disobey it – even though his original expectations . . . are verified? . . . [o]ur answer is that the optimal plan of the present moment is generally one which will not be obeyed, or that the individual's future behaviour will be inconsistent with his optimal plan . . . .[t]he rational individual will do one of two things . . . he may 'precommit' his future behaviour . . . or he may modify his chosen plan to take account of future disobedience. (Strotz, 1955/6, p. 165)

In the context of this volume, hysteresis in preferences arises in the insider–outsider models considered in chapters 7,9 and 15. Here the preferences of insiders are defined over real wages and the probability of employment which are not state variables but rather change with the history of unemployment. Thus the preferences of workers, or groups of workers, change endogenously in response to experience of the economic environment.

Other Examples of Hysteresis in Economic Analysis

Other explanations of economic phenomena which have explicitly invoked hysteresis can be found in international trade theory and the political economy literature. In the content of trade theory:

labour moves from Europe to America in search of higher wages . . . time preference or interest rates are positive . . . migration must cease unless the present discounted value of the perpetual wage differential exceeds the costs of migration. . . . [t]he result is that a whole range of geographical equilibria can prevail, depending on initial locations. . . . . [o]ur most interesting conclusion concerns the possible multiplicity of long-run equilibria . . . . (Kemp and Wan, 1974, pp. 221–2)

In the context of the political economy:

Is it possible . . . to erase even a very small part of man's recent hysteresis, as the physicist can do for a magnet? . . . [c]an the socialist man be created so as not to show any hysteresis trace of his bourgeois or peasant past?' (Georgescu-Roegen, 1971, p. 126)

Hysteresis and the Natural Rate of Unemployment

The received account of the 'natural' rate of unemployment, which achieved a status of conventional wisdom soon after the term was coined by Milton Friedman in 1968, is ahysteretic, depending on state variables alone:

> the 'natural rate of unemployment' . . . is the level that would be ground out by the Walrasian system of general equilibrium equations, provided there is embedded in them the actual structural characteristics of the labour and commodity markets, including market imperfections, stochastic variability in demands and supplies, the cost of gathering information about job vacancies and labour availabilities, the costs of mobility, and so on. (Friedman, 1968, p. 8)

The implications of ahysteresis in the natural rate are far reaching: governments wishing to change the natural or equilibrium rate of unemployment can do so only by changing the state variables involved, and not by altering the path taken by actual unemployment. The irony is that Friedman's subsequent positively sloped Phillips curve conjecture does introduce a form of hysteresis: the condition for no hysteresis is

> that inflation is steady or at least no more variable at a high rate than at a low . . . that the inflation is . . . open, with all prices free to adjust; . . . when a country initially moves to higher rates of inflation these requirements will be systematically departed from . . . and such a transitional period may well extend over decades. (Friedman, 1977, p. 465)

Friedman, however, is still concerned to remove the traces of hysteresis from long-run equilibrium: 'I am inclined to retain the long-long-run vertical Phillips curve' (Friedman, 1977, p. 464).

The puzzle for the historian of ideas in economics is why the ahysteretic account of the natural or equilibrium rate of unemployment has, until recently, attracted more attention than the alternative hysteretic account of the natural rate proposed by Edmund Phelps in 1972, shortly after he and Friedman had coined the natural or equilibrium rate concept (see Cross, 1987, for an account of these two species of natural rate theory). In the Phelps analysis the natural rate depends on history, as well as state variables, the natural rate being partly determined by the actual unemployment experienced during the movement from one steady rate of inflation to another:

> the transition from one equilibrium to the other tends to have long-lingering effects on the labour force, and these effects may be discernible in the equilibrium rate of unemployment for a long time. . . .[t]he natural rate of unemployment at any future date will depend upon the course of history in the interim . . . such a property is sometimes called hysteresis. (Phelps, 1972, p. xxiii)

Phelps would not dissociate himself from the version of the natural rate hypothesis which says that the equilibrium rate of unemployment is independent of the expected rate of inflation (letter to the author, 20 October 1986). Subsequent contributions which employ a hysteretic version of the natural rate of unemployment include those of Cross (1979), Hargreaves Heap (1980), Buiter and Gersovitz (1981) and Gregory (1982), though earlier contributions by such as Tobin (1965) involve hysteresis but without the formal terminology.

The chapters in this volume investigate the hysteresis theory of equilibrium unemployment initiated by the insight of Phelps, and form part of the sequel to the ahysteresis of Friedman's natural rate. The rest will be history, so to speak.

ACKNOWLEDGEMENT

We would like to thank Edmund Phelps, Paul Samuelson and James Tobin for their help in the preparation of this chapter: they are not necessarily implicated in what appears herein. We are most grateful to Serena Yeoward, who put us on the track of Ewing; to Juliet Shaughnessy, who helped with the detective work; to Peter Clark, for help with the philosophy literatures sources; to Antoni Chawluk and Harold Hutchinson for discussion of the issues involved; and to Keith Cross and David Mason for help with etymological matters. The errors are our own.

REFERENCES

Buiter W. H. and Gersovitz M., 1981: Issues in controllability and the theory of economic policy. *Journal of Public Economics*, 15.1, 33–44.

Coleman J. 1973: *The Mathematics of Collective Action*. New York.

Cross R. 1979: Aggregate Demand and the Natural Rate of Unemployment. University of St Andrews, mimeo.

Cross R. 1987: Hysteresis and instability in the natural rate of unemployment. *Scandinavian Journal of Economics*, 89.1, 71–89.

Duffin W. J. 1980: *Electricity and Magnetism*, 3rd edn. New York: McGraw-Hill.

Elster J. 1976: A note on hysteresis in the social sciences. *Synthese*, 33, 371–91.

Ewing A. W. 1939: *The Man of Room 40: The Life of Sir Alfred Ewing*. London: Hutchinson.

Ewing J. A. 1881a: The effects of stress on the thermoelectric quality of metals, Part I. *Proceedings of the Royal Society of London*, 32, 399–402.

Ewing J. A. 1881b: On the production of transient electric currents in iron and steel conductors by twisting them when magnetised or by magnetising them when twisted. *Proceedings of the Royal Society of London*, 33, 21–3.

Ewing J. A. 1885: Experimental researches in magnetism. *Philosophical Transactions of the Royal Society of London*, 176.II, 523–640.

Ewing J. A. 1893: *Magnetic Induction in Iron and Other Metals*. London: D. Van Nostrand.

Friedman M. 1968: The role of monetary policy. *American Economic Review*, 58, 1–17.

Friedman M. 1977: Nobel lecture: Inflation and unemployment. *Journal of Political Economy*, 85, 451–72.

Frisch R. 1936: On the notion of equilibrium and disequilibrium. *Review of Economic Studies*, V, 100–5.

Georgescu-Roegen, N. 1966: *Analytical Economics: Issues and Problems*. Harvard, MA: Harvard University Press.

Georgescu-Roegen, N. 1971: *The Entropy Law and the Economic Process*. Harvard, MA: Harvard University Press.

Glazebrook R. T. 1935: James Alfred Ewing 1855–1935: *Obituary Notices of Fellows of the Royal Society of London*, 1, 475–92.

Goodwin P. B. 1977: Habit and hysteresis in mode choice. *Urban Studies*, 14, 95–8.

Gregory R. G. 1982: Work and welfare in the years ahead. *Australian Economic Papers*, 21, 219–43.

Haavelmo T. 1944: The probability approach in econometrics. *Econometrica*, supplement.

Hargreaves Heap S. P. 1980: Choosing the wrong natural rate: Accelerating inflation or decelerating employment and growth. *Economic Journal*, 90, 611–20.

Kaldor N. 1933: A classificatory note on the determinateness of equilibrium. *Review of Economic Studies*, II, 122–36.

Kemp M. C. and Wan H. Y. Jr. 1974: Hysteresis of long-run equilibrium from realistic adjustment costs. In Horwich, G. and Samuelson, P. A. (eds), *Trade, Stability and Macroeconomics*, New York: Academic Press,

Loemker L. E. (ed.) 1969: *Leibniz: Philosophical Papers and Letters*. Dordrecht.

Lotka A. J. 1925: *Elements of Mathematical Biology*. Baltimore: William and Wilkins.

Page L. and Adams N. I. 1969: *Principles of Electricity*, 4th edn, Princeton: D. Van Nostrand.

Phelps E. S. 1972: *Inflation Policy and Unemployment Theory*. London: Macmillan.

Pippard A. B. 1985: *Response and Stability*. Cambridge: Cambridge University Press.

Samuelson P. A. 1965: Some notions of causality and teleology in economics. Reprinted in Merton, R. C. (ed.) (1972): *The Collected Scientific Papers of Paul A. Samuelson*, Vol. III. Massachusetts: MIT Press.

Samuelson P. A. 1968: What classical and neoclassical monetary theory really was. Reprinted in Merton, R. C. (ed.) 1972: *The Collected Scientific Papers of Paul A. Samuelson*, Vol.III. Massachusetts: MIT Press.

Schumpeter J. A. 1934: *The Theory of Economic Development*. Harvard: Harvard University Press.

Strotz R. H. 1955/6: Myopia and inconsistency in dynamic utility maximisation. *Review of Economic Studies*, XXIII, 165–80.

Tobin J. 1965: Money and economic growth. *Econometrica*, 33, 671–84.

Part III
The Characteristics of the Unemployed

4

Real Wage Adjustment and Long-term Unemployment

ALAN BUDD, PAUL LEVINE and PETER SMITH

Introduction

One of the striking aspects of the rise in unemployment in the UK since 1980 has been the even more rapid rise of long-term unemployment. In 1967 the ratio of long-term to total unemployment was only 0.1 and since then there appear to have been three periods when this ratio was in approximate steady state; around 0.16 in 1969–72, 0.23 from 1977 to 1979 and 0.4 from 1984 to the present.

Why should we be so concerned with this phenomenon? First, there are grounds of *equity*. Not only are the benefits from the recent recovery concentrated within the employed 'insiders' but, in addition, within the unemployed 'outsiders' the costs are very unevenly distributed. This disparity can be clearly stated by looking at the expected average duration of unemployment. For the newly unemployed the expected duration is around 11 months. Those who have been unemployed for 12 months can expect on average to be unemployed for another 21 months (Budd et al., 1985).

Second, there are grounds of *macroeconomic inefficiency*. An increase in unemployment which is increasingly concentrated at the long-term end of the duration spectrum cannot be attributed to an increased mobility of the labour force. Indeed the rise in long-term unemployment reflects the fact that almost all recent changes in unemployment in the UK can be accounted for by a drop in the flow out

of unemployment (Pissarides, 1986). It follows that any resource allocation gains associated with the present high level of unemployment are
likely to be small.

Finally there is the question of *wage inflation.* There appears to be
considerable evidence within the OECD countries that long-term
unemployment exerts less downward pressure on wage increases than
short-term unemployment (Coe, 1986; Layard and Nickell, 1985). This
helps to explain why real wages are rising in the UK and elsewhere at
such high levels of unemployment. It also has important implications for
macroeconomic policy, a point we pursue further in the section on
model properties.

In the next section a model is presented to explain the duration profile
of unemployment. In this model a key parameter is the outflow rate
from unemployment, which can be thought of as the average probability
of leaving the register. Flow data for the UK indicate that this average
probability of finding a job within a given quarter is considerably less for
the long-term than for the short-term unemployed (see Budd et al.,
1985). The model shows that this differential is crucial for explaining the
recent sharp rise in the ratio of long-term to total unemployment.

We believe that this fall in probability is associated with both a reduction in the intensity of job search and with a reluctance of employers to
hire the long-term unemployed. The process can be understood by
analogy with a flower shop. The seller has, on day 1, a stock of fresh
flowers. Suppose there is no price variation. Then the most popular
varieties will sell first, leaving on day 2, a cohort consisting of a higher
proportion of the less fashionable flowers, which in addition, are a day
older. These in turn will compete with a new supply of fresh flowers, so
that over time a cohort will develop which consists mainly of the less
popular varieties which are also fading.

Something of the same process may be happening in the labour
market. The unemployed with the most favourable labour market
characteristics will be the first to find jobs. The cohort of those who fail
to find jobs will increasingly consist of those with less favourable qualifications. In addition the experience of unemployment on both the
unemployed and on emloyers' perceptions will reinforce the deteriorating prospects of this cohort.

It is important to distinguish between the two reasons for the
probability of leaving unemployment to fall with unemployment
duration. One cause is the initial heterogeneity of the unemployed. The
other is the effect of unemployment on the individual. For example,
skills may become rusty or obsolete; work habits may be weakened. In
addition employers may use the history of unemployment as a signal to
indicate employee productivity.[1]

In the section on long-term unemployment and the *U–V* curve we
show that if the second 'deterioration of human capital' effect is

significant, then this can help to explain the considerable shifts in the relationship between unemployment and vacancies (the '*U–V* curve') which have been observed in some OECD countries.

By the same token if the experience of unemployment is having an effect on the unemployed this can also explain the differential Phillips curve effect on wage adjustment. In the section on the complete labour market we pursue this point by outlining a complete model of the labour market in which a real wage equation includes the ratio of long-term to total unemployment as well as total unemployment.

The next section presents the estimated labour market model which now constitutes part of the London Business School (LBS) macro-economic model of the UK economy. The final section concludes the chapter by presenting and discussing simulations on the LBS model with alternative wage equations.

The Model of Long-term Unemployment

We begin by writing down the identity

$$U_{t+1} - U_t = I_t - O_t \tag{4.1}$$

where U_t is the level of unemployment at the beginning of period t and I_t and O_t are inflows and outflows into and out of unemployment. Inflows I_t consist of workers who have been fired or made redundant plus those who have quit, plus those who are new entrants or re-entrants into the labour market without jobs. The outflows O_t consist of workers who have been hired plus those who have retired and others leaving the register.

Let us introduce the following definitions:

u_t^τ=the stock of unemployed at the beginning of period t who have been unemployed for τ periods.
π_t^τ=the proportion of those who were unemployed for periods at the beginning of period t leaving the register during period t.

Then we may write

$$u_{t+1}^{\tau+1} = (1 - \pi_t^\tau) u_t^\tau, \quad \tau > 0 \tag{4.2}$$

which is an identity which states that those unemployed for duration $\tau+1$ at the beginning of period $t+1$ are those who were unemployed for duration τ at the beginning of period t minus those in this group, $\pi_t^\tau u_t^\tau$ in number, who left the register during period t.

Let us define long-term unemployment, U_t^{LT}, as those who have been unemployed for T period or longer. Then total U_t can be written as the sum of short-term and long-term unemployment,

$$U_t = \sum_{\tau=0}^{T-1} u_t^\tau + \sum_{\tau=T}^{\infty} u_t^\tau. \tag{4.3}$$

(We ignore the upper limit on the duration of unemployment due to mortality and retirement.)

We are interested in the ratio of long-term to total unemployment.

$$R_t = \frac{U_t^{LT}}{U_t} = \frac{\sum_{\tau=T}^{\infty} u_t^\tau}{\sum_{\tau=0}^{\infty} u_t^\tau}. \tag{4.4}$$

Those who have just become recorded as unemployed at the beginning of period t are the inflows during the previous period, i.e. $u_t^0 = I_{t-1}$. (We exclude from I_t those in the inflow who leave unemployment during period t.) Then from equation (4.2)

$$u_t^\tau = (1-\pi_{t-1}^{\tau-1})\,(1-\pi_{t-2}^{\tau-2}) \ldots (1-\pi_{t-\tau}^{0})\, I_{t-\tau-1} \tag{4.5}$$

for $\tau \geq 1$. Equation (4.5) relates the unemployment of duration τ at time t to the inflow into unemployment $\tau+1$ periods earlier. It says that unemployment of duration τ equals the flow $\tau+1$ periods ago minus those finding employment in the intervening period.

Now consider a steady state described by $U_t = \bar{U}$, $I_t = O_t = \bar{I}$, $U_t^\tau = \bar{U}^\tau$, $\pi_t^\tau = \bar{\pi}^\tau$ and $R_t = \bar{R}$. Suppose also that the probabilities of leaving unemployment $\bar{\pi}^\tau$ are constant with respect to duration τ. Letting $\bar{\pi}^\tau = \bar{\pi}$ we then have from equation (4.5) that

$$U_t^\tau = (1-\bar{\pi})^\tau\, \bar{I} \tag{4.6}$$

so that substituting into (4.4) we obtain the steady-state ratio of long-term to total unemployment as

$$\bar{R} = (1-\bar{\pi})^T. \tag{4.7}$$

It is of interest to note that $\bar{R}$ depends only on the probability of leaving the register and not on the inflow rate.

To get some feel of the model so far it is instructive to compute current values of $\bar{R}$ for some OECD countries for which the steady state seems to have been reached. In the steady state $\bar{I}=\bar{O}=\bar{\pi}\bar{U}$. Data are available for R_t, U_t and I_t for the countries listed in table 4.1. From the table we can see that the model's value for $\bar{R}$ is rather low varying form 65 per cent of the actual value for West Germany and France to 78 per cent for the Netherlands. One possible reason for this is that π^τ in fact varies with τ. We now refine the model to take into account this variation.

Table 4.1 *Calculations of $\bar{R}$ for constant $\pi^\tau=\bar{\pi}$, 1985q4.*

Country	Inflow per month, $\bar{I}$ (thousands)	Unemployment $\bar{U}$ (thousands)	$\bar{\pi}=\dfrac{\bar{I}}{\bar{U}}$	$\bar{R}$ given by eqn (4.7)	$\bar{R}$ actual
West Germany	277	2149	0.13	0.19	0.29
France	259	2505	0.10	0.27	0.41
Netherlands	47	743	0.06	0.46	0.51
UK	316	3277	0.10	0.30	0.40

Source: EUROSTAT

In order to keep the analysis tractable we shall approximate π^τ by a simple function of the form

$$\begin{aligned} \pi^\tau &= \pi_1 \qquad \tau \le T_1 < T \\ &= \pi_2 < \pi_1 \tau > T_1. \end{aligned} \tag{4.8}$$

We shall focus only on the steady-state value for R_t, $\bar{R}$, which now becomes, after a little algebra

$$\bar{R} = \frac{\pi_1(1-\pi_1)^{T_1+1}(1-\pi_2)^{T-1-T_1}}{[\pi_2(1-(1-\pi_1)^{T_1+1})+\pi_1(1-\pi_1)^{T_1+1}]} . \tag{4.9}$$

We are interested in the effects of unequal probabilities between duration of unemployment cohorts. We shall therefore choose π_1, π_2 so that the average probability

$$\bar{\pi} = \sum_{\tau=0}^{\infty} \pi_t^\tau u_t^\tau / \sum_{\tau=0}^{\infty} u_t^\tau$$

remains the same. Again some algebra then implies that

$$\bar{\pi} = \frac{\pi_1\pi_2}{\{\pi_2[1-(1-\pi_1)^{T_1+1}]+\pi_1(1-\pi_1)^{T_1+1}\}} . \tag{4.10}$$

Then clearly $\pi_1 > \bar{\pi} > \pi_2$ and equation (4.9) becomes

$$\bar{R} = \frac{\bar{\pi}(1-\pi_1)^{T_1+1}(1-\pi_2)^{T-1-T_1}}{\pi_2}. \tag{4.11}$$

In table 4.2 we demonstrate the effect of a non-constant π^τ. The exercise is based on UK data from which quarterly values for π^τ can be calculated (Budd et al., 1985).

Table 4.2 *Calculations of $\bar{R}$ for non-constant π^τ (T= 4, T_1=3 quarters). UK Data, 1984*

$\bar{\pi}$	π_1	π_2	$\bar{R}$
0.26	0.26	0.26	0.30
0.26	0.30	0.20	0.31
0.26	0.32	0.17	0.33
0.26	0.35	0.13	0.37
0.26	0.36	0.11	0.40

Source: Employment Gazette

We take T_1=3 and T=4 quarters and choose π_1 and π_2 to be close to their observed average UK values for unemployment durations ≤ 3 quarters and >3 quarters respectively. Then with $\bar{\pi}$ kept at 0.26 (per quarter) based on $\bar{R}$=0.40, $\bar{R}$ turns out to be consistently determined at its observed value 0.40.

What then do the results of the model say about the labour market and the characteristics of the unemployed? To go back to the simple step-function, equation (4.8), the pair of probabilities (π_1, π_2) is a statement about the labour market characteristics of different duration cohorts of unemployed. Of those who become unemployed or enter or re-enter the labour market the best qualified and most determined push to the front of the queue. By this process of selection the cohort who have been unemployed for a long period increasingly consist of the less qualified and less determined. Our model demonstrates the crucial importance of this 'queue-jumping' for explaining the extremely high proportion of long-term to total unemployment.

Another possible additional explanation of the non-constant π^τ is that the *experience of unemployment* itself reduces the probability of re-entering employment. As well as obvious demoralization there may be a process of deskilling at work here with the unemployed losing their initial skills through inactivity and/or technological change rendering the original skills inappropriate. In the next section we explore this possibility in the context of a re-examination of the debate concerning the outward shift in the unemployment/vacancies relationship.

Long-term Unemployment and the U–V Curve

Let us return to the identity equation (4.1) which equates net flows into unemployment with the increase in unemployment.

Let $I_t = I^l_t + I^e_t$ where I^l_t are inflows into unemployment from the 'labour reserve' consisting of new entrants or of re-entrants into the labour market and I^e_t are inflows from employment. Similarly define $O_t = O^l_t + O^e_t$ where O^l_t are outflows from unemployment who leave the register but do not enter employment and O^e_t are the outflows into employment. If we now write $O^e_t = \pi_t U_t$ where π_t is the outflow rate from unemployment into employment, and $I^e_t = s_t N_t$ where N_t is total employment and s_t is the outflow from employment into unemployment, then equation (4.1) becomes

$$U_{t+1} - U_t = s_t N_t - \pi_t U_t + I^l_t - O^l_t. \qquad (4.12)$$

Following Jackman et al. (1985) we can also write $O^e_t = p_t V_t$ where p_t is the rate at which vacancies are filled by the unemployed. Then $\pi_t = p_t V_t / U_t$ provides the connection between the two approaches. What then determines p_t? In much of the literature (for example Hall, 1977) it is assumed that p_t, the proportion of vacancies filled by the unemployed per period, is a function of the ratio of job-seekers to vacancies. If the proportion of the unemployed who are searching per period is c_t, this implies that $p_t = f(c_t U_t / V_t)$, $f' > 0$.

Another interpretation of c_t is that it measures the willingness on the part of the unemployed to accept the available jobs. A fall in c_t increases the number of 'effective vacancies' per period, V_t / c_t, and so reduces p_t. This immediately suggests that employers' willingness to fill jobs from available applications may also be an important determinant of p_t. So let the proportion of job applicants accepted per period be d_t. We then respecify $p_t = f(c_t U_t / V_t, d_t)$ with $f_1, f_2 > 0$.

Our discussion and equation (4.12) now give a long-run or steady-state 'U–V curve'

$$I^l_t - O^l_t + s_t N_t = f(c_t U_t / V_t, d_t) V_t. \qquad (4.13)$$

From equation (4.13) we can deduce four possible explanations as to why an outward shift in the U–V relationship should occur. First the net inflow into unemployment from the labour reserve, $I^l_t - O^l_t$, rises.

Second, the turnover rate s_t rises. Third the search intensity c_t falls. Finally the choosiness of employers rises which means that the acceptance rate d_t falls.

Empirical evidence for the UK (Jackman et al., 1985; Layard and Nickell, 1985) suggests that a fall in c_t and d_t provides the most convincing explanation for the outward shift in the $U–V$ curve in that country. But why should search intensities and acceptance ratios fall? This brings us to long-term unemployment.

We have seen from the first section that the exit probabilities of leaving unemployment are less for the long-term than for the short-term unemployed in the UK. This would clearly arise if search intensities and acceptance ratios were less for the long-term unemployed. But this *in itself* does not imply that the *average* search intensity and acceptance ratio falls as long-term unemployment rises.

To pursue this important point let us focus on the search intensity (the same argument applies to the acceptance rate). Let R_t be the ratio of long-term to total unemployment at the beginning of period t. For convenience we drop the subscript t and write the average search intensity

$$c=(1-R)c^{ST}+Rc^{LT} \tag{4.14}$$

where c^{ST} and c^{LT} are the average search intensities for the short-term and long-term unemployed respectively. It would then appear that if $c^{ST}>c^{LT}$ then as R increases c decreases. But this is misleading.

To see this suppose there are n types of unemployed workers grouped according to their labour market characteristics and thus their ability to leave unemployment. Let u_{it}^{τ} be the cohort of unemployed of type i who at the beginning of period t have been unemployed for τ periods. As in equation (4.14) we still drop the subscript t in what follows. Dividing the duration cohorts into short-term and long-term groups, we then have

$$c^{ST}=\frac{\sum_i c_i^{ST}\, u_i^{ST}}{\sum_i u_i^{ST}} \tag{4.15}$$

with a corresponding expression for c^{LT}. Then putting $\sum u_i^{ST}=(1-R)U$ (total short-term unemployment) and $\sum u_i^{LT}=RU$ (total long-term unemployment) and substituting for c and c^{LT} into equation (4.14) we obtain

$$c=\sum_i c_i^{ST}(1-R_i^{LT})\frac{U_i}{U}+\sum_i c_i^{LT}R_i^{LT}\frac{U_i}{U} \tag{4.16}$$

where $R_i^{LT} = \dfrac{U_i^{LT}}{U_i}$ and $U_i = U_i^{ST} + U_i^{LT}$ (i.e. R_i^{LT} is the ratio of long-term

to total unemployment, U_i, for group i).

Equation (4.16) rather than (4.14) is the appropriate one for examining the effect of long-term unemployment on the average search intensity. Suppose that unemployment rises so that in the absence of a sufficient increase in vacancies, exit probabilities of leaving unemployment fall for all groups. Then R_i^{LT} rises for all i (see Budd et al, 1985). The effect on c is found by differentiating equation (4.16) to give

$$\frac{\partial c}{\partial R_i^{LT}} = (c_i^{LT} - c_i^{ST}) \frac{U_i}{U} \qquad . \qquad (4.17)$$

Clearly then if $c_i^{LT} = c_i^{ST}$ or, in other words, if long-term unemployment has no effect on search intensitites *for individual groups* then the average search intensity will not be affected either. If on the other hand $c_i^{LT} < c_i^{ST}$ then a rise in long-term unemployment will cause the average search intensity to fall. The crucial issue then is the relative size of c_i^{ST} and c_i^{LT} and, since the same argument applies to acceptance ratios, the relative size of d_i^{ST} and d_i^{LT}. If the experience of unemployment causes search intensitites of individual groups to fall and the choosiness of employers to rise, then the average search intensity c_t and the average acceptance ratio d_t in equation (4.13) will fall. A rise in long-term unemployment will then cause the U–V curve to shift outward provided that there is no countervailing fall in $I_t^l - O_t^l + s_t N_t$.

This last caveat is an important one. As long-term unemployment increases one would expect an increasing number of this group to retire, possibly prematurely. Then O_t^l rises and the U–V curve shifts inward. Given that older workers are disproportionately represented in the long-term unemployed this effect may be strong enough to dominate any reduction in average search intensity. Thus, on theoretical grounds, an increase in long-term unemployment has an ambiguous effect on the U–V curve. If the 'withering effect' dominates, it shifts outwards. If the 'retirement effect' dominates then the shift is in the opposite direction.

The Complete Labour Market

In this section we assess the importance of changes in long-term unemployment in a complete model of the labour market. This, in turn, forms part of the LBS macroeconomic model of the UK economy (London Business School, 1986).

Long-term Unemployment

The number of long-term unemployed is, by definition, equal to the unemployed one year ago who have not found jobs since. Therefore we may write

$$U_t^{LT}=f(U_t/V_t, R_t, X_t)\ U_{t-4}\quad f_1, f_2 > 0 \tag{4.18}$$

where $f(.)$ is the average probability of the unemployed at time $t-4$ not finding a job between $t-4$ and t. As we have seen in the previous section the ratio of unemployment to vacancies is expected to be one determinant of this probability. Another determinant should be the search intensity which our analysis suggests will be negatively related to R_t. Both these effects may have lags going back four periods. (In equation (4.18) as in the equations that follow we omit the details of lag structure.) Candidates for exogenous variables x_t are replacement ratios, especially those relevant to the long-term unemployed.

The U–V Curve

The analysis of the previous section suggests a steady-state U–V curve of the form

$$U=f(V, R, X)\quad f_1 < 0, f_2 > 0. \tag{4.19}$$

Potential candidates for X include the separations rate s, the change in the working population, replacement ratios and mismatch indices (see Jackman et al., 1985; Budd et al., 1985).

The Real Wage

In the LBS model there are three sectors of the labour market – manufacturing, non-manufacturing excluding public sector services, and the public sector. Wage determination in the latter is considered as exogenous. The real wage equation for the remaining two private sectors takes the form

$$W/PC^e=f(U, R, W^o/PC^e, X)\quad f_1 < 0, f_2 \cdot f_3 > 0 \tag{4.20}$$

where W is the nominal wage rate, PC^e is the expected consumer price index and W^o is the nominal wage rate in the other sector. There are a large number of possible candidates for the exogenous variables X. Possible candidates are replacement ratios, tax rates affecting both employers and employees, mismatch indices and trade union membership. The innovative feature of equation (4.20) as far as the LBS model is concerned is the inclusion of the ratio of long-term to total unemployment which captures the view that the long-term unemployed exert less downward pressure on wages than the short-term unemployed (see, for example, Layard, 1986).

The Demand for Labour

The demand for labour in the two private sectors is determined by an equation of the form

$$L=f[W/P(1+t),X] \quad f_1<0 \qquad (4.21)$$

where L is employment, P is the producer price index and t the employers' national insurance contribution rate. Exogenous variables (exogenous, that is, to the labour market) include relative factor prices and aggregate demand.

Labour Supply

The total labour force $N=L+U$ is modelled in terms of the differential supply decisions of both males and females. The male labour force is assumed to follow the male population of working age. The female labour supply function takes the form

$$\frac{N^f}{POP^f}=f\left[U, \frac{W}{PC^e}(1-\tau), X\right] \quad (f_1 \gtrless 0, f_2 > 0) \qquad (4.22)$$

where POP is the total population of working age, f superscript refers to females and τ is the direct tax rate. Thus female participation depends on unemployment and the average after tax level of the expected real wage. The effect of unemployment on labour supply is ambiguous. High unemployment may discourage women from registering but the effect of unemployment on household incomes could have the opposite effect. Included in exogenous variables is the relative earnings of females to males.

The equation system outlined above can be solved to give unemployment, real wages and employment in two sectors, the total labour force, and long-term unemployment given PC^e, P, t, τ POP and the remaining exogenous variables in X. Many of these latter variables are of course endogenous to the LBS model itself and the assessment of long-term unemployment effects requires a full simulation of the entire model. This we consider in the final section.

Estimation

Estimates of the equations outlined in the previous section are shown in tables 4.3–4.7. The data on which they are estimated are generally for the period 1965/q2 to 1984/q4 and are described in full in the data appendix. In each of the columns of the tables we present the various point estimates along with the steady-state forms of the equations. We also report some summary test statistics to give an indication of their statistical adequacy. In all cases we find that the equations have serially uncorrelated errors and acceptable stability properties. More detailed explanation of their derivation is made in Holly and Smith (1987), and Budd et al. (1985).

In the equation determining the number of long-term unemployed (table 4.3) we find that the data are well explained by a combination of past values of the average probability S, the ratio of unemployment to vacancies and the ratio of long-term unemployment to the total. In no case did we find a significant role for replacement ratios. This may reflect the inadequacy of the measurement of replacement ratios and average benefit levels. The effects of the measures of tightness in the labour market (U/V) and of the degree of search intensity (R) are highly significant, however, in the short run and steady state.

The U–V curve (table 4.4) is found to be a less than proportional relationship between the unemployment and vacancy rates, which has shifted out over time and is significantly affected by the ratio of long-term unemployment to the total. The increase in the ratio of long-term unemployment explains over half of the shift in the U–V curve over the late 1970s. The estimates are structurally stable and well determined. We found that there was no significant effect of the separations rate, the change in the working population, replacement ratios or mismatch indices. These alternatives, as well as the derivation, are discussed more fully in Budd et al. (1985).

The expected real wage equations for manufacturing and non-manufacturing are shown in table 4.5. In the case of manufacturing we find that the unemployment rate and the ratio of long-term to total unemployment have a significant effect on wages.[2] The positive coefficient on the ratio R implies that the long-term unemployed exert a much smaller effect on real wages than the short-term. The full implications for real wage growth will be examined in the final section of the chapter using simulations of the model of the labour market within the structure of a large macroeconometric model of the UK. We find that unemployment benefits and expected real wages in the non-manufacturing sector do not affect manufacturing wages. However, incomes policies have affected the level of weages in the past. In non-manufacturing we find that manufacturing wages have a 'leading-sector' effect in addition to real unemployment benefit. Unemployment appears significantly in this equation but we failed to find an independent effect of long-term unemployment. The differential impact of long-term unemployment will, however, affect non-manufacturing wages through the effect on wages in manufacturing.

Table 4.3 *Long-term unemployment equation (estimation period: 1972/q1–1985/q4; method of estimation: OLS)*

	$\log S_t$
$\log S_{t-1}$	0.8432
	$(9.41)^a$
$\log S_{t-3}$	−0.4705
	(3.36)
$\log S_{t-4}$	0.4900
	(4.24)
$\log (u/v)_{t-3}$	−0.06094
	(2.27)
$\log R_{t-1}$	−0.4218
	(5.05)
$\log R_{t-3}$	0.4392
	(4.78)
constant	−0.2541
	(1.68)

Test statistics	
$\bar{R}^2$	9.955
s.e.	6.16%
DW	2.02
$LM(5)^b$	11.52
$Z_1(4)^c$	0.161

Steady-state coefficients	
$\log (U/V)$	0.444
$\log R$	0.127
constant	−1.851

Variables
S:average probability of unemployed at $t-4$ finding a job between $t-4$ and $t=U_t^{LT}/U_{t-4};U$: unemployment level; u: unemployment rate$=U/N;N$: total labour force; V: vacancy level; v: vacancy rate$=V/L;$ L: total employment; U^{LT}: long-term unemployment; R: ratio of long-term unemployment to total$=U^{LT}/U$

[a] *t*-statistics in brackets
[b] LM(5): Lagrange Multiplier test for up to fifth-order autocorrelation (95% critical value=11.07)
[c] Z_1 (4): Chow test of within-sample parameter stability (95% critical value: F (4,41)=2.60)
Data sources: in appendix

Table 4.4 *U–V curve (estimation period: 1972/q1–1985/q4; method of estimation: TSLS)*

	$\log u_t$
$\log u_{t-1}$	1.266
	(20.2)
$\log u_{t-3}$	−0.4149
	(8.01)
$\log v_t$	−0.09366
	(2.48)
$\log R_{t-2}$	0.1571
	(4.28)
$1/\text{time}^2$	−720.10
	(2.96)
constant	0.5253
	(8.15)
Test statistics	
$\bar{R}^2$	0.998
s.e.	2.78%
DW	2.20
LM(5)	8.41
$Z_1(4)$	0.129
$Z_2(7)^a$	1.20
Steady-state coefficients	
$\log V_t$	0.629
$\log R_t$	1.055
constant	3.528

[a] $Z_2(n)$ is a test for the validity of the n instruments used, additional instruments are $\log v_{t-1}$, $\log v_{t-2}$, $\log v_{t-3}$.

The estimates of the employment functions in table 4.6 show that producer cost real wages have a signficant effect on the level of employment in both manufacturing and non-manufacturing. In addition, output in both sectors and the real cost of other inputs in manufacturing have a significant impact. The real wage elasticity is higher in non-manufacturing as noted in Holly and Smith (1987). In both equations we treat real wages and output as endogenous right-hand side variables and use instrumental variable estimation with some valid instruments of OECD variables. We also use *IV* estimation for the *U–V* curve.

Table 4.5 *Real wage equations (estimation period: 1965/q2–1984/q4; method of estimation: OLS)*

	Manufacturing $\log (Wm/PC^e)_t$	Non-manufacturing $\log (Wn/PC^e)_t$
$\log (W/PC)_{t-1}$	0.9431 (13.75)	0.3761 (2.97)
$\log (W/PC)_{t-2}$		0.1444 (1.10)
$\log (W/PC)_{t-3}$	−0.1897 (2.90)	−0.3433 (2.94)
$\log [Wm^*(1-TAX)/PC]_{t-1}$		0.1343 (1.82)
$\log u_{t-1}$	−0.1002 (3.53)	−0.1135 (2.33)
$\log u_{t-2}$	0.1365 (3.68)	0.2004 (2.34)
$\log u_{t-3}$		−0.1319
$\log u_{t-4}$	−0.06136 (3.75)	(2.73)
$\log (UBEN/PC)_{t-1}$		0.07386 (1.67)
$\log R_{t-4}$	0.02186 (2.09)	
$\log (1+TAX3)_t$	−0.4475 (1.91)	
$\log (1+TAX3)_{t-2}$	0.5321 (2.18)	
IPOL	−0.00763 (1.68)	−0.004981 (0.70)
time	0.001454 (2.97)	0.003598 (4.43)

Test statistics		
$\bar{R}^2$	0.997	0.982
s.e.	0.83%	1.77%
DW	1.96	2.06
LM(5)	11.03	7.13
$Z_3(4)$	3.71	5.16

Steady-state coefficients		
$\log [Wm(1-TAX2)/PC]$		0.163
$\log u$	−0.213	−0.0734
$\log R$	0.0886	
$\log (UBEN/PC)$		0.0898
$\log (1+TAX3)$	1.710	
IPOL	−0.0309	−0.00605
time	0.00590	0.00437

Variables used ((in addition to table 4.3):
Wm: wages in manufacturing; *Wn*: wages in non-manufacturing; *PC*: consumption deflator; *PC^e*: expected consumption deflator; TAX2: direct tax index; TAX3: indirect tax index; UBEN: unemployment benefit index; IPOL: incomes policy dummy
$Z_3(4)$ test of the outside sample parameter stability (95% critical value $\chi^2(4)=9.49$).

Table 4.6 *Employment equations (estimation period: 1965/q2–1984/q4; method of estimation: TSLS)*

	Manufacturing log Lm_t	Manufacturing log Ln_t
$\log L_{t-1}$	1.185	1.350
	(7.39)	(3.29)
$\log L_{t-2}$	−0.2847	−0.4142
	(1.94)	(3.29)
$\log Y_t$	0.08342	0.1827
	(4.25)	(3.40)
$\log Y_{t-1}$		−0.1174
		(3.28)
$\log [W/P(1+TAX1)]_t$	−0.2099	
	(3.88)	
$\log [W/P(1+TAX1)]_{t-1}$	0.1368	
	(2.46)	
$\log [W/P(1+TAX1)]_{t-2}$		−0.0709
		(2.93)
$\log (P^m/P)_t$	0.04099	
	(1.90)	
$\log (P^m/P)_{t-1}$	−0.04084	
	(2.55)	
Test statistics		
$\bar{R}^2$	0.998	0.534
s.e.	0.392%	0.476%
DW	1.99	2.22
LM (5)	0.027	9.06
Z_3 (8)	9.03	7.34
Z_2 (12)	7.14	8.96
Steady-state coefficients		
$\ln[(W/P)(1+TAX1)]$	−0.733	−1.085
$\ln Y$	0.837	1.0
$\ln(P^m/P)$	−0.0745	—

Variables (in addition to table 4.3):
Lm: employment in manufacturing; *Ln*: employment in non-manufacturing; *Ym*: output in manufacturing; *Yn*: output in non-manufacturing; TAX1: employers' national insurance contributions rate; *P^m*: price of non-manufacturing output.
Additional instruments used: current values and lags of world GNP, money supply, real world price of raw materials.

Table 4.7 *Female participation rate equation (estimation period=1965/q2–1984/q4; method of estimation: OLS)*

	$\triangle log\ N_t^f$
$\triangle \log N_{t-1}^f$	−0.1810
	(1.26)
$\triangle \log N_{t-2}^f$	−0.5230
	(3.56)
$\log (N_{t-3}^f/P_{t-1}^f)$	−0.7467
	(5.76)
$\log u_t$	−0.06235
	(3.54)
$\log u_{t-1}$	0.05184
	(1.98)
$\log u_{t-2}$	−0.05756
	(3.51)
$\log [WSI^*(1-TAX2)/PC]_t$	0.05884
	(1.98)
$\log [WSI^*(1-TAX2)/PC]_{t-3}$	0.04582
	(2.25)
$\log (W^f/W^m)_{t-1}$	0.1448
	(2.25)
$\log (W^f/W^m)_{t-3}$	0.2295
	(3.02)
time	0.001986
	(4.68)

Test statistics	
$\bar{R}^2$	0.581
s.e.	0.319%
DW	1.80
LM (5)	10.92
Z_3 (8)	8.12

Steady-state coefficients	
$\log P^f$	1.0
$\log u$	−0.091
$\log (WSI^*(1-TAX2)/PC]$	0.40
$\log (W^f/W^m)$	0.5013
time	0.0027

Variables (in addition to table 4.3):
N^f: female labour force; P^f: female participation of working age; WSI: wage and salary index; W^f/W^m: relative female to male wage rates.

The female participation rate is found to be a negative function of unemployment and a positive function of both absolute and relative female/male real wages (table 4.7). The discouragement effect of unemployment on female labour supply dominates any household income effect in our estimates. The time trend is intended to pick up demographic and other excluded effects. We found no significant effect for any benefit ratios or a dummy for the Equal Pay Act; any missing effect is picked up by the equation dynamics.

The estimates presented thus provide a complete estimated model of the UK labour market. Whilst the individual equations can be solved for both short-run and steady-state values of the conditionally exogenous variables, the solution is best observed through a simulation of the model within the structure of the LBS model of the UK. This is presented in the final section.

Model Properties

We first consider the steady-state properties of the U–V curve and the long-term unemployment equation taken together. In the steady-state $S_t = U_t^{LT}/U_{t-4} = U_t^{LT}/U_t = R_t$. Thus from table 4.3 we have

$$\log R = -2.12 + 0.51 \log u/v. \tag{4.23}$$

From table 4.4 as $t \to \infty$ the effect of the time trend disappears and we have

$$\log u = 3.52 - 0.63 \log v + 1.06 \log R. \tag{4.24}$$

For a given unemployment rate (determined through the workings of the entire model) we may solve equations (4.23) and (4.24) for steady-state values of R and v. It is instructive however to first consider equation (4.23) separately. Table 4.8 shows long-run values for R

Table 4.8 *Long-run values of R given by equation (4.23)*

$\dfrac{u}{v}$	R (%)
1	12
10	39
15	47
20	55

corresponding to different values for u/v. Recently u/v has fluctuated between 15 and 20, in which case R will eventually settle somewhere between 4.7 per cent and 5.5 per cent. The most recent figure for R (1986/q2) is 41 per cent so our equation suggests we have not yet reached the steady-state.

Solving equations (4.23) and (4.24) for R and v, given u, we obtain

$$
\begin{bmatrix} \log R \\ \log v \end{bmatrix} = \begin{bmatrix} -2.69 & 0.71 \\ 1.09 & -0.39 \end{bmatrix} \begin{bmatrix} 1 \\ \log u \end{bmatrix}.
\tag{4.25}
$$

This implies that if u remains at the 1986/q3 figure of 13 per cent[3] steady-state values of R and v will be 42 per cent and 1.09 per cent respectively. The latter figures compares with a vacancy rate around 0.7 per cent in 1986/q1, so that a further outward shift in the u–v curve is predicted by our system.

In addition to this steady-state analysis of part of the model, we can also examine the short-term dynamic paths of all the variables in the labour market model. We do this by embedding the model outlined in the sections on the complete labour market within the LBS model of the UK. The simulation that we examine is that of an increase in government expenditure on procurement of £600m (at 1980 prices) per quarter which we assume is made unexpectedly and permanently in the first quarter of 1987. Table 4.9 shows the effects of this policy change on each of the endogenous variables in the labour market plus some variables whose behaviour impinges on the labour market. The expansionary fiscal policy change is assumed to be accommodated by an increase in the money supply sufficient to keep short-term nominal interest rates constant throughout. The impact on GDP is expansionary over the first 5 years with the peak during the second year.

Unemployment falls by 125,000 after one year and by 235,000 after 4 years. Short-term unemployment takes up the bulk of this fall for the first year. This may be due to queue jumping by the short-term unemployed or reduced inflows into short-term unemployment. In either case the result is that the ratio of long-term unemployment to the total rises for the first 2 years before falling, as falling unemployment and rising vacancies reduce long-term unemployment. The ratio falls by 2.2 per cent after 8 years. Vacancies rise by 38,000 after two years. This increase arises from a movement along the U–V curve as unemployment falls and an offsetting reduction, later on, due to an inward shift of the U–V curve as the long-term unemployment ratio R falls.

The impact on wages of this expansionary policy is that they rise over the path of the simulation both in nominal and real terms. The depreciation of the exchange rate leads to higher prices than expected and an adaptive response of money wages in both manufacturing and

Table 4.9 *Simulation of £600/quarter permanent increase in government procurement (1980 prices)*

	Year 1	Year 2	Year 4	Year 8
Unemployment				
Rate (% points)	−0.51	−0.62	−0.67	−0.33
Total	−125	−213	−235	−122
Short term	−86	−113	−87	−2
Long term	−39	−100	−148	−120
LT ratio (% points)	0.64	0.19	−1.71	−2.20
Vacancies				
Rate (% points)	0.126	0.185	0.126	−0.023
Total	25.9	37.5	24.1	−7.0
Employment				
Total (%)	0.68	1.14	1.32	0.66
Manufacturing	77.1	126.3	155.6	65.9
Non-manufacturing	94.7	167.6	192.5	111.4
Labour force (%)	0.17	0.28	0.39	0.18
Consumer prices (%)	1.25	2.56	4.89	6.87
Wages (%)				
Manufacturing (nominal)	0.90	2.86	5.64	7.46
(real)	−0.35	0.30	0.75	0.59
Non-manufacturing (nominal)	1.09	2.80	5.40	7.19
(real)	−0.15	0.24	0.51	0.32
Exchange rate (%)	−7.90	−7.98	−7.56	−3.69
GDP (%)	1.56	1.88	1.42	0.33

All figures given as thousands except where indicated; deviations from base forecast.

non-manufacturing. Money wages rise by 5 to 6 per cent after four years and by 7 to 8 per cent after eight years. Real (consumer price) wages rise by 0.6 per cent after eight years in manufacturing and by 0.3 per cent in non-manufacturing.

The differential impact of long- and short-term unemployment on wage determination can be well observed from table 4.10. In column one the figures from table 4.9 are reproduced. In column two the figures for the same variables are shown where we replace the equation for manufacturing wages with one that does not distinguish the effects of long-term unemployment (i.e. omits R from the specification). The result of replacing the wage equation is that wages rise by less in the short run (i.e. over the first year) and by more over the longer run (i.e. over 8 years). In the short run the inclusion of the long-term

Table 4.10 *Comparison of simulation results*

	Year 1	Year 2	Year 4	Year 8
Unemployment				
Total I	−125	−213	−235	−122
II	−155	−254	−232	−104
Long term I	−39	−100	−148	−120
II	−46	−110	−155	−114
Real wages				
Manufacturing I	−0.35	0.30	0.75	0.59
II	−1.92	−0.62	0.87	1.25
Non-manufacturing I	−0.16	0.24	0.51	0.32
II	−0.38	0.18	0.50	0.37

I: simulation results using equation from table 4.5.
II: simulation results using equation for wages in manufacturing which omits differential effect of long-term unemployment. This equation is estimated on the same basis as that in table 4.5:

$$\log (Wm/PC^{\,e})_t = 1.116 \log (Wm/PC)_{t-1} - 0.07565 \log (Wm/PC)_{t-2}$$
$$\qquad\quad (14.68) \qquad\qquad\qquad (0.77)$$
$$-0.2130 \log (Wm/PC)_{t-3}$$
$$(2.90)$$
$$+0.06885 \log U_{t-1} - 0.1054 \log U_{t-2} - 0.05799 \log U_{t-3}$$
$$(2.40) \qquad\qquad (2.08) \qquad\qquad (2.07)$$
$$+0.0205 \log (UBEN/PC)_{t-1} - 0.01316 \, IPOL + 0.00149 \, time$$
$$(0.76) \qquad\qquad\qquad (3.40) \qquad\qquad (4.42)$$
$$\bar{R}^2 : 0.997 \quad DW: 1.95 \quad Z_3(4): 3.28$$
$$\text{s.e.: } 0.93\% \quad LM(5): 5.27$$

unemployment ratio means that the immediate larger fall in short- rather than long-term unemployment and consequent rise in R leads to higher wage growth than otherwise. Over the longer term the fall in R leads to lower real wage growth than in the case where R is omitted from the equation. The impact on unemployment of these differential effects is of a somewhat smaller fall in unemployment in the first year and an increased fall by the sixth year. We conclude that the inclusion of long-term unemployment in the wage equation has important implications for the dynamic properties of the LBS model.

The labour market is of crucial importance for any macromodel. The introduction of long-term unemployment into the wage equation not only has important effects on the behaviour of the LBS model; it will also enable us to examine the effect of targetting jobs on the long-term unemployed in the context, say, of an increase in public sector employment.

NOTES

The authors are grateful for the comments of Sean Holly and their other colleagues at the Centre for Economic Forecasting (CEF) and to Francis Breedon for assistance. The research was carried out under ESRC grant number B0125 0012.
1 Lockwood (1986) has formalized this idea in a screening model of decisions on falling vacancies.
2 It should be noted that this equation encompasses, in the sense that the equation has a lower standard error, a similar equation which omits the effect of long-term unemployment. The structure of this alternative equation is shown in table 4.10.
3 This is on the definition of unemployment rate up to October 1986. Under the new definition the 1986/q3 figure is 11.

DATA APPENDIX

L	m	Employment in manufacturing
	n	Employment in non-manufacturing
		(full-time equivalent=Ln*NMHOURS/40)
		,000 CSO

W m Wages in manufacturing

$$W=E/(1.3*HOURS-0.3*NHOURS)$$

E		Average earnings in manufacturing
W	n	Average earnings in non-manufacturing
		(full-time equivalent=Wn*NMHOURS/40)
		1980=100 DEG

WSI   Wages and salaries per employee (whole economy)
                   1980=100   CSO

W^f/m Ratio of average female to male full-time earnings (whole economy)
                   1980=100   NES

Y	m	Output in manufacturing
	n	Output non-manufacturing
		1980=100 ET

P Producer price: manufacturing output
                   1980=100   ET

pm Wholesale price: manufacturing inputs
                   1980=100   ET

PC	Price of private consumption 1980=100 ET	

$UBEN$ Unemployment benefit index
1980=100   SSS

U Total adult unemployment in UK
,000   DEG

U^{LT} Total of those unemployed for more than 52 weeks
,000   DEG

V Total number of vacancies registered at Job Centres
adjusted by the average of the ratio of the outflow of
registered vacancies to engagements and the ratio of the
inflow of registered vacancies to total separations
,000   DEG

N Working population
N^f :female
N^m :male
,000   DEG

P Population of working age
P^f :female
P^m :male
,000   AAS

TAX1   Employment tax rate on employers %, [(YEC+TNIS)/
YWS]
       where YEC: Employers' contributions   ET
            TNIS: National Insurance surcharge   FINS
            YWS: Total wage and salary bill   ET
       includes SET where appropriate

TAX2   Direct tax rate on workers
%, [TJYP/YJTAX]
       where TJYP: Personal income tax payments   ET
            YJTAX: Personal taxable income   CSO

TAX3   Indirect tax rate
%, (TEAX/C£)
       where TEAX: VAT, specific duties etc   FINS
            C£: Consumers' expenditure   ET

HOURS   Average hours worked in manufacturing

NHOURS   Normal hours worked in manufacturing
1980=100   DEG

NMHOURS   Average hours worked in non-manufacturing
Hours/week   NES

All data are seasonally adjusted.

Sources:
      AAS —Annual Abstract of Statistics
      CSO —Central Statistical Office
      DEG —Department of Employment Gazette
      ET   —Economic Trends
      FINS —Financial Statistics
      NES —New Earnings Survey
      SSS   —Social Security Statistics

All data are available from the authors on request.

REFERENCES

Budd, A. P., Levine, P. and Smith, P. N. 1985: Unemployment, vacancies and the long-term unemployed. Centre for Economic Forecasting Discussion Paper No. 154 (revised).

Coe, D. T. 1986: Tests for Hysteresis in Aggregate Wage Equations. OECD, mimeo.

Hall, R. E. 1977: An aspect of the economic role of unemployment. In Harcourt G. C. ed., *The Microeconomic Foundations of Macroeconomics*. London; Macmillan.

Holly, S. and Smith, P. N. 1987: A two-sector analysis of the UK labour market. *Oxford Bulletin of Economics and Statistics* (forthcoming).

Jackman, R., Layard R. and Pissarides, C. 1985: On vacancies. Centre for Labour Economics, London School of Economics, Discussion Paper No. 165.

Layard, R. 1986: *How to Beat Unemployment*. Oxford: OUP.

Layard, R. and Nickell, S. J. 1985: The causes of British unemployment. *National Institute Economic Review*, 111.

Lockwood, B. 1986: Adverse Selection and the Duration of Unemployment. Birkbeck College, mimeo.

London Business School 1986: The London Business School Quarterly Econometric Model of the United Kingdom Economy. Mimeo.

Pissarides, C. 1986: Unemployment flows in Britain: Facts, theory and policy. *Economic Policy*, 3.

5

Characteristics of the Long-term Unemployed: Evidence from the Labour Force Survey

STEPHEN W. CREIGH

Introduction

This chapter reviews the information available on the characteristics of unemployed people using Department of Employment (DE) data and research. The discussion will focus on how the long-term unemployed differ from people unemployed for shorter periods. The long-term unemployed are defined as unemployed for 1 year or more.

Popular discussion of unemployment and time-series analyses focus on the Department's administrative records. However, in recent years this series has been subject to considerable revision and provides only limited information (duration, school-leaver status, age, sex and location) on the unemployed. These claimant records are discussed in the first section of this chapter. In-depth studies of particular aspects of the claimant data and sample surveys have been undertaken. However, such studies in turn raise their own problems, notably limited sample sizes and the tendency to concentrate upon youth unemployment rather than the older age groups where (as we shall see) long-term unemployment is more prevalent.

These considerations make the other major Departmental data source on unemployment – the annual Labour Force Survey (LFS) – a very attractive analytical tool. In the final section of the chapter, information on some selected characteristics of the unemployed is presented. The richness of the LFS database is illustrated by comparing the short-term and long-term unemployed in terms of marital status, job search methods, qualification/education levels and health.

Claimant Data

The most commonly used statistics on long-term unemployment are of course the official Department of Employment figures – hereafter referred to as *claimant unemployment*. This series covers people claiming benefits (unemployment benefit, supplementary allowances or national insurance credits), who declare that they are unemployed and available for work on the relevant count date (normally the second Thursday in each month).

As a source of information on the unemployed this series has certain clear advantages for the analyst:

1 it provides a monthly time series of claimant unemployed;
2 the exact count of claimant unemployed meeting certain defined criteria raises no sampling issues and provides detailed local data.

Currently the DE publishes data on the long-term claimant unemployment count every quarter i.e. January, April, July and October. Monthly figures are not produced because of the work involved in the processing of the remaining (10 per cent) non-computerized records. In recent years the official claimant unemployment statistics have been affected by various changes in coverage, which make the production of a fully comparable time series on long-term unemployment (or indeed unemployment generally) difficult.

The main changes affecting the claimant series began in October 1982. Thereafter unemployment statistics are based on records of claimants held at the Unemployment Benefit Offices (UBOs) of the DE. This followed from the introduction of voluntary registration of claimants at Job Centres and Careers Offices. The new voluntary system followed recommendations of a 'Rayner' scrutiny of benefit payment arrangements and was designed to avoid the need for visits to more than one office and so reduce waste and duplication of effort.

The new computerized claimant records differ from the previous manual count of Job-Centre registrants in several key ways:

1 persons not claiming benefit are excluded from the claimant count;
2 severely disabled people previously excluded are now included in the claimant series;
3 computerized information means that there is less delay between a person finding work and that fact being reflected in the official series.

During the year preceding the switchover the new system yielded a figure 2.5 per cent (78,000) less than the old method. The definitional changes of October 1982 reduced recorded unemployment by a further 3.7 per cent (112,000), giving an average reduction of over 6 per cent (200,000) compared with the old Job Centre-based clerical count in the year to October 1982.

Measures announced in the 1983 Budget meant that men aged 60 and over were no longer required to sign on at a UBO to secure national insurance credits. In addition men over 60 receiving supplementary benefit could receive this at the higher long-term rate without the need to sign on. This affected the long-term unemployed, disproportionately reducing the number of claimant unemployed recorded as claiming for 1 year or more by 25,000 by April 1983 (the total effect was around 29,000). Between April and October 1983 97,000 long-term unemployed claimants were affected (129,000 claimants in total).

Around 20,000 persons per working day enter and leave the unemployment claimant count. Until March 1986 a 1 week waiting period separated the 'count date' and the shut down for compilation of statistical returns. This was adequate to allow for the late arrival of information on new claimants but not sufficient to prevent over-recording due to delays in claimants informing their UBO that they have ceased to be unemployed. Claimants were assumed to still be unemployed on the count date unless they informed their UBO to the contrary by the time figures were compiled. The DE estimates that over-recording on this basis averaged around 65,000 (all but 5,000 on the computerized records).

From the March 1986 count an additional 2 weeks' delay (making 3 weeks in all) was introduced between the count date and the compilation of the unemployment statistics. This reduces recorded unemployment by around 50,000 with some residual over-recording being justified by the requirement to process and publish the information promptly.

In July 1985 the DE produced a seasonally adjusted time series for unemployed excluding school leavers on the then current basis extending back to 1971. Back figures incorporating the effects of the March 1986 changes are now also available in recent issues of the *Employment Gazette*.

In table 5.1 time series for total claimant unemployment and for long-term claimants are presented for the period October 1982 to April 1986. The data on total unemployed are the comparable time series (excluding school leavers). The second and third columns cover the long-term unemployed – the recorded count and quarter to quarter changes adjusted approximately for changes in collection method. Thus, for example, the decline of 15,000 in recorded long-term unemployed numbers between January and April 1986 is almost entirely due to the change in collection method made in March 1986.

Table 5.1 *Trends in United Kingdom 1982–1986*

	Total[a] unemployed (thousands)	Claimants unemployed for 1 year and over (thousands)	
		Recorded level[c]	Best estimate of change allowing for discontinuities[d]
1982			
October	2,715	1,029[b]	—
1983			
January	2,790	1,107	+78
April	2,844	1,143	+62
July	2,889	1,103	+53
October	2,899	1,143	+46
1984			
January	2,928	1,188	+45
April	2,959	1,218	+30
July	2,999	1,234	+16
October	3,047	1,277	+43
1985			
January	3,075	1,316	+39
April	3,121	1,334	+18
July	3,121	1,327	−3
October	3,120	1,352	+25
1986			
January	3,153	1,372	+20
April	3,202	1,357	−1

[a] Seasonally adjusted excluding school leavers.
[b] Estimated level taking account of Civil Service dispute.
[c] Not adjusted for seasonality or discontinuities.
[d] Estimated to allow for Civil Service dispute of 1981, the 1983 Budget Measures, discontinuity of July 1985 in Northern Ireland and change in compilation method in March 1986.
Source: DE *Gazette* and unpublished estimates

The mounting total of UK long-term unemployed from 1983 to 1985 is evident in table 5.1.

The Department also publishes flow data on claimant unemployed which reflect the dynamics underlying the monthly count. An average of some 400,000 people join the register each month (around 20,000 per working day) and the outflow is similar. Many of the individuals leaving the count gain employment. However, some leave for a variety of other reasons, e.g. retirement, training, exit from the labour force or exhaustion of benefit/social security entitlement. The annual inflows and outflows total 4.7 million.

For the period January 1985 to January 1986 analyses of outflows show that almost half of newly unemployed claimants left the register within 3 months of joining it. Two-thirds left the register within 6 months and four-fifths left within 1 year. The remaining fifth (about 70,000 people per month) flow into long-term unemployment.

The probability of leaving the unemployment count tends to decline as the spell of unemployment increases, but the outflows are still appreciable among the long-term unemployed. After 18 months 10 per cent of the inflow remain with 90 per cent having left. By 24 months 93 per cent have left the count and after 36 months this rises to 96 per cent.

Each quarter the DE publishes analyses of unemployment duration by age and sex. Full monthly duration data are not produced due to the remaining clerical records used in the claimant count system and the consequent work load involved in more frequent analysis.

The available stock data on long-term unemployed by age group and sex are summarized in tables 5.2 to 5.5. April 1985 is the latest date for which comparable LFS data are available (for the Spring of 1985) while April 1986 is the most recent claimant count currently available. The pattern does not vary greatly between these dates.

Taking April 1986 as the benchmark it is clear that most of the 1.3 million claimant unemployed were males (over 76 per cent), with adult males (25 years and over) making up just under 60 per cent of the total.

Table 5.2 *Distribution of long-term claimant unemployment by age and sex April 1985 and April 1986 (United Kingdom)*

	Percentage share of group in total unemployed over 1 year			
	Males		Females	
	April 1985	April 1986	April 1985	April 1986
Under 25 years	18.1	16.4	8.7	8.1
25–54	47.1	48.2	11.3	12.1
55 years and over	11.5	11.6	3.3	3.6
All ages	76.7	76.2	23.3	23.8

N(000s)=1,334 in April 1985 and 1,357 in April 1986.
Changes between April 1985 and April 1986 were affected by the change in the compilation system in March 1986.
Source: DE *Gazette* (various issues)

Table 5.3 *Distribution of long-term claimant unemployment by age and sex, April 1985 and April 1986 (United Kingdom)*

	Unemployed for over 1 year (thousands)			
	Age group			
	Under 25 years	25–54	55 years and over	All ages
Males				
April 1985	242 (30)	629 (51)	153 (52)	1,024 (45)
April 1986	223 (30)	653 (52)	157 (52)	1,033 (45)
Females				
April 1985	117 (24)	149 (32)	44 (63)	310 (31)
April 1986	109 (24)	163 (33)	49 (64)	324 (31)
Total				
April 1985	359 (28)	778 (46)	197 (54)	1,334 (41)
April 1986	332 (28)	819 (46)	206 (54)	1,357 (41)

See note table 5.2.
Figures in brackets denote percentages of all unemployed in age group.
Source: DE

Long-term unemployed comprise 41 per cent of all claimant unemployed (45 per cent of all male claimants).

It is of course important to remember that the long-term unemployed claimant count comprises individuals with very diverse claimant records. Some may only just have crossed the 1-year 'threshold' while others have been claimants for extremely long periods. The duration pattern in April 1986 is summarized by age and sex in table 5.4.

So far as males over 25 are concerned over 50 per cent have been claimants for a year or more, over one-third for 2 years or more and more than a quarter for over 3 years. Among younger male claimants short-term unemployment is predominant, with almost 70 per cent having claimed for less than a year.

Given the coverage of the data it is not surprising to find female claimants more heavily concentrated in the short-term group (almost 69 per cent claiming for less than a year). Adult married women with a working spouse are not eligible for supplementary benefit once their own unemployment benefits are exhausted, although they may continue to sign on to obtain National Insurance credits. The only group of

Table 5.4 *Claimant unemployment by age, sex and duration, April 1986 (United Kingdom)*

Number of claimants (in thousands)

Duration	Males				Females			
	Under 25 years	25–54	55 years and over	All ages	Under 25 years	25–54	55 years and over	All ages
Under 1 year	508 (69.5)	603 (48.0)	146 (48.2)	1,257 (54.9)	344 (75.9)	341 (67.3)	27 (35.5)	712 (68.8)
Over 1 year	223 (30.5)	653 (52.0)	157 (51.8)	1,033 (45.1)	109 (24.1)	166 (32.7)	49 (64.5)	324 (31.3)
of which								
1 to 2 years	112	204	46	362	60	76	14	150
over 2 years	111	450	111	671	49	90	35	174
Over 2 years	111 (15.2)	450 (35.8)	111 (36.6)	671 (29.3)	49 (10.8)	90 (17.8)	35 (46.1)	174 (16.8)
of which								
2 to 3 years	50	129	32	211	23	34	10	68
over 3 years	61	321	79	461	26	56	25	106
Over 3 years	61 (8.3)	321 (25.6)	79 (26.1)	461 (20.1)	26 (5.7)	56 (11.0)	25 (32.9)	106 (10.2)
of which								
3 to 4 years	31	99	25	155	14	22	9	45
over 4 years	30	222	54	306	12	34	16	62
Over 4 years	30 (4.1)	222 (17.7)	54 (17.8)	306 (13.4)	12 (2.6)	34 (6.7)	16 (21.1)	62 (6.0)
of which								
4 to 5 years	17	83	19	119	7	14	7	28
over 5 years	13	139	35	187	5	20	10	34
All claimants	731	1,256	303	2,290	453	507	76	1,035

Source: DE Gazette

Table 5.5 Estimated claimant unemployment rates by age, sex and duration, April 1986 (United Kingdom)

Percentage rates

	Males			Females		
	Unemployed less than 1 year	Unemployed 1 year and over	All unemployed	Unemployed less than 1 year	Unemployed 1 year and over	All unemployed
Under 25 years	15.6	6.8	22.4	12.8	4.1	16.9
25–54	6.8	7.4	14.2	5.4	2.6	8.0
55 years and over	7.1	7.6	14.7	2.1	3.8	5.9
All ages	9.0	7.4	16.4	7.0	3.1	10.1

Rates were expressed as a percentage of all employed and unemployed.
While figures are presented to one decimal place this should not be taken to imply precision. The denominators used are the sum of mid–1984 estimates of employed employees and the unemployed and have not yet been revised to take into account new employment data.

females where long-term claimants form the majority is that covering older claimants (55 and over) which includes widows eligible for supplementary benefits in their own right who are available for work.

Overall claimant unemployment rates by age and sex are published in the Employment *Gazette* using estimates of the relevant active populations. The results of a similar exercise are presented in table 5.5 where the numbers of short-term and long-term unemployed are expressed as a percentage of the estimated number of employed and all unemployed in each age and sex category.

Because of the assumptions made in calculating them such rates must be treated with caution and the single decimal place used should not be taken to indicate such precision. However, the figures do show that about 1 in 13 of economically active males had been claiming benefits for 1 year or more in April 1986.

As well as the data on the age and sex of claimants, information is available on their geographical location. The April 1986 count data are summarized in table 5.6 where the shares of the 11 UK standard regions in all unemployment and long-term unemployment are presented.

For both sexes the three regions of Southern England all have smaller shares in national long-term unemployment than in total unemployment. The only other region with a below average rate of male

Table 5.6 *Long-term claimant unemployed by region, April 1986*

	Percentage share in UK total			
	Males		*Females*	
	Unemployed 1 year or more	*All unemployed*	*Unemployed 1 year or more*	*All unemployed*
South East	20.8	24.7	23.0	25.0
East Anglia	2.0	2.6	2.5	2.9
South West	4.8	6.2	6.4	7.1
West Midlands	12.0	11.1	12.0	10.4
East Midlands	6.1	6.4	6.1	6.4
Yorks and Humberside	9.5	10.3	9.3	9.3
North West	15.2	14.6	14.3	13.1
North	8.2	7.9	7.3	6.7
Wales	5.7	6.0	5.3	5.2
Scotland	10.9	11.3	10.5	10.6
Northern Ireland	4.8	4.3	3.3	3.2

Source: DE *Gazette*

unemployment – the East Midlands – also has a smaller share of long-term unemployment than of total unemployment. Across the other regions the pattern is less clear. So far as males are concerned some regions with above average overall unemployment rates have greater shares in long-term unemployment (e.g. the North) while this is not so for others (e.g. Scotland).

In recent years DE/MSC have sponsored several studies of aspects of unemployment. Some of these have either used the claimant database or drawn samples of the long-term unemployed and undertaken detailed interviews and/or postal surveys. Samples have typically been limited to 2,000/3,000 individuals due to the cost involved in such detailed survey work. Several of these studies have focused on youth rather than the long-term unemployed in general.[1]

Social and Community Planning and Research (SCPR) has been commissioned to carry out a survey of the destinations of long-term unemployed leaving the claimant register. This study will fill an important gap in our knowledge of the termination of claimant unemployment. A two-stage survey is planned beginning with an interview (in 1986) and with a postal follow-up (in 1987). Sample sizes will be around 2,000 outflows and 1,000 people remaining on the register. A comprehensive questionnaire is currently being developed and piloted.

The Labour Force Survey

The LFS is a voluntary household survey designed to collect information on the labour force. In Britain it is carried out by the Office of Population Censuses and Surveys (OPCS) on behalf of the Department of Employment. A similar survey is carried out in Northern Ireland and there are comparable surveys based around a common core of questions and definitions in all European Community (EC) member states during the Spring of each year.

Since 1983, Labour Force Surveys have been carried out annually (previously they were every 2 years). The latest results relate to the Spring 1985 survey which covered 60,000 private households in Britain during the March to May period. This is equivalent to about 1 in every 350 households.

Since the Spring of 1984 the British LFS has consisted of two elements – a major Spring survey covering 45,000 households and a continuous quarterly survey of 15,000 households. Together these provide the 60,000 household annual Spring survey giving information on around 120,000 people aged 16 and over.

Broad summaries of LFS results are published in the *Employment Gazette* together with occasional specialized in-depth studies of particular issues. EC-wide results are also published by SOEC. Annual data tapes are made available to Government Departments in the Spring following the survey and copies are deposited in the ESRC survey archive at Essex University a year later.

Unemployment as conventionally defined in the context of British labour force estimates covers *persons without a job who were looking for work during a particular reference week*. People who were not seeking work in that week because they were temporarily sick or on holiday, or were waiting the result of a job application or waiting to start a new job already obtained, are treated as if they were seeking work. Students seeking work but not available to start a job within 2 weeks because they have to complete their education are excluded, as are Youth Training Scheme (YTS) trainees (but not TOPS participants who are seeking work). On this basis some 2.8 million persons were unemployed in Great Britain in April 1985. All LFS estimates in this chapter will relate to this conventional definition.

LFS data on unemployment have certain advantages over the claimant count:

1 Information on unemployment can be related to a very wide range of background information – not simply age, sex, duration and region as in the claimant count.
2 Information is provided on job seekers not claiming benefit payments.

Like any other data source the LFS has its limitations:

1 it is a sample survey subject to sampling error;[2]
2 around one-third of information is provided by a related adult member of the same household where a household member is not available for interview.

Nevertheless the LFS provides a valuable and rich data source with a much larger achieved sample (around 8,000 unemployed) than specialist surveys (typically covering 2,000 or so individuals). The LFS provides labour market information on a large sample of the long-term unemployed which can be directly compared to other specified sub-groups.

Unemployed LFS respondents were asked how long they had been looking for paid work using nine categories ranging from under 1 month to 4 years or more. These declared duration of search categories form the basis for the information on long-term and short-term unemployment presented in the remainder of this chapter.

The pattern of long-term unemployment across EC countries is shown in table 5.7. These data relate to April 1983, the latest date for which EC-wide information is available. They show that the UK had the

Table 5.7 *Duration of search by unemployed job seekers, LFS Spring 1983*

	Percentage with declared duration of search 12 months or more			
	Males	Females	Total	Total long-term job seekers (thousands)
West Germany	40.7	37.7	39.3	657
France	39.4	44.9	42.5	698
Italy	53.6	58.4	56.3	1,014
Netherlands	49.0	49.9	49.4	316
Belgium	60.0	70.3	65.8	293
Luxembourg	36.8	31.1	33.9	—
United Kingdom	52.3	36.0	46.6	1,310
Irish Republic	42.3	24.8	36.4	67
Denmark	27.3	37.4	32.2	70
Greece	24.6	44.6	34.8	99
Europe 10	47.2	46.0	46.6	4,525

Unemployed persons were those who in the reference week had no employment and:
1 were actively looking for paid employment and were immediately available to start work or,
2 were looking to set up in self-employment or,
3 were waiting to be called back to a job from which they had been laid off or,
4 had found a job to start after the reference week.
Duration estimates can only be regarded as an approximation since in many cases respondents may not be able to fix or recall an exact start date. Duration estimates may overestimate unemployment since job search may have started while still holding a job or unavailable immediately for other reasons.
Source: LFS 1983 in SOEC (1985b) T68 and 69

largest number of long-term unemployed of any EC country – with about 29 per cent of all the EC's long-term unemployed. The long-term unemployed accounted for over 52 per cent of UK male unemployment, a larger share than in any other EC economy except Belgium and Italy. However, the share of long-term unemployed in female unemployment was lower than in any other country except the Irish Republic and tiny Luxembourg.

The pattern of long-term unemployment (as defined in the LFS) by sex and age group for Great Britain in the Spring of 1985 is shown in table 5.8. Comparable data for claimants in April 1985 are given in parentheses. The LFS-sample-based estimates are subject to standard errors. However, even allowing for these it is clear that the numbers of long-term unemployed males and adult males are significantly lower than the comparable claimant counts. In contrast the numbers of long-term unemployed females and prime age females considerably exceed the relevant claimant figures.

LFS respondents were asked directly if they are currently (last week) signing at an Unemployment Benefit Office to claim unemployment benefit, supplementary allowance or National Insurance Credits. This information on the declared claimant status of the unemployed as defined in the LFS is summarized in table 5.9.

Among long-term unemployed males all but 8.6 per cent declared themselves to be current claimants and consequently they form a sub-set of the DE's claimant count. Given the restrictions on benefit claims by married women, it is not surprising to find that some 40.9 per cent of long-term unemployed women were non-claimants (among prime age women current claimants form only a minority – 45.7 per cent).

Table 5.8 *Distribution of long-term unemployed by age and sex, LFS Spring 1985 (Great Britain)*

	Unemployed for over 1 year (thousands)			
	Age group			
	Under 25	*25–54*	*55 and over*	*All ages*
Males	257	520	120	898
(claimants)	(229)	(595)	(149)	(973)
Females	121	210	34	365
(claimants)	(112)	(144)	(43)	(299)
Total	378	730	154	1,262
(claimants)	(341)	(739)	(192)	(1,272)

LFS data relate to duration of job search (see also note to table 5.7) while claimant data relate to duration of benefit claim.
Source: 1985 LFS and DE *Gazette* for Claimant data (April 1985)

Table 5.9 *Declared claimant status of LFS unemployed by age, sex and duration Spring 1985 (Great Britain)*

	Males (thousands)					
	Unemployed less than 1 year			Unemployed 1 year and over		
	Non-claimant	Claimant	DN Apply/ no response	Non-claimant	Claimant	DN Apply/ no response
Under 25	66	280	—	11	246	—
25–54	43	316	—	31	487	—
55 and over	13	50	—	35	81	—
All ages	122	646	*	77	814	*

	Females (thousands)					
Under 25	101	185	—	18	103	—
25–54	234	140	—	114	96	—
55 and over	17	*	—	15	13	—
All ages	352	334	*	147	212	*

* indicates estimate less than 10,000.
Some 44,000 unemployed males and 40,000 unemployed females are excluded from this analysis as their duration of unemployment is not known. Some 52 per cent of these males were claimants and 27 per cent of the females.
Source: LFS 1985

A recently published DE analysis investigated the relationship between labour force estimates and claimant count data for all unemployed. In addition to the LFS unemployed who were claiming benefits it is estimated that some 1.08 million persons (640,000 males and 440,000 females) were claimants but were not unemployed in conventional LFS terms. This was because some 200,000 individual claimants (110,000 males) had done some work in the relevant period and 880,000 (530,000 males) had not been actively looking for work (in the last week). Unfortunately comparable estimates are not available for the long-term unemployed.

Data on the age, sex and marital status of LFS unemployed by duration are summarized in tables 5.10 and 5.11. The predominant group among long-term unemployed are married men who accounted for 37.4 per cent of all long-term job seekers and 17.4 per cent of total unemployment. The next two most numerous groups are short-term

Table 5.10 *Unemployed persons by age, sex, duration and marital status, LFS Spring 1985 (Great Britain)*

	Males (thousands)					
	Single		Married		Previously married	
	Unemployment duration					
Age	Less than 1 year	1 year and over	Less than 1 year	1 year and over	Less than 1 year	1 year and over
Under 25	308 (77.6)	205 (60.3)	37 (11.2)	50 (10.6)	*	*
25–54	82 (20.6)	120 (35.3)	241 (73.0)	339 (71.6)	36 (83.7)	61 (71.7)
55 and over	*	15 (4.4)	52 (15.8)	84 (17.8)	*	22 (25.9)
All ages	397 (100.0)	340 (100.0)	330 (100.0)	473 (100.0)	43 (100.0)	85 (100.0)
	Females (thousands)					
Under 25	202 (89.3)	102 (72.4)	82 (20.3)	19 (11.9)	*	— (—)
25–54	22 (4.7)	35 (24.8)	304 (75.2)	125 (78.7)	48 (80.0)	50 (76.9)
55 and over	*	*	18 (4.5)	15 (9.4)	*	15 (23.1)
All ages	226 (100.0)	141 (100.0)	404 (100.0)	159 (100.0)	60 (100.0)	65 (100.0)

Percentages of relevant totals in brackets.
— Widowed, divorced and separated
* indicates estimate less than 10,000.
Source: LFS 1985

unemployed married women (14.8 per cent of all unemployed) and single males (14.6 per cent of the total).

The LFS provides several important pieces of information on the labour market characteristics of the unemployed. In the remainder of this chapter I shall review the data on job search activity, qualifications/ education and the limitations on work because of health. Other relevant 1985 data, such as the occupation/industry in which the unemployed person last worked, were not available at the time of writing but will be processed and released in due course.[3]

Respondents were asked which of a range of nine job search methods they had used in the last 4 weeks and also to indicate their main (or only) method. Their responses on main job search method are summarized in table 5.12.

Table 5.11 *Share in total unemployment by age, sex, duration and marital status, LFS Spring 1985 (Great Britain)*

Percentage share in total unemployed

Males

Age	Single Less than 1 year	Single 1 year and over	Married Less than 1 year	Married 1 year and over	Previously married† Less than 1 year	Previously married† 1 year and over
Under 25	11.3	7.5	1.4	1.8	0.1	0.1
25–54	3.0	4.4	8.9	12.4	1.3	2.2
55 and over	0.3	0.6	1.9	3.1	0.1	0.8
All ages	14.6	12.5	12.1	17.4	1.6	3.1

Females

Age	Single Less than 1 year	Single 1 year and over	Married Less than 1 year	Married 1 year and over	Previously married† Less than 1 year	Previously married† 1 year and over
Under 24	7.4	3.7	3.0	0.7	0.1	—
25–54	0.8	1.3	11.2	4.6	1.8	1.8
55 and over	0.1	0.1	0.7	0.6	0.3	0.6
All ages	8.3	5.2	14.8	5.8	2.2	2.4

† Widowed, divorced and separated.
Source: LFS 1985

For all the sub-groups of unemployed males, visiting an MSC Job Centre or an Employment Office was the most common main job search method. Some 38.9 per cent of short-term unemployed males and 44.9 per cent of long-term unemployed males used this method most. Studying situations vacant columns in newspapers was the next most common method for males, being used by 17.8 and 20.0 per cent of short-term and long-term unemployed respectively.

Of the remaining options only three were named as their main job search method by substantial numbers of unemployed males. Direct approaches to firms/employers, personal contacts and answering advertisements were all selected by about 11 per cent of all short-term unemployed males. Personal contacts were the third most common main search method among long-term unemployed males (11.4 per cent) followed by direct approaches to firms/employers (8.7 per cent) and answering advertisements (8.6 per cent).

Table 5.12 Job search methods of the unemployed by age, sex and duration, LFS Spring 1985

Main job search method	Males (thousands)							
	Less than 1 year				1 year and over			
	16–24	25–54	55 and over	All ages	16–24	25–54	55 and over	All Ages
Visit Job Centre, employment office etc.	160 (46.0)	120 (33.4)	20 (31.7)	300 (38.9)	141 (54.7)	219 (42.0)	42 (35.0)	403 (44.9)
Name on private agency books	*	*	—	10 (1.3)	*	*	—	*
Advertising in newspapers	*	*	—	*	*	*	—	*
Answering advertisements	26 (7.4)	49 (13.7)	*	83 (10.7)	14 (5.4)	49 (9.4)	14 (11.7)	77 (8.6)
Studying situations vacant column in newspapers/	57 (16.3)	65 (18.1)	14 (22.2)	137 (17.8)	48 (18.6)	100 (19.2)	32 (26.7)	179 (20.0)
Direct approach to firms/ Employers	39 (11.1)	40 (11.1)	*	85 (11.0)	20 (7.7)	52 (10.0)	*	78 (8.7)
Personal contacts	30 (8.6)	47 (13.1)	*	84 (10.9)	23 (8.9)	64 (12.3)	16 (13.3)	102 (11.4)
Other methods								
Waiting for job application results	*	*	*	15 (1.9)	*	*	—	*
Other	*	*	*	12 (1.5)	*	*	*	10 (1.1)
No answer	*	*	*	10 (1.3)	*	*	*	14 (1.6)
DNA	14 (4.0)	15 (4.2)	*	33 (4.3)	*	12 (2.3)	*	21 (2.3)
Total	349 (100)	359 (100)	63 (100)	772 (100)	258 (100)	521 (100)	120 (100)	897 (100)

Table 5.12 (continued)

Females (thousands)

Main job search method	Less than 1 year				1 year and over			
	16–24	25–54	55 and over	All ages	16–24	25–54	55 and over	All Ages
Visit Job Centre, employment office etc.	115 (40.1)	86 (22.9)	*	205 (29.7)	66 (53.7)	59 (28.1)	10 (30.3)	135 (36.8)
Name on private agency books	*	11 (2.9)	*	16 (2.3)	*	*	*	*
Advertising in newspapers	*	*	—	*	—	*	—	*
Answering advertisements	32 (11.1)	55 (14.7)	*	91 (13.2)	11 (8.9)	26 (12.4)	*	38 (10.4)
Studying situations vacant column in newspapers	63 (21.9)	122 (32.5)	10 (35.7)	195 (28.2)	27 (22.0)	78 (37.1)	16 (48.5)	121 (33.0)
Direct approach to firms/ Employers	24 (8.4)	24 (6.4)	*	50 (7.2)	*	*	—	17 (4.6)
Personal contacts	21 (7.3)	29 (7.7)	*	52 (7.5)	*	15 (7.1)	*	23 (6.3)
Other methods Waiting for job application results	*	*	—	16 (2.3)	*	*	—	*
Other	*	*	*	*	*	*	—	*
No answer	*	*	*	*	—	*	*	*
DNA	16 (5.6)	30 (8.0)	*	50 (7.2)	*	*	*	11 (3.0)
Total	287 (100)	375 (100)	28 (100)	691 (100)	123 (100)	210 (100)	33 (100)	367 (100)

Percentage in brackets.
* indicates estimate less than 10,000.
Source: LFS (1985)

So far as males in the predominant 25 to 54 years age group are concerned, it is clear that job search methods differ between short-term and long-term job seekers. The short-term unemployed are significantly less likely to rely on visits to a Job Centre as their main job search method (33.4 per cent did so) than the long-term unemployed (42.0 per cent).

Among males aged 25–54 relying on visits to the Job Centre as their main job search method further differences exist in terms of other (secondary) search methods. For both long- and short-term unemployed males, studying the situations vacant columns in newspapers is the most common other method, with no significant difference in popularity between the long-term unemployed (74.9 per cent) and short-term unemployed (79.3 per cent). However, when more active methods are considered it is clear that the long-term unemployed males are less likely to have used personal contacts (50.7 per cent had done so against 58.1 per cent of the corresponding group of short-term unemployed males), to have approached an employer directly (35.8 per cent against 42.8 per cent for the short-term unemployed) or to have answered newspaper advertisements (37.9 per cent against 47.7 per cent of the short-term unemployed).

Given the limited social security entitlements of married women, it is not surprising to find that studying situations vacant columns in newspapers is generally a more common main job search method than for men. This is especially true for adult women (aged over 25 years) in both the short-term and long-term unemployed groups. Nevertheless, when all ages are considered, long-term unemployed women are more likely to indicate visits to a Job Centre as their main job search technique (36.8 per cent did so) than short-term unemployed women (29.7 per cent).

A series of LFS questions yield data on the education and training of respondents. The answers of the unemployed in terms of qualifications held, age at which full-time education was completed and whether a recognized apprenticeship was completed (or in progress) by sex and age for the two key duration categories are summarized in tables 5.13, 5.14 and 5.15 respectively.

Information on the educational qualifications of unemployed job seekers is set out in table 5.13. In general long-term unemployed report fewer qualifications than short-term job seekers. For prime age males (25 to 54 years) the long-term unemployed are noticeably more likely to have no qualifications at all (65.9 per cent) than short-term job seekers (46.4 per cent). Only 27.3 per cent of all employed males in the age group did not have any qualifications.

The relative lack of qualifications among the long-term unemployed is underlined by the data on age at which full-time education was completed, which are summarized in table 5.14. Some 87.8 per cent of

Table 5.13 *Qualifications of unemployed persons by age, sex, and duration, LFS Spring 1985 (Great Britain)*

	Males (thousands)											
	16–24				25–54				55+			
	Less than 1 year	%	1 year or more	%	Less than 1 year	%	1 year or more	%	Less than 1 year	%	1 year or more	%
Higher degree	*	—	—	—	*		*		—		—	—
First degree	*	—	*	—	14	3.9	*		*		*	
Other degree level:												
Qual. (Grad. member of Prof. Inst. etc.)	—	—	*	—	*		*					
HNC/HND/BEC (Higher) TEC/Higher	—	—	*	—	*		*		*		*	
Teaching qualification	—	—	—	—	*		*		*		*	
Nursing qualification	—	—	—	—	*		—		*		—	
ONC/OND/BTEC (Nat or Gen)/TEC (Nat or Gen)	*	—	*	—	*		*		*		—	
City and Guilds	28	8.0	15	5.9	44	12.2	39	7.6	*		*	
A Level or equivalent	25	7.2	16	6.3	16	4.4	12	2.4	*		*	
O Level or equivalent	79	22.7	37	14.5	32	8.9	32	6.3	*		*	
CSE (other than grade 1)	56	16.1	42	16.4	12	3.3	15	2.9	*		*	
Other qualification	*	*	*	—	20	5.6	23	4.5	*		11	9.2
No qualification	112	32.2	124	48.4	167	46.4	336	65.9	29	44.6	67	55.8
Not known if qualifications	*	*	*	—	*		13	2.5	*		*	
No answer	*	—	*	—	*		*		*		*	
Did not apply	17	4.9	12	4.7	23	6.4	26	5.1	12	18.5	25	20.8
All qualifications	348	100	256	100	360	100	510	100	65	100	120	100

Table 5.13 (continued)

Females (thousands)

	16–24				25–54				55+			
	Less than 1 year	%	1 year or more	%	Less than 1 year	%	1 year or more	%	Less than 1 year	%	1 year or more	%
Higher degree	*	—	—	—	*		*		—	—	—	—
First degree	*	—	*	—	14	3.7	*		—	—	—	—
Other degree level:												
Qual. (Grad. member of Prof. Inst. etc.)	—	—	—	—	*		*		—	—	—	—
HNC/HND/BEC (Higher) TEC/Higher	*	—	—	—	*		*		—	—	—	—
Teaching qualification	*	—	—	—	11	2.9	*		*	—	*	—
Nursing qualification	*	—	*	—	16	4.3	*		*	—	*	—
ONC/OND/BTEC (Nat or Gen)/TEC (Nat or Gen)	*		*		*		*					
City and Guilds	13	4.6	*		*		*		*			
A Level or equivalent	24	8.4	*		20	5.3	25	11.9				
O Level or equivalent	87	30.4	28	23.5	76	20.3	11	5.2				
CSE (other than Grade 1)	53	18.5	29	24.4	20	5.3	13	6.2			*	—
Other qualification	*		*		28	7.5	*				*	
No qualification	73	25.5	46	38.7	138	36.8	108	51.4	12	41.4	13	39.4
Not known if qualifications	*		*		*		*					
No answer	*		*		*						*	—
Did not apply	12	4.2	*	4.2	28	7.5	20	9.5	12	41.4	15	45.5
All qualifications	286	100	119	100	375	100	210	100	29	100	33	100

Source: LFS 1985

Table 5.14 Age on leaving full-time education of unemployed persons by age, sex and duration, LFS Spring 1985 (Great Britain)

Males (thousands)

Age left full-time education	16–24 Less than 1 year		16–24 1 year and over		25–54 Less than 1 year		25–54 1 year and over		55+ Less than 1 year		55+ 1 year and over	
	Numbers	%	Numbers	%	Numbers	%	Numbers	%	Numbers	%	Numbers	%
Under 15	*		*		31	8.7	69	13.3	38	62.3	76	63.3
15	20	5.8	29	11.3	166	46.5	254	49.0	*		*	
16	227	65.2	181	70.4	97	27.2	132	25.5	*		*	
17	28	8.0	18	7.0	16	4.5	20	3.8	*		*	
18	15	4.3	12	4.6	16	4.5	16	3.1	*		*	
19–24	23	6.6	13	5.1	23	6.4	18	3.5	—		*	
25–9					*		*		—		—	
Still in cont. full-time education	32	9.2	*		—		*		—		*	
Never had full-time education	—		—		*		*		*		*	
All ages	348	100	257	100	357	100	518	100	61	100	120	100

Table 5.14 (continued)

	16–24				25–54				55+			
	Less than 1 year		1 year and over		Less than 1 year		1 year and over		Less than 1 year		1 year and over	
Age left full-time education	Numbers	%	Numbers	%	Numbers	%	Numbers	%	Numbers	%	Numbers	%
Under 15	*	—	—	—	18	4.8	23	11.1	12	42.9	16	50.0
15	25	8.8	13	10.8	144	38.4	98	47.3	*	*	*	*
16	155	54.6	84	69.4	104	27.7	49	23.7	*	*	*	*
17	33	11.6	13	10.7	32	8.5	13	6.3	*	—	—	—
18	28	9.9	*	—	28	7.5	10	4.8	—	—	—	—
19–24	16	5.6	*		44	11.7	12	5.8	—	—	*	*
25–9	—	—	—	—	*	—	*	—	—	—	—	—
Still in cont. full-time education	26	9.1	*	—	—	—	—		—	—	—	—
Never had full-time education	—	—	—	—	*	—	*	—	—	—	—	—
All ages	284	100	121	100	375	100	207	100	28	100	32	100

— includes no answer/did not apply in totals.
* indicates estimate less than 10,000.
Source: LFS 1985

Table 5.15 *Apprenticeship record of unemployed persons by age, sex and duration, LFS Spring 1985 (Great Britain)*

Males (thousands)

Apprenticeship	Less than 1 year			1 year and over		
	16–24 yrs	*25–54 yrs*	*55+ yrs*	*16–24 yrs*	*25–54 yrs*	*55+ yrs*
Apprenticeship completed	28 (8.0)	92 (25.8)	18 (28.1)	12 (4.7)	97 (18.7)	23 (19.0)
Apprenticeship not completed (still doing)	*	*	—	—	—	—
No apprenticeship (and discontinued)	295 (84.5)	263 (73.7)	41 (64.1)	242 (94.5)	418 (80.5)	83 (68.6)
No answer	—	*	—	*	*	—
Did not apply	23 (6.6)	—	*	*	—	14 (11.6)
Total	349 (100.0)	357 (100.0)	64 (100.0)	256 (100.0)	519 (100.0)	121 (100.0)

Females (thousands)

Apprenticeship	Less than 1 year			1 year and over		
	16–24 yrs	*25–54 yrs*	*55+ yrs*	*16–24 yrs*	*25–54 yrs*	*55+ yrs*
Apprenticeship completed	*	16 (4.3)	—	—	11 (5.3)	*
Apprenticeship not completed (still doing)	*	—	—	—	—	—
No apprenticeship (and discontinued)	260 (90.6)	356 (95.2)	19 (65.5)	118 (98.3)	198 (94.7)	24 (70.6)
No answer	*	*	—	*	—	—
Did not apply	17 (5.9)	—	10 (34.5)	—	—	*
Total	287 (100.0)	374 (100.0)	29 (100.0)	120 (100.0)	209 (100.0)	34 (100.0)

Percentages in brackets.
Source: LFS 1985

long-term unemployed males age 25 to 54 years left full-time education at the age of 16 or younger compared to 82.4 per cent of short-term unemployed males in that age group. For employed males the corresponding figure was only 69.5 per cent.

The extent to which the various sub-groups of the unemployed had completed a recognized apprenticeship is shown in table 5.15. Given the very limited extent to which women participate in the apprenticeship system in Britain (outside hairdressing) it is not surprising to find that only 3.5 per cent of all unemployed females had completed an apprenticeship. For males the figure was 16.2 per cent. Within the 25 to 54 years age group short-term unemployed males were more likely to have completed an apprenticeship (25.8 per cent had done so) than the long-term employed (18.7 per cent).

Respondents were also asked whether they suffer from any of 14 specified health problems or disabilities, and then whether any of these problems limit the kind of paid work the respondent can do. The results for the short-term and long-term unemployed are summarized in table 5.16.

At least half the unemployed in all the sub-groups considered reported no health problems or disabilities. Not surprisingly the percentage reporting no health problems tended to decline with age, e.g. for long-term unemployed males it fell from 79.5 per cent for 16 to 24 year olds to 53.7 per cent for those aged 55 years and more.

So far as prime age males are concerned the short-term unemployed are more likely to report no health problems (72.3 per cent) than their long-term contemporaries (62.0 per cent). Some 19.7 per cent of long-term unemployed males aged 25–54 reported health problems which limited the kind of work they can do compared to only 12.9 per cent of comparable short-term unemployed males.

Conclusion

In this chapter the latest available evidence on the characteristics of the long-term unemployed has been reviewed using two Department of Employment data sources – the claimant count and the Labour Force Survey. The annual LFS survey is clearly a rich and valuable source providing far more information than the quarterly claimant count which is limited to age, sex and geographical location.

The results from the 1985 LFS presented in this chapter illustrate the type of analysis which is possible. They show that the long-term unemployed are generally less qualified in terms of formal educational qualifications, time spent in full-time education and completed apprenticeships than the equivalent groups of short-term unemployed. The long-term unemployed are more likely to have their work limited by

Table 5.16 Health limitations on job choice of unemployed persons by age, sex and duration, LFS Spring 1985 (Great Britain)

Males (thousands)

	Less than 1 year						1 year and over					
	16–24 years		25–54 years		55+ years		16–24 years		25–54 years		55+ years	
Limited	24	(6.9)	46	(12.9)	19	(29.7)	24	(9.3)	102	(19.7)	32	(26.5)
Not limited	36	(10.4)	52	(14.6)	13	(20.3)	28	(10.9)	93	(17.9)	23	(19.0)
No health problems	285	(82.1)	258	(72.3)	32	(50.0)	205	(79.5)	322	(62.0)	65	(53.7)
Did not apply	*		*		—		*		*		*	
Total	347	(100.0)	357	(100.0)	64	(100.0)	258	(100.0)	519	(100.0)	121	(100.0)

Females (thousands)

	Less than 1 year						1 year and over					
	16–24 years		25–54 years		55+ years		16–24 years		25–54 years		55+ years	
Limited	21	(7.3)	44	(11.8)	5	(17.2)	11	(9.2)	41	(19.6)	7	(20.6)
Not limited	41	(14.3)	75	(20.1)	5	(17.2)	16	(13.3)	41	(19.6)	6	(17.6)
No health problems	224	(78.3)	253	(67.8)	19	(65.5)	93	(77.5)	126	(60.3)	21	(61.8)
Did not apply	—		*		—		—		*		—	
Total	286	(100.0)	373	(100.0)	29	(100.0)	120	(100.0)	209	(100.0)	34	(100.0)

* indicates estimates less than 10,000.
Source: LFS 1985

health problems or disabilities and so rely on visits to a Job Centre as their main job search method.

The LFS survey has only operated on an annual basis since 1983 and is as yet relatively little used by researchers. However, data tapes are made available through the ESRC's survey archive located at the University of Essex. In future it may supplement or replace time consuming and expensive specialist surveys.

Work is continuing on the extension of the annual LFS surveys. A simplified questionnaire has formed the basis for smaller scale quarterly surveys since 1984. The results of these surveys are currently being evaluated and in future it may be possible to link successive surveys so as to produce flow data on changes in status. Thus the LFS is likely to become an even more valuable tool for labour market analysis in the future.

NOTES

The views expressed in this chapter are personal and do not reflect those of the Employment Market Research Unit (EMRU) or the Department of Employment.

1 For instance, the DE commissioned a comprehensive longitudinal survey of less qualified urban youth. Results from the first wave are summarized in Banks et al. (1984).

2 The importance of standard errors is illustrated below for different estimates of unemployment level.

Estimate	95 per cent confidence interval Males	95 per cent confidence interval Females
50,000	+/−9,100	+/−8,300
100,000	+/−12,900	+/−11,700
200,000	+/−18,200	+/−16,500
500,000	+/−28,700	+/−26,100
1,000,000	+/−40,300	+/−36,600

Thus, for example, with a sample survey estimate of 100,000 unemployed males we can be confident that in 19 cases out of 20 the actual figure lies between 87,100 and 112,900.

3 Data on occupation/industry of last job is collected in the LFS. However, the preliminary results for 1985 used in this chapter do not include such information. In any case such data may be of limited value when considering long-term unemployment since no information is collected where the last job held was more than 3 years ago.

REFERENCES

Banks, M., Ullah, P. and Warr, P. 1984: Unemployment and less qualified urban young people. *Employment Gazette*, 92 (8), 343–6.

Department of Employment 1982: Changed basis of the unemployment statistics. *Employment Gazette*, 90 (12), 520.

—1985a: Unemployment adjusted for discontinuity and seasonality. *Employment Gazette*, 93 (7), 274–7.

—1985b: Unemployment: Estimates from the Labour Force Survey compared with the monthly claimant count. *Employment Gazette*, 93 (10), 393–6.

—1986a: Change in the compilation of the monthly unemployment statistics. *Employment Gazette*, 94 (3), 107–8.

—1986b: Labour Force Survey for 1985: Preliminary results. *Employment Gazette*, 94 (4), 135–44.

Structural Office of the European Communities EUROSTAT 1985a: *Labour Force Sample Survey Methods and Definitions*. Luxembourg: SOEC.

—1985b: *Labour Force Sample Survey 1985*. Luxembourg: SOEC.

6

Unemployment, Irreversibility and the Long-term Unemployed

PETER R. HUGHES
and GILLIAN HUTCHINSON

Introduction

It is by now well known that the number of unemployed and the unemployment rate have reached record levels for the post-war period during the most recent economic cycle. What is less well known is that the proportion of the unemployed who are long-term unemployed (with spells in excess of 1 year) has also reached record levels. Figure 6.1 shows this fraction, for males in Great Britain, increasing with a regular procyclical pattern during the period from 1957 to 1986, from 9 per cent to 44.1 per cent (see appendix for data from which figures were drawn). The time series at January each year for the stock of unemployed males, based on the JUVOS, or claimants, definition is also shown in this figure, the numbers having increased from 273,700 in 1949 to 2,254,000 in 1986.

It is within this long historical context that we take the view that these unemployment figures reveal the feature of irreversibility. Since 1949 a wide variety of economic policy measures have been used, from Keynesian aggregate demand intervention and Stop-Go, to Prices and Incomes Policies, Special Employment Measures and Supply Side economics. These have been partly responsible for the pronounced cyclicality evident in figure 6.1, although in such an open economy as the British one we should not omit the role of foreign influences on domestic fluctuations. Nevertheless, the trend shown in the figure is inexorably upwards, from a rather low average to the striking increase which is evident since 1976, and at no time during this period is there

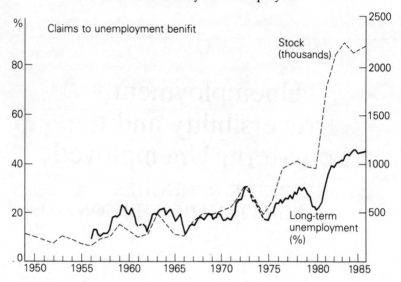

Figure 6.1 *Unemployment stock, and long-term unemployment (>52 weeks) as % of total unemployment. Males, Great Britain, Jan 1949 to Jan 1986*

evidence of any marked secular reduction in the numbers of unemployed males.

In order to concentrate on the trends in unemployment, it is of interest to abstract from the effects of the cycle. The averaged figures for the latest four cycles and the last 5 years (which constitute an incomplete cycle) are given in table 6.1 for the male[1] unemployment stock, unemployment rate and the long-term unemployed proportion. The cycles are defined from trough to trough as given by the CSO's co-incident indicator series. In the first half of the period, from 1963 to 1975, there is already evident a doubling of the unemployment stock and a near doubling (from 2.2 per cent to 4.3 per cent) of the unemployment rate. The proportion of the unemployed who are defined as long-term unemployed did not rise with anything like that magnitude in the 1960s and early 1970s but during the 1980s it has risen very steeply. In the last half of the period covered in table 6.1 the numbers and rate of the unemployed have more than trebled, while the fraction which is long-term unemployed has more than doubled over the whole period.

These secular trends are a cause for great concern and are far from being well understood. In this chapter we shall discuss a disaggregated analysis of the male labour force which indicates that such rising trends may be very difficult and costly to reverse. We shall present evidence that the stock of the long-term unemployed consists increasingly of men

Table 6.1 *Cyclically averaged male unemployment trends, Great Britain, 1963–1986*

Time period	Male unemployment stock (thousands)	Male unemployment rate (%)	Long-term unemployed as a % of all unemployed
Jan 1963–Jan 1967	297.7	2.2	17.9
Apr 1967–Oct 1971	493.4	3.5	17.0
Jan 1972–Jul 1975	634.8	4.3	23.5
Oct 1975–Jan 1981	1044.6	7.4	24.3
Apr 1981–Apr 1986	2084.9	15.2	39.0

Source: *Employment Gazette* and *British Labour Statistics: Historical Abstract*

with some skills aged 45 years and over who, because of their experience and productivity, did not expect to lose their jobs but who are not easily re-employable. Because of the shorter pay back period, increasing problems of ill-health and wage rigidities which prevent the remuneration of older workers from falling with their decreasing marginal product, they are rarely viewed as desirable workers or trainees. Conventional expansionary fiscal or monetary measures are unlikely to be very effective in helping the re-employability of this group and are likely to result in inflationary pressures as employers seek to expand by hiring the limited stock of younger labour. We shall argue that targetted policies aimed at this particular group are the most cost-effective way of combatting long-term unemployment and, finally, we shall consider the current experience of this type of special employment measure.

A Disaggregated Analysis of Male Unemployment

The absence of a regular and adequate data set covering the characteristics of the unemployed, and particularly of the long-term unemployed,[2] has meant that policymakers have been at something of a disadvantage when designing targetted employment policies. The excellent DHSS cohort study of the unemployed (1978) and the MSC's cohort data (1980) provide a comprehensive 'still' picture but they are inappropriate for examining changes over time, that is, for understanding the dynamics of the unemployment-generating process. The regularly produced unemployment series, whether from Job Centre data (pre-1982) or on a claimants basis (from 1982 onwards), provides little information on the characteristics of the inflow and outflow and, in order to study the dynamics of what is, essentially, a sorting process, it is the flows which are of prime interest.

Currently there is a stock of over 2,250,000 unemployed males, and about 800,000 flow in and out of unemployment each quarter. Most enter and leave quickly but some are trapped for reasons of age, lack of skill or other unfavourable labour market characteristics which signal low productivity to employers. This sorting process has been likened to a flower shop (Budd et al., 1985), in which new flowers enter regularly but it is always the freshest flowers which are selected and, at the end of the week, the most wilted flowers remain unsold. Our model is rather more complex since even on entry we suggest that some flowers will not be as attractive as others and so will stand a lesser chance of being selected. The long-term unemployed fall into this category, and because the sorting process is a continuous operation the unemployed with poorer prospects will make up the preponderant part of the stock, even though they may be a minority part of the flow.

In this section we shall examine the evidence available and that which can be inferred concerning the changing composition of the long-term unemployed. Because of the paucity of direct information over a reasonably long time period the sorting process must be modelled. The starting point for this is a simple disaggregation of the labour force into groups which share similar intra-group unemployment flow character-istics, but with significant inter-group differences. These groups, which are suggested by the DHSS and MSC cross-section data sources, are shown in table 6.2

The applicability of this two-way bimodal disaggregation is discussed and supported in many varied studies (see Hughes, 1984). Testing for other distributions of the outflow probabilities such as a Gamma distribution, for example, and for a trimodality rather than a bimodality in that distribution led to their rejection. Similarly, tests for different 'skill' definitions (such as combining social classes IV and V as the 'unskilled' group for the latest cycle) were rejected. Perhaps the most telling evidence for the bimodality of the outflow distribution comes at operational level from the managers of Unemployment Benefit Offices. Bowers (1982), when analysing the duration of unemployment by age and sex, refers to the Department of Employment's occasional surveys of the unemployed and comments of 'Employment Exchange Managers apparently experiencing no difficulty in classifying their registrants into those who should and should not experience difficulty in finding employment'.

The proportions of the active labour force shown in table 6.2 are the figures from the 1971 Census, and these proportions stayed remarkably stable in the 1970s, except that the proportion of unskilled has been falling over time. We have, therefore, reduced the figure from 8 per cent (at 1971) to 6 per cent, matching this with 2 per cent increase in the

Table 6.2 *Disaggregation of male labour force into groups sharing unemployment flow characteristics (percentages of active labour force)*

		Probability of leaving unemployment		
		Low	High	Total
Probability of becoming unemployed (inflow)	Low	Old[a] and skilled[b] 36.9	Prime aged[a] and skilled 39.7	76.6
	High	All the unskilled 6.0	Young[a] and skilled 17.4	23.4
	Total	42.9	57.1	100.0

[a] Old, prime aged and young refers to those workers aged 45 and over, 25–44 and under 25, respectively.
[b] Skilled refers to those workers defined in the Census of Population as social classes I–IV. The unskilled include labourers, messengers, lorry drivers' mates and kitchen hands.

prime-aged and skilled. Recalculation of parameter estimates using the precise 1981 weights produces very little change.

The outflow probabilities are the most straightforward to calculate since the quarterly cumulative duration distribution is a regularly produced Department of Employment statistic. These can be calculated for each of the last four complete economic cycles as defined, trough-to-trough, by the CSO's co-incident indicator series (for a full description, see Hughes and Hutchinson, 1986). The estimated parameters are, therefore, representative of, or averaged over, the particular cycle of interest. The inflow probabilities are then solved analytically, their solution depending upon the imposition of the equilibrium, or steady-state, condition that total inflows to the unemployment stock equals total outflows.

Although the analysis was performed over the last four complete cycles there was little change in any parameters for the first three of these. There were, however, striking changes during the 1970s, as aggregate unemployment soared, and we shall focus, therefore, on the two latest complete cycles, 1972–5 and 1975–81. Table 6.3 shows the changes in the flow probabilities.

There are, clearly, two large changes shown in table 6.3. The low inflow probability has risen tenfold, from 0.008 per cent per week to 0.070 per cent per week, and the high outflow parameter has more than halved. Although there is still a marked difference between the low and

Table 6.3 *Joint distribution of inflow and outflow probabilities and representative unemployment rates*

		1972–75	1975–81
Likelihood of becoming unemployed	Low	0.008	0.070
(% per week)	High	1.688	1.497
Likelihood of ceasing to be	Low	2.2	1.8
unemployed (% per week)	High	20.1	9.6

high probabilities, it is those with the 'good' characteristics whose positions have deteriorated. This deterioration is reflected in the changes in the representative or equilibrium unemployment rates.

Once inflow and outflow probabilities have been estimated over a given cycle it is possible to infer the steady-state unemployment rates. If I_i, $i=1$, 2 are the inflow probabilities and O_j, $j=1$, 2 are the outflow probabilities, then the steady-state unemployment rate for group i, j is given by

$$\frac{I_i}{I_i+O_j}.$$

The advantage of this segmented approach is that any changes in these unemployment rates can be traced directly to changes in either the inflow or outflow behaviour (or both) and, by associating these flow parameters with different age and skill groups, policy measures may more accurately be targetted.

Using the above relation, and inflow and outflow probabilities (shown in parentheses in table 6.4) calculated for cycles January 1972 to July 1975 and October 1975 to January 1981, we obtain the representative rates shown in table 6.4.

These steady-state rates are derived from the model which generates the estimates of inflow and outflow probabilities. How do these estimated rates compare with survey and Census evidence?

Ideally, we would wish to take comparable independent survey evidence about the age/skill composition of male unemployment in Great Britain for each of the cycles and compare actual rates with the predictions from the model. Although not ideal, we do have information from the 1984 LFS about the age/skill composition of the unemployed and from the 1981 Census of Population about the employed, as set out in table 6.5.

Table 6.4 *Representative unemployment rates, males, Great Britain*

1972–75	Low outflow probability (0.022)	High outflow probability (0.201)	1975–81	Low outflow probability (0.018)	High outflow probability (0.096)
Low inflow probability (0.00008)	0.4%	0.0%	Low inflow probability (0.00070)	3.7%	0.7%
High inflow probability (0.01688)	43.1%	7.8%	High inflow probability (0.01497)	45.3%	13.5%

Table 6.5 *Age/skill composition of the employed and unemployed, males, Great Britain*

%	Census of Population (1981)				LFS (1984)			
Employed	Low outflow probability	High outflow probability	Total	Unemployed	Low outflow probability	High outflow probability	Total
Low inflow probability	34.6	43.6	78.2	Low inflow probability	15.2	23.5	38.8
High inflow probability	5.2	16.5	21.8	High inflow probability	43.0	18.2	61.2
Total	39.8	60.2	100.0	Total	58.3	41.7	100.0

With this information and information about the stock of employed and unemployed, it is possible to derive unemployment rates for males in Great Britain, by age/skill as shown in table 6.6.

Clearly, the rates reported above are only approximations to actual age/skill rates since the proportions employed are 1981-based while the proportions unemployed and the totals employed and unemployed are 1984-based. They are, however, the closest we can get to actual rates on currently available information. A comparison with the model predictions for 1975/81 is set out in table 6.7.

Table 6.6 *Unemployment rates, males, Great Britain, 1984*

%	Low outflow probability	High outflow probability
Low inflow probability	6.3	7.6
High inflow probability	55.9	14.5

Aggregate unemployment rate=13.3%

Stock of unemployed (2,109,600) is defined as average male unemployment, n.s.a., including school leavers, in 1984 – see table 2.2, *Employment Gazette*.

Table 6.7 *Representative unemployment rates, males, Great Britain*

%	Model (1975/81)	Survey/Census (1981, 1984)
Old/skilled	3.7	6.3
All the unskilled	45.3	55.9
Prime-aged/skilled	0.7	7.6
Young/skilled	13.5	14.5
Total	6.7	13.3

Old, prime aged and young refers to those workers aged 45 and over, 25–44 and under 25 respectively. Skilled refers to workers defined in the Census of Population as social class I–IV.

We would not expect the actuals which refer to 1984 unemployment to match the predictions which relate to an earlier period when labour market conditions were more favourable. But perhaps some qualitative comparisons can be made which allow for changed market conditions and other influences, such as changes in the level and direction of the Government's special employment and training measures, and differences of definition between the way the model counts the unemployed and LFS definitions.

Since 1975–81, the Government has expanded measures to help the long-term unemployed (e.g. Community Programme) and has expanded its youth training commitments with YTS. These initiatives would improve the prospects of the under 25s (YTS) and of the old/skilled and unskilled (Community Programme). They would not affect the prospects of the prime-aged and skilled, which are likely to have deteriorated through a fall in the outflow probability.

It is also necessary to consider differences in definitions. The model is based on numbers registering as unemployed. For males, this is not much different from the number of claimants which, since October 1982, is the basis of the official count. The LFS definition is not the same as the official definition. It includes unemployed persons seeking work who are not claiming benefits (mostly married women) and excludes claimants who are inactive, that is, who were not looking for work in the reference week. Table 15, p. 141, *Employment Gazette*, May 1986, reveals that over 500,000 male claimants would be excluded from the LFS definition of unemployment for this reason. If we can assume that the claimants inactive are principally older or unskilled people, then this exclusion will tend to improve the unemployment rates of these groups when the rates are measured using the LFS.

If the above reasoning is correct, then we would expect the 1984 unemployment rate for prime-aged skilled men to have increased the most since the effects of worsening labour market conditions are not offset by targetted employment/training measures and there are no definitional offsets. This is indeed revealed to be the case since the rate is higher by a factor of ten. For the unskilled, rates are always high and further deterioration is unlikely to be other than gradual. Moreover, there is an offset to a rise in the rate from the expansion of YTS and CP. We observe that the rate rises, but not by any large amount, which accords with what we would expect.

We now consider the two remaining groups – the old/skilled and the young/skilled. Worsening economic conditions would raise the rates (higher inflow for old/skilled, lower outflow for young/skilled), but there would be offsets from Government measures (CP, YTS) and (for the old/skilled) from definitional changes. It is not possible to predict the scale of these effects. We observe, however, that the rate for old/skilled has not quite doubled, while there is only a small change in the young/skilled rate, possibly because of YTS. Sensible comparisons between the 1984 'actuals' and the model predictions are possible, therefore, and the model predictions appear to survive the comparisons quite well.

Comparing the rates for the 1975–81 period with those for the earlier period, reported in table 6.4, we see that the greatest proportionate change is to the old and skilled. This group has traditionally been cushioned from unemployment by their experience, skills, legislation which offers employment protection to those with longer duration in a job, by union negotiation and seniority lay-off rules and by other institutional arrangements. Members of this group did not expect to lose their jobs but once they have done so they have a low probability of re-employment. The other people who have been particularly badly affected are the young and skilled. The young, in general, have typically experienced frequent short spells of unemployment (often of a frictional nature) as they sample different jobs, industries, employers and even locations. During the last cycle, however, they have been finding it more difficult to find new jobs to sample, their unemployment duration has more than doubled and this is reflected in their unemployment rate.

Characteristics of the Long-term Unemployed

The long-term unemployed are defined as those with an unemployment spell whose duration exceeds 52 weeks. This is not a completely arbitrary definition but applies to all who have exhausted their entitlement to unemployment benefit and must rely on supplementary benefit and other means-tested benefits.

The outflow parameters calculated as described above can be used to deduce the characteristics and changes in the composition of the long-term unemployed in the 1970s. More recent information is available (although on a somewhat different definitional basis) from the annual Labour Force Surveys.

Let $P(U_j>52)$ be the probability that an individual with outflow parameter, O_j, experiences an unemployment spell greater than 52 weeks. Since

$$P(U_j>1)=1-O_j \text{ and}$$

$$P(U_j>2)=(1-O_j)^2,$$

$$\text{then } P(U_j>52)=(1-O_j)^{52}.$$

This is a geometric distribution, with an exponential continuous time approximation of

$$P(U_j>52)\simeq e^{-O_j\,0.52}.$$

For each of our four groups, disaggregated by age and skill, we may obtain the number who are long-term unemployed as $e^{-O_j\,0.52}.\,U_{ij}$, where U_{ij} is the unemployment stock of each of our four groups, and by summing these four numbers, and dividing by the total unemployment stock we obtain the total number of the long-term unemployed as a proportion of all the unemployed (LU). Thus

$$LU=P(U>52)=\frac{\sum\limits_{ij}P(U_j>52).U_{ij}}{U}=\frac{\sum\limits_{ij}e^{-O_j\,0.52}U_{ij}}{U}.$$

These calculations permit the four-way disaggregations of the flow into long-term unemployment, the stock of the long-term unemployed and the *LU*, the proportion of all the unemployed who are long-term unemployed, for the latest two complete cycles, as shown in table 6.8. The results show that *LU* has increased from 20.9 per cent to 24.0 per cent and the model described in the previous section permits an investigation of this change. It is only the group with the *low* probability of outflow who contribute to this result and the main change has arisen through the increased *inflow* into the stock of the skilled aged 45 years and over. They exert a substantial weight on the result since they comprise 37 per cent of the active labour force and their contribution to the stock of the long-term unemployed has risen more than twelvefold, by almost 77,000 (see table 6.9). The unskilled of all ages have also

Table 6.8 *Characteristics of the long-term unemployed segmented by age and skill, 1972–1981*
(males, Great Britain)
(all numbers are rounded to the nearest thousand and nearest percentage point)

		1972/75			1975/81		
		Low outflow probability	*High outflow probability*	*Total*	*Low outflow probability*	*High outflow probability*	*Total*
Flow into long-term unemployment (thousands per week and (percentages))	Low inflow probability	0 (5)	0 (0)	0 (5)	2 (32)	0 (1)	2 (32)
	High inflow probability	3 (95)	0 (0)	3 (95)	3 (63)	0 (5)	3 (68)
	Total	3 (100)	0 (0)	3 (100)	5 (94)	0 (6)	5 (100)
Stock of long-term unemployment (thousands and (percentages))	Low inflow probability	7 (5)	0 (0)	7 (5)	84 (33)	0 (0)	84 (33)
	High inflow probability	125 (95)	0 (0)	125 (95)	165 (66)	2 (1)	167 (67)
	Total	132 (100)	0 (0)	132 (100)	248 (99)	3 (1)	251 (100)
LU (Stock of long-term unemployed as a proportion of all unemployment)			20.9%			24.0%	

Table 6.9 *Changes in the stock of long-term unemployed 1972/75 to 1975/81 (thousands)*

	Low outflow probability	High outflow probability	Total
Low inflow probability	76.7	0.3	77.0
High inflow probability	39.3	2.4	41.8
Total	116.0	2.7	118.8

contributed to the total increase but they are a relatively small group (6 per cent of the active labour force) and their contribution, an increase of about 30 per cent, is smaller, at 39,300.

The results so far presented in this section are derived from the estimated parameters of the model and they are averaged over, or representative of, a complete cycle. Although the current cycle has not yet been completed it is possible to give some indications of recent developments using the Labour Force Survey data. Let us consider the 1984 information on the age/skill characteristics of the long-term unemployed.

The analysis divides males, in Great Britain, who are unemployed for more than 1 year into 12 age categories (16–19, 20–4, 25–9, 30–4, 35–9, 40–4, 45–9, 50–4, 55–9, 60–4, 65–9, 70+) which for our purposes are aggregated into three age groups, 24 and under, 25–44 and 45 and over. Skill is defined according to Census social class definitions, the unskilled being defined as social class V and the skilled classes I–IV.

The analysis is, unfortunately, unable to produce a clear divide between skilled and unskilled and two residual categories are reported – Armed Forces/inadequately described/no reply and 'Does not apply'. The latter category is a large group which covers people unemployed for 3 years or more who are not asked about social class.

The LFS definition of unemployed is a survey definition which does not coincide with the official claimants definition. The differences are discussed in the *Employment Gazette* (1986), table 15, and the comparison for males is reproduced in table 6.10.

Unemployed persons on LFS definitions are those without a job who were looking for work in the reference week or prevented from seeking work by temporary sickness or holiday, or who were waiting for the results of a job application or waiting to start a job. People who were claimants but who had not looked for work in the reference week would not be counted as unemployed. This category is quite large (some 25 per cent of the official count).

Table 6.10 *Comparison of the male unemployment count, LFS and claimants basis, Spring 1985 (millions)*

Labour Force estimate of unemployed persons seeking work of which:	1.71
Not claiming benefit	0.18
Claiming benefit[a]	1.53
Claimants not unemployed[a] of which:	0.64
Inactive	0.53
In employment	0.11
Claimants count	2.17

[a] Sum of

The number of claimants 'inactive' who are omitted from the LFS count will need to be added back in if the LFS distribution of age/skill characteristics is to be used as a proxy for the official count, especially if, as is likely, the characteristics of the 'inactive' are biased towards older age groups.

Table 6.11 sets out the 1984 LFS distributions by age/skill for the two categories of unemployed described above – the LFS unemployed and the claimant inactive. Two categories are inadequately described and have had to be arbitrarily allotted to a particular skill category. 'DNA' is included with the unskilled, and Armed Forces/other with skilled. This presumes that the larger part of those who have been unemployed more than 3 years will be unskilled. Among the older very long-term unemployed, some could be skilled but there is no means of disaggregating. Overall, the older (45 and over) DNAs are 25 per cent of total DNA. Comparing the two halves of table 6.11 we see that the distribution of long-term unemployed by age/skill is very different. The claimants inactive are biased towards the older skilled person at the expense of the unskilled, particularly the younger unskilled. Combining the distributions we obtain an age/skill picture which approximates to the official count. This is shown in table 6.12, where the groups are now comparable with the four groups of our model.

Table 6.12 shows the fourfold increase in the total number of the long-term unemployed since the previous cycle, from about a quarter of a million to over 1 million males. For our four groups the numbers can be compared with the stock numbers in table 6.8, although we consider these LFS segments to be indicative only. It seems as if the deteriorating

Table 6.11 *Long-term unemployed, males, Great Britain, 1984*

1 LFS definitions (males unemployed more than 1 year)

Age	Class V	DNA[a]	Sub-total	Other classes	Armed Forces/ other[b]	Sub-total	Grand total
Under 25	28,061	168,767	196,828 (20.2)	107,199	4,463	111,662 (11.5)	308,490 (31.7)
25–44	34,254	192,458	226,712 (23.3)	171,551	3,052	174,603 (17.9)	401,315 (41.2)
45 and over	12,152	125,773	137,925 (14.2)	125,076	1,487	126,563 (13.0)	264,488 (27.1)
All ages	74,467	486,998	561,465 (57.6)	403,826	9,002	412,828 (42.4)	974,293 (100.0)

2 Claimant inactive (males whose last job was more than 1 year ago)

Age	Class V	DNA[a]	Sub-total	Other classes	Armed Forces/ other[b]	Sub-total	Grand total
Under 25	3,603	··	3,603 (3.1)	12,160	784	12,944 (11.0)	16,547 (14.1)
25–44	5,722	..	5,722 (4.9)	22,250	348	22,598 (19.2)	28,320 (24.1)
45 and over	4,640	..	4,640 (3.9)	67,804	362	68,166 (57.9)	72,806 (61.9)
All ages	13,965	..	13,965 (11.9)	102,214	1,494	103,708 (88.1)	117,673 (100.0)

[a] DNA – 'Does not apply' refers to those unemployed more than 3 years who are not asked about social class.
[b] Armed forces/other. 'Other' is inadequately described, no reply.

position of those groups which previously rarely experienced long-term unemployment has continued. It is the young skilled and prime-aged/ skilled who, in the very recent years, are sharing increasingly the burden of long unemployment spells. The number of old and skilled in this category has more than doubled but the proportion has fallen. For the unskilled the position is similar, with their absolute number more than trebling but their proportion continuing the fall which has been evident for more than a decade. Without placing too much credence in the actual numbers, the figures in table 6.12 suggest a continuation of the process whereby, at a time of rapidly rising aggregate unemployment,

Table 6.12 *Long-term unemployed males, Great Britain, 1984 LFS*
(LFS definitions and claimants inactive)

	Low outflow probability	High outflow probability	Total
Low inflow probability	194,729 (17.8%) Old and skilled	197,201 (18.1%) Prime-aged and skilled	391,930 (35.9%)
High inflow probability	575,430 (52.7%) All the unskilled	124,606 (11.4%) Young and skilled	700,036 (64.1%)
Total	770,159 (70.5%)	321,807 (29.5%)	1,091,966 (100%)

those with 'good' labour market characteristics are finding that their position has worsened considerably.

In this section we have focused on the inferences which can be drawn from the segmented model concerning the characteristics of the long-term unemployed. These workers have become a source of some concern in recent years, as their number and proportion in the unemployment stock have grown rapidly. They will have exhausted their claim to unemployment benefit and many will face problems of low income, depreciating skills, boredom, decreasing motivation and feelings of lowered self-worth. In the next section we examine and suggest policies specifically aimed at the long-term unemployed.

Conclusion and Policy Implications for the Long-term Unemployed

This chapter has singled out specific groups among the male labour force who, once unemployed, will experience particular difficulties in finding re-employment. These are the unskilled of any age and men with some skills aged 45 years and older. We saw in the previous section that these groups form the great part of the long-term unemployed, i.e. those unemployed more than 12 months. We believe it might be difficult or costly to reverse this unemployment using conventional policy measures – an easing of fiscal and monetary policy – and that targetted policies are called for.

Conventional policy assumes that if there is an excess supply of labour at current rates of pay an expansion in aggregate demand will generate new jobs and remove the excess supply. If labour supply were homogeneous and skills were available to match vacancies, this expansion in demand need not be inflationary. If, however, there is mismatch in skills and if there are market imperfections such that a large proportion of the unemployed are not acceptable for filling new jobs, then the expansion in demand may be ineffective as well as being costly.

We emphasize in this chapter that the excess supply of labour (the unemployed) are not a homogeneous group and that only a minority of the stock (though a majority of the flow) are likely to be helped by conventional policies. These are the young and skilled and prime-aged and skilled whose duration of unemployment is responsive to improved economic conditions. For the majority of the stock – the unskilled and the old and skilled – conventional policies would have some effect on the rate of inflow, but for reasons discussed below would not do much for the existing stock of unemployed.

British governments are well aware of the problems faced by specific groups in finding re-employment and a range of special employment and training measures have been devised, starting with Community Industry (jobs for disadvantaged young people) in the mid-1970s. Moreover, analyses of the costs and benefits of such measures confirm their effectiveness relative to general reflation. The House of Commons Employment Committee's First Report (1986), for example, compares the costs of creating a job by tax cutting methods (estimated by Gavyn Davies at £47,000 in the second year) with the costs of special employment measures (estimated by Department of Employment at £2,650 or less).

For these specific policies to be effective in creating sustainable new jobs it is clearly necessary to consider what has caused the unemployment and what are the obstacles to re-employment of those people who would most benefit from the measures. The groups we consider for targetting can be divided into three parts:

1 The young/prime aged and unskilled
2 The old and unskilled
3 The old and skilled.

A problem in devising programmes for these groups is the lack of any British evidence about whether the loss of employability occurs because of a deskilling/demotivation effect as unemployment is prolonged or whether there is a stigma effect which is not related to the intrinsic productivity characteristics of the potential employee. Depending on which of the effects dominates, the emphasis should be upon training or work experience respectively.

The mix of current measures for the unskilled combines both of these elements. For the under 18s, the emphasis is upon training (YTS, non-advanced further education (NAFE) and the technical and vocational education initiative (TVEI)). Those over 18 are less well served with Community Programme, a work experience programme for the longer duration unemployed, the major programme catering for this group.

The group, however, which we wish to focus upon in this chapter is the third group – the old and skilled. We have seen that the stock of long-term unemployed consists increasingly of men with some skills aged 45 years and over who, because of their experience and productivity, did not expect to lose their jobs but who are not easily re-employable. Perhaps the chief obstacle to re-employment of this group is the existence of internal labour markets, especially in large public and private sector enterprises, with their restricted ports of entry, internal screening and promotion rules (see Doeringer and Piore, 1971; George and Shorey, 1985). It should be noted, however, that such markets, while imposing an imperfection on the labour market as a whole may, internally, be quite efficient (see Williamson et al., 1975).

The shorter payback period and the likelihood of some deterioration in health as the person ages beyond 45 are further reasons for a loss of re-employability. The 1985 LFS (see table 16, Creigh, 1986) reports the age/morbidity profile shown in table 6.13.

Though on-the-job training continues throughout a person's working life, new hires are likely to involve a relatively high specific investment by the firm which, with the older person, needs to be recouped over a shorter payback period. This raises the amount by which total expected marginal value product must exceed the expected wage (see Oi, 1962) and in the presence of wage rigidities will be an impediment to re-employment.

Human capital theory predicts that increments to a person's skill endowments from on-the-job training will dwindle with age until at some point the losses of productivity due, for example, to depreciation outweigh gains. This explains the concave shape seen in all cross-section surveys of earnings distributions by age. If the curvature is insufficiently steep to reflect the diminished marginal product of the older worker then there is indirect evidence of wage rigidities. Table 6.14 shows typical cross-section earnings profiles by age for manual and non-manual males, Great Britain, taken from NES 1978, 1980 and 1985, section E.

Table 6.13 *Unemployed experiencing health limitations on job choice Males, Great Britain*

Age	16–24	25–54	55+	Total
%	7.9	16.9	27.6	14.8

Table 6.14 *Median gross weekly earnings, males, full-time pay, not affected by absence*

£/Week	Under 18	18–20	21–4	25–9	30–9	40–9	50–9	60–4
1985								
Manual	65.4	101.9	133.8	149.3	164.5	166.2	154.7	142.6
Non-manual	63.8	92.0	134.3	176.2	215.9	236.1	214.9	181.5
1980								
Manual	45.5	73.4	94.2	103.7	111.2	110.0	103.3	95.2
Non-manual	44.6	65.7	88.8	113.7	136.2	143.7	134.0	117.3
1978								
Manual	33.5	53.9	69.9	76.9	81.2	80.3	75.7	69.2
Non-manual	31.6	46.3	65.0	82.9	98.8	102.7	95.8	83.3

Source: NES, section E, table 126

We see that the curvature is more pronounced for non-manuals than for manuals, which is to be expected since the loss of capital endowment is potentially greater and the need to make a compensating adjustment to pay greater also. However, the curvature is still not much evident until after age 60 and, if we can assume that these median earnings reflect the going rate for existing employees and new hires, arguably does not offset the loss of productivity, especially if a change of job brings with it some destruction of human capital and the need to re-invest in specific skills.

We have singled out a particular group – the old and skilled – who are increasingly flowing into long-term unemployment and we have identified various reasons why once a job is lost re-employment is particularly difficult. We advocate targetted policies for this group since conventional policy measures – an easing of monetary and fiscal policy – are inappropriate. Moreover, policies targetted at these groups appear to exert little pressure on wages and costs (see Layard and Nickell, 1985).

Various government special employment and training measures are already targetted at the long-term unemployed. How well are they matched to the older skilled worker? Clearly, Community Programme which offers work experience and is increasingly a programme for the single under 25s is not helping this group. This leaves Jobstart and the Restart programme. Jobstart is a supply-side scheme which supplements the income of the long-term unemployed who take full-time jobs below a given income level (currently set at earnings of less than £80 per week). Arguably, this is pitched at too low a level to influence the skilled job-seeker.

The most promising scheme is Restart. This offers invitations for in-depth counselling interviews to the long-term unemployed with the prospect of an offer of training, advice and assistance in seeking a job or self–employment. The scheme is open-ended in that it can point to a variety of routes to help the long-term unemployed. For the old and skilled, it would seem that opportunities for self-employment or to participate in voluntary projects are particularly appropriate policies. Failing these avenues, perhaps access to eased early retirement is required. Finally, we would suggest the possibility of subsidizing employers to screen older skilled workers in order to undo the stigma which may be attached, often unfairly, to those longer term unemployed.

NOTES

This work is not related to Dr Hughes' official duties at the Department of Employment. We would like to acknowledge contributions from Linda Derrick in a joint (unpublished) paper.

1 We do not address the problem of rising female unemployment because the data are poor, largely due to the changes in registration behaviour following the change in National Insurance regulations from the early 1970s onward.

2 The new annual Labour Force Survey is a partial solution to this problem although unemployment is measured differently from other regular statistics and there is a heavy dependence on proxy information by whichever member of the household is present when the interview is given. The General Household Survey is marred by small sample sizes within the categories of interest, particularly so in the case of the long-term unemployed.

APPENDIX 1

Unemployment stock (January figures) and long-term unemployment as per cent of unemployment, males, Great Britain

Year	Unemployment stock (thousands)	Long-term[a] unemployment (%)	Year	Unemployment stock (thousands)	Long-term unemployment (%)
1949	273.7		– 3		21.2
1950	258.0		– 4		18.9
1951	223.7		1966 – 1	261.6	16.4
1952	536.3		– 2		17.6
1953	265.6		– 3		19.2
1954	233.3		– 4		14.4
1955	185.4		1967 – 1	420.8	11.0
1956	164.6		– 2		12.2
1957 – 1	237.5	9.0	– 3		14.2
– 2		12.9	– 4		14.8
– 3		13.0	1968 – 1	493.8	14.4
– 4		11.0	– 2		16.0
1958 – 1	268.3	9.8	– 3		18.0
– 2		11.1	– 4		17.7
– 3		11.0	1969 – 1	494.2	16.6
– 4		11.4	– 2		17.8
1959 – 1	403.9	13.2	– 3		19.6
– 2		17.7	– 4		19.1
– 3		18.1	1970 – 1	523.6	16.9
– 4		17.9	– 2		17.7
1960 – 1	327.5	18.9	– 3		19.6
– 2		23.1	– 4		19.2
– 3		22.1	1971 – 1	572.1	16.7
– 4		19.8	– 2		16.8
1960 – 1	260.0	19.1	– 3		17.6
– 2		21.5	– 4		17.3
– 3		18.9	1972 – 1	779.8	16.6
– 4		15.3	– 2		18.8
1962 – 1	316.7	14.1	– 3		23.1
– 2		14.1	– 4		24.8
– 3		15.1	1973 – 1	660.6	25.2
– 4		14.2	– 2		28.3
1963 – 1	487.0	11.5	– 3		30.5
– 2		14.8	– 4		30.4
– 3		19.1	1974 – 1	[485]	30.4
– 4		19.3	– 2		24.4
1964 – 1	363.5	18.3	– 3		24.6
– 2		20.8	– 4		22.9
– 3		21.4	1975 – 1	[649]	
– 4		21.6	– 2		18.5
1965 – 1	278.9	18.7	– 3		17.2
– 2		20.1	– 4		16.9

Year	Unemployment stock (thousands)	Long-term[a] unemployment (%)
1976 – 1	961.3	16.7
– 2		19.4
– 3		19.6
– 4		23.4
1977 – 1	1034.0	23.4
– 2		25.1
– 3		23.4
– 4		25.8
1978 – 1	1070.2	25.5
– 2		27.0
– 3		25.4
– 4		28.2
1979 – 1	989.9	27.2
– 2		30.2
– 3		28.8
– 4		30.0
1980 – 1	970.4	27.2
– 2		26.0
– 3		22.2
– 4		21.8
1981 – 1	1647.1	20.5
– 2		22.0
– 3		24.0
– 4		28.8
1982 – 1	2123.7	32.1
– 2		36.2
– 3		37.5
– 4		39.3
1983 – 1	2270.6	38.2
– 2		40.0
– 3		40.4
– 4		41.1
1984 – 1	2156.6	40.9
– 2		43.1
– 3		44.0
– 4		43.7
1985 – 1	2226.8	43.2
– 2		44.6
– 3		45.5
– 4		45.7
1986 – 1	2254.0	44.1
– 2		44.7

[Interpolated]

[a] Pre-1962, 1=March Post-1962, 1=January
2=June 2=April
3=September 3=July
4=December 4=October

REFERENCES

Bowers, J. K. 1982: The Duration of Unemployment by Age and Sex 1976–1981. University of Leeds, mimeo, November 1981.

Budd, A., Levine, P. and Smith, P. 1985: Unemployment, Vacancies and the Long-term Unemployed. Centre for Economics Forecasting, Discussion Paper No. 154.

Creigh, S. 1986: Characteristics of the Long-term Unemployed. Evidence from the Labour Force Survey. Paper presented at University of St Andrews Conference on Hysteresis and Unemployment, July.

Doeringer, P. B. and Piore, M. 1971: *Internal Labour Markets and Manpower Analysis*. Lexington, MA: Heath.

George, K. D. and Shorey, J. 1985: Manual workers, good jobs and structured internal labour markets. *British Journal of Industrial Relations*, 23 (3), 425–47.

House of Commons 1986: First Report from the Employment Committee, Session 1985–6. *Special Employment Measures and the Long-term Unemployed*. London: HMSO.

Hughes, P. R. 1984: Flows to and from unemployment: Is the register bimodal?. In Hutchinson, G. and Treble, J. (eds), *Recent Advances in Labour Economics*, London: Croom Helm, 179–202.

Hughes, P. R. and Hutchinson, G. 1986: The changing picture of male unemployment in Great Britain, 1972–1981. *Oxford Bulletin of Economics and Statistics*, 48 (4): 309–29.

Layard, R. and Nickell, S. 1985: The causes of British unemployment. *National Institute Economic Review*, 111, 62–85.

Oi, W. Y. 1962: Labor as a quasi-fixed factor. *Journal of Political Economy*, December, 538–55.

Williamson, O. E., Wachter, M. L. and Harris, J. E. 1975: Understanding the employment relation: The analysis of idiosyncratic exchange. *Bell Journal of Economics and Management Science*, 6, 250–79.

IV
Analysis of Hysteresis Effects

7

Union Activity, Unemployment Persistence and Wage-Employment Ratchets

ASSAR LINDBECK and
DENNIS J. SNOWER

Introduction

The idea underlying this chapter is quite simple. Consider a labour market containing firm-specific unions facing labour demand shocks which are transient (in the sense that the distribution of shocks has a constant mean and finite variance). After an adverse shock, firms reduce the size of their workforces (through dismissals or failure to replace retiring employees) and unemployment rises. The remaining incumbent employees are now in a better position than previously: since they are smaller in number but face the same distribution of shocks, their chances of retaining their jobs have risen. Now, acting through their unions, they respond to this enhanced job security by driving up their wages. However, the unemployed workers cannot underbid on account of labour turnover costs. At the new higher wages, the firms will employ fewer workers (for any given new labour demand shock) than they would otherwise have done. In this way, unions help perpetuate the initial rise in unemployment. We will explore how this unemployment persistence is related to the degree of union power and how unions may generate wage–unemployment ratchets.

A number of recent studies[1] have presented various analytical frameworks in which unions (or, simply, workers with market power) may be responsible for unemployment persistence. Yet unlike the present chapter, these studies do not show how unemployment persistence is related to the degree of union power; nor do they explore how union activity may give rise to wage–unemployment ratchets.

Our model of union behaviour is an outgrowth of 'insider–outsider analysis' (for a survey see Lindbeck and Snower, 1986), which presumes that labour turnover costs give a group of privileged, employed workers ('insiders') more favourable conditions of work than the unprivileged, unemployed workers ('outsiders'). The insiders exercise market power on their own behalf in the process of wage determination.

Applying this approach to labour union activity, we distinguish between two types of insiders: union members and employed non-members. The former have some influence on wage determination, the latter do not. Our model has two salient, distinguishing features:

1 firms must bear some labour turnover costs whenever they fire current employees and hire other workers instead, and
2 union members exert market power (generated by the above labour turnover costs) in wage determination, without taking other workers into account.

Wages, Employment and Unemployment

For simplicity, we focus on a single firm whose insiders belong to a single union. Let work be a discrete activity, with each employee providing one unit of work. The firm's production function is $Q = \varepsilon \cdot f(L)$, $f' > 0$, $f'' < 0$, where Q is output, L is the number of employees (union members and employed non-members) and ε is a random variable with a time invariant distribution $[G(\varepsilon)]$ with zero mean and finite variance.

We assume that, in each period, labour market decisions are made in two stages. First, the wage (W) is set before the realized value of ε is known (but with full information about $G(\varepsilon)$). Second, the employment decision is made after ε is observed. We call a worker an 'incumbent insider' if he or she is an employed union member in the current period before ε is revealed. The wage is assumed to be the outcome of a Nash bargain between the firm and the union, which consists of incumbent insiders. The employment decision is assumed to be made unilaterally by the firm.

Consider the second stage of decision making first. Given the known values of W and ε, the firm sets employment so as to maximize its profit: $\varepsilon \cdot f(L) - W \cdot L$, which yields the labour demand equation

$$L = l(W/\varepsilon), \quad l' < 0. \tag{7.1}$$

Now turn to the first stage of decision making. Suppose that the incumbent insiders are risk neutral and that each of them faces the same probability of being retained by the firm. Moreover, suppose that the union is run by a majority voting rule and that the majority of union members are employed. Thus, in the first stage of decision making, the union's objective is to maximize an incumbent insider's expected utility.

For simplicity, suppose that if the worker is employed in the current period, he or she experiences utility of $U(W)$, where $U'>0$, $U''<0$;[2] yet if the worker is fired, then his or her utility is zero. Let σ be the incumbent insider's expected probability of being retained. Then the union's objective is $\sigma \cdot U(W)$ and its threat point is zero.

Let L^I be the number of incumbent insiders in the current period and let $l(W/\hat{\varepsilon})=L^I$. Then σ may be defined as

$$\sigma= \int_{-\infty}^{\hat{\varepsilon}} (L/L^I) \cdot G(\varepsilon)d\varepsilon+ \int_{\hat{\varepsilon}}^{\infty} G(\varepsilon)d\varepsilon. \qquad (7.2a)$$

Here we implicitly assume that the union is able to give its members an advantage over the non-members in retaining their jobs, so that when the firm fires incumbents, non-members are fired first.[3] By implication,

$$\sigma=\sigma(L^I, W), \qquad (7.2b)$$
$$(-) \, (-)$$

for any density $G(\varepsilon)$ which is strictly positive between a minimum and maximum value of ε.[4] (In other words, the more incumbents there are in the firm and the higher their wage, the lower is each incumbent's chance of being retained).

The firm's objective in the wage bargain is to maximize its profit. If an agreement with the union is reached, whereby the wage W is accepted and no incumbent insiders are replaced by outsiders, the firm's expected profit is

$$\pi(W)= \int_{-\infty}^{\infty} \{\varepsilon \cdot f[l(W/\varepsilon)]-W \cdot l(W/\varepsilon)\} \cdot G(\varepsilon)d\varepsilon , \qquad (7.3)$$

where we assume that π', $\pi''<0$.

Let T be the firm's turnover cost (i.e. the cost of firing an incumbent insider and hiring an outsider instead), which we assume to be a constant. (For a microeconomic derivation of T, see Lindbeck and Snower, 1984a and b, 1985.)[5] Let R be the reservation wage (at which a worker is indifferent between employment and unemployment).[6] Then, for simplicity, we specify the firm's threat-point profit as $\pi=\pi(R+T)$. (The $\pi(R+T)$ function may be interpreted as the profit which the firm earns upon replacing all its insiders by outsiders.)

Let $B=\pi(W)-\pi(R+T)$ be the firm's objective in wage negotiation and let $C=\sigma \cdot U(W)$ be the union's objective. Then the negotiated wage may be expressed as the solution to the following generalized Nash bargaining problem:

$$\underset{W}{\text{Max}} \quad \Omega = B^a \cdot C^{1-a}, \text{ subject to } W \geqslant R, \quad \pi(W) \geqslant \pi(R+T), \quad \pi(W) \geqslant 0, \tag{7.4a}$$

where R and T are exogenously given to both negotiating parties, and the constant a $(0 < a < 1)$ measures the (exogenously given) bargaining strength of the firm relative to that of the union. Note that the turnover cost poses a threat to the firm, without which the union would have no bargaining power. The first constraint of problem (7.4a) ensures that union members prefer employment to unemployment; the second and third constraints ensure that the firm has no incentive to replace its insiders by outsiders or to close down its operations, respectively. By equation (7.3), it is evident that the second constraint implies that

$$W \leqslant R + T. \tag{7.4b}$$

The first-order condition for an interior solution is

$$A = C_W + \delta \cdot (C/B) \cdot B_W = 0 \tag{7.4c}$$

where $\delta = a/(1-a)$. From this condition, along with some restrictions on the density G and the production function f (see the appendix), we can show that the wage depends on the number of incumbent insiders (L^I) and on $(R+T)$ in the following way:

$$W = \phi \ (L^I, R+T) \tag{7.5a}$$
$$(-) \ (+)$$

for values of W in the range

$$R \leqslant W \leqslant \min[R+T, \pi^{-1}(0)] = W^{\max}, \tag{7.5b}$$

(with $\pi^{-1}(0)$ given by equation (7.3)). The larger the number of incumbent insiders, the lower the retention probability, and thus the lower the wage is set. Also, the greater $(R+T)$, the lower the firm's threat-point profit, and the higher the wage.

Having analysed wage formation, we now turn to the determinants of the firm's current incumbent workforce, L^I. Let r be the retirement rate (a positive constant), so that $r \cdot L^I_{-1}$ of last period's incumbent insiders retire. Let $h[(1-r) \cdot (L_{-1} - L^I_{-1})]$ be the 'entry–exit function', which describes how many of the firm's non-retired, employed non-members ($(1-r) \cdot (L_{-1} - L^I_{-1})$ when $L_{-1} > L^I_{-1}$) become union members or how many of the non-retired insiders who have been dismissed ($(1-r) \cdot (L^I_{-1} - L_{-1})$ when $L_{-1} < L^I_{-1}$) exit from the union. Then the current incumbent insider workforce is

$$L^I = (1-r) \cdot L^I_{-1} + h[(1-r) \cdot (L_{-1} - L^I_{-1})]. \tag{7.6}$$

The entry–exit function has the following properties:

$$h=0 \text{ if } L^I=L^I_{-1};$$ (7.6a)

$$h=1 \text{ if } L_{-1}<L^I_{-1},$$ (7.6b)

(i.e. when incumbent insiders are dismissed, they lose their influence in wage determination, since, as noted, union behaviour is determined by majority vote, with the majority consisting of the employed members), and

$$0{\leqslant}h{\leqslant}1 \text{ if } L_{-1}>L^I_{-1},$$ (7.6c)

(i.e. a fraction of the non-retired, employed non-members enter the union).[7,8]

In short, our model of the labour market consists of the labour demand function (7.1) (pictured in figure 7.1a), the wage determination conditions (7.5a) and (7.5b) (pictured in figure 7.1c) and entry–exit function (7.6) (pictured in figure 7.1d), which specifies the incumbent insider workforce. To characterize the labour market equilibrium in a particularly simple way, we make the following assumptions. First, we suppose that the labour market contains a fixed number of identical firms, union members, employed non-members and outsiders. Then the wage-employment activity within an individual firm may be seen as a microcosm of that for the entire labour market. Second, we assume that the parameters of our model are such that, for any given value of ε, there exists a unique, stable, stationary equilibrium $(\hat{W}, \hat{L}, \hat{L}^I)$, where $\hat{L}^I=\hat{L}^I_{+1}$ in the figure. Finally, we suppose that each realization of ε persists for long enough so that this equilibrium is reached. Such an equilibrium is illustrated by the points E_1 in figure 7.1.

The Influence of Union Power on Economic Resilience

We now show how the exercise of union power in wage bargaining may make the labour market less 'resilient' in the face of cyclical swings in employment. We specify this loss of resilience in terms of

1 an 'unemployment persistence effect', whereby the union influences the wage in such a way that any random variation in current labour demand tends to create a persistent change in unemployment (e.g. an adverse random variation means that the future employment will be lower than it otherwise would have been, ceteris paribus) and
2 a 'wage–employment ratchet effect', whereby random variations in labour demand through time lead to an upward trend in the wage and

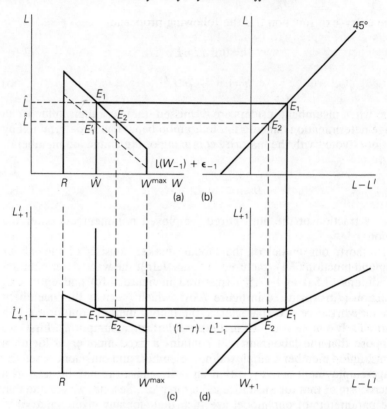

Figure 7.1 *Labour market equilibrium and unemployment persistence effect*

unemployment rates (because favourable variations lead to larger wage changes, per unit of employment, than unfavourable variations).

Consider the unemployment persistence effect first. Assume that given the level of ε, the initial equilibrium wage ($\hat{W}$) lies strictly between the upper and lower bounds given in condition (7.5b). Now consider what happens when there is a transient adverse shock to labour demand – genereated by a fall in ε – after the current wage $\hat{W}$ has been negotiated. In other words, the labour demand curve in figure 7.1a shifts downwards, so that for the current wage ($\hat{W}$), current employment ($\hat{L}$) is lower (as shown by point E'_1 in figure 7.1a). Assuming that $h>0$ (so that the right-hand segment of the entry–exit function in figure 7.1c has a positive slope), the current incumbent insider workforce ($\hat{L}^I$) falls (as shown by point E_2 in figure 7.1c). Since a fall in the incumbent workforce (under the same distribution of employment shocks, ε, as before) raises each incumbent's retention probability, the union negotiates a higher wage. Thus, the wage rises above $\hat{W}$, as shown by point E_2 in figure 7.1d (where the new wage is less than $W^{\max}$). The wage increase discourages the firm from employing as many workers as it would otherwise have done. Thus, for any given ε_{+1}, current employment will be lower than it would otherwise have been.

Given that the economy has n workers and m firms and that the negotiated wage (W) exceeds the reservation wage (R), the level of involuntary unemployment is $(n - m \cdot L)$. Then the argument above implies that once an employment slump occurs, the wage-setting activity of unions tends to make it persist, provided that $h > 0$ and $W < W^{\max}$.[9,10]

Note that once the wage hits $W^{\max}$ (given by equation (7.5b)), the unemployment persistence effect disappears, in the sense that no further adverse shock in employment leads to a rise in the wage. (The reason is, of course, that if the union would allow the wage to exceed this maximum level, the firm would respond either by replacing the insiders by outsiders or by closing down.) In other words, the unemployment persistence effect is bounded from above.[11]

We now consider the influence of union bargaining power on the magnitude of this unemployment persistence effect. In our analysis, a rise in such power is mirrored in (a) a fall in a (and hence δ) in equation (7.4c) (reflecting a fall in the bargaining strength of the firm relative to that of the union) and/or (b) a rise in the firm's labour turnover cost, T.[12] It can be shown that each of these phenomena not only raises the wage (W), but makes the wage more responsive to changes in the incumbent insider workforce (L^I) (i.e. each increases the absolute value of $(\partial W / \partial L^I)$ in equation (7.5) and thereby augments the unemployment persistence effect. This proposition is proved formally in the appendix. Intuitively, when δ falls or T rises in the bargaining solution (7.4c), a given drop in L^I calls forth a larger rise in W, because now the firm's loss from a wage increase is weighted less heavily (relative to the union's associated gain) in the Nashian objective function. By implication, the $W - L^I$ schedule in figure 7.1c become flatter. Thus, when there is an adverse employment shock, the resulting wage increase and the associated employment decrease are larger than they would otherwise have been. In this way a rise in union power strengthens the unemployment persistence effect.[13]

Figure 7.1 also indicates how union influence on wage bargaining may generate a 'wage–employment ratchet effect'. In order for this effect to operate, it is necessary that there is less than 'free entry' (i.e. $h < 1$) and that the random variations in labour demand are 'large' relative to the incumbent insider workforce, i.e. adverse swings cause $L_{-1} < L^I_{-1}$ and favourable swings cause $L_{-1} > L^I_{-1}$.

To see this, observe that when $h < 1$, the left-hand branch of the entry–exit locus in figure 7.1d is steeper (45 degrees) than the right-hand branch. In other words, the insiders who are dismissed all relinquish their influence on wage determination (since the union is assumed only to represent the interests of employed members), but the entrants who are hired do not all gain influence on wage determination (because when $h<1$, some entrants do not promptly join the union). Consequently, the random variations in labour demand lead to a downward trend in the incumbent insider workforce and, by implication, an upward trend in the wage and unemployment rates. The greater union power (viz. the lower δ or the greater T) and the smaller h, the larger this wage–employment ratchet effect, ceteris paribus. The ratchet is bounded from above by $W \leqslant W^{max}$. Once the wage hits W^{max}, adverse swings reduce employment while the wage remains rigid.

Concluding Remarks

Our analysis indicates that (a) unions' power over wages may, to some extent, hinder an economy in recovering from a recession and (b) the greater the unions' power (as reflected in their bargaining strength and the magnitude of labour turnover costs), the bleaker the economy's recovery prospects may become. In this light, the more widespread and intensive influence of unions in Europe than in the United States may help explain the drastically different product wage trajectories in these two parts of the world and Europe's comparative lack of success in reducing its unemployment after the recession of the early 1980s.[14,15] Thus, our analysis may help explain why unemployment rates in Europe and the US have had an upward trend since the early 1970s. It also provides some microeconomic underpinning for the notion that European unemployment is more closely related to 'excessive wages' than American unemployment.

NOTES

This chapter was first written as a paper for the session on 'Labor Contracts' (organized by J. Malcomson) at EEA Congress, Vienna, August 1986. We are indebted to Nils Gottfries and Alan Manning for insightful comments. The support of the ESRC, Leverhulme Trust and the Swedish Council for Research in the Humanities and Social Sciences is gratefully acknowledged. This was originally published in *European Economic Review* (Paper and Proceedings) 1987.

1 Gottfries and Horn (1986) and Blanchard and Summers (1986a) consider unemployment persistence in the context of a union whose members have uncertain employment prospects, whereas Lindbeck and Snower (1985) deal with persistence due to labour turnover costs arising from the discrimination against outsiders by insiders by way of non-cooperation and harassment activities of insiders (who may or may not be unionized). Horn (1983) shows

how an expansion of the government sector leads to lower employment and higher wages in the private sector, but a government contraction leaves the private sector unable to absorb the layed-off workers in the public sector. Finally, Drazen (1985) considers how unemployment persistence can occur through the attrition of human capital in a recession.

2 Note that the concavity of the utility function does not contradict our assumption of risk neutrality since W is not a random variable in our model.

3 At the opposite extreme, the union is unable to do so, and thus the retention probabilities of members and non-members are identical. In that case 'L^I' must be replaced by 'L_{-1}' (last period's total labour force) in equation (7.2a). This amendment does not affect our qualitative conclusions with regard to the unemployment persistence effect, but it does imply that there is no wage-employment ratchet.

4 We do no not exclude the possibility that these minimum and maximum values of ε may be $-\infty$ and $+\infty$, respectively.

5 In general, the firm's costs of altering its workforce may be divided into two categories: (a) the cost of replacing current employees by outsiders and (b) the cost of expanding or contracting the workforce. Per employee, the former costs (which may involve litigation costs, severance pay and a drop in the morale of the remaining employees) are usually much greater than the latter (pertaining to temporary layoff and subsequent recall). Our analysis forces attention on the former costs (as a threat which the union uses in wage negotiation) and ignores the latter.

6 We assume all workers to have the same utility function and thus the same reservation wage.

7 How many of such workers join the union in the real world depends on laws, social norms, transaction costs, inertia in non-members' behaviour – all of which lie beyond the influence of the union itself (and beyond the scope of this chapter).

8 Note two extreme cases. On the one hand, there is 'free entry', where each of last period's employed non-members becomes a union member in the current period if he or she retains his or her job. Here, $h=1$ for all $(L_{-1}-L^I_{-1})$, so that $L^I=(1-r)\cdot L_{-1}$. On the other hand, there is the case of 'no entry', where employed non-members have no opportunity of joining the union. Here $h=0$ for $L_{-1}-L^I_{-1}\geq0$, so that $L^I=(1-r)\cdot L^I$ over this range.

9 Of course, insider market power is not the only conceivable rationale for such an effect. Other rationales include the depreciation of human and non-human capital during prolonged periods of unemployment, and changes in workers' tastes and job search behaviour over such periods (in particular, an increased preference for leisure relative to work and a loss of self-confidence in job search).

10 Observe that this result is superficially similar to that of Blanchard and Summers (1986) in this volume. However, their unemployment persistence rests on a fundamentally different relation between wages and labour demand: in our model, unions may be responsible for excessive real wages and 'deficient' employment due to production processes characterized by diminishing returns to labour; in their model, unions may give rise to excessive nominal wages, implying excessive product prices and thereby leading to deficient product demand for labour.

11 Observe, furthermore that if $h<1$ when $L_{-1}>L^l_{-1}$ and if adverse employment swings lead to shrinkage of the labour force while favourable swings lead to net hiring, then the unemployment persistence effect tends to be weaker in a boom than in a slump. Blanchard and Summers (1986a) find empirical confirmation of this phenomenon.

12 Note that the degree of union power, as defined here, does not necessarily have anything to do with the degree of centralization in bargaining.

13 As the appendix shows, these are not the only channels whereby a fall in δ or a rise in T may influence the relation between W and L^l. Suffice it to say that the other channels pull in the same direction.

14 The same may be said of the sectors within these economies. For example, unions play a comparatively important role in wage determination of the steel and automobile industries in the US: and it has been these industries that have witnessed relatively low employment rates.

15 It is worth noting that the unemployment persistence effect also works in reverse: union wage setting tends to perpetuate favourable random variations in employment, and the stronger the unions are, the more pronounced this effect will be. Thus, it may be argued that whereas a rise in union power generally leads to higher wages and lower employment (both in the comparative static terms and via the bounded ratchet effect), union wage setting is more harmful in a recession than in a boom on account of the unemployment persistence effect.

APPENDIX

The effect of the incumbent workforce on the wage:
Rewriting equation (7.4c):

$$A=(\sigma\cdot U\,'+\sigma_{l'}\cdot l'\cdot U)+\delta\cdot(\sigma\cdot U/B)\cdot\pi'(W)=0.$$

In order for the second-order condition for optimality to be fulfilled, we need to assume that $[(\sigma_{ll}\cdot l'/\sigma_l)-(l''/l')]$ exceeds some negative critical value. For the sake of algebraic simplicity below, however, we suppose that $l''=0$, $\sigma_{ll}<0$ and $\sigma_{lL}=0$. These conditions may be derived by imposing the appropriate restrictions on the density G and the production function f

$$(\partial W/\partial L^l)\,\big|\,_{A=0}=-A_L/A_W, \text{ where}$$

$$A_W=(\partial A/\partial W)$$

$$=-l'\cdot[\sigma\cdot U\,'+\sigma_{ll}\cdot l'\cdot U+\delta_1\cdot\pi'(W)\cdot\sigma\cdot U/B]$$

$$+\sigma\cdot U\,''+\sigma_{l'}\cdot l'\cdot U\,'+(\delta\cdot\sigma/B)\cdot[\pi'(W)\cdot U\,'-(\pi'(W)\cdot U/B)-U\cdot\pi''(W)]$$

which must be negative in order for the second-order condition for optimality to be fulfilled. We assume that $\sigma_{ll}<0$ to ensure this; furthermore, assuming $\sigma_{lL}=0$ for simplicity,

$$A_L=(\partial A/\partial L^I)=\sigma_L\cdot[U~'+(\delta\cdot U\cdot\pi'(W)/B)]<0.$$

Thus, $(\partial W/\partial L^I)\mid_{A=0}<0$.

The effect of $(R+T)$ on the wage:

$$[\partial W/\partial(R+T)]\mid_{A=0}=-A_{R+T}/A_W, \text{ where}$$
$$A_{R+T}=[\partial A/\partial(R+T)]=-\delta\cdot(\sigma\cdot Y/B^2)\cdot\pi'(W)\cdot[\partial B/\partial(R+T)]>0.$$

Thus, $[\partial W/\partial(R+T)]\mid_{A=0}>0$.

The effect of δ on the wage:

$$(\partial W/\partial\delta)_{A=0}=-[\sigma\cdot U\cdot\pi'(W)]/B\cdot A_W<0.$$

The effect of T on the responsiveness of W to L^I:

Note that
$$(A_W/A_L)=-l'+(\zeta/A_L)=D, \text{ where}$$
$$\zeta=\sigma\cdot U~''+\sigma_l\cdot l'\cdot U~'+(\delta\cdot\sigma/B)\cdot\{\pi'(W)\cdot U~'-[\pi'(W)\cdot U/B]-U\cdot\pi''(W)\}.$$

Then
$$\frac{\partial D}{\partial D}=\frac{\zeta_\delta\cdot A_L-A_{L\delta}\cdot\zeta}{(A_L)^2}, \text{ which is positive because}$$

$$A_{L\delta}=\sigma_L\cdot\pi'(W)\cdot U/B<0,$$
$$\zeta_\delta=(\pi'(W)\cdot\sigma/B^2)\cdot[U~'\cdot B-\pi'(W)\cdot U]+(\sigma\cdot U\cdot\pi''(W)/B)<0$$

and thus

$$\zeta_\delta\cdot A_L-A_{L\delta}\cdot\zeta=\zeta_\delta\cdot[\sigma_L\cdot U~'-\sigma''\cdot l'\cdot U]$$
$$-A_{L\sigma}\cdot[\sigma\cdot U~''+\sigma_l\cdot l'\cdot U~']>0.$$

Hence $\partial[(\partial W/\partial L^I)\mid_{A=0}]/\partial\delta>0$.

REFERENCES

Blanchard, O. and Summers, L. 1986a: Hysteresis in unemployment. *European Economic Review*. 31 (1/2), 288–95.

Blanchard, O. and Summers, L. 1986b: Hysteresis and the European Unemployment Problem. Mimeo.

Drazen, A. 1985: Cyclical determinants of the natural level of economic activity. *International Economic Review*, 26 (2), 387–97.

Gottfries, N. and Horn, H. 1986: Wage Formation and the Persistency of Unemployment. Seminar Paper No. 347. University of Stockholm: Institute for International Economic Studies.

Horn, H. 1983: Imperfect Competition in Models of Wage Formation and International Trade, PhD Dissertation. Monograph No. 15. University of Stockholm: Institute for International Economic Studies.

Lindbeck, A. and Snower, D. J. 1984a: Involuntary Unemployment as an Insider–Outsider Dilemma. Seminar Paper No. 282. Forthcoming in Beckerman, W. (ed.) *Wage Rigidity and Unemployment,* London: Duckworth.

Lindbeck, A. and Snower, D. J. 1984b: Labor Turnover, Insider, Moral and Involuntary Unemployment. Seminar Paper No. 310. University of Stockholm: Institute for International Economic Studies.

Lindbeck, A. and Snower, D. J. 1985: Cooperation, Harassment, and Involuntary Unemployment. Seminar Paper No. 321. University of Stockholm: Institute for International Economic Studies.

Lindbeck, A. and Snower, D. J. 1986: Wage setting, unemployment, and insider–outsider relations. *American Economic Review,* 76 (2).

8

A Simple Model of Imperfect Competition with Walrasian Features

HUW DIXON

Imperfect competition is a pervasive part of modern industrial economies, where high levels of concentration in product markets often coexist with unionized labour markets. Most standard macroeconomic models, however, assume that markets are perfectly competitive. This chapter provides a *simple* framework in which we are able to explore some of the implications of imperfect competition for the macro-economy, and to evaluate the adequacy of competitive macroeconomic models as 'convenient simplifications'. The results of the chapter suggest that whilst some general features of competitive macromodels do carry over to an imperfectly competitive framework, others do not. Imperfect competition in the labour and product markets can have a significant impact on the level of employment and the effectiveness of macro-economic policy. Imperfect competition provides an explicit account of price and wage determination, and thus gives us a far greater insight into the microeconomic structure of macroeconomic equilibrium than is possible in competititve models.

This chapter presents a simple model of imperfect competition with Walrasian features. The model is 'Walrasian' both in some of its assumptions,[1] and also in the properties of the model. What we have attempted to do is to take a standard neoclassical synthesis macromodel (e.g. Patinkin, 1965; Branson, 1979) and introduce imperfect competition into the product and labour markets. We feel that this is a useful exercise for two reasons. Firstly, it provides a simple macromodel of imperfect competition in which the causal mechanisms are very clear. In general, models of imperfect competition have tended to be rather complex, despite a recent trend towards simpler versions (e.g. Hart,

1982; d'Aspremont et al., 1985). Secondly, by adopting the standard neoclassical synthesis framework, it is easy to relate the model of imperfect competition to more familiar models.

Imperfect competition in the product market is modelled using conjectural-variations Cournot equilibrium which captures a wide range of possible market solutions, encompassing perfect competition, Cournot competition and joint profit maximization as special cases. This approach contrasts with existing models which adopt a Chamberlinian framework with differentiated prices and price-setting firms (Blanchard and Kiyotaki, 1985; Layard and Nickell, 1985; Svensson, 1985), and generalizes Hart's (1982) assumption of Cournot competition. We explore the model with a competitive labour market in the next two sections, and with a unionized labour market in the final section.

With an imperfectly competitive product market and competitive labour market, we can use familiar aggregate demand and aggregate supply analysis to evaluate the influence of the degree of imperfect competition on the level of employment, the government expenditure multiplier and the neutrality of money. There are three main results. Firstly, equilibrium employment is inversely related to the degree of monopoly in the product market. With perfect competition employment is at its Walrasian level. Since the labour market is competitive there is no involuntary unemployment and this deviation of employment from its Walrasian level can be interpreted as underemployment. Secondly, if money is neutral the underlying Walrasian equilibrium will also be neutral in the imperfectly competitive equilibrium. This follows since the behavioural equations are all homogeneous to degree zero (Hodo) in money and prices. Thirdly, the government expenditure multiplier is in a very precise sense 'Walrasian' in this model. By this we mean that the mechanisms underlying the Walrasian multiplier are the same with imperfect competition. There will be crowding out, and the multiplier has the Walrasian value as its lower bound, is strictly less than unity and strictly increasing in the degree of monopoly. In the next section the model is presented assuming constant returns to scale, a convenient simplification which enables us to derive an explicit solution to the model. In the section following, however, we make the more orthodox assumption of diminishing returns: the analytical properties of the model are not affected by this.

In the final section we consider the impact of unions in an imperfectly competitive macromodel. A union may wish to set the wage above the market clearing level, so that there may be 'excess supply' in both the labour and product markets.[2] In this sense the economy has a 'Keynesian' equilibrium. However, we consider two alternative models of wage determination (bargaining, monopoly union) for which the equilibrium is very un-Keynesian in its implications for macroeconomic policy. Both fiscal and monetary policy are neutral,[3] so that macroeconomic policy has even less impact here than in a Walrasian economy, despite the presence of excess supplies. The basic reason is that the equilibrium level of employment and real wages are unaffected by government policy, so that changes in the money supply or government expenditure feed through entirely into nominal wage and price increases. The only role for macroeconomic policy in a unionized economy in the examples presented is in the presence of multiple equilibria: macroeconomic policy can be used to ensure that the equilibrium with the highest level of employment is attained rather than a low employment equilibrium. The results of this section relate most closely to Layard and Nickell's (1985) model of NAIRU. The main conceptual difference between the two models is that Layard and Nickell adopt an essentially partial equilibrium approach for the purpose of deriving a tractable econometric model. The model we present adopts an explicit – if simple – general equilibrium framework. As we discuss, the model in the final section gives a theoretical justification for some of Layard and Nickell's assumptions. For example, when combined with fixed wages in the short run, only surprises in government expenditure influence output.

Whilst the models presented in this chapter are very specific, and have no claim to generality, we believe that the results should not be dismissed as simply special examples. Most of the assumptions made are absolutely standard, and the originality of the chapter depends not on the ingredients but on the recipe. For this reason we believe the specific models presented have conceptual implications over and beyond their mathematical implications.

Imperfect Competition with a Competitive Labour Market

We shall first lay out the basic assumptions about households, firms and the government.

The Household

There is one price-taking household which has initial endowments of money M^o and leisure T and derives utility from consumption C, real money balances M/p and leisure l (money is being used as numeriare). The household also receives all the profits from the two firms in the economy. The household has Cobb–Douglas utility:

$$U = \alpha \log C + \beta \log l + \gamma \log \frac{M}{p}. \tag{8.1}$$

The household is a price taker, and so maximizes (8.1) subject to the budget constraint:

$$p.C+l.w+M \leq w.T+M^o+\pi, \tag{8.2}$$

where π are distributed profits, to be explained below. The solution to equations (8.1) and (8.2) yields the familiar Walrasian demand functions for money and consumption, and supply of labour $N=T-l$. Whilst equation (8.1) is assumed throughout the chapter, we shall often write these demand functions in general form:

$$C=C(\frac{w}{p}, \frac{M^o+\pi}{p}) = \alpha \frac{(wT+M^o+\pi)}{p} \tag{8.3}$$

$$N=N(\frac{w}{p}, \frac{M^o+\pi}{p}) = T(1-\beta) - \frac{\beta p}{w}(\frac{M^o}{p}+\frac{\pi}{p}) \tag{8.4}$$

$$\frac{M}{p} = \frac{M}{p}(\frac{w}{p}, \frac{M^o+\pi}{p}) = \gamma(\frac{wT}{p}+\frac{M^o+\pi}{p}). \tag{8.5}$$

As is clear from equation (8.3), the household's demand for consumption has a unit elasticity (as do (8.4) and (8.5)). Furthermore, all the demand functions are homogeneous of degree zero (Hodo) in prices, money balances and profits (P,w,M^o,π). This is because (a) the budget constraint (8.2) is unaffected by an equiproportionate change in (p,w,M^o,π) (b) utility is Hodo in (p, M). Of course, we might prefer to interpret the model as being a temporary equilibrium, in which case *nominal* rather than real money balances would enter the household's utility function. The conditions for an indirect utility function to be Hodo in (p, M) are very restrictive (see Grandmont, 1984). However, it suits our purposes to have real money balances in the utility function because we aim to demonstrate that imperfect competiton per se does not invalidate the 'classical dichotomy': if the underlying competitive equilibrium is unaffected by the money supply M^o, then so will the imperfectly competitive economy be. The treatment of profits in imperfectly general equilibrium models is problematic (see Hart, 1985).

The Firm

There are two firms in the output market (this obviously generalizes). They are price takers in the labour market and there is a conjectural variations Cournot model in the output market. The assumption of price taking in the labour market and price making in the output market can be justified by the fact that the firm is 'small' in the labour market (there are lots of firms from the many output markets), but 'large' in its particular product market. Furthermore, the firms have no 'general equilibrium' awareness: in taking their output decisions, they do not calculate the effects of this on the labour market (this contrasts with models such as Hart, 1979 and Roberts, 1980 where firms do calculate the full effect). However, the firms know the 'true' household demand curve (taking w as given), which from equation (8.3) has unit elasticity. In this section it is assumed that firms have constant return to scale production with one input – labour. This is a convenient simplification that enables us to derive explicit results; in the next section we show that the introduction of diminishing returns does not invalidate our analytical results. The output-labour ratio is normalized to unity:

$$y_i = N_i \tag{8.6}$$

where y_i and N_i are the i firm's output and employment respectively. Under equation (8.6) firms have constant marginal cost w. We further assume that firms have the same conjectural variations parameter ϕ. With two firms, unit elasticity demand, and constant marginal cost we have the equilibrium price–cost margin μ:[4]

$$\mu = \frac{p-w}{p} \equiv \frac{1+\phi}{2} \tag{8.7}$$

and hence real wages and profits:

$$\frac{w}{p} = 1 - \mu \qquad \frac{\pi}{p} = \mu . N. \tag{8.8}$$

For the competitive case with Bertrand conjectures ($\phi = -1$) $w/p = 1$ and $\mu = 0$, there are no profits, and all income is wages. In the Cournot case ($\phi = 0$), $w/p = \mu = 1/2$, wages are half of income. For ϕ close to 1, the equilibrium price-cost margin μ becomes close to 1 and real wages close to 0 (note that for $\phi \geq +1$ no conjectural variation equilibrium exists with unit elastic demand). Following Lerner (1934), we shall call μ the 'degree of monopoly'.

Government

Government expenditure can be in two forms: levels of *real* expenditure g which are predetermined, or *nominal* levels ('cash limits'). Whether government expenditure is planned in real or nominal terms will have a big influence on the effects of that expenditure on the macroeconomy (this is discussed in more detail in Dixon, 1986). The results of this chapter will apply to *real* government expenditure plans, as is standard in the macroeconomic literature. The simplest way to model g is to conceive of the government purchasing output at a price p_g determined by bilateral bargaining between the industry and government, the corresponding mark-up being μ_g. The important point is that the price which the government pays is not (directly) influenced by, and will not influence the price paid by the household. This assumption seems reasonable: the government is a big buyer, and does not enter the market as a price taker.

Since p_g is determined independently of p, the conjectural variations equilibrium μ (8.7) will not be influenced by g (since the revenue gained from government contracts is fixed at $p_g.g$, it does not enter into *marginal* revenue). Again, purely for simplicity, we assume that although independently determined, $p_g=p$, the price paid by government and households happens to be equal. This can easily be relaxed.[5] For a wide range of industrial products, bilateral contracts between firms and government are more realistic than the usual treatment of simply adding g to industry demand.

Lastly, there is the question of the government's budget constraint: how does it finance its expenditure? This is not analysed in any detail here. However, the results of this chapter are consistent with a proportional profits tax. Alternatively, the government can be viewed as financing the expenditure by printing money, which appears in the next period's money balances. Neither of these possibilities is made explicit, since our main interest does not lie in the government finance policy.

Equilibrium and Macroeconomic Policy

We have now outlined the assumptions underlying the model. Since the household is unrationed in all markets, consumption, employment and the demand for money are all given by notional demands (8.3)–(8.5). The equilibrium in the economy can be represented by four equations:

$$y = N \left(\frac{w}{p} , \frac{M^{\circ}+\pi}{p} \right) \tag{8.9}$$

$$y = c \left(\frac{w}{p} , \frac{M^{\circ}+\pi}{p} \right)+g \tag{8.10}$$

$$\frac{w}{p} = \frac{1-\phi}{2}=1-\mu \tag{8.11}$$

$$\frac{\pi}{p} =\mu.y . \tag{8.12}$$

Equation (8.9) is the equilibrium condition for the competitive labour market (y is total output); equation (8.10) is the equilibrium condition for output (output is demand determined); equation (8.11) is the real wage determined by the equilibrium price–cost margin; equation (8.12) is total real profits determined by the equilibrium price–cost margin and output. We omit the money market equilibrium condition, since equations (8.3)–(8.5) satisfy Walras' Law. The endogenous variables determined by the equilibrium are $\{w, p, y, \pi, N\}$, and the exogenous variables are $\{M^o, \phi, g\}$.

The equilibrium in this economy can be represented by the usual aggregate supply and demand equations in (p, N) space (see figure 8.1). From the price–cost equation (8.7), the mark-up of price over the wage is fixed due to CRTS, hence things look the same in (w, N) and (p, N) space. The aggregate supply curve (AS) is derived by combining equations (8.9) and (8.12):

$$AS \; N = N(1-\mu, \; \mu N + \frac{M^o}{p}) \; . \tag{8.13}$$

By total differentiation:

$$\frac{dN}{dp}\bigg|_{AS} = \frac{-N_2.M^o}{p^2(1-N_2.\mu)} > 0 \tag{8.14}$$

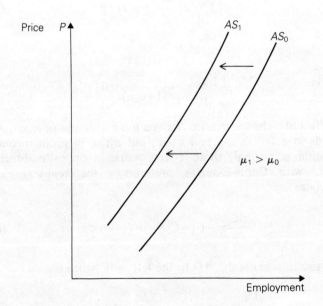

Figure 8.1 *Aggregate supply and the degree of monopoly*

where $N_2=dN/dW<0$ from equation (8.4). If the price rises *given the real wage*, then the real balance effect will elicit an increased supply of labour (since with Cobb–Douglas preferences (8.1), leisure is normal). Note that the AS curve is upward sloping not due to the presence of 'money illusion', but rather due to the real balance effect which operates in the labour supply (with leisure a normal good). In many received textbook accounts, the labour supply depends only on the real wage w/p, which implicitly suppresses the real balance effect. The resultant vertical AS function is at best a misleading hueristic device (the origin of this 'simplification' is probably Patinkin, 1965: 202–5). Similarly:

$$\frac{dN}{d\mu}\bigg|_{AS} = \frac{-(N_1-N_2N)}{1-N_2.N}<0 \tag{8.15}$$

At a given price, a rise in the mark-up μ will reduce the real wage and increase profits for any level of employment. Both of these effects lead to a reduction in the labour supply at a given price. Thus the AS function is upward sloping, and a rise in μ shifts it to the left, as in figure 8.1.

The analysis of aggregate demand is a little more complicated. The real balance effect will of course lead to a downward sloping aggregate demand curve (AD), which is defined by

$$N=C(1-\mu, \frac{M^{\circ}}{p}+\mu N)+g. \tag{8.16}$$

Hence:

$$\frac{dN}{dp}\bigg|_{AD} = \frac{-C_2M^{\circ}}{p^2(1-c_2\mu)}<0. \tag{8.17}$$

The effect of a change in μ on N given p is a little less obvious. A rise in μ leads to a fall in the real wage, but a rise in profit income. If consumption is normal, these effects work in opposite directions. However, with Cobb–Douglas preferences the real-wage effect predominates:

$$\frac{dC}{d\mu} = -C_1+C_2N=\alpha(N-T)<0. \tag{8.18}$$

Hence a rise in μ shifts the AD to the left as in figure 8.2.

$$\frac{dN}{d\mu}\bigg|_{AD} = \frac{-(C_1-C_2N)}{1-C_2\mu}<0. \tag{8.19}$$

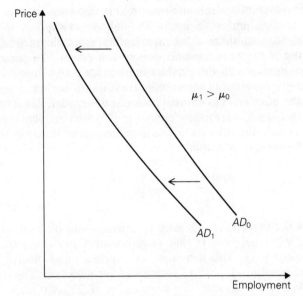

Figure 8.2 *Aggregate demand and the degree of monopoly*

(Note that $1-C_2\mu>0$, since from equation (8.3) C_2, the marginal propensity to consume from real balances, is of course less than unity.)

An equilibrium in this economy is represented by the intersection of the aggregate demand and aggregate supply functions. Inspection of equations (8.13) and (8.16) reveals that the classical dichotomy holds in this model since the equilibrium equations are homogeneous of degree zero (Hodo) in w,p,m. The classical dichotomy thus stems from homogeneity, and not from a vertical AS curve nor the assumption of a competitive economy.

Proposition 1: Let $\lambda>0$. If $\{w^*, p^*, \pi^*, N^*\}$ is an equilibrium given M^o, then $\{\lambda w^*, \lambda p^*, \lambda\pi^*, N^*\}$ is an equilibrium given λM^o.

Whilst the introduction of imperfect competition into this model does not upset the homogeneity of the economy, the level of equilibrium employment is decreasing in the degree of monopoly.

Proposition 2: Equilibrium employment is inversely related to the degree of monopoly μ.

Proof: Total differentiation of equations (8.13) and (8.16) yields:

$$\frac{\mathrm{d}N}{\mathrm{d}\mu} = \frac{N_2C_1-N_1C_2}{C_2-N_2}<0. \qquad \text{QED}$$

The maximum employment attained in this economy occurs at the Walrasian equilibrium, with $\mu=0$. The labour market is of course competitive, so that there is no involuntary unemployment (in any possible sense of the word), merely underemployment. The presence of imperfect competition in the product market leads to a lower level of equilibrium employment in the competitive labour market.

What of the effectiveness of fiscal policy in this model? If we consider equations (8.13)–(8.16) which define the *AS* and *AD* curves, fiscal policy affects only the *AS* curve. The fiscal multiplier *taking μ and p as given* is a 'Keynesian' multiplier:

$$\left.\frac{dN}{dg}\right|_{AD} = \frac{1}{1-C_2\mu} > 1 \tag{8.20}$$

where C_2 is the marginal propensity to consume out of (real) income. Essentially, what happens is that government expenditure increases profits initially by μg. This increases consumption, and this leads to a feedback from output to profits to increased consumption. The increase in output due to an increase in g in equation (8.20) is represented in figure 8.3 by a shift from initial position A to B. However, the increase in output at initial price p_0 leads to excess demand for labour, and hence

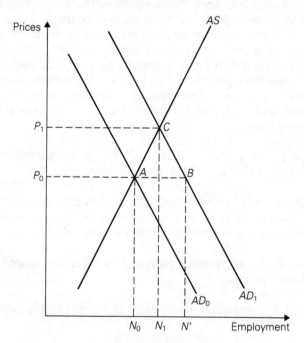

Figure 8.3 *Fiscal policy*

wages and prices will rise. The full fiscal multiplier can be derived if we totally differentiate the AS and AD functions with respect to g:

$$\begin{bmatrix} 1-N_2\mu & N_2\,\dfrac{M}{p^2} \\[2ex] 1-C_2\mu & C_2\,\dfrac{M}{p^2} \end{bmatrix} \begin{bmatrix} dN/dg \\[2ex] dp/dg \end{bmatrix} = \begin{bmatrix} 0 \\[2ex] 1 \end{bmatrix}$$

Using Cramer's rule this yields:

$$\frac{dN}{dg} = \frac{-N_2}{C_2-N_2} > 0, \tag{8.21}$$

$$\frac{dp}{dg} = \frac{p^2 C_2(1-N_2\mu)}{M^o C_2-N_2} > 0. \tag{8.22}$$

Clearly, the fiscal multiplier is less than one and strictly positive.

Using equations (8.3) and (8.4) the explicit solution is:

$$\frac{dN}{dg} = \frac{\beta}{\beta+(1-\mu)\alpha}. \tag{8.23}$$

Using equation (8.7) we can relate firms' conjectures ϕ to the mark-up μ and hence the mulitplier by equation (8.23). This is done in table 8.1.

Table 8.1 *Imperfect competition (duopoly) and the fiscal multiplier*

Conjecture	Mark-up μ	Multiplier
-1 (Bertrand)	0	$\dfrac{\beta}{\beta+\alpha}$
0 (Cournot)	1/2	$\dfrac{2\beta}{2\beta+\alpha}$
1 (Cartel)	1	1

Recall that when $\phi=1$ there is no equilibrium in the product market: we include $\phi=1$ since from equation (8.23) as μ tends to 1 from below, the multiplier tends to unity. The cartel is then a limiting result. As is clear from equation (8.23) and table 8.1, the greater the degree of monopoly μ, the more effective is fiscal policy. In general since $-1 \leqslant \phi < +1$,

$$1 > \frac{dN}{dg} \geqslant \frac{\beta}{\alpha + \beta}. \tag{8.24}$$

Whilst the value of μ does influence the fiscal multiplier, there is always crowding out. Furthermore, the mechanisms underlying the multiplier are essentially the same – as indicated by the general formula in equation (8.21). In this sense, the multiplier is basically 'Walrasian' rather than Keynesian. We summarize the foregoing discussion in proposition 3.

Proposition 3: For $0 \leqslant \mu < 1$ the fiscal multiplier is

$$\frac{dN}{dg} = \frac{-N_2}{C_2 - N_2} = \frac{\beta}{\beta + (1-\mu)\alpha}.$$

Hence

$$\frac{\beta}{\beta + \alpha} \leqslant \frac{dN}{dg} < 1$$

and is *increasing* in μ.

We shall now show that a profits tax will leave these results unaffected. This is important, since it shows that we are justified in not treating the government budget constraint explicitly. Suppose we assume that only a proportion t of profits appears in households' budget constraints (8.2) (where $0 \leqslant t \leqslant 1$). In this case, AD and AS become:

$$N - C(1-\mu, \frac{M_o}{p} + t\mu N) - g = 0 \qquad AD(t),$$

$$N - N(1-\mu, \frac{M^o}{p} + t\mu N) = 0 \qquad AS(t).$$

Total differentiation of $AD(t)$ on $AS(t)$ with respect to t shows that $dN/dt = 0$. The equilibrium is unaffected by the proportion of profits distributed to the shareholder. Furthermore, total differentiation with respect to g yields the *same* fiscal multiplier as in equations (8.21) and (8.23). The effectiveness of fiscal policy is not influenced by the proportion of profits distributed. This is a surprising result given that the aggregate demand multiplier derived from $AD(t)$ holding price constant is sensitive to t (e.g. if no profits are distributed, and $t=1$, then $dN/dg|AD=1$). The crucial point here is that if t increases, real distributed profits at the equilibrium output fall by $\Delta t.\mu.N$. The price level will fall so that real balances increase by $\Delta p.M^o/p^2$. The increase in real balances exactly offsets the fall in real distributed profits, so that total wealth remains unchanged. Since the real wage remains constant, equilibrium output and employment are unaltered. In one sense, therefore, an ad valorem profits tax can be said to have no real effects, only nominal effects. Similar exercises can be conducted for an employment tax (which reduces the real wage and share of profits in income), a (real) lump sum tax (which increases equilibrium output via the wealth effect) and an income tax (which alters the real wage and the proportion of profits which households receive). The imposition of these taxes to finance government expenditure would alter the specific results stated in this chapter, as they would in a Walrasian economy. However, we hope to have convinced the reader that the Walrasian features would still shine through.

Imperfect Competition with Diminishing Returns

In the previous section, we made the simplest possible assumptions that enabled us to derive explicit formulae for policy multipliers. One of these – the 'Walrasian' assumption of constant returns – is not standard in textbook macroeconomics. Since Keynes, it has been usual to view the macroeconomic equilibrium as occurring in the 'short run'; capital is fixed. This leads to the standard assumption that there are diminishing returns to labour-output is a concave function of employment; $y=f(N)$; $f'>0>f''$.

In this section we shall see that constant returns was merely a convenient simplification. Whilst we are unable to derive explicit formulae for the multiplier, the overall logic and conclusions of the previous section are not changed.

With diminishing returns, the only additional complexity is that the real wage becomes a function of employment as well as the degree of competition in the product market. The profit maximizing duopolist chooses its output so that marginal revenue equals marginal cost. Rather than being constant, marginal cost increases with output, and is given by w/f':

$$\mu=\frac{p-w/f'}{p}=\frac{1+\phi}{2} \tag{8.25a}$$

$$\frac{w}{p}=f'.\frac{(1-\phi)}{2}=f'.(1-\mu). \tag{8.25b}$$

In the case of a perfectly competitive product ($\phi=-1$), this simply means that the real wage equals the marginal product of labour. With imperfect competion, however, labour receives less than its marginal product. In the case of Cournot duopoly ($\phi=0$) the real wage equals only one half of the marginal product. Equation (8.25a) is often referred to as the 'demand curve' for labour. This is misleading, as we shall discuss below. Rather, it simply tells us the relationship between nominal wages, prices and employment that must hold with imperfectly competitive product markets.

If we now define the real wage $\omega=w/p$, the real wage in our macroeconomic system becomes:[6]

$$Y=c(\omega, \frac{M^{\circ}}{p})+g \tag{8.26}$$

$$Y=f(N) \tag{8.27}$$

$$\omega=w/p=f'.(1-\mu) \tag{8.28}$$

$$N=N(\omega, \frac{M^{\circ}}{p}). \tag{8.29}$$

Note that we are omitting profits from our analysis for simplicity.

Aggregate demand and supply analysis is still valid in this framework, so long as we include the real-wage equation (8.28). Turning first to aggregate demand (AD) in (N,p) space, we have the three equations (8.26)–(8.28). As the price increases, this reduces real balances as before, but also leads to an increase in the real wage. To see this, substitution reduces equations (8.26)–(8.28) to the AD relation:

$$AD \ f(N)=c(f'(N).1-\mu, \frac{M^{\circ}}{p})+g. \tag{8.30}$$

Total differentiation of equation (8.30) yields

$$\frac{dN}{dp}\bigg|_{AD} = \frac{-c_2}{f'-f''.(1-\mu).c_1}<0. \tag{8.31}$$

Note that since $c_1>0$ (leisure is normal) then the 'real wage' effects of increases in price via the price cost equation (8.28) reinforces the real balance effect. As in the Walrasian model, an increase in monopoly μ shifts the AD curve to the left in (N,p) space.

Aggregate supply (AS) is defined by equations (8.28) and (8.29). For comparison with textbooks, we can consider the AS relationship in real wage/employment space. Equation (8.28) gives the real wage as a function of employment, as in figure 8.4. The supply of labour is upward sloping in the real wage. However, because of real balance effects, there are a family of labour supply curves which correspond to different price levels. The higher the price level, the lower are real balances, and the higher the labour supply at any given real wage (in terms of figure 8.4, $p_0 < p_1$). Thus for the price level p_0, the corresponding employment is N_0, and N_1 corresponds to p_1.

The *AS* function is upward sloping, as can be verified by total differentiation of equations (8.28) and (8.29):

$$\frac{dN}{dp}\bigg|_{AS} = \frac{-N_2 \cdot \dfrac{M^o}{p^2}}{1 - N_1 \cdot f'' \cdot (1-\mu)} > 0. \tag{8.32}$$

Note that an increase in the degree of monopoly (a decrease in ϕ) will shift the relationship between real wages and employment to the left. In figure 8.5 we depict the relationship for $\phi = 1$ (perfect competition, $\phi = -1$) and $\phi = 1/2$ (Cournot). There is an inverse relationship between the degree of monopoly and employment.

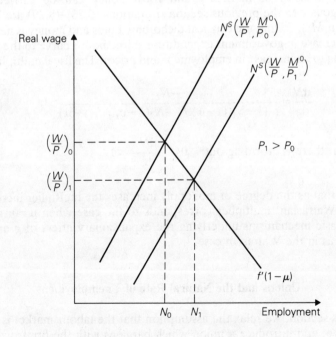

Figure 8.4 *Real wages, employment and the price level*

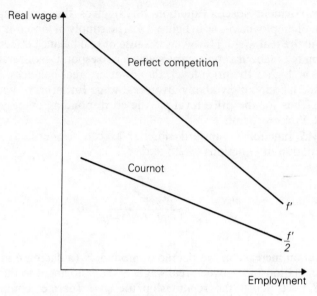

Figure 8.5 *Real wages and employment*

The analysis of monetary and fiscal policy can be carried out analogously to the previous section. Equations (8.26)–(8.29) are Hodo in (w, p, M^o), so that the classical dichotomy holds and money is neutral. An increase in government expenditure shifts the AS curve to the right, leading to an increase in employment and prices. The fiscal multiplier is:

$$\frac{dN}{dg} = \frac{-N_2}{c_2(1 - N_1.(1 - \mu).f'' - N_2(f' - c_1.f''.(1 - \mu)} > 0. \qquad (8.33)$$

Again, there is crowding out: $0 < \dfrac{dN}{dg} < 1$.

Note that as the degree of monopoly increases the multiplier increases. The 'Walrasian' multiplier corresponds to the case when $\mu = 0$: again, the basic mechanisms underlying the expansionary effect of g are the same as in the Walrasian case.

Unions and the Natural Rate of Unemployment

In this section, we relax the assumption that the labour market is competitive, and introduce a union which bargains with the firms over the nominal wage w. This introduces the possibility of an excess supply of labour: the union can push up the nominal wage, and hence the real wage, above the market clearing level. The resultant equilibrium will be 'Keynesian' in the sense that there will be an excess supply in both the product and labour markets. However, as we shall demonstrate, the model is very un-Keynesian in that the classical dichotomy still holds (money is neutral) and fiscal policy can be less effective than in the Walrasian case. Indeed, we provide examples in which the fiscal policy multiplier is zero, and there is complete crowding out.

The model presented seems a good interpretation of Friedman's conception of the natural rate of unemployment (NRH) (Friedman, 1968, 1975). Friedman's original article on the natural rate defined it as 'the level . . . ground out by the Walrasian system of general equilibrium equations, provided that there is embedded in them the actual structural characteristics of labour and product markets, including market imperfections, the cost of gathering information about job vacancies and so on' (1968: 8). Some economists have focused on the word 'Walrasian' in the above quote, and interpreted the NR as simply the Walrasian equilibrium (e.g. Hahn, 1980: 293). Others focus on search models of unemployment (Mortenson, 1970; Diamond, 1985; Pissarides, 1985; Lockwood, 1985). The model here focuses on imperfect competition in the labour and product markets – the NR as a non-Walrasian equilibrium. At the end of this section we will show how the equilibrium can be interpreted as the natural rate.

How should unions be introduced into this model? A first point is that we can no longer think of there being one 'representative' household. There will be two types of households in equilibrium: the employed and the unemployed. The union may act in the interests of its employed members, to maximize their welfare. Secondly, since there will be rationing in the labour market, the notional consumption function will have to be altered to become an *effective* demand function. We will first outline the model of the household and labour market, and then the union.

Households

There is a continuum H of households with identical preferences and money balances as represented by equations (8.1)–(8.5), except that for simplicity profits are not distributed. This corresponds to the idea that each household is very 'small' and that to obtain market demand/supply you have to add up (in fact integrate) each household's demand/supply. If we look first at the labour supply, we integrate over the set H of households, so that market supply is given by:

$$N^s(\omega, M^o/p) = \int_H N^s(\omega, M^0/p, h)\, \mathrm{d}h. \tag{8.34}$$

If there is insufficient demand for the labour supplied, we assume that the first households in the queue (or seniority system) are employed, and the rest are unemployed. Thus if labour demand is N, then the employment and unemployment rates are:

$$e = N/N(\omega, M^o/p) \tag{8.35a}$$

$$u = 1 - e \tag{8.35b}$$

Those households which are employed will receive income consisting of wages from employment plus money balances; the unemployed live off their money balances. Since households have Cobb–Douglas preferences, we can aggregate over employed and unemployed households. Consumer demand in the product market is thus:

$$c^d\left(w, \frac{M^o}{p}, N\right) = e.c(w/p, M^o/p) + (1-e).\frac{\alpha}{\alpha+\gamma}.\frac{M^o}{p}. \tag{8.36}$$

The effective demand function still has unit elasticity of demand, so our analysis of the firm in the first section still holds good.

For a given level of (w, M^o) then, the macroeconomic equilibrium is determined by:

$$y = c^d\left(\omega, \frac{M^o}{p}, N\right) + g \tag{8.37}$$

$$y = f(N) \tag{8.38}$$

$$\omega = w/p = f'.(1-\mu) \tag{8.39}$$

plus (implicitly) the three equations (8.34)–(8.36) used to derive c^d. Equation (8.37) tells us that output is determined by *effective* demand $c^d + g$, which takes account of the fact that some households may be rationed in the labour market. Using equations (8.37)–(8.39) we can determine output, employment and prices *given* the nominal wage, money balances and government expenditure. We will define the aggregate demand function as solving equations (8.37)–(8.39) for employment, $AD(w, M^o, g)$. If we hold (M^o, g) as fixed, this yields the true 'demand for labour' relationship. Total differentiation of equations (8.36)–(8.39) yields:

$$\left.\frac{dN}{dW}\right|_{AD} = \frac{-c_2^d.f'.(1-\mu).M^o}{w^2[f'-f''(1-\mu)]c_1^d + c_2^d f''(1-\mu)\dfrac{M^o}{w} + c_3^d} < 0. \tag{8.40}$$

Thus a higher nominal wage leads to a lower level of employment. This is because a higher nominal wage leads to higher prices, and a higher real wage. As in the previous section, a rise in the degree of monopoly μ leads to an inward shift in the AD curve. The AD curve is the union's real demand curve: it shows the level of employment that will result if a particular nominal wage is set. Equations (8.36)–(8.39) also tell the union the real wage that will result. As in the previous sections, the behavioural equations are all Hodo in (w, p, M°), as is the AD function.

The Union

Given the relationships between nominal wages, real wages and employment contained in the AD curve and equations (8.36)–(8.39), how is the equilibrium determined? We need a model of nominal wage determination. In this section, we shall consider two different models: the monopoly-union model where unions have the power to set unilaterally the nominal wage, and a model where firms and unions bargain over the nominal wage. Given the nominal wages set, firms choose outputs and thus prices. This seems very reasonable: in practice unions have a direct say only on the wages they get, not on the prices which firms set.

There are many alternative assumptions that can be made about the union's objectives in the wage determination process. In the bargaining model we adopt the simple yet plausible assumption that the union seeks to maximize the real wage. The rationale for this is that the union seeks to maximize the utility of those households which are employed – who presumably make up its membership. As Oswald (1984) argues, if there is a seniority system such as LIFO (Last-in, First-out) which determines who gets laid-off, then majority voting will lead to real wage maximization. In the context of the monopoly union model, however, the assumption of real wage maximization is rather extreme (with diminishing returns, real wages are maximized with one employee), so we allow for a general utility function defined on employment as well as real wages (as is common – see Oswald, 1985; Pencavel, 1984).

Bargaining Over the Nominal Wage

The firms and the union bargain over the nominal wage. The wage bargain is made at the industry level, so that the two firms act together. Given the nominal wage chosen, price is determined by the non-cooperative behaviour of firms in the product market. The firms' objectives are profits: the unions real wages. Out of the many possible bargaining solutions we will adopt the simple Nash bargain. Thus the nominal wage is chosen to maximize the product of profits and real wages. Since (from the AD relation) there is a one-to-one relationship between nominal wages and employment, it is most convenient to represent the bargain as a choice of *employment*. Real wages are $f'(1-\mu)$: profits are $f-f'.(1-\mu)N$. Hence the Nash product is:

$$\max_{N} (f-f'(1-\mu)N).f'(1-\mu) \qquad (8.41)$$

$$\text{s.t. } N \leqslant N^s(f'(1-\mu), M^o/p). \qquad (8.42)$$

Constraint (8.42) represents the notion that the union cannot force people to work, and p is given through equations (8.37)–(8.39). We will assume that equation (8.42) never binds, so that from the first-order conditions for equation (8.41) we have for an interior maximum:

$$N = \frac{f'^2\mu + f.f''}{2f'.f''(1-\mu)} \qquad (8.43)$$

(the second-order condition will generally be satisfied – a sufficient condition is that $f'''\leqslant0$). Given the equilibrium level of employment, the nominal wage is set so that AD yields N using equations (8.37)–(8.39). Of course an interior solution to equations (8.41) and (8.42) need not exist: however, that is not of interest here.[7] What is of interest is that the equilibrium level of employment defined by equation (8.43) is determined solely by the degree of monopoly μ, and the technology represented by the production function $f(N)$. If equation (8.42) is binding, then the labour market clears and we revert to the equilibrium examined in the second section.

Suppose we consider a concrete example. Let $y=N-\delta N^2$, where we choose δ small enough so that $dy/dN=1-2\delta N$ is positive for relevant N (e.g. $1/2\delta$ is greater than the Walrasian level of employment). In this case we can solve equation (8.43) for the equilibrium employment level (assuming equation (8.42) is not binding). In table 8.2 we have calculated the solution for different values of μ (the second-order conditions are satisfied at these values, which give the global maxima over relevant ranges of N). In the second row we express the equilibrium employment levels as a percentage of the level when $\mu=0$. In this example, the degree of monopoly in the product market has a very strong influence on the equilibrium level of employment.

A generalization of the classic Nash solution is to allow for differential bargaining power, and have a *weighted* Nash bargain. The objective function then becomes:

$$\max_{N} (f-f'N(1-\mu))^\lambda.(f'(1-\mu))^{(1-\lambda)} \qquad (8.44)$$

Table 8.2 *Equilibrium employment and the degree of monopoly: example*

| | | The degree of monopoly | | |
Equilibrium employment	Competitive $\mu=0$	$\mu=1/4$	Cournot $\mu=1/2$	Cartel $\mu=1$
N	$\dfrac{1}{3\delta}$	$\dfrac{1}{\delta\sqrt{12}}$	$\dfrac{1}{4\delta}$	$\dfrac{2-\sqrt{3}}{2\delta}$
% of $\mu=0$ (3.s.f.)	100	86.8	75.1	40.2

where a smaller λ represents greater union bargaining power, and $1\geqslant\lambda\geqslant0$. Equation (8.44) yields the first-order condition:

$$N=\frac{\lambda.\mu f'+(1-\lambda).f.f''}{f'.f''(1-\mu)}.\qquad(8.44a)$$

Letting $\mu=0$ a quadratic production function yields $N=\lambda/\delta(1+\lambda)$. Thus the greater the bargaining power of unions (the smaller λ) the lower the equilibrium level of employment.[8]

In the particular model of bargaining we have considered, there is no role for macroeconomic policy to influence the equilibrium level of employment. Unions and firms are locked into a bargaining process, the outcome of which is not influenced by monetary or fiscal policy.[9]

A Monopoly Union Model

An alternative assumption to a wage bargain is that the union sets nominal wages. Thus the union sets (nominal) wages and firms set prices given the wages set. A higher nominal wage causes lower employment (through aggregate demand) and a higher real wage. The real wage equation (8.39) gives the feasible combinations of real wages and employment. We could assume a general union utility function defined on the real wage and employment (see Oswald, 1985 for a survey). In this case, the union maximizes its utility subject to the real wage equation.

$$\max_{N} u(\omega, N)\qquad(8.45)$$

$$\text{s.t. } \omega=f'(1-\mu).\qquad(8.46)$$

Should a solution to equations (8.45) and (8.46) exist, government monetary and fiscal policy will not affect the equilibrium level of employment. The impact of an increase in government expenditure is to crowd out the consumption of households, since the resultant price rise reduces the value of their real balances.[10]

These strong results of fiscal neutrality stem from the assumptions made about the union's objective function. Although household utility depends upon consumption and leisure, it also depends upon real balances. In the two examples given above, the union's objective was expressed purely in *real* terms: the nominal price level played no direct role. This suppression of the real balance effect may seem a very reasonable step: after all, how many unions worry about the impact of wage settlements on their members' real balances? However, the introduction of real balances to the union's objective function would undermine the fiscal neutrality result, although homogeneity and hence monetary neutrality still hold.

We have considered two models of nominal wage determination in a unionized economy. With a union influencing wage determination, and firm's prices, the resultant equilibrium can have excess supply in both the output and labour markets. In this sense the equilibrium is very Keynesian. However, the policy implications for the economy are very un-Keynesian: money is neutral, and the fiscal multiplier can be zero. The basic idea behind the classical dichotomy still holds in a unionized economy. The monopoly union case is depicted in figure 8.6. The equilibrium level of employment is determined in the labour market. Given the equilibrium level of employment, the nominal wage w^* is set to achieve this given AD. Since the AD function is Hodo in (w, M^o), an increase in M^o to $M^{o\prime}$ will lead to an equiproportionate rise in the nominal wage set by the union, from w^* to w^1.

To what extent do models of imperfect competition with unionized labour markets yield a model of the 'natural rate'? There are perhaps five crucial features of the NRH: (a) there exists a unique equilibrium in the economy, in which (b) agents' expectations are confirmed and (c) money is neutral, (d) trade unions can influence the unique equilibrium,[11] and (e) the theoretical model is a general equilibrium model (this seems to be the import of Friedman's use of the phrase 'Walrasian system'). Any equilibrium concept which has properties (a)–(e) will very much resemble Friedman's notion of the NRH.

Clearly, the model of imperfect competition in a unionized economy which we have presented satisfied (b)–(e). Uniqueness is, however, rather less easy to guarantee. If we turn to the case of a Nash bargain between firm and unions, over the nominal wage, uniqueness may or may not hold, depending on the nature of the production function. In the case of the monopoly union, uniqueness can only be guaranteed by fairly strong restrictions on both the production function and the union's

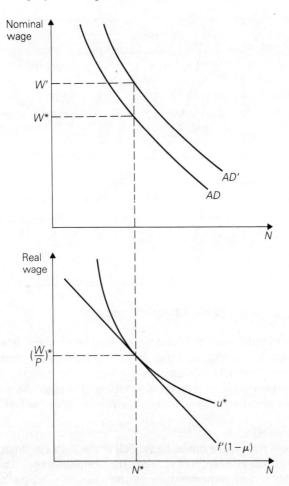

Figure 8.6 *The monopoly union: real wages, nominal wages and employment*

utility function. For example, if the marginal product of labour is non-concave then there may be two or more 'tangencies' with the union's indifference curve, as in figure 8.7. Recall that the concavity of the production function merely requires the marginal product of labour to be decreasing, so for any shaped union indifference curve it is possible to construct multiple equilibria (a sufficient condition to ensure uniqueness given that the union utility is quasiconcave is $f''' \leq 0$).

Whilst non-uniqueness goes very much against the spirit of Friedman's NRH, it does not imply that the model is Keynesian, in the sense that there are multiplier effects. However, it is possible to conceive of macroeconomic policy causing the economy to switch from one equilibrium to another. Consider the following argument. In figure 8.7 there is a high-employment equilibrium at N_h, and a low-

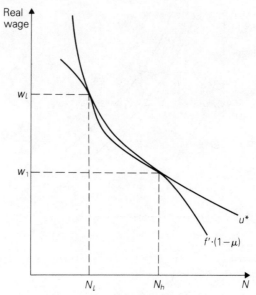

Figure 8.7 *Multiple equilibria*

employment equilibrium at N_l. Suppose that the economy is at the low-employment equilibrium, and that wages are fixed in the short run due to fixed-term contracts. Given initial government policy (M^o, g), the union has set wage w_1, as in figure 8.8. Given this wage, the government can alter its macroeconomic policy to some $(M', g'))$, such that:

$$N_h = AD(w_1, M', g').$$

With the new policy, the union finds itself at the high-employment equilibrium, and has no incentive to alter the nominal wage. This story is very plausible, and indicates that in the case of multiple equilibria, macroeconomic policy can be used to ensure that the highest level of equilibrium employment is attained, avoiding the low-employment equilibria.

If we put aside problems of uniqueness, it is possible to generate the long-run Phillips curve model if we assume that wage bargains are fixed in the short run and unions (and firms) have rational expectations. We can impose the following two-stage temporal structure on the model. In the first stage, unions and firms bargain over the nominal wage, or the union chooses w. In the second stage, the nominal wage is fixed: the government announces its money supply and firms choose their output and employment (this structure of moves is used by Layard and Nickell, 1985). The agents in the economy have point expectations about the government's policy (M^e, g^e). Given the desired level of employment N^*, w is chosen to attain this given expectation, so w solves:

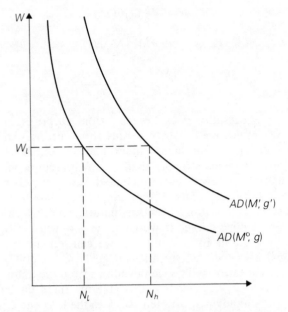

Figure 8.8 *Macroeconomic policy with multiple equilibria*

$$N^*=AD(w,\ M^e,g^e).$$

Given the wage set, actual employment is given by:

$$N=N^*+(M^o-M^e).\partial AD/\partial M+(g-g^e).\partial AD/\partial g, \qquad (8.47)$$

where the derivatives of AD are obtained by total differentiation[12] of equations (8.36)–(8.39), and will include standard multiplier effects. Thus if monetary or fiscal policy are more expansionary than expected, employment will be higher than the equilibrium where they are fully anticipated (this model can be seen as a theoretical justification for the econometric model employed by Layard and Nickell, 1985, in which only surprises in fiscal policy are effective). From the price–cost equation (8.39), $p=w/f'(1-\mu)$. Hence an increase in employment will give rise to an increase in prices, due to diminishing marginal productivity:

$$\left.\frac{\mathrm{d}p}{\mathrm{d}N}\right|_w = \frac{-\ f'^{2}.(1-\mu)}{f''.w} >0. \qquad (8.48)$$

Hence it is possible to represent the deviation of actual from expected employment as a function of the deviation of actual from expected prices:

$$N=N^*+\beta(p-p^e) \tag{8.49}$$

or
$$p=p^e+(1/\beta).(N-N^*) \tag{8.50}$$

where
$$\beta=\frac{dp}{dN}.\frac{\partial AD(M^o-M^e)}{\partial M}+\frac{\partial AD(g-g^e)}{\partial g}.$$

Of course, the causality does not run from surprises in prices to deviations in employment: rather it runs from surprises in aggregate demand to deviations in employment and prices. Note that this neutrality result is much stronger than in a Walrasian economy where money is neutral, but even fully anticipated fiscal policy is not.

Given the basic set-up of fixed-wage contracts, we are able to provide a rigorous story of deviations from the 'natural rate', which is in effect the short-run Phillips curve. If we combine this with an appropriate model of expectations formation, then we can tell the usual stories. With rational expectations, surprises in government policy will be a white-noise error term, and hence deviations from the natural rate will be purely transitory. With adaptive expectations, there can be short-run deviations, but employment will tend back to the long-run equilibrium.

Conclusion

This chapter has explored some of the implications of imperfect competition for macroeconomic policy within the simplest possible macroeconomic model with proper microeconomic foundations. In the product market there is a conjectural variations Cournot oligopoly model which allows for a wide range of competitive behaviour from perfect competition to joint profit maximization. In the labour market we considered the case of perfect competition and two models of wage determination in a unionized labour market. Whilst it is dangerous to draw general conclusions from specific models, we feel that the following broad lessons can be drawn.

Imperfect competition matters. Not only does imperfect competition influence the equilibrium levels of employment and prices, it also influences the effectiveness of fiscal policy. With a competitive labour market the fiscal multiplier is larger the less competitive is the product market (though there is still crowding out). With a unionized labour market we presented two examples where there was complete crowding out. All three examples presented point towards 'classical' conclusions about fiscal policy – there is partial or complete crowding out. Of course, it may well be possible that alternative assumptions might yield more Keynesian results.

Perhaps the most crucial assumption made in the models presented is that there is only one sector. In Dixon (1986) we present a two-sector model of a unionized economy. A monopoly union in each sector sets its wage, given the wage set by the other union. Prices and employment are then determined given these wages. With two sectors the unionized equilibrium does not have a unique natural rate of employment, but rather a *natural range* of employment. Fiscal policy is not ineffective, and can be used to attain a clearly defined range of employment levels. Thus the natural rate property of the present chapter seems to be sensitive to the assumption that there is only one sector.

There is one aspect of a perfectly competitive economy that can carry over to an imperfectly competitive economy: the neutrality of money. The basic justification for neutrality is the homogeneity of the underlying behavioural equations. This homogeneity is unaffected by imperfect competition per se. However, even in a perfectly competitive economy homogeneity is an extremely strong assumption (see Grandmont, 1984). Whilst we have adopted a basic framework that includes homogeneity for simplicity, it is no more plausible here than in competitive macromodels.

Imperfect competition has an ambiguous relationship to Keynesian economics. If firms set prices, and unions wages, it is possible to have a macroeconomic equilibrium which is Keynesian in the sense that if agents were price takers, they would like to sell more at equilibrium prices. Imperfect competition leads to a non-Walrasian equilibrium. The implications for macroeconomic policy can be very non-Keynesian. In the examples presented of a unionized economy, fiscal policy had no effect on equilibrium employment, because an increase in government expenditure causes wages and prices to rise, crowding out private consumption by the real balance effect.

Certainly, the models of a unionized economy presented seem to have some affinity with Friedman's natural rate. We argued that the imperfectly competitive equilibrium can be seen as a natural interpretation of the natural rate, and one of which Friedman is aware. If we combine the model of the unionized economy with short-run wage rigidity, the usual Phillips curve stories arise. The only scope for macroeconomic policy in this context appears to be in the case of multiple equilibria. If wages are fixed in the short run, the government can ensure that the equilibrium with the highest level of employment is attained.

NOTES

I would like to thank Ben Lockwood and Dennis Snower for many useful conversations. The first section of the chapter was used for the MSc. macroeconomics course at Birkbeck in March 1985. The current revision owes much to comments made at the time. Faults, alas, remain my own. Financed by ESRC project No. B00 26 0037; originally published in *Oxford Economic Papers*, 1987.

1 These Walrasian assumptions include that of Leontief technology in the first section. It is often forgotten that Walras made wide use of 'coefficients de-fabrication' in his work.

2 The use of the terms 'excess supply' and 'market clearing' are the subject of disagreement. My own favoured uses are (a) market clearing means competitive – hence any non-competitive equilibrium is a non-clearing equilibrium, (b) excess supply means that at a given price suppliers would like to sell more than they do. Others who dislike this may translate into their own terminology.

3 Throughout this chapter we will use the term 'fiscal neutrality' to mean that the fiscal multiplier is zero. We do not use the term in the technical sense of monetary theory, i.e. that no real variables are affected (although money is neutral in this sense too).

4 Those unfamiliar with the conjectural variations model of Cournot oligopoly are referred to Waterson (1984: 18–19). The equilibrium condition that marginal revenue equals marginal cost is:

$$p.(1+ \frac{1+\phi}{2})=w$$

from which equation (8.7) comes directly. The mark-up μ is constant because with Cobb–Douglas preferences there is constant elasticity of demand. For those who dislike conjectural variations, the mark-up with Cournot competition will vary with the number of firms n: $\mu=1/n$.

5 For example, a common form for government contracts is cost-plus, in effect a mark-up μ_g. The model would then simply require a different mark-up for government and private consumption. For example, profits would become: $\pi=\mu_g.g+\mu.(N-g)$ (see equation (8.12)).

6 There is an aggregation problem here which is skirted around, as is usual. In equation (8.25) the marginal productivity condition holds for the firm's production function. In equations (8.27) and (8.28) we have the aggregate production function. So long as firms are identical and the equilibrium symmetric, as here, there is no problem. Let the firm's production function be defined as $g(N_i)$, and the economy's as $f=2.g(N/2)$: then $f'=g'$.

7 No solution may exist at all, since the lower bound on N is given by the strict inequality $N>g$ (there is no upper bound on nominal wages). If a solution does exist, it may have equation (8.42) binding.

8 When $\lambda=0$, $N=0$ and the real wage is maximized: when $\lambda=1$ then $N=1/2\delta$ and profits are maximized. Clearly, we would expect the labour supply constraint to become effective for $\lambda<1$, with the labour market clearing (as in the first section).

9 This is only true for an interior solution (8.43) or (8.44a), when equation (8.42) is not binding.

10 Consumption by employed workers is $c(w/p, M^o/p)$; by the unemployed $(\alpha/\alpha+\gamma)M^o/P$.

11 'Trade unions play an important role in determining the position of the natural level of unemployment' Friedman (1975: 30).

12 Equation (8.47) can be seen as a linear approximation if derivatives are evaluated at (M^e,g^e), or an exact expression by the mean value theorem if derivatives are evaluated at some intermediate value.

REFERENCES

d'Aspremont, C., Ferriera, R. and Varet, L. 1985: Monopolistic Competition and Involuntary unemployment. CORE, mimeo.

Blanchard, O. and Kiyataki, N. 1985: Monopolistic Competition and Aggregate Demand Externalities. NBER working Paper 1770.

Branson, W. 1979: *Macroeconomic Theory and Policy*. New York: Harper and Row.

Diamond, P. 1985: Wage determination and efficiency in search equilibrium. *Review of Economic Studies*, 52.

Dixon, H. 1986: Unions, Oligopoly, and Macroeconomic Policy. Forthcoming Discussion Paper, Birkbeck College.

Friedman, M. 1968: The role of monetary policy. *American Economic Review*, March.

Friedman, M. 1975: Unemployment Versus Inflation. Occasional Paper 44.

Grandmont, J. 1984: *Money and Value*. Cambridge: CUP.

Hahn, F. 1980: Unemployment: A theoretical viewpoint, *Economica*, 47, 285–98.

Hart, O. 1979: Monopolistic competition in a large economy with differentiated products. *Review Of Economic Studies*, 46, 1–30.

Hart, O. 1983: A model of imperfect competition with Keynesian features. *Quarterly Journal of Economics*, 97, 109–38.

Hart, O. 1985: Imperfect competition in general equilibrium: An overview. In Arrow K. J. and Honkapohja S. (eds), *Frontiers of Economics*, Oxford: Blackwell.

Layard, R. and Nickell, S. 1985: The causes of British unemployment. *NIER*, Feb, 62–85.

Lerner, A. 1934: On the concept of monopoly and the measurement of monopoly power, *Review of Economic Studies*, 1.

Lockwood, B. (1985): Transferable skills, job matching, and the inefficiency of the natural rate of unemployment. *Economic Journal*, forthcoming.

Mortenson, D. 1970: Job search, the duration of unemployment, and the Phillips curve, *American Economic Review*, 60, 847–62.

Oswald, A. 1984: Efficient Contracts are on the Labour Demand Curve. Oxford, mimeo.

Oswald, A. 1985: The economic theory of trade unions. *Scandinavian Journal of Economics*, 87, 160–93.

Patinkin, D. 1965: *Money, Interest, and Prices*, 2nd edn. Harper and Row.

Pencavel, J. 1984: The trade-off between wages and employment in union objectives. *Quarterly Journal of Economics*, 99, 215–32.

Pissarides, C. 1985: Taxes, subsidies, and equilibrium unemployment, *Review of Economic Studies*, 52, 121–34.

Roberts, K. 1980: The limit points of monopolistic competition. *Journal of Economic Theory*, 22, 112–27.

Snower, D. 1983: Imperfect competition, underemployment, and crowding out. *Oxford Economic Papers*, 35, 245–70.

Svensson, L. 1985: Fiscal Policy, Sticky Prices and Resource Utilisation. Mimeo, University of Stockholm.

Waterson, M. 1984: *Economic Theory of the Industry*. Cambridge: CUP.

9

Unemployment and Worker Quality

SIMON PRICE

Introduction

This chapter examines the relationships between worker quality, unemployment and wages. We find we can provide a justification for the notion of 'Keynesian' low-level equilibria without arbitrary restrictions on price or wage-setting behaviour. This enables us to proffer an explanation for the apparent rise in the 'natural' rate of unemployment in Western economies, and particularly in Britain, without needing to posit an exogenous change in the underlying structure of the economy. In particular, we need not call upon a rise in unemployment benefits or exogenous attitudinal changes to explain the rise (although clearly such changes will alter the equilibrium rate). Because of the structural relationships between the demand for labour and aggregate wages and unemployment we find that the 'natural' rate may plausibly have a number of equilibrium levels.[1] The section of the chapter from which these results first emerge also formalizes the notion of unemployment 'hysteresis'; that is, that the path of unemployment alters the equilibrium level.[2] A simple model of aggregate supply with the long-run properties of full information and complete wage and price flexibility is developed, where in equilibrium all unemployment is voluntary. The competitive equilibrium is shown to result in an inefficiently high level of unemployment, and the possibility of Pareto-ranked multiple equilibria is established. In this case an employment subsidy is always optimal while aggregate demand management may also be effective in permanently reducing unemployment, despite the existence of long-run vertical aggregate supply curves; if this is possible, then this is also a Pareto-improving policy. However, we note that hysteresis effects are not sufficient to guarantee the existence of multiple equilibria.[3]

We also examine three related models that incorporate versions of the 'efficiency wage' hypothesis. That is, worker productivity is increasing with the wage. It may be justified by appealing to sociological arguments (Akerlof, 1983), the existence of unobservable effort (Shapiro and Stiglitz, 1983; Price, 1985) or individual investments in human capital. We explicitly derive three different effort supply loci. Here, unemployment may be involuntary in the sense that the return to unemployment is less than the return to employment. The wage will be set at a level in excess of the return to unemployment; this may imply an unemployment rate *lower* than that which would prevail at a lower level of wages. The resulting unemployment rate will generally be inefficient. These models all share a common feature in that multiple equilibria are a possibility, so that the economy may be trapped in a low-level equilibrium.

The plan of the chapter is that in the next section four microeconomic models of 'effort supply' are examined. In the succeeding section, the equilibrium properties of each function are examined. Finally, we draw some conclusions.

Effort Supply Functions

In this section, we consider four 'effort supply' or 'worker quality' functions.

Model A: Hysteresis

Throughout the chapter we consider two classes of agent, workers and firms. Workers are risk neutral and (at this stage of the chapter) derive utility only from consumption. Workers may either be employed or unemployed. Consumption in each state is given by the real wage, $w = W/p$ (where W is the nominal wage and p the price level) or by the real return to being unemployed, b. The latter return may be thought of as the level of consumption enjoyed in the 'informal economy'.[4] All workers are identical, and spend a proportion of their time in the unemployed state. This proportion is given by

$$u = \frac{M-N}{M} \tag{9.1}$$

where u is the rate of unemployment, M is the size of the fixed labour force and N is the number employed. The notion that unemployment is a phenomenon experienced by all workers may be justified by specifying unemployment as a stochastic process. Each period, a proportion s of the N employed workers are randomly separated from their jobs by some exogenous process. For example, there may be exogenous bankruptcies taking place. There is no search as such; instead, unemployed workers passively wait for a job vacancy to arrive, which they then take. If $N=M$, then this waiting period is of zero duration. We assume that the 'search technology' is such that firms can costlessly locate the unemployed; thus workers have no bargaining power (unlike, say, in Diamond, 1982). Thus competition between the employed and unemployed drives down the wage to the point where the expected present value of being unemployed is just equal to the expected present value of being employed.[5] This is easily shown to imply that $w=b$. We now posit that workers may be characterized by their quality and that the experience of unemployment causes a reduction in this quality; high unemployment results in low productivity. Proposed explanations of this phenomena include deterioration of human capital, an erosion of the work ethic and an induced, socialized change in the marginal utility of unemployed leisure (see Tobin, 1972; Hargreaves Heap, 1980; and discussion elsewhere in this volume). This assumption has been criticized on two grounds. Firstly, the unemployed are drawn primarily from the unskilled, who by definition have little human capital and can quickly be trained. However, while the unskilled may have little specific human capital it is still the case that the most unskilled worker has general human capital; for example, the ability to understand instructions or good time-keeping. It may be motivation that is crucial here. Secondly, from micro studies of the unemployed there appears to be little evidence that there is state dependency, in the sense that the conditional probability of unemployment does not fall with duration. For recent evidence for the UK, see Narendranathan et al. (1985) who find no state dependency; but also see Lynch (1984) who does find such evidence in a sample of unemployed youths. The argument (as expressed in the conclusion to Narendranathan et al.) is that the reservation wage of the unemployed falls with unemployment to compensate for the human capital effect. If this is the case, this is consistent with the model presented here, where the marginal product falls with unemployment (although there is no search over a perceived distribution of wage offers in our model). Thus we assume that worker quality (or 'effort'),[6] e, is a diminishing function of the unemployment rate:

$$e=e(u) \quad e'\leq 0. \tag{9.2}$$

For completeness we allow the marginal effect of unemployment on effort to be zero for some values. Thus

$$e_N=e'(-1/M)\geq 0. \tag{9.3}$$

This is our first and basic model of effort supply.

Model B: An Effort Supply Locus with Observable Effort

A standard justification (Malcolmson, 1981; Calvo, 1979; and Yellen, 1984) of the efficiency wage hypothesis in modern economies[7] is that wages are required not only to induce workers to participate in the labour force, but also to induce effort. The first case we examine is where effort is perfectly observable to firms. With a suitable choice of units, we now introduce (unpleasant) effort into the utility function, v, in the simplest possible way:

$$v = c - e. \tag{9.4}$$

We assume risk neutrality and separability of consumption, c, and effort. Firms who value effort will offer a simple contract:

$$w = \frac{w \text{ for } e \geq \mathbf{E}}{0 \text{ elsewhere.}} \tag{9.5}$$

The wage offered will simply be the minimum wage at which workers are prepared to offer themselves for work at effort level $\mathbf{E}$, defined by the wage such that

$$v = w - \mathbf{E} = b. \tag{9.6}$$

Thus effort supply is given by

$$e = w - b$$
$$= e(w, b) \; ; \; e_w = -e_b = 1, \; e_{ij} = 0 \tag{9.7}$$

or, for the more general utility function $v(w, e)$ with standard partial derivatives,

$$e = e(w, b) \; ; \; e_w \geq 0, \; e_b \leq 0, \; e_{ww} < 0. \tag{9.8}$$

This is our second effort supply function.[8,9]

Model C: An Effort Supply Locus with Observable Effort and Human Capital

In our third model we consider the role of human capital. We now introduce an initial period when our infinitely lived workers decide how much worker quality to invest in. Worker quality is costly to acquire. The cost is given by the function $C(e)$, $C' > 0$, $C'' > 0$. Thereafter, firms offer the same contract as in model B. Utility is only a function of consumption; the only disutility of effort is the initial cost. In the initial period workers form a view about the proportion of their lifetimes they will spend working. This proportion is given by u in equilibrium. Assuming intertemporal additive separability and a rate of time preference r, expected lifetime utility is given by

$$v=w(1-u)/r-C(e)+ub/r. \qquad (9.9)$$

Again, employers simply choose a wage to elicit any desired level of effort consistent with $v=b/r$. Thus

$$e=e[(w-b)(1-u)]. \qquad (9.10)$$

From the properties we assume for the $C(e)$ function, it follows that $e'>0$ and $e''<0$. Note that this effort supply function reintroduces the hysteresis effects of the first model.

Model D: An Effort Supply Locus with Unobservable Effort

This model is closely related to that of Shapiro and Stiglitz although we allow effort to be a continuous variable. The flow of utility per period is given by

$$v=c-e \qquad (9.11)$$

or over a lifetime for infinitely lived workers

$$v= \sum_{t=1}^{t=\infty} (c_t-e_t)/(1+r)^t. \qquad (9.12)$$

We are assuming that wages or the return from unemployment are received at the end of the period and that e is the value of effort discounted to the end of the period. Effort can be thought of as the degree to which workers slack on the job. If they are detected slacking to any degree, then they are sacked – the only penalty available to firms. Firms will always use this penalty given our previous assumption of costless hires. Firms cannot observe output directly – for example, production may take place in teams – and can only detect slackers with uncertainty. For simplicity we assume an exogenous detection technology[10] which determines the probability, s, of being sacked at the end of any period:

$$s=s(e) \; ; \; 0<s\leq1 \; ; \; s'<0. \qquad (9.13)$$

The harder workers work, the less likely they are to be sacked. We further assume that $s''>0$. If a worker is unemployed, then he or she may be hired at the end of the period with probability h. In a steady state where unemployment inflows equal outflows, this will be

$$h = SN/(M-N)$$
$$= S(1-u)/u \tag{9.14}$$

where S is the aggregate separation rate, equal to s only in equilibrium. Next we define $V(E)$ and $V(U)$ as the expected value of being in employment and unemployment respectively at any time:

$$V(E) = \frac{w - e + sV(U) + (1-s)V(E)}{1+r} \tag{9.15}$$

$$V(U) = \frac{b + hV_0(E) + (1-b)V(U)}{1+r}. \tag{9.16}$$

$V_0(E)$ is the expected return from joining a new firm from the unemployed pool. In equilibrium it will be equal to $V(E)$ but we will not impose this at this stage. Although $V_0(E)$ is a function of e next period, it is independent of the current choice of e. Hence $V(U)$ is parametric. Workers will choose e to

$$\max V(E) = \frac{w - e + sV(U)}{r+s}$$
$$\text{s.t. } s - s(e) = 0. \tag{9.17}$$

For this problem to have an interior solution we require that $s'' > 2s'^{2/(r+s)}$. If this is not satisfied then effort is either zero or infinity. We assume it holds.[11] It is easily shown that the effort supply function is given by

$$e = [w - rV(U)] + (r+s)/s'. \tag{9.18}$$

Unemployment in this model is involuntary as any unemployed person would be willing to take a job at less than the going wage rate – the value of employment is greater than the value of unemployment. However, employers will not be prepared to hire workers at less than the optimal wage. If we use the flow equilibrium condition we can derive a function.

$$e = e[w, b, u, S, V_0(E)] \tag{9.19}$$

where $e_w > 0$, $e_b < 0$, $e_u > 0$, $e_s < 0$ and $e_{v_0(E)} < 0$. The intuition underlying the signs of these partial derivatives is straightforward. An increase in w

raises the penalty associated with being sacked: a fall in u or an increase in b, $V_0(E)$ or S (which determines the outflow rate from unemployment) lowers it. Note that unemployment can never fall to zero, as if it were to do so then the threat of dismissal would be ineffective (the probability of being rehired is unity). This function contains a hysteresis effect, but one which is opposite in sign to that we assumed in model A.

Equation (9.19) is the effort supply function that faces any firm at each instant in time. However, in equilibrium all firms and workers must act identically. This implies that the equilibrium value of $V(E)$ is

$$V(E)=\frac{(w-e)(r+h)+sb}{r(r+h+s)}.\qquad(9.20)$$

Thus the relationship determining effort supply in equilibrium is given by substituting equation (9.20) into equation (9.19):

$$e=w-\frac{rb}{(r+h)}-\frac{h(w-e)}{(r+s+h)}-\frac{sbh}{(r+h)(r+s+h)}+\frac{r+s}{s'}\qquad(9.21)$$

where

$$h=s(1-u)/u\qquad(9.22)$$

or, in general functional form,

$$e=e(w,b,u).\qquad(9.23)$$

However the effort supply function relevant to the firm remains equation (9.19).

Equilibrium Models

In this section we take the effort supply functions from the previous section and explore the properties of the resulting equilibria.

Model A: Hysteresis

We assume that the number of (identical) firms in the economy is large enough for them to face parametric wages and prices. The representative firm produces output Q with a fixed stock of capital according to the following production function:

$$Q=Q(N,e)\ ;\ Q_1>0,\ Q_2\geq0,\ Q_{11},\ Q_{22}<0\qquad(9.24)$$

where capital is suppressed. Note that for completeness we allow for the possibility that the marginal return to effort may become zero at some point. Firms take e as parametric and wish to maximize profit. As vacancies arising from the exogenous separations are costlessly filled, the firm's problem is the standard static one, so that employment is chosen such that the real wage is equal to the marginal product (for a constant level of effort, $\mathbf{e}$).

$$w = Q_1(N, \mathbf{e}). \tag{9.25}$$

In equilibrium the wage is equal to b, so for the interesting case when $Q_1(M, \mathbf{e}) < b$, the return to unemployment determines employment.[12] We now have a family of demand curves, each conditional on a particular level of effort, itself determined by N. The long-run or equilibrium relationship between the marginal product and the quantity of labour is therefore given by

$$Q_1 = Q_1[N, e(N)]. \tag{9.26}$$

Note that the total derivative of output with respect to N, Q_N, is generally greater than Q_1 (see equation (9.29) below). The gradient of the long-run relationship is given by the following expression:

$$\frac{dQ_1}{dN} = Q_{11} + Q_{12}e_N. \tag{9.27}$$

We cannot give a sign to Q_{12} a priori but it is natural to assume that it is positive. Thus over at least some of the relevant range

$$\frac{dQ_1}{dN}$$

may be positively sloped. One possible realization is illustrated in figure 9.1. Three possible equilibria are shown. We assume that when the marginal produce Q_1 (for given e) lies above (below) the wage b firms will expand (contract) employment, thus increasing (decreasing) e. Consequently A and C are stable equilibria; B is unstable. C is socially preferable to A, in the following sense. We assume that profits are distributed to owners of the firms who have identical utility functions to workers. Workers are indifferent between employment and unemployment, so as output is unambiguously higher at C than at A, equilibrium C is Pareto superior to A.[13] The equilibrium at A is an example of a 'low level' equilibrium; low, that is, in output and employment but high in unemployment.

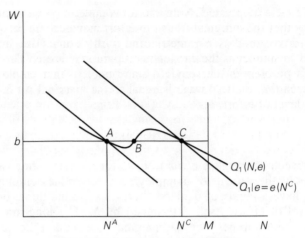

Figure 9.1 *Labour demand and effort*

As in the 'matching' literature, there is an externality which results in both the possibility of multiple equilibria and in the local inefficiency of these equilibria. By increasing employment, an individual firm reduces unemployment, which raises productivity in the entire economy. However, the social return exceeds the private return and employment is too low. If we define the efficient level of employment as that which maximizes the sum of output and the return from being unemployed, than a planner [14] would choose N such that

$$\max_{N} V = Q(N,e) + b(M-N)$$

$$st \qquad e - e(N) = 0 \qquad\qquad (9.28)$$

$$M - N \geq 0.$$

From this we have that for $M > N$ optimal employment will satisfy[15]

$$b = Q_N = Q_1 + Q_2 e_N. \qquad\qquad (9.29)$$

The government could attain the appropriate level of employment by a Pigovian subsidy to output or employment financed by (say) a tax on capital, which will have no allocative effects. As $Q_2 e_N > 0$ it follows that $Q_N > Q_1$ and optimal employment (unemployment) is greater than (less than) that achieved in a private or competitive equilibrium.

Even with locally optimal taxation (in the sense that a fixed subsidy ensures that the private cost of hiring an extra worker is equated to the social cost) the possibility of a low-level equilibrium remains. We can illustrate this with a simple model of aggregate demand and supply. Suppose we are initially at equilibrium A in figure 9.1. So far the price level p has been assumed exogenous. We will now endogenize p by introducing a government that costlessly issues a stock of money. Money is required solely to peform transactions. The transactions demand for money is assumed proportional to income. This underlies the aggregate demand curves (AD_1) in figure 9.2. Aggregate supply may be determined by the standard procedure of assuming an information asymmetry between firms and workers: firms know the price level with certainty but workers must form (inelastic) expectations of it, p^e; b is fixed by assumption, so labour supply is infinitely elastic at the nominal wage W equal to $p^e b$. Thus short-run aggregate supply is given by the solution to the following equations:

$$W = p^e b$$
$$W = p Q_1(N, \mathbf{e}) \qquad (9.30)$$
$$Q = Q(N, \mathbf{e})$$

where aggregate supply is increasing in prices, as in SRASA in the figure; $\mathbf{e}$ is parametric in the short run. In the long run, price expectations are fulfilled and e is endogenous. For small changes in prices, the long-run aggregate supply curve is vertical, as at ASA and ASC. Output Y^A and Y^c correspond to output at points A and C in figure 9.1. If the government now increases the money supply so that aggregate demand shifts from AD_1 to AD_2 then we move along the short-run aggregate supply schedule. Ultimately as expectations adjust short-run aggregate supply shifts up. If the initial shock was sufficient we

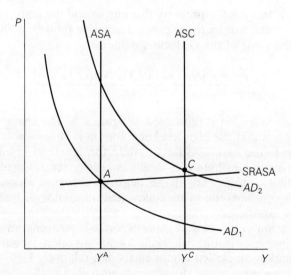

Figure 9.2 *Aggregate demand and supply*

move to a new and permanent level of output, Y^c, which is Pareto superior to Y^A. This will hold only for increases in demand that are sufficiently large; otherwise we will remain on ASA. We are of course only comparing static equilibria here: we do not attempt to specify the dynamic path. The government could equally reduce demand to reverse the process.

It remains to decide whether multiple equilibria are in any sense likely. The hysteresis effect is not a sufficient condition for there to be multiple equilibria. It is entirely possible that over the range of nominal aggregate demand observed in the post-War period there were only unique stable equilibria at each point in time.[16] Stable multiple equilibria require two sign changes in expression (9.27). Furthermore it is not even necessary that unemployment equilibria exist.

For example, assume a Cobb–Douglas technology where

$$Q=N^a e^b \; ; \; a,b,a+b<1$$

$$e=N^c \quad ; \; c<1$$

(9.31)

where a, b and c are parameters. For this case there is a unique equilibrium. Another simple case is

$$Q=N^a(e^b-e^c) \; ; \; a,b,c,a+b<1, \; b>c, \; N\geq 1$$

$$e=N^d \qquad ; \; d<1.$$

(9.32)

For $b+c>1$, this has the property that output and the marginal product of labour exhibit first increasing then decreasing returns to effort. If we evaluate the slope of the Q_1 locus we find

$$\frac{dQ_1}{dN} = \frac{aN^a[N^{db}(bd+a-1)-N^{dc}(cd+a-1)]}{N^2}.$$

(9.33)

A possible realization is illustrated in figure 9.3. The characteristic of this solution is that the high-level equilibrium is either stable or at full employment (the case illustrated) while the low-level equilibrium is unstable even in the absence of locally increasing returns to effort. This suggests that a sufficiently large negative shock to demand might engender a continual rise in unemployment; this is not inconsistent with recent UK experience.

An extension of the model can incorporate heterogeneous labour. In particular, we may distinguish 'skilled' and 'unskilled' labour. Assume that the market for skilled labour clears at a relatively high wage, and there is no unemployment. However, the unskilled market clears only at a wage below the return to unemployment, so that b sets a floor to

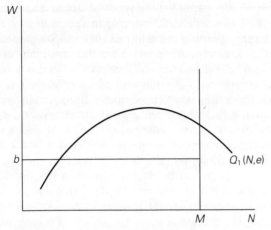

Figure 9.3 *Possible equilibrium positions*

wages in this market. The unemployed are therefore drawn from among the unskilled and low paid.[17] The previous model is modified slightly: production is now given by

$$Q = Q(L^s, L^u) \ ; \ Q_1, Q_2 > 0, \ Q_{11}, Q_{22} < 0 \tag{9.34}$$

where L^s and L^u are labour services from skilled and unskilled labour. Labour services are determined by

$$L^i = L^i(N^i, e^i) \ ; \ L_1^i, L_2^i > 0, \ L_{11}^i, L_{22}^i < 0 \tag{9.35}$$

(where $i = s, u$). As in the case for a single market for labour, we have

$$e^i = e^i(u^i) \quad e^{i\prime} < 0$$
$$u^i = \frac{M^i - N^i}{M^i}. \tag{9.36}$$

We assume that supplies of each type of labour are fixed although this is clearly inadequate for long-run analysis unless ability is entirely innate. For perfectly competitive profit-maximizing firms, labour demand satisfies the following equations:

$$\frac{w^s}{p} = Q_1(M^s, -) > b$$
$$\frac{w^u}{p} = Q_2(N^u, e^u, -) = b \tag{9.37}$$

where w^s and w^u are wages for the types of labour and firms take e^u as parametric. This is scarcely different from the results of the previous section, with firms ignoring the effect of their employment decisions on the rest of the economy. Again we have the possibility of a low-level equilibrium; figures 9.1 and 9.2 still hold (with figure 9.1 referring now to the unskilled sector). One question of some interest is to ask what happens to relative wages when we move from a high- and low-level equilibrium. Unskilled wages are pegged at the level of benefits. It is unclear what the effect on skilled wages is. If skilled and unskilled labour are sufficiently substitutable then skilled wages could actually rise, despite the fall in output. Such a relative shift in wages has occurred over the course of the last few years in Britain. Note that for empirical purposes, if we were investigating the relationship between employment (or unemployment) and the real wage, then the relevant wage would be the marginal wage for unskilled labour, which is not necessarily connected to the usual measures of average wages. This analysis may explain why the existence of an aggregate relationship between employment and the real wage has been so hard for empirical investigators to track down (but see Symons, 1985 for a neoclassical demand for labour function for the manufacturing sector).

Model B: Observable Effort

We now take the simplest version of the efficiency wage hypothesis. As above, we have

$$Q=Q(N,e) \; ; \; Q_1>0, \; Q_2 \geq 0, \; Q_{11}, \; Q_{22}<0. \qquad (9.38)$$

Our effort supply function is

$$e=e(w) \; ; \; e' \geq 0, \; e''<0. \qquad (9.39)$$

We are suppressing the b term for convenience. Previously we derived this function formally. However, we note that it may be justified by sociological theory as in Akerlof (1983). The rest of the economy is as specified above. We begin by considering a competitive economy, in the sense that wages are bid down to the return from unemployment. This is unrealistic as it assumes that firms are unaware of the relationship in equation (9.39) and serves merely as a benchmark, although we might still wish to examine this case if we consider equation (9.39) as a long-run relationship of which firms are unaware. The equilibrium demand for labour for $M>N$ is simply given by[18]

$$b=Q_1[N,e(b)]. \qquad (9.40)$$

Hitherto, we have thought of b as being the real return to unemployment. We will now allow the government to make transfer payments to the unemployed. If they do, then b rises. The gradient of the locus (9.40) is indeterminate. It is given by

$$\frac{db}{dN} = \frac{Q_{11}}{1-Q_{12}e'}. \tag{9.41}$$

It is clearly possible for (9.40) to slope upward to the right: if so, then a rise in benefits will *lower* unemployment.

While this result is of some interest, it is clearly more appropriate for firms to choose w. In this case, the problem for the firm is now to maximize profits, π;

$$\max_{w,N} \pi = Q(N,e) - wN$$

$$s.t. \ e - e(w) = 0$$

$$w - b \geq 0. \tag{9.42}$$

For $M > N$ and $w > b$, the first-order conditions are

$$Q_1 - w = 0 \tag{9.43}$$

$$Q_2 e' - N = 0. \tag{9.44}$$

The gradient of (9.43) is simply (9.41) and is indeterminate. The gradient of (9.44) is

$$\frac{dw}{dN} = \frac{1-Q_{21}e'}{Q_{22}e' + Q_2 e''} \tag{9.45}$$

and is also indeterminate; however, the gradients of both (9.43) and (9.44) must be the same sign. The second-order conditions for a maximum require that the absolute slope of (9.43) exceeds that of (9.44). The loci are illustrated for the upward sloping case in figure 9.4. Note that for this case the level of employment, N^*, is above that which would hold if wages were equal to b, N^c. Both loci having gradients with the same sign suggests that multiple equilibria are possible. Unlike the previous section, we no longer require a sign change in the gradient for a multiple solution to exist.

We can use the informational assumptions we employ above to generate a plausible short-run aggregate supply curve, where an increase in prices will temporarily increase output. If the price level falls

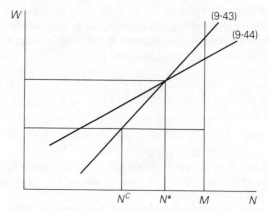

Figure 9.4 *Employment-wage loci*

then to maintain equilibrium a proportionate fall in wages is required. But workers will mistake a drop in the nominal wage for a fall in real wages. For the downward sloping case, this shifts the loci as illustrated in figure 9.5. Thus in the short run after a drop in the price level employment falls to N_1, generating an upward sloping (but not vertical) short-run aggregate supply locus[19] and allowing 'equilibrium' demand management as in figure 9.2.

There are two interesting features of these equilibria. Firstly, all unemployment is involuntary, in the sense that any worker who is unemployed would strictly prefer to be in employment. Job offers would never be rejected. Secondly, the level of unemployment is invariant to

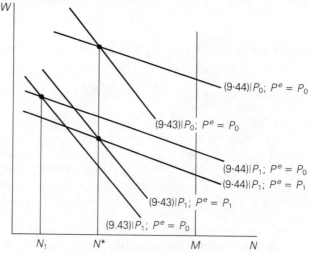

Figure 9.5 *Labour supply and the price level*

the return from unemployment, so long as $w>b$. Thus the government could choose to pay unemployment benefits with no loss in output or rise in unemployment. This implies that if some version of the model applies to the real economy, then empirical investigators may find that there is no relation between unemployment benefits and unemployment. Certainly, the cross-sectional evidence for the UK is far from robust (Atkinson et al., 1984) and the time-series evidence, which may be more relevant for our purposes, is full of contradictions and may be consistent with the absence of any effects. However, both these conclusions rely on the assumption that the effort supply function is a sociological phenomenon and will not hold if our microeconomic justification of the supply function is true.

It is easy to show that the level of unemployment is not optimal. Using the same criterion as before, we assume a planner would wish to maximize total output:

$$\max_{N,w} V=Q(N,e)+b(M-N)$$

$$s.t.\ e-e(w)=0$$

$$M-N\geq0 \qquad (9.46)$$

$$Q(n,e)-wN\geq0.$$

For this maximand, if there is a solution at less than full employment $(M>N)$ then

$$Q_1=b+\frac{Q_2e'(Q_1-w)}{Q_2e'-N}. \qquad (9.47)$$

When $Q-wN>0$, Q_1 is simply equal to the return from unemployment, as Q_2e' (the multiplier on the second constraint) is zero. This simply states that the wage will be pushed up until either the total product is exhausted or the extra product from an increase in the wage is zero. If the product is exhausted, then a rise in N will reduce the wage (the average product falls with increasing N) which in turn reduces effort. The second term is in fact $-(Q_ee_ww_N)$ at the point where $w=Q/N$.

The policy conclusion is that the government should subsidize wages to the point where Q_2e' is zero or the product is exhausted, assuming there are no efficiency losses from financing the subsidy.

If, however, the effort supply function (9.7) holds then the problem becomes

$$\max_{N,w}\ \ V=Q(N,e)+b(M-N)-Ne$$

$$s.t. \ w-e-b=0$$

$$M-N\geq 0 \tag{9.48}$$

$$Q(n,e)-wN\geq 0.$$

For this case the private equilibrium is given as above by

$$w-Q_1=0 \tag{9.49}$$

$$Q_2-N=0 \tag{9.50}$$

but the public optimum is undefined for $Q_2e'>0$. Any level of output is consistent with maximization of V; this can be seen immediately by substituting the constraints into the maximand. Intuitively, as workers are indifferent between an extra unit of consumption and less effort, and as wages will exhaust the product, the planner does not care what level of output is achieved.

Model C: Observable Effort with Human Capital

This model reintroduces hysteresis effects. Suppressing the b term, we had

$$e=e[w(1-u)] \ ; \ e'\geq 0, \ e''<0. \tag{9.51}$$

Given a 'competitive' assumption firms will choose optimal levels of the wage and employment but will treat u as parametric. The first-order conditions are

$$Q_1-w=0 \tag{9.52}$$

$$Q_2e'(1-u)-N=0. \tag{9.53}$$

The solutions are very similar to those of the previous models, and we will not spell them out in detail; equations (9.52) and (9.53) are practically identical to equations (9.43) and (9.44). As in model B, the intersection of the two loci yields the profit-maximizing levels of the wage and employment. As above, the gradients of the two loci are indeterminate but share the same sign, and the second-order conditions for a maximum have the same implications about relative gradients as previously. The hysteresis effects imply that for a market equilibrium we must also consider the effects of changing employment on productivity. There are now two 'long-run' loci whose intersection determines equilibrium. We note that the derivation of the effort supply locus was for infinitely lived individuals investing in 'quality' only at the start of their lives. Shifts in unemployment on the path to equilibrium are somewhat hard to fit into this framework, so this is a somewhat artificial model. Nevertheless, differentiating equations (9.52) and (9.53) while allowing u to change we find that the gradients of the loci are given by equations (9.54) and (9.55) respectively:

$$\frac{dw}{dN} = -\frac{[Q_{11}-(Q_{12}e'w/M)]}{Q_{12}e'(1-u)-1} \tag{9.54}$$

$$\frac{dw}{dN} = -\frac{[Q_{21}e'(1-u)+Q_2e''(1-u)^2+Q_2e'/M-1]}{(Q_{22}e'^2+Q_2e'')(1-u)^2}. \tag{9.55}$$

The signs of the gradients of these loci are ambiguous. Once again, there is no reason to rule out the possibility of multiple equilibria.

Model D: Unobservable Effort

In this case, unemployment has the opposite effect to that in our hysteresis model. The problem for the representative firm is to

$$\max_{w,N} \pi = Q(N,e)-wN$$

$$s.t. \ e-e(w,b,\bar{N})=0 \tag{9.56}$$

$$w-b\geq 0$$

where $\bar{N}$ is aggregate employment which each firm treats parametrically. Here the first constraint is equation (9.19). We have rewritten this equation suppressing all the variables taken parametrically by the firm except aggregate employment. The first-order conditions are now

$$Q_1-w=0 \tag{9.57}$$
$$Q_2e_1-N=0. \tag{9.58}$$

In equilibrium we require that N is equated to aggregate employment.[20] Differentiating, we find that the slopes of the two loci are indeterminate:

$$\frac{dw}{dN} = \frac{Q_{11}+Q_{12}e_2}{1-Q_{12}e_1} \tag{9.59}$$

$$\frac{dw}{dN} = \frac{1 - Q_{21}e_1 - Q_2 e_{12} - Q_{22}e_2 e_1}{Q_{22}e_1{}^2 + Q_2 e_{11}}.$$ (9.60)

These two loci correspond to equations (9.43) and (9.44) but are modified by the effect of aggregate unemployment on efficiency. There is nothing to rule out any combination of slopes, so that both may be positive, in which case unemployment is lower at the ruling wage than if it had been set at b, and there is the possibility of multiple equilibria.

Welfare may be examined as before. In this case there is a clear case for including effort in the maximand. Hence we assume the planner will

$$\max_{N,w} V = Q(N,e) + b(M-N) - Ne$$

$$s.t.\ e - e'(w,b,N) = 0$$

$$M - N > 0$$

$$Q(N,e) - wN \geq 0.$$ (9.61)

The labour supply constraint must hold with strict inequality. The optimal conditions are similar to those derived above for model B:

$$Q_1 = b + e + \frac{(Q_2 - N)(Ne_3/e_1 + Q_1 - w)}{(Q_2 - N/e_1)} \text{ for } Q = wN$$

or

$$Q_1 = b + e \qquad\qquad \text{for } Q > wN.$$ (9.62)

The third term (for $Q = wN$) has a similar interpretation to the second term in equation (9.47). In each case the planner would wish to set wages and employment such that the marginal product net of effort is equal to the opportunity cost of employment net of the lost output from the efficiency effect of expanding employment.

Conclusions

There are two main conclusions. The first is that if any of the posited relationships between worker quality, unemployment and wages actually hold, then the equilibrium rate of unemployment is likely to be wrong and possibly too high. Government subsidies to employment or to the unemployed are called for. The other main conclusion is that the possibility of multiple equilibria, possibly unstable, exists in each case which suggests that the recent rise in unemployment, which many argue is due to overly restrictive government fiscal policy (for example, Buiter

ınd Miller, 1984), may not be a transitory but a permanent phe-
ıomenon, unless an equally large stimulus to demand occurs. This is
essentially an empirical question. Several testable hypotheses have
emerged in the chapter. It would be interesting to test these hypotheses
for the UK, and especially the notion that there has been an endogenous
switch to a new, low-level equilibrium in recent years.

NOTES

I am grateful to the participants at the conference, and to Dr Andrew Oswald,
Professor David Ulph and Dr Jeff Frank for their helpful comments. The
normal caveats apply.

1 This suggests that the term 'equilibrium' is to be preferred to the 'natural'
rate, which may be neither unique nor optimal.
2 We note however that in our essentially static models the notion of the past
path of unemployment is somewhat vague. Throughout, we compare static
equilibria.
3 This section of the chapter is related to a paper by Hargreaves Heap (1980).
Hargreaves Heap argues, as we do, that the actual rate of unemployment
affects the 'natural' rate; however, he gives no particular explanation of why
unemployment occurs and his model has the somewhat unsatisfactory
property that there is a unique but unstable equilibrium; hence the title of his
paper.
4 The return b might also be interpreted as the consumption equivalent of the
value of unemployed leisure. It is *not* to be thought of as a transfer payment
from the government, although in the next section we shall consider such
transfers.
5 We discuss the derivation of these values below. At this stage, none of our
results hinge on them.
6 While 'effort' is a convenient concept to have in mind, it implies the
existence of a disutility of work which for simplicity we will not take into
account when we consider the optimal level of employment below. However,
later in the chapter 'effort' becomes a much more relevant interpretation and
is incorporated into the utility function.
7 In developing economies where the hypothesis was first suggested, there are
obvious physical and nutritional explanations for the phenomenon (Leibenstein, 1957).
8 Although we have yet to fully model the behaviour of firms or to introduce
taxes, it is obvious that e is determined by the real wage net of tax.
9 Note that we could equally have derived a conventional neoclassical labour
supply function. That too would be increasing in wages (assuming consumption and the negative of effort are normal) and could potentially sustain an
unemployment equilibrium.
10 We are assuming that the level and cost of supervision are not under the
firm's control, that effort or output levels cannot be specified in a contract
and that more complex contracts are inadmissable (e.g. the firm cannot fine
slacking workers, although in our set-up with costless hires the firm will not
wish to).

11 The Shapiro and Stiglitz model has effort at 0 or 1. We can derive a similar result by allowing $s(E)=0$ for some $E>0$ and assuming a corner solution. A linear $s(e)$ function would ensure this; for example, $s=(1-e/E)$. In such cases, the 'No Shirking Condition' of Shapiro and Stiglitz holds. There is a critical wage W such that for $w \geq W$, $e=E$; $e=0$ elsewhere. In Shapiro and Stiglitz $E=1$.

12 Note that all unemployment is 'benefit induced' in this model. However, we would stress that the optimal policy is not a reduction in unemployment benefits (equivalent to a tax on the return to unemployment in our model), but a subsidy to employment or in some cirucmstances a rise in aggregate demand (see below).

13 Output at C must exceed that at A as $e(N^c)>e(N^A)$. Consequently the Q_1 locus that passes through C is higher than that passing through A (or any level of employment less than N^c) for any employment level. Thus output (the integral of Q_1) is greater than C.

14 Our definition of the planner or the social optimum is necessarily second best. At this stage the point is unclear as the microeconomics of the effort supply function are not spelt out but we are restricting the planner to affecting effort only through the same incentive channels that exist in the unplanned economy.

15 This would be the condition that would hold under the extreme case of a complete monopoly, for the usual reason that the monopolist would internalize the externality. In this case there is no welfare loss from monopoly production, as p is still assumed parametric and the wage is determined by b.

16 This issue is an empirical one. Suppose that, as here, in equilibrium the demand for labour function has unemployment as an explanatory variable. If we assume that there are (say) two stable equilibria around which observations are clustered then the model might be estimated using a 'switching' condition, where the endogenous switch point is determined by point B in figure 9.1, say. We note that were one to estimate (say) the real wage/employment relationship without this condition then the equation would be mis-specified; this may explain why reported attempts to test the hysteresis hypothesis by adding lagged (un)employment to the employment equation have not met with success (for example, in Layard and Nickell, 1985). Carruth and Oswald (in this volume) use an alternative approach where non-linearities are introduced into the long-run relationships underlying the short-term dynamic model and fail to find multiple equilibria. Clearly work in this area is at an early stage.

17 There is plenty of empirical support for this assumption: for example, see Nickell (1979).

18 Where $e=e(-)$ in equation (9.7) effort would be zero.

19 However, the short-run aggregate supply locus for the upward sloping case is negatively sloped.

20 We take this approach for exegetic convenience as this is not a complete characterization of the equilibrum. The function $e(-)$ alters with the exogenous variables. The complete solution involves taking the specific form of equation (9.19) and imposing equation (9.20) as an equilibrium condition.

REFERENCES

Akerlof, G. 1983: Labor contracts as partial gift exchange. *Quarterly Journal of Economics,* 97, 543–69.

Atkinson, A. B. et al. 1984: Unemployment benefit, duration and incentives in Britain: How robust is the evidence?. *Journal of Public Economics,* 23, 3–26.

Buiter, W. H. and Miller, M. H. 1984: The macroeconomic consequences of a change in regime: The UK under Mrs Thatcher. *Brookings Papers on Economic Activity.*

Calvo, G. 1979: Quasi-Walrasian theories of unemployment. *American Economic Review,* 69, 102–7.

Diamond, P. A. 1982: Wage determination and efficiency in search equilibrium. *Review of Economic Studies,* 49, 217–27.

Hargreaves Heap, S. P. 1980: Choosing the wrong natural rate: Accelerating inflation of decelerating growth?. *Economic Journal,* 90, 239–53.

Layard, P. R. G. and Nickell, S. J. 1985: The causes of British unemployment. *National Institute Economic Review,* 111, 62–85.

Leibenstein, H. 1957: *Economic Backwardness and Economic Growth.* New York: Wiley.

Lynch, L. 1984: State dependency in youth unemployment: A lost generation. Centre for Labour Economics (LSE) *Discussion Papers,* No. 184.

Malcolmson, J. M. 1981: Unemployment and the efficiency wage hypothesis. *Economic Journal,* 91, 848–66.

Narendranathan, W., Nickell, S. J. and Stern, J. 1985: Unemployment benefits revisited. *Economic Journal,* 95, 307–29.

Nickell, S. J. 1979: The effect of unemployment and related benefits on the duration of unemployment. *Economic Journal,* 89, 34–49.

Price, S. G. 1985: *Aspects of the British Labour Market,* chapter 5, PhD thesis, University of Essex.

Shapiro, C. and Stiglitz, J. 1983: Unemployment as a worker discipline device. *American Economic Review,* 73, 433–44.

Symons, J. S. V. 1985: Relative prices and the demand for labour in British manufacturing. *Economica,* 52, 37–50.

Tobin, J. 1972: Inflation and unemployment. *American Economic Review,* 62, 1–19.

Yellen, J. L. 1984: Efficiency wage models of unemployment. *American Economic Review,* 74, 200–5.

10

Screening in Labour Markets with Heterogeneous Workers

INGE TÖTSCH

Introduction

Unemployment in most Western economies has been rising at least since the mid-1970s. This trend was hardly surprising during times of great turbulence and general recession, e.g. the oil price shocks, but has become a major puzzle, when the economy in general is improving again. This phenomenon is in apparent contradiction to the 'natural rate theory of unemployment'. Unemployment seems not only to depend on demand conditions, but to depend on its own history as well. As unemployment was steadily increasing and traditional models were failing to explain this trend, a new strand of research developed, the hysteresis literature.

The basic approach is concerned with the distinction between outsiders (the unemployed or at least the long-term unemployed) and insiders (the employed and possibly short-term unemployed). If outsiders are not perfect substitutes for the insiders, there is no pressure for the economy to return to previous employment levels, once the level of long-term unemployment has increased.

Gregory (1985) for example found, in an econometric investigation of the Australian economy, wages to be hardly influenced by the unemployment rate, but to be strongly influenced by the actual capital utilization in the firm. The low substitutability allows 'inside labour' to be scarce and consequently wages to be high, even though unemployment prevails in the economy. This approach is also supported by the empirical observation that the share of long-term unemployment has been rising with the 'natural rate' of total unemployment, while at the same time the job acquisition rates were distinctly higher for workers with short compared to long unemployment duration.

The usual approach is to have wage bargaining between the insiders and the firm which is hardly influenced by the outsiders, because of the limited substitutability. This chapter is also founded on the low substitutability between the long- and short-term unemployed, but does not use the collective bargaining approach, as in Blanchard and Summers (1985). It rather assumes search problems to be important in preventing unemployed workers from finding a job immediately.

Different explanations for the low substitutability between short- and long-term unemployed workers have been given. One explanation is the depreciation of productivity during unemployment. Technology changes but also the lack of chance to practice skills reduce productivity during unemployment. Another argument is not concerned with the depreciation of productivity but with the decreased ability to acquire a job during unemployment. This could be explained by helpful contacts who are a result of previous employment, and who as time passes, become less and less valid. A still different explanation concerns membership rules of labour unions. After being unemployed for so long a worker loses membership, which greatly reduces his or her chances of getting a job. This argument is explored by Blanchard and Summers (1985).

The focus of this chapter is a sorting effect, which takes place during unemployment. Suppose better workers are leaving unemployment at a higher rate than others. Firms can then expect average productivity to be negatively related to unemployment duration and will make their employment decision accordingly. These are in fact valid considerations for firms deciding whether job applicants should be invited for an interview or not. The reasoning usually is that long unemployment duration might either be due to a low efficiency when searching or, which might be just as disqualifying, is the result of being rejected after previous interviews. Prospective employers, lacking any other information, then have to take unemployment duration as an indication of low quality. Despite the fact that a good worker might just have been unlucky, the firm will expect a worker's quality to be lower, the higher the unemployment duration. These conditional expectations are a result of the adverse sorting effect. This chapter argues along the line of the second sorting effect. Here the screening by previous potential employers is not a result of information obtained during an interview, but of self-selection. Any other screening device would have the same effect.

Suppose workers differ in efficiency of labour, which can be monitored on application by some but not all firms. For example, in reality there are tests which are organized by government agencies or big companies to screen workers. To avoid the possibility of screening by third parties we assume that efficiency of labour can only be monitored on the job. Self-selection is then used to yield a screening device within a general equilibrium framework.

If firms are primarily interested in workers of high efficiency, screening will cause the job-acquisition rate to depend positively on a worker's efficiency. Workers of different efficiency levels will then have different probabilities of finding a job in a given period and the average efficiency of an unemployment cohort will deteriorate with its duration of unemployment.

In this two-sector model partial sorting is the result of the wage and job-termination structure which induces self-selection in one but not the other sector. If firms suffer losses when employing low-efficiency workers unknowingly, they will only accept applicants with an unemployment history which allows them to expect an efficiency level high enough to yield a non-negative surplus on average. In this model a single individual's productivity does not worsen during times of unemployment, but the composition of the unemployment cohort does. This adverse effect is enough to reduce the average efficiency to a level where non-screening firms are not willing to hire at wages above the reservation wage of high-efficiency workers. Their reservation wages will depend on unemployment benefits but also on their job opportunities with firms in the screening sector.

This chapter develops a two-sector model with heterogeneous workers which yields the above structure for appropriate parameters. It then imposes an exogenous business cycle on this economy. The minimum expected productivity for profitable hiring at a high-efficiency worker's reservation wage will vary over the business cycle. Thus employment behaviour in the non-screening sector will vary as well. As will be shown, employment behaviour by the screening firms will not necessarily change with the business cycle. The adverse effect on the average productivity of a cohort will then be smaller, but nevertheless still occur during a recession.

Consider the cohort which was at the margin of being accepted in the non-screening sector, but then was not hired during the recession. Workers of this cohort might not only experience a postponement of their employment possibilities, but could actually lose their last chance to enter the non-screening sector, if average productivity has decreased by too much.[1] The number of unemployed in this cohort would then always remain above the level it would have had without the shock. The absolute difference between its post-shock and steady-state levels will decrease over time, as some of those who would have entered the non-screening sector without the shock, find employment in the screening sector or die. An 'extra' share of unemployed workers is only gradually reduced over time.

It is this feature of the unemployment pool which causes the unemployment level to depend on its own history. The inheritance of a large unemployment pool will stay with an economy even after a recession, unless a positive shock above the steady-state values reduces it appropriately.

The next section develops a stationary model where self-selection induces the described sorting effect. The dynamic reaction to temporary real shocks due to changes in the terms of trade are explored in the section entitled 'Unemployment and the Business Cycle'. The following section briefly notes how the number of firms can be derived endogenously. This closes the model except for the exogenous terms of trade. The final section draws conclusions to the chapter.

A Stationary Model

Workers

There are two types of workers, with an efficiency of labour A or B with $A>B=1$. All workers work fixed hours, which are normalized to one. A highly efficient worker then supplies A efficiency units of labour per period, a less efficient worker supplies one.

The share of highly efficient workers in the total population P is q. Both types face a probability of death z each period. zqP individuals of type A, the high-productivity workers, and $z(1-q)P$ individuals of type B, the low-productivity workers, are born each period. Thus the overall working population remains constant.

Independent of type, all workers have the same von Neumann–Morgenstern utility function $u(w)=w$ which depends on the real wage w only.[2] The discount rate $\tilde{r}$ is constant over time and independent of type as well.

All individuals receive the same unemployment benefit when out of a job. Utility then is g.

Firms

The country is small and takes world prices as given. The terms of trade, and with them the real value per unit of output, are therefore exogenous. The country is active in two production sectors, a 'high-technology' sector, e.g. manufacturing of computers, and a normal sector, e.g. services. Labour is the only factor of production. The production functions of both sectors are linear in efficiency units of labour.[3]

The manufacturing sector m faces fixed costs k_m per worker each period. One interpretation is that there is a fixed quantity of capital which must be available to each worker. For simplicity these fixed costs are assumed to be zero for services.

Compared with the production of services, manufacturing also has higher fixed costs per firm each period k_i, i.e. $k_m>k_s$, which can only be avoided if the firm stops production.[4] In return, manufacturing has a higher real return per efficiency unit of labour.

Define b_i, $i=m, s$ as the value of output per period that a less efficient worker produces in sector i. Define a_i analogously for a highly efficient worker. Then

$$a_i=b_iA>b_i. \tag{10.1}$$

Firms maximize expected profits and have the same discount rate $\bar{r}$ as workers. Hiring and firing can only take place at the beginning of a period.

Information Structure

Workers have a list of firms. Because of turnover among firms, they do not know which are still in business.[5] Before actually applying at a particular firm the workers have no idea which sector the firm belongs to nor whether it is active or not. Workers know their own productivity.

Firms have no other information about potential workers other than the duration of their present unemployment spell d. The model can be generalized to allow richer information to be made available to firms, for example past employment. The algebra would be different, but the structure of the model would remain unchanged. If parameters are such that nobody will ever leave a job voluntarily, once they are employed, d contains all relevant information.

A worker's productivity is only revealed after working for one period. This information is then private to the firm and cannot be transferred to another firm.

Job Search

Unemployed workers can sample one firm per period.[6] Search on the job is assumed to be impossible.[7]

Applications and hiring only take place at the beginning of a period.

Wage Bargaining on the Job

A worker's type is revealed after the first period of work. Afterwards wage bargaining under complete information takes place. This bargaining takes place at the same time as the unemployed apply for new jobs. This implies the worker is unemployed for at least one period if no agreement is reached. Assume no other exogenous reasons besides death exist for job separation. The surplus of a job match with a highly efficient worker in sector i then is:[8]

$$(a_i-k_i) \sum_{t=0}^{\infty} (1-z)^t/(1+\bar{r})^t-U^*(0)=(a_i-k_i)(1+\bar{r})/(\bar{r}+z)-U^*(0). \tag{10.2}$$

For a less efficient worker we get the analogous expression

$$(b_i-k_i) \sum_{t=0}^{\infty} (1-z)^t/(1+\tilde{r})^t - V^*(0) = (b_i-k_i)(1+\tilde{r})/(\tilde{r}+z) - V^*(0), \quad (10.3)$$

where $\tilde{r}$ is the discount rate and z the probability of death per period. $U^*(d)$ is the expected utility, if a high-productivity worker with unemployment duration d does not accept or have a present job offer, but stays unemployed and waits for another offer. $V^*(d)$ is defined analogously for low-efficiency workers.

Workers of known efficiency can secure the share $h<1$ of a non-negative future surplus.[9] Their wages $w_j(i)$ will then depend on type j and sector i

$$w_a(i)=h(a_i-k_i)+(1-h)rU^*(0)/(1+r) \quad (10.4)$$

$$w_b(i)=h(b_i-k_i)+(1-h)rV^*(0)/(1+r) \quad (10.5)$$

where r is defined by

$$(1+r)=(1+\tilde{r})/(1-z)>(1+\tilde{r}). \quad (10.6)$$

r is the subjective rate of time preference, which also includes the per period probability of death z. z reduces the value of future utility, because with $z>0$ it is not certain whether future consumption can be enjoyed or a future surplus can actually be generated. Thus r and not $\tilde{r}$ is the relevant discount factor for infinitely lived firms when deriving the potential surplus of a worker.

Present Value of Job Offers and Unemployment

Let N be the total number of firms listed, S the number of firms active in services and M the number of firms active in manufacturing. The probability of finding an active firm in manufacturing, when searching for one period is

$$m=M/N. \quad (10.7a)$$

Similarly we get for s the probability per period of finding a firm active in services

$$s=S/N. \quad (10.7b)$$

Some applications involuntarily go to firms which are already out of business, because the information about closures takes time to spread.

If there is no turnover among firms or no informational problem about which firm is still active, we could alternatively assume that workers can only search with a probability less than unity each period. In either case the probability of getting a job offer in a given period will be smaller than unity. This feature is crucial to the model, because all high-efficiency workers would otherwise leave the unemployment pool after one period of unemployment.

Define $U^i(d)$ as the present value of a job offer in sector i to a good worker with unemployment duration d and $V^i(d)$ as the same for a less efficient worker in the same unemployment cohort. For the given information and search structure, these can be derived as follows

$$U^i(d)=\begin{cases} w_o(i,d)+U^*(0)/(1+r) \text{ for } (a_i-k_i)(1+r)/r<U^*(0) \\ w_o(i,d)+h(a_i-k_i)/r+(1-h)U^*(0)/(1+r) \text{ otherwise.} \end{cases} \quad (10.8)$$

$$V^i(d)=\begin{cases} w_o(i,d)+V^*(0)/(1+r) \text{ for } (b_i-k_i)(1+r)/r<V^*(0) \\ w_o(i,d)+h(b_i-k_i)/r+(1-h)V^*(0)/(1+r) \text{ otherwise.} \end{cases} \quad (10.9)$$

As mentioned above $U^*(d)$ and $V^*(d)$ are the present values of unemployment for a highly or for a less efficient worker with unemployment duration d. $w_o(i,d)$ is the first-period wage paid in sector i to a member of the unemployment cohort d. First-period wages will in general be different from $w_a(i)$ or $w_b(i)$, the on-the-job wages, because either it is in the interest of both types of workers to apply, or $w_o(i,d)$ must be set to induce self-selection. Also $U^*(d)$ or $V^*(d)$, the worker's status quo point, will in general be different from $U^*(0)$ or $V^*(0)$. We assume $(a_i-k_i)(1+r)/r>U^*(0)$ for both sectors. So high-efficiency workers will never want to leave a job. For the less efficient workers we assume $(b_m-k_m)(1+r)/r<V^*(0)$. They will then be fired from a job in manufacturing or, which is equivalent, be offered wages below their opportunity costs, as soon as their efficiency is revealed. Both possibilities, $(b_s-k_s)(1+r)/r$ and larger or smaller $V^*(0)$, will be discussed below.

The first-period wage, wage bargaining on the job and the workers' alternative options influence which kind of workers will accept a job offer. First-period wages affect a firm's profits via costs but also by influencing the expected productivity of a job match. Two distinctions have to be made:

$$U^*(d)-(1-h)U^*(0)/(1+r)-h(a_i-k_i)/r<$$

or
$$V^*(d)-V^*(0)/(1+r)-\max\{0;h[(b_i-k_i)/r-V^*(0)/(1+r)]\} \quad (10.10a)$$

$$U^*(d)-(1-h)U^*(0)/(1+r)-h(a_i-k_i)/r>$$

$$V^*(d)-V^*(0)/(1+r)-\max\{0;h[(b_i-k_i)/r-V^*(0)/(1+r)]\}. \quad (10.10b)$$

The left-hand sides of equations (10.10a) and (10.10b) are a good worker's reservation wage for the first period of employment in sector i, $R_a(i,d)$. A less efficient worker's reservation wage $R_b(i,d)$ is given on the right-hand side. These reservation wages leave the workers indifferent between accepting and rejecting the job offer. In the case of equation (10.10a), first-period wages can be set to attract only the highly efficient workers. Given equation (10.10b) only the less efficient workers will enter, if first period wages are low enough.

Incentive Compatibility and Profitability of an Unscreened Match

$$q(d)(a_i-k_i)+[1-q(d)](b_i-k_i)+T_i\geq R_a(i,d) \quad (10.11a)$$

$$q(d)(a_i-k_i)+[1-q(d)](b_i-k_i)+T_i\geq R_b(i,d) \quad (10.11b)$$

where T_i is the discounted value of expected future profits from an unscreened job match. The left-hand side of equations (10.11a) and (10.11b) give the firm's willingness to pay for an unscreened worker in the first period. The right-hand sides of equations (10.11a) and (10.11b) are the reservation wages for the high- (equation 10.11a), and low- (equation 10.11b) efficiency workers, as defined in equations (10.10).

To derive T_i we need to know which type of worker would stay on the job. We assumed employment of the highly efficient workers to be profitable in all sectors. Due to the high capital costs, employment of workers known to be of low efficiency is not profitable in manufacturing. Thus T_m is given by

$$T_m=q(d)(1-h)[(a_m-k_m)/r-U^*(0)/(1+r)]. \quad (10.12a)$$

There are two possibilities for low-efficiency workers in the services sector. First $b_s(1+r)/r$ can be greater than $V^*(0)$, i.e. the less efficient workers produce a surplus on the job above searching for a new job. They would then stay with the firm after the first period of employment. This will not be the case if the probability of finding another job offer is high, the productivity on the job b_s is not much bigger than unemployment benefits g and/or first-period wages are considerably higher than on-the-job wages. First-period wages can be higher than on-the-job wages if they are also supposed to attract high-efficiency workers, whose type has not been revealed. Their reservation wages set a lower limit to first-period wages. The second possibility in the services sector is $b_s(1+r)/r<V^*(0)$, i.e. less efficient workers leave the firm after the first period of work. This can be relevant if a good worker's reservation wage is high and search costs are low for the less efficient workers.

T_s will be different in these cases.

$$T_s= \begin{cases} q(d)(1-h)[a_s/r-U^*(0)/(1+r)] \text{ for } b_s(1+r)/r<V^*(0) \\ q(d)(1-h)[a_s/r-U^*(0)/(1+r)]+ \\ [1-q(d)](1-h)[b_s/r-V^*(0)/(1+r)] \text{ otherwise.} \end{cases}$$ (10.12b)

A match will not result in acceptance by highly efficient workers if neither equation (10.10a) nor equation (10.11a) hold for the particular sector and cohort, that is, if screening is impossible and unscreened employment is unprofitable. It then might be possible for the less efficient workers to agree with the firm on a still smaller wage, if $(b_i-k_i)(1+r)/r\geq V^*(d)$ or $(b_i-k_i)+V^*(0)/(1+r)\geq V^*(d+1)$. So screening of low-efficiency workers can be profitable either because of a sufficient productivity or to regain a fresh unemployment record. In this case self-selection of the less efficient workers and their employment is still possible.

If self-selection of good workers is possible (equation (10.10a)) and profitability of unscreened employment is given (equations (10.11a) and (10.11b)), it depends on the bargaining outcome whether self-selection is enforced or not.

Our interest is in the case where self-selection of highly efficient workers is enforced in manufacturing, but not in the services sector. To avoid analysing the bargaining process we assume equation (10.11b) not to hold for m and all d.

The net product of highly efficient workers depends only on $a=(Ab_m-k_m)$. The net product of a less efficient worker $(-L)$, L for losses, with $(-L)=(b_m-k_m)$ can be set completely independent of a, as long as $A>1$. b_m and k_m would then have to be

$$b_m=(L+a)/(A-1)$$ (10.13a)

$$k_m=(LA+a)/(A-1).$$ (10.13b)

Losses (L) of any magnitude are compatible with a large a. The larger a, the lower the reservation wage of a good worker, because future surpluses are worth an entrance fee which can take the form of low or negative first-period wages. For a high enough net product of good workers in manufacturing, their self-selection will be possible, because of their lower reservation wage. This is restated in equation (10.14).

$$U^*(d)-(1-h)U^*(0)/(1+r)-h(a_m-k_m)/r<$$

$$V^*(d)-V^*(0)/(1+r). \tag{10.14}$$

Recall the firm's willingness to pay for first-period employment of an unscreened worker, as given on the left-hand side of equation (10.11). This can be rewritten in terms of L and a, the surplus of a good worker's output above the capital costs. This is done in equation (10.15). The firm's willingness to pay will be smaller than a less efficient worker's reservation wage, if L is large enough.

$$q(d)a-[1-q(d)]L+q(d)(1-h)[a/r-U^*(0)/(1+r)]\leq$$

$$V^*(d)-V^*(0)/(1+r). \tag{10.15}$$

In this case the first-period wage $w_o(m,d)$ in manufacturing will be equal to $[V^*(d)-V^*(0)/(1+r)]$, the highest wage, which just deters the less efficient workers from entering. The on-the-job result $w_a(m)$ is not attainable. Even though accepting a job in manufacturing identifies a worker as being highly efficient, first-period wages have to be lowered to $[V^*(d)-V^*(0)/(1+r)]$ to make self-selection and profitable production possible.

In the services sector we assume equation (10.10b) to hold for all d and equation (10.11a) to hold for $d=1$. This causes self-selection of good workers to be impossible for all cohorts and unscreened hiring from the youngest cohort to be profitable. In addition we assume it to be more profitable for a firm to employ an unscreened worker with $d=1$, than to enforce self-selection of low-efficiency workers by lowering the first-period wage offered for services to applicants of the youngest cohort, $w_o(s,1)$. In this case low-efficiency workers yield a higher surplus, above the alternative of looking for another job in services, than high-productivity workers. Then high-efficiency workers will only enter manufacturing while less efficient workers only enter the services sector.[10] This is not the constellation we are interested in. Thus we assume unscreened hiring from young cohorts to be in the interest of firms in the services sector.

As the proportion of high-efficiency workers $q(d)$ decreases, the firm's willingness to pay, the left-hand side of equation (10.11a), will decrease as well, while the reservation wage, the right-hand side, is only affected if future employment possibilities change. We assume the productivity of a low-efficiency worker in services to be too low compared to a good worker's to allow the excessive first period wage to be covered by their own contribution to the firm's future profits. An unscreened worker who turns out to be of low efficiency thus imposes a loss to the firm, due to the excessive first-period wage. Define $\bar{d}$ as the lowest value of unemployment duration d for which equation (10.11a) does not hold in the services sector. For services, unscreened hiring will be unprofitable at the good workers' reservation wages for cohorts with $d>\hat{d}-1$. In general even some cohorts with $d<\hat{d}$ will not be employed unscreened. The expected profit to the firm is zero for unscreened hiring, if equation (10.11a) holds with equality. At the same time the firm can get the share $(1-h)$ of a surplus made, if a less efficient worker enters a job. This will be the case if $b_s>g$, i.e. the worker's product is larger than unemployment benefits g, or $V^*(0)$ is much bigger than $V^*(\hat{d})$.[11] In the latter case the firm just 'sells' a new unemployment record. Thus there might be room for some d with $1<d<\hat{d}$ for which the firm chooses to enforce self-selection of low-productivity workers even though (10.11a) is not violated. Define δ as the lowest value of d for which unscreened employment is denied in services. For $d\geq\delta$ the first-period wage in the services sector will be such that only the less efficient workers will enter and $V^s(d)$ is constant for all $d\geq\delta$.

In this case we also have to assume s, the probability of finding a firm active in services, to be smaller than m, the probability of finding a firm active in manufacturing. This guarantees the average efficiency of a cohort will worsen with unemployment duration d, if only the high-efficiency workers of a cohort enter jobs in manufacturing and only the low-efficiency workers of the cohort enter the services sector. If, however, the highly efficient workers enter both sectors, their share $q(d)$ is definitely decreasing in duration. With hiring of workers known to be of low efficiency being unprofitable, $q(d)$ will be decreasing in d, as long as $m>0$. $s<m$ then is not necessary.

If it is not profitable to employ workers known to be of low efficiency, the situation in this sector is analogous to the Weiss (1980) model. The higher reservation wage of high-efficiency workers makes screening impossible and prohibits wage competition by the less efficient. Even though the highly efficient workers of old cohorts would produce a positive surplus in services, they are only offered wages below their reservation level. This is due to the fact that they are mixed with too many less efficient workers, from whom they cannot be distinguished.

Unemployment of high-productivity workers in young cohorts is only the result of not being able to find an active firm. Unemployment in old cohorts is also due to search problems, but in addition is the result of the signalling effect of unemployment duration d.

Given the self-selection in the high-technology sector and a maximum length of unemployment for unscreened hiring, $U^*(d)$ and $V^*(d)$, the present values of unemployment can be derived as

$$g+mU^m(d+1)/(1+r)+sU^s(d+1)/(1+r)+$$

$$U^*(d)= \begin{cases} (1-m-s)U^*(d+1)/(1+r) & \text{for } d<\delta \\ g+mU^m(d+1)/(1+r)+(1-m)U^*(d+1)/(1+r) & \text{otherwise.} \end{cases} \quad (10.16)$$

$$V^*(d)= \begin{cases} g(1+r)/r & \text{for } V^s(d)>V^*(d) \\ g+sV^s(d+1)/(1+r)+(1-s)V^*(d+1)/(1+r) & \text{otherwise.} \end{cases} \quad (10.17)$$

Young high-efficiency workers have access to two sectors. Their output per unit of labour is higher in manufacturing than in services. For the assumed bargaining and information structure this causes wages after the first period of work to be higher in manufacturing than for services. This difference in future earnings causes the first-period reservation wage to be lower in manufacturing. As the present value of a job in manufacturing increases, the reservation wage for services rises, because the alternative to accepting a job in services, continued search, becomes more attractive. Suppose employment in services can only compete with the search for a job in manufacturing if high-efficiency workers get the whole value of their output as wages. The reservation wage could then rise to a_s with later wages $w_a(s)=a_s$ as well.

In this situation, hiring of good workers cannot take place in services, as long as less efficient workers are in the market also. The less efficient workers, lacking alternative employment opportunities, would be eager to enter at the same first-period wage, inducing losses to the firm.

This discussion already indicates the constellation necessary to make self-selection of highly efficient workers in services impossible, but allowing at the same time the share of good workers, for which unscreened employment is profitable, to be well below unity. If the worker's share of the surplus when bargaining under complete information is low, the loss per hired low-efficiency worker can be relatively large for a given share of good workers q. It has to be small, though, if workers get a larger share of a surplus. Otherwise, good workers cannot have high reservation wages for services while firms make non-negative profits from unscreened hiring of cohorts, which include quite a few low-efficiency workers.

The model leads to the following structure of a static equilibrium. Due to their job-acceptance behaviour, workers with higher efficiency leave the unemployment pool at a higher rate. The negative dependence of the proportion of high-efficiency workers on unemployment duration is a result of differences in the job-acquisition rates. In this model these are induced by self-selection. Any other screening device, which is only available to some firms but not all, will have the same effect. Firms who do not have access to a screening mechanism and depend on a sufficient share of good workers, if unscreened hiring is to be profitable, will not try to hire high-productivity workers from old unemployment cohorts.

First-period wages are a crucial factor in generating self-selection in this model. They essentially determine the cost of screening on the job. If these costs are low, the availability of another screening device, for example self-selection, loses its importance. First-period wages might not seem to be a serious cost factor at first glance. However, suppose output is stochastic and productivity cannot be monitored directly. In this case quite a bit of time might be necessary to make a reasonable inference from output about a worker's efficiency. Alternatively suppose labour laws are such as to make recontracting or firing very difficult. In both cases the contracted starting wage will be very important.

In any case the details of this model should not be taken too seriously. Any other mechanism leading to self-selection or any other screening device, for that matter, can lead to an adverse effect of unemployment duration on the average efficiency of an unemployment cohort. This might induce firms to stop unscreened hiring after a maximum unemployment duration, because it becomes unprofitable. These phenomena are both realistic and can help to explain the low job-acquisition rates of the long-term unemployed.

Unemployment and the Business Cycle

Regarding the real value per unit of output in sector i, b_i, as the exogenous but variable world price is sufficient to transfer the stationary model into a world with an exogenous business cycle. Assume all goods to be non-storable. The real value of output per efficiency unit of labour in sector i then equals b_i. A change in b_i thus represents an exogenous real shock to the economy.

The subscript t is added to all variables which vary with the business cycle. Variables without t still stand for their steady-state values.

Negative Shocks

Consider the manufacturing sector first. Only high-productivity workers are willing to enter this sector. Employment behaviour in this sector is not changed by a general recession or a relative price drop which is small enough to leave the surplus of a job match in this sector big enough to pay wages above the reservation levels for all cohorts. This is equivalent to

$$(Ab_{mt}-k_s)+(1-h)(Ab_m-k_m)/r+U^*(0)/(1+r)> $$
$$U^*(d)-U^*(0)/(1+r)-h(Ab_m-k_m)/r+U^*(0)/(1+r) \qquad (10.18)$$

for all d. In our framework there is no marginally accepted worker in manufacturing, because technology is linear and, due to self-selection, expected efficiency is the same for all workers. If equation (10.18) does not hold, the firms would also want to fire all workers who have been hired in previous periods. A small recession affects the current starting and on-the-job wages, $w_{ot}(m,d)$ and $w_{at}(m)$, but all applicants are accepted.

This is not the case in the services sector. The required share of high-efficiency workers needed to break even at wages above the reservation levels rises as the value per unit of output b_{st} falls.

Suppose we are starting from a steady-state equilibrium, with x the steady-state value of the maximum unemployment duration accepted for unscreened hiring δ. The share of high-efficiency workers in cohort d, $q(d)$, is independent of time in the steady-state equilibrium, because employment behaviour has been constant and the arrival of new workers by birth is constant by assumption. Now the value per unit of output b_{st} falls temporarily and causes δ to fall by one for one period. In the following period bs, $t+1$ is up again to its steady-state value.

During the period of the adverse shock, firms in the normal sector would not accept any unscreened applicants of the cohort with $x-1$ at the time. Firms in the high-technology sector were still hiring high-productivity workers. $q_{t+1}(x)$, the share of good workers in cohort x at time $t+1$ will then be:[12]

$$q_{t+1}(x)=(1-m)q_t(x-1)/[(1-s)+(s-m)q_t(x-1)]<q_t(x-1). \quad (10.19)$$

The quality effect on an affected cohort is smaller during a recession than during normal times, as is shown in equation (10.20). Despite this, the sorting effect during a recession can prohibit the high-efficiency workers of these cohorts from getting another chance in the services sector after the shock, if the profitability constraint (10.11a) was close to binding before the shock, or if the shock is persistent.

$$(1-m)q_t(x-1)/[(1-s)+(s-m)q_t(x-1)]>$$
$$(1-m-s)q_t(x-1)/[1-s-mq_t(x-1)]=q_t(x). \quad (10.20)$$

Consider a temporary shock which is severe enough to reduce the maximum unemployment duration accepted for unscreened hiring δ by $c>1$. Those cohorts with $x-c-1<d<x-1$ at the time will be allowed to enter the normal sector right after the shock. But when they finally have $d=x$ their $q(x)$ will be as described in equation (10.19). So for them the $(x-1)$th chance of entering the normal sector also may be gone.

Reduced hiring during the shock, which is not fully corrected by increased hiring afterwards, permanently reduces the employment level. If one or more chances of obtaining a job in services are lost, the number of unemployed high-efficiency workers will be higher at each period afterwards than it would have been without the shock. Only as the absolute size of these cohorts is reduced by death or by entering a job will this effect vanish.

This hysteresis result is common to all models with an adverse effect of unemployment duration on average efficiency, whether it is caused by a depreciation of the individual efficiency or by an adverse sorting effect. Temporary shocks have long-term consequences and the economy does not revert to the previous equilibrium immediately afterwards. The policy implications are very interesting. Temporary employment programmes not only reduce present unemployment, but increase future employment and with it future productive capacity as well.

Positive Shocks

As above, consider a steady-state equilibrium as a starting point. A shock only influences employment behaviour if it is big enough to change the marginally accepted cohort for unscreened hiring δ.

Recall the profitability constraint (10.11a). The right-hand side is a high-productivity worker's first-period reservation wage $R_a(s,d)$ for services. The left-hand side is the firm's willingness to pay for the first period of unscreened employment $W(q,b_s)$. In the steady state $U^*(\delta-1)=U^*(\delta)=U^*(\delta+1)$ and $q(\delta)=(1-m-s)q(\delta-1)/[1-s-mq(\delta-1)]<q(\delta-1)$.

The derivative with respect to a temporary change in the value of output, b_s, of this willingness to pay $W[q(d), b_{st}]$ then depends negatively on unemployment duration d. It is $q(d)(A-1)$.

A larger shock in b_s is needed to induce the same change on $W[q_t(d),b_{st}]$ as on $W[q_t(d-1),b_{st}]$. Because $U^*(\delta)=U^*(\delta-1)$, a good worker's reservation wage $R_a(s,d)$ is the same for δ and $\delta-1$.

Suppose we are starting with b_s such that

$$W[q(\delta-1),b_s]-R_a(s,\delta-1)=-\{W[q(\delta),b_s]-R_a(s,\delta)\}>0. \quad (10.21)$$

Then the same positive change in $W[q(\delta),b_{st}]$, the willingness to pay for an unscreened worker with $d=\delta$, is needed to make their hiring just profitable, as the necessary negative change of $W[q(\delta-1),b_{st}]$ to make their employment become just unprofitable.

Consider a negative temporary shock of magnitude y, which causes the willingness to pay for an unscreened worker of cohort $\delta-1$, $W[q(\delta-1),b_s-y]$ to equal the highly efficient workers' reservation wage $R_a(\delta-1)$, i.e.

$$-yq(\delta-1)(A-1)+W[q(\delta-1),b_s]-R_a(\delta-1)=0. \quad (10.22)$$

A negative shock of this magnitude decreases δ by one for one period. A positive shock of the same magnitude then does not increase the maximum unemployment duration accepted for unscreened employment, δ, by one, because

$$yq(\delta-1)(A-1)>yq(\delta)(A-1).\tag{10.23}$$

If the real value per unit of output b_{st} is distributed symmetrically around its steady-state level b_s, δ will be reduced by a higher probability rather than increased.

In this example we started from a special kind of 'symmetry', namely condition (10.21). Suppose b_s to be such that

$$b_s=(b_{s-}+b_{s+})/2\tag{10.24}$$

where b_{s-} and b_{s+} are implicitly defined as follows

$$W[q(\delta),b_{s+}]-R_a(\delta)=0,\tag{10.25}$$

$$W[q(\delta-1),b_{s-}]-R_a(\delta-1)=0.\tag{10.26}$$

Now small symmetric changes in the value per unit of output b_s will cause symmetric changes in δ. If shocks can be large enough to change δ by more than one, the same asymmetry applies as above. Smaller changes above (b_s-b_{s-}) are sufficient to decrease δ by c, more so than changes above $(b_{s+}-b_s)$ are to increase δ by c.

If shocks are symmetric around the steady-state value per unit of output b_s, positive changes of δ by c will be less frequent than negative changes by the same c. This effect could be partially or completely reversed, if the distribution of the shocks is symmetric in percentage changes, which is not totally unreasonable for prices.

Magnitude and Persistence of a Temporary Change in δ

Compare the effect of shocks on the unemployment level which increase or decrease the maximum unemployment duration accepted for unscreened hiring δ by one for one period (see table 10.1). $P(d)$ is

Table 10.1 *Changes in unemployment numbers of high-efficiency workers*

Period	Negative shocks	Positive shocks
0	$-sq(\delta-1)P(\delta-1)$	$+sq(\delta)P(\delta)$
1	$-(1-m)(1-z)sq(\delta-1)P(\delta-1)$	$+(1-z)sq(\delta)P(\delta)$
2	$-(1-m)^2(1-z)^2sq(\delta-1)P(\delta-1)$	$+(1-z)^2sq(\delta)P(\delta)$
j	$-(1-m)^j(1-z)^jsq(\delta-1)P(\delta-1)$	$+(1-z)^jsq(\delta)P(\delta)$

defined as the number of unemployed high-efficiency workers with unemployment duration d at the original steady-state level.

Figure 10.1 draws the sequence of $P(d)$ for the cohort with $d=\delta-1$ at the time of the temporary shock. The solid line represents the sequence relevant without the shock. The actual sequence, if the shock occurs when $d=\delta-1$ and if the last employment chances in the services sector are not only postponed but lost, follows the solid line until $d=\delta-1$ but then is higher, as represented by the broken line.[13]

Figure 10.2 shows the sequence of $P(d)$ for the cohort with $d=\delta$ at the time of the temporary shock. Again the solid line traces the sequence, if no shock occurs. This cohort is only affected by the shock if it is a positive one. If a positive shock is strong enough to allow for profitable hiring of unemployed workers with $d=\delta$, the sequence of $P(d)$ follows the solid line until δ and afterwards follows the broken line.

Using the knowledge about the exit pattern, we get

$$q(\delta-1)P(\delta-1)-q(\delta)P(\delta)=(1-z)mq(\delta-1)P(\delta-1)>0 \quad (10.27)$$

i.e. first-period effects are higher for a negative than for a positive shock. After the period of the shock these first-period effects on high-efficiency workers are reduced by different rates. Unemployment is left by death or entering a job in manufacturing. Higher employment numbers are only reduced by death. After a certain number of periods a positive effect will have left larger traces on the unemployment and employment levels of high-efficiency workers than negative effects will.

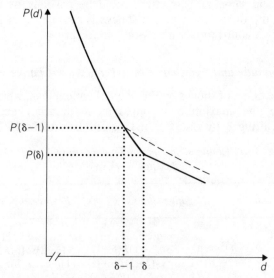

Figure 10.1 *Effect of a shock when $d=\delta-1$*

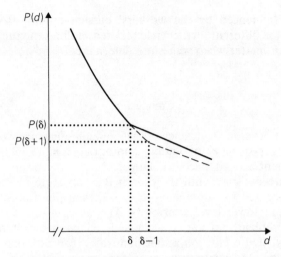

Figure 10.2 *Effect of a shock when* $d=\delta$

It can be argued that positive shocks on employment are more likely to occur and are stronger on impact, than negative shocks. The picture of the long-term effects of temporary shocks is reversed. But note that this reversal takes place when absolute numbers have decreased already.

Turnover and the Number of Firms

With the above information structure the number of new applicants to a firm is stochastic. In the presence of fixed costs per period and limited credit, unfortunate firms will go bankrupt. This effect is supported in the services sector by the losses experienced when low-efficiency workers are hired unknowingly. A bankruptcy will then happen despite the fact that these firms have a positive expected profit for the future. The assumption that debts are constrained by an upper limit on credits is crucial to this argument. For this model, restrictions on the credit market are only necessary to create turnover among firms and thus a probability of finding a potential job offer lower than unity. If this probability is lower than unity for some other reason, credit markets could be imperfect.

The average number of applicants to a firm depends on the number of firms and the number of unemployed workers. Since profits depend on the number of workers, expected net profits can only be positive for a finite number of firms, if fixed costs K^i are positive.

Obviously profits also depend on the wages which have to be offered to the particular groups of applicants. For the given bargaining structure wages are influenced by the workers' outside option. Because job matches in the different sectors yield different utilities the sum $s+m$ and the ratio s/m matter when wages are determined.

Conclusion

This chapter developed a framework where high-efficiency workers face a decreasing possibility of finding appropriate employment as their unemployment record becomes longer. More specifically, their job prospects are constant until they reach the maximum unemployment duration accepted for unscreened hiring δ, then jump downward and remain at this lower level afterwards. This adverse effect is due to a signalling problem and not to an actual reduction of an individual's productivity. Different job-acquisition rates for different types of workers change the composition of an unemployment cohort over time. This in turn influences future employment possibilities. If δ is very large the efficiency loss due to this phenomenon will not be serious, because the affected unemployment cohorts will be small. δ will be smaller, the lower the surplus a high-efficiency worker can produce in services above the expected utility from continued search. It increases with the share of a good worker's profits accruing to the firm.

The long-term effects on unemployment caused by temporary shocks can help to explain some of the now much discussed hysteresis phenomenon. Past recessions have undesirable bootstrap effects on the present and future, by bequesting a higher level of long-term unemployed. These long-term unemployed cause unemployment to remain higher, even for improved demand, because their average productivity has deteriorated to the point where unscreened employment becomes unprofitable to firms.

NOTES

I am indebted to Charles Bean and John Moore for many helpful discussions.
1 In a world where screening is the only adverse effect on average productivity during unemployment, this result depends on the fact that the screening sector is still hiring during the recession. In this case it seems to be appropriate, because screening, self-selection, is costless.
2 Risk neutrality, or equivalently the possibility of insurance, is assumed for simplicity. The model would easily generalize to risk-averse workers without access to insurance.
3 As with the form of the utility function, the form of the production function is chosen purely for convenience. It is straighforward to introduce a more complex technology.

4 K_i is introduced to endogenize the number of firms and to induce turnover among firms by bankruptcies later on.

5 This structure could be supported by the following story. When leaving the market, firms do not care whether they are assumed to be still producing or not. So this information takes time to reach every unemployed worker. To be able to receive workers and start production, new firms on the other hand make every effort to become known as active, i.e. to enter the list.

6 Together with the turnover argument this assumption produces an application rate at active firms smaller than unity as in many other papers of the literature, e.g. Stiglitz (1985) and Pissarides (1985). The present combination of assumptions is felt to be more plausible than a frequency of search lower than one. It seems more reasonable to have uncertainty about finding an active firm when searching, rather than flipping a coin each period whether to actually search or not.

7 This assumption could be relaxed. Search on the job could lead to wage differentials among firms of the same sector and change the evaluation of the present value of a specific job match by workers and firms. The structure is explained in Stiglitz (1985). It still allows for self-selection in some of the firms but not all. This source of wage differentials is not the topic here and the above assumption is made to ease the analysis and concentrate on the topic of the informational content of unemployment duration.

8 The derivation of this surplus and of the present value of job offers implicitly assumes that bankrupt firms will operate under new ownership and firms can 'sell' the existing firm at its present value. In this case workers and firms do not have to take the possibility of bankruptcy into account.

9 As will become clear, we only need wages to be higher than the reservation wage. Without getting into bargaining theory it seems reasonable that both sides get some part of a surplus. Since it is not clear who would be the first to move in a Rubinstein bargaining game, and commitments could probably not last forever, this assumption seems to be justified. For the structure of the model it is sufficient for both sides to get some part of a surplus. Constant shares independent of the size of this surplus are not necessary. Constant shares simplify the algebra and are assumed purely for this reason.

10 Despite $a_s > b_s$ this is possible, as long as $U^*(0)$ is high enough, due to the employment opportunities in manufacturing.

11 We are only going through the pain of considering these different cases because we want to allow for the possibility that low-efficiency workers can stay once they have entered a job in services. This unfortunately implies $b_s(1+r)/r > V^*(0)$ and makes screening of low-efficiency workers profitable for old unemployment cohorts.

12 In the following discussion about reactions to shocks, we assume the less efficient workers to be able to stay on the job for all realizations of world prices. Then the share of good workers in the youngest cohort $q_t(0)$ is independent of t. Otherwise we would have to account for repercussions over time, because $q(0)$ would go up for one period after a negative temporary shock, since fewer less efficient workers would have been hired previously and re-enter with a new unemployment record. At the time when this new cohort is at the margin of being accepted for unscreened hiring, their $q(0)$ can make the difference between whether they get another chance to enter

unscreened or not. This effect would be more important the larger the services sector.

13 If the sorting effect during the recession is small, employment chances are only postponed for one period. The number of unemployed will then only be above the normal value during the recession and again be at the normal value right afterwards.

REFERENCES

Blanchard, O. J. and Summers L. 1985: A Model of Unemployment Hysteresis. Mimeo.

Gregory, R. G. 1985: Wages Policy and Unemployment in Australia. Australian National University, mimeo.

Guasch, J. L. and Weiss A. 1981: Self-selection in the labour market. *American Economic Review*.

Heap, H. 1980: Choosing the wrong 'natural' rate: Accelerating inflation or decelerating employment and growth? *Economic Journal*.

McDonald, I. M. and Solow, R. M. 1981: Wage bargaining and employment. *American Economic Review*.

Meyerson, R. 1979: Incentive compatibility and the bargaining problem. *Econometrica*.

Pissarides, C. A. 1985: Short-run equilibrium dynamics of unemployment, vacancies and real wages. *American Economic Review*.

Rothschild, M. and Stiglitz, J. 1976: Equilibrium in competitve insurance markets: An essay on the economics of imperfect information. *Quarterly Journal of Economics*.

Salop, J. and Salop, S. 1976: Self-selection and turnover in the labour market. *Quarterly Journal of Economics*.

Salop, S. 1979: A model of the natural rate of unemployment. *American Economic Review*.

Stiglitz, J. 1985: Equilibrium wage distributions. *Economic Journal*.

Weiss, A. 1980: Job queues and layoffs in labor markets with flexible wages. *Journal of Political Economy*.

Yellen, J. 1984: Efficiency wage models of unemployment. *American Economic Review*.

Part V

Hysteresis Effects and the Explanation of Aggregate Unemployment

11

Labour Force Participation: Timing and Persistence

KIM B. CLARK and LAWRENCE H. SUMMERS

Much of the development of applied economic theory since the late 1950s has emphasized the importance of viewing economic decisions in a life-cycle context. Consumption decisions are today frequently viewed as being determined by wealth or permanent income. The human capital revolution has brought life-cycle considerations to the forefront of modern labour economics. While the life-cycle dynamics of labour force participation decisions have important implications for macroeconomic theory and policy, they have received relatively little empirical attention. With the notable exceptions of Lucas and Rapping (1969) and Hall (1980), none of the large body of work on cyclical fluctuations in employment has explicitly relied on a dynamic model of labour supply.[1]

This chapter uses several types of data to examine two elements of participation dynamics. The first is the aspect of 'timing' which is implicit in the work of Lucas and Rapping, and in Mincer's (1966) early discussion of hidden unemployment. The timing argument, which is presented most explicitly in Ghez and Becker (1975), holds that leisure is easily substitutable across periods. Hence relatively small transitory movements in the perceived real wage or real rate of return can have large effects on the path of labour supply as individuals time their participation to coincide with periods of high transitory wages. On the other hand, permanent changes, because they do not affect the timing decision, are expected to have a much smaller effect on participation.

It is this view of labour supply which underlies new classical macroeconomic models. The dependence is made explicit in Lucas (1975), who claims that 'what we do know indicates that leisure in one period is an excellent substitute for leisure in other nearby periods'. The ability of classical macroeconomic models to explain fluctuations in employment depends on the presence of strong intertemporal substitution effects.

Unless leisure is very substitutable across periods, large observed cyclical variations in employment could not possibly be caused by the response of labour supply to the relatively small fluctuations which are found in real wages and real interest rates.

It is by now clear that models in which only timing elements are present cannot fully account for cyclical fluctuations. The restrictions imposed by rationality imply that the expectational errors which generate business cycles are serially uncorrelated. The serial correlation which is characteristic of business cycles can only be explained in terms of mechanisms which cause shocks to be propagated over several periods. While Lucas (1975), Blinder and Fischer (1980) and Sargent (1980) have considered alternative explanations of persistence in the demand for labour, little attention has been devoted to the question of persistence in labour supply. To a substantial extent, a demonstration of substantial persistence in labour supply decisions undercuts the plausibility of models based on a high elasticity of labour supply with respect to transitory wage movements since it is difficult to see why a long-run decision should be strongly responsive to transitory developments.

The second element of labour force dynamics which we consider is embodied in the 'persistence' hypothesis. In this view, past work experience is a key determinant of current employment status. Because of high separation costs and costs of finding new employment, those who are employed tend to remain employed. Persistence of unemployment might also be rationalized on human capital grounds. Those who are employed longer tend to accumulate more human capital, which raises the return to work in the future relative to leisure. Those out of the labour force may also develop household specific capital or commitments (i.e. children) which reduce the return to working relative to remaining outside the labour force. There is also some reason to believe that the taste for work may be affected by work experience. Such habit formation effects have been well documented in demand analysis.[2]

This aspect of labour force dynamics appears to be quite important in microeconometric studies of employment patterns. Freeman (1977) presents extensive evidence indicating that the probability of separation from employment declines with the duration of employment. This result is obtained separately for voluntary separation (quits) in Freeman (1977) and for involuntary separations (lay-offs) in Medoff (1979). Of course it is possible that this pattern results from individual heterogeneity. Those with high withdrawal possibilities are less likely to be observed as employed than those with low probabilities. Heterogeneity has been considered by Heckman (1978) and Yatchew (1977) as an explanation of persistence in labour force participation; both conclude that at least for married women, true state dependence exists. Chamberlain (1978) has devised a methodology for estimating the size of the persistence effect. He finds that, after controlling for individual differences, prior experience raises the odds of participation by a factor of seven. Other researchers have found evidence that persons with employment experience are more likely to be re-employed quickly when unemployed. Persistence effects of this magnitude imply that any measure which affects employment will have important long-run effects.

The differing macroeconomic implications of models in which timing or persistence effects predominate are highlighted by the following example. In an economy which is initially in equilibrium, the government unexpectedly undertakes expansionary policy.[3] Irrespective of whether timing or persistence predominates, the initial impact of the change is an increase in employment and labour force participation. However, timing and persistence effects are opposite in the longer run. An extreme version of the timing hypothesis would hold that individuals desire to spend a fixed proportion of their lives in the labour force which they schedule to coincide with periods of maximum opportunity. If this is the case, labour supply after the shock will be less than it would have been had the shock never occurred, as individuals 'schedule' themselves out of the labour force.

Such scheduling effects have been used to counter arguments that the fluctuations in participation that accompany changes in the unemployment rate imply a significant discouraged worker effect.[4] What appears to be discouragement is actually the effect of individuals timing their participation to coincide with periods of maximum opportunity. When timing predominates, output gains from expansionary policy are illusionary. They will be cancelled by a reduction in subsequent output as workers time their withdrawal from the labour force. Thus, models with strong intertemporal substitution effects imply that a transitory increase in the real wage will reduce subsequent labour supply. Moreover, a permanent upgrading of opportunities in a timing world implies a much smaller increase in participation than observed in the short run because scheduling effects would no longer occur.

Persistence effects, however, yield a long-run increase in labour supply. Short-run increases in employment will tend to persist as workers remain in the labour force because of habit formation, adjustment costs or human capital accumulation. Hence, concurrent changes on this view understate the total increment to output from expansionary policy. The effects of persistence described here potentially complement the process of worker upgrading discussed in Okun (1973) and Thurow (1976).[5]

The relative empirical importance of timing and persistence effects in labour supply is an issue with important implications for macroeconomic theory and policy. Both effects essentially deny the 'natural rate' hypothesis as a medium-run proposition. They imply that policy can have an extended impact on the rate of employment without repeatedly fooling economic agents, because in both views labour supply is conditioned by past employment.[6] It is this link which translates short-run policy effects into longer run impacts. As is clear from the preceding discussion, timing and persistence effects have exactly the opposite implications for the long-run direction of expansionary policy. This chapter is directed at determining their relative importance in economic fluctuations.

The next section of the chapter examines a natural experiment which potentially can shed light on the question at hand. During the Second World War, the level of female employment and participation rose precipitously. We examine the aftermath of the conflict to see whether the war had a positive or negative impact on subsequent female participation. The third section of the chapter lays the groundwork for the econometric analysis, by outlining a simple model of life-cycle labour supply which is capable of embodying both timing and persistence effects. The model developed in this section can be examined using several types of data. The fourth section of the chapter uses the model to examine the relative importance of timing and persistence effects in accounting for the time-series behaviour of the aggregate labour force participation rate. The fifth section of the chapter examines the timing and persistence effects using cross-section data. Essentially, the analysis relies on the observation that differences in unemployment over time are dominated by transitory movements, whereas geographical differences are for the most part permanent. The sixth section of the chapter summarizes the empirical results and discusses their implications.

The Impact of the Second World War

Before developing a formal model of life-cycle labour supply, it is instructive to examine the one natural experiment which history has provided. The Second World War period and its aftermath offer an ideal testing ground for timing and persistence effects. From 1940 to 1944 real output in the United States increased 46.4 per cent while the unemployment rate fell from 14.6 per cent to 1.2 per cent and averaged 1.3 per cent from 1943–5. The expansion in real output occurred at a time when large numbers of men were drawn into the Armed Forces, increasing the job prospects and potential earnings of women. After 1945, unemployment rose slightly but remained below 4.0 per cent through 1948. In the recession of 1949, the unemployment rate rose 2.1 points to 5.9 per cent. The decade of the 1940s provides a good example of a large spurt in aggregate demand followed by a return to normal growth.

In perhaps the first statement of the timing hypothesis Milton Friedman underscored the instructive quality of the World War period:

. . . the reaction to a higher wage rate expected to be temporary and then to revert to a lower level will tend to be very different than the reaction to a higher wage rate expected to be permanent. The temporarily higher wage would seem more likely to bring forth an increased quantity of labour from a fixed population than a permanently higher one, since there would be strong temptation to take advantage of the opportunity while it lasts and to buy leisure later.

An interesting case in point is the experience of the United States during World War II, when both the fraction of the population in the labour force and the average number of hours worked per week were substantially higher than during the pre-war period.[7]

Friedman provides no explicit empirical analysis of changes in participation over the period, yet it is implicit in his discussion that the Second World War marked a period of transitory wage gains which ought to be followed by an increased purchase of leisure in later years. This effect should have been accentuated by the large build-up of wealth which took place during the war. In contrast, if persistence effects were dominant market attachment would have increased with increased work experience, and the Second World War would have had a long-run positive impact on observed participation.

The issue of long-run versus transitory effects seems particularly important for the female labour force, and particularly for married women. Since almost all able males are always in the labour force, there is little variation in male participation and thus little to be learned about the impact of transitory movements in job opportunities and wages. Females participate much less than men, and their behaviour appears to be much more sensitive to labour market conditions. Moreover, because of the large increase in the Armed Forces and the consequent increase in job opportunities, women were particularly affected by the expansion of demand during the Second World War.

The impact of the Second World War on the participation of adult women is documented in table 11.1.[8] From 1890 to 1940, the participation rate of adult women aged 25–64 increased from 13.9 to 25.7 per cent, a compounded annual rate of increase of 1.2 per cent per year. In striking contrast between 1940 and 1944, the participation rate rose 23.5 per cent (25.7 to 32.5) or 6.0 per cent per year. Among married women, partipation increased 2.5 per cent per year from 1890 to 1940 (4.6 to 15.6), but a remarkable 11.3 per cent from 1940 to 1944 (15.6 to 23.9). The marked increase in participation of married women was not confined to a specific age group. After rising very slowly in the 20-year period before 1940, for example, participation by married women ages 45–64 more than doubled in the early years of the war.

The data in table 11.1 suggest that the war had a major impact on the market behaviour of adult women, particularly those who were married.[9] The data also suggest that the increase in participation was

Table 11.1 *Participation of adult women by marital status and age 1890–1950*

	1890	1900	1920	1930	1940	1944	1947	1950
(1) Adult women 25–64	13.9	16.0	19.6	21.8	25.7	32.5	28.8	31.1
(2) Married women	4.6	5.6	9.0	11.7	15.6	23.9	20.0	23.0
Marital status by age								
(3) Women 25–44	15.1	17.5	21.7	24.6	30.5	36.1	31.2	33.3
Married	—	—	9.0	13.9	16.1	28.8	—	24.3
Single	—	—	—	75.4	76.8	82.0	—	77.7
(4) Women 45–64	12.1	13.6	16.5	18.5	20.2	27.1	25.3	28.8
Married	—	—	6.2	7.3	9.0	21.4	—	19.1
Single	—	—	—	47.5	56.6	59.1	—	64.8

Source: Line 1 is a weighted average of participation rates for women aged 25–44 and 45–64 taken from census data in *Historical Statistics of the United States (1975)*, Part 1, Series D38–D39, p. 132. Populations weights were taken from the same source. The values for 1944 and 1947 are based on CPS data and have been *reduced* to make them comparable to the Census definitions. We assumed that the growth rate of participation in the CPS data 1944–50 was accurate; we thus extrapolated the growth rates back from the 1950 census value. The CPS values are 36.1 for 1944 and 32.0 for 1947.

Line 2 is series D60 from p. 133 of *Historical Statistics*. The data are for women aged 15 and over from 1890–1930, and 14 and over, 1940–50. Married refers to all married women whether husband is present or not. As in line 1, the data for 1944 and 1947 were adjusted to accord with Census definitions. The CPS values were 25.6 for 1944 and 21.4 for 1947.

The data in lines 3 and 4 were taken from Census publications as follows:

1920: US Census, 1920 vol. 4, p. 694, table 5 – data refer to married women with no distinction based on absence or presence of spouse. The entry for women aged 45–64 is the rate of participation of women 45 and over.

1930: US Census, 1930, vol. 5, General Report on Occupation, chapter 5, table 5, p. 274–data refer to all married women.

1940: US Census, 1940, *Employment and Family Characteristics of Women –* Special Report, table 1. p. 9 and table 2, p. 10. Data refer to married women, spouse present.

1950: US Census, 1950, Special Report P-E, No. 1-A, *Employment and Personal Characteristics,* table 10, p. 1A-101. Data refer to married women, spouse present. Data for 1950 suggest that the category married-spouse present dominates the married-total group. Total married participation rates were 25.8 for women 25–44, and 20.4 for women 45–64.

not short-lived. Table 11.2 presents projected values of labour force participation, based on trends estimated over the periods 1890–1930 and 1890–1940, for married women and adult women aged 25–64. Comparison of actual and predicted values confirms the long-term effects of the war. For adult women aged 25–64, the trend fitted through 1940 predicts the 1940 participation rate, but the actual rate remains above the trend throughout the subsequent decade. The results for married women are even more striking; the actual rate averages 24.7 per cent above the trend for the three time periods noted.[10]

The failure of the participation rate to fall below the trend after the transitory developments of the war had passed seems to be evidence that persistence effects dominated the effects of timing. It is important to note that both effects seem to have been present. The fact that we observe a decline in participation after 1945 suggests that a significant number of women responded to the extraordinary opportunities of that period, and then scheduled themselves out of the labour force in subsequent years. Yet there is little support for a strong version of the timing hypothesis, which would have predicted a fall of labour supply below trend after the war. It seems evident that strong peristence effects were at work. Indeed, the labour force participation rate of women, especially married women, appears to have been permanently increased by the Second World War.[11]

Two alternative explanations of the apparent positive long-run effect of the war experience deserve further comment. First, it is frequently argued that the war brought changes in social attitudes towards women in the workplace. However, these changes were caused in large part by the increase in the number of women working during the war. Changes in attitudes should be viewed as factors through which the effect of employment experience on long-run increases in participation

Table 11.2 *Predicted trends in participation 1940–1950*

	Adult women 25–64			Married women		
	Actual	*Predicted 1890–1940 trend*	*Predicted 1890–1903 trend*	*Actual*	*Predicted 1890–1940 trend*	*Predicted 1890–1930 trend*
1930	21.8	22.3	21.9	11.7	11.8	11.5
1940	25.7	25.4	24.4	15.6	15.1	14.6
1944	32.5	26.3	25.5	23.9	16.7	16.0
1947	28.8	27.3	26.4	20.0	17.9	17.2
1950	31.1	28.2	27.3	23.0	19.3	18.4

Source: Table 11.1

is mediated. That work experience during the war affected attitudes is evident in a 1944 survey conducted by the United Auto Workers.[10] Half of the women surveyed, who had never worked in a factory before the war, professed a desire to continue in a factory after the war. Over 85 per cent desired to remain employed in some capacity.[11] The view that the increased participation of women was due to a general change in attitudes rather than the conditioning effect of wartime experience is also belied by a comparison of cohort participation rates. The participation rate of women aged 20–4, who were not directly affected by the war, actually fell between 1940 and 1950. If the change in attitudes was general, it would have been expected to rise along with other participation rates.

A second explanation of the long-run increase in female participation following the war relies on the argument that reduced discrimination and increased productivity led to a rise in the permanent relative wage of women following the Second World War, and thus to an increase in participation. Insofar as this reflected human capital accumulation during the war, it is consistent with persistence effects. However, there is not much evidence that the male–female wage differential fell between the immediate pre- and post-war periods.[12]

The results presented in this section, while quite suggestive, are based on relatively fragmentary data. While there is an indication in the data that persistence effects dominated timing effects, this conclusion deserves much more careful scrutiny. In the next section we develop the model which underlies the more sophisticated econometric analysis of the timing and persistence effects presented in subsequent sections.

The Model

This section outlines the model which provides the basis for the empirical work in this study. The model follows closely that of Lucas–Rapping (1969). However, it does differ in several respects, notably the treatment of expectations and our focus on participation rather than aggregate labour supply. Because much of the focus of this study is on how past behaviour as well as expected future developments influence participation, it is necessary to employ a three-period framework, rather than the more·common two-period formulation.

Individuals are assumed to maximize an intertemporal utility function of the form:

$$U = U(c_{t-1}, l_{t-1}, c_t, l_t, c_{t+1}, l_{t+1}), \tag{11.1}$$

where c represents consumption and l represents leisure, measured as a proportion of total time endowment. The period $t-1$ is assumed to represent the entire past, and the period $t+1$ embodies the whole future. It is assumed that the individual at time t takes consumption and labour supply decisions in period $t-1$ as given.

Individuals maximize the utility function (11.1), taking as predetermined previous employment experience, and the level of assets A_t, which may be positive or negative. The solution to the maximization problem will depend on their expectations of future nominal wages, w_{t+1}, future prices p_{t+1} and the interest rate r_t. The budget constraint holds that lifetime consumption cannot exceed lifetime earnings.

Since the focus of this analysis is on the participation decision, the first-order conditions for the maximization of (11.1) are of little concern. It suffices to observe that an interior maximum with positive participation will occur if the market wage w_t exceeds the reservation wage w_t^*, the minimum wage at which an individual will supply a positive amount of labour, that is, join the labour force.

For the moment we assume, following Lucas and Rapping, that the labour market is in equilibrium, though this assumption will be relaxed subsequently. If the labour market is in equilibrium, the prevailing market wage is potentially available to any possible participants. The reservation wage will depend on tastes, past employment, future opportunities and assets. This may be written as:

$$w_t^* = f\left[(1-l_{t-1}), p_t, \frac{w_{t+1}^e}{(1+r)}, \frac{p_{t+1}^e}{(1+r)}, A_t\right]. \qquad (11.2)$$

Notice that we assume here that economic agents know the true price level at each point in time and so rule out misperceptions of the types stressed in some recent macroeconomic models.

The central question of this chapter can be posed in terms of the signs of the derivatives of w_t^* with respect to the arguments in (11.2). The standard assumption that leisure is a normal good yields the unambiguous conclusion that $f_4 > 0$, that is, an increase in wealth, *ceteris paribus*, raises the reservation wage. The signs of the effects of the other variables in (11.2) depend on the form of the utility function (11.1).

Consider first the sign of f_1, the impact of previous employment experience on current labour supply. With assets held constant, previous employment will affect the reservation wage only insofar as it affects the marginal rate of substitution between current leisure and consumption. The types of arguments usually put forward in discussions of intertemporal substitution suggest that $\partial w_t^*/\partial(1-l_{t-1})$ is negative. Increases in previous work effort raise the marginal disutility of current labour. Formulations adopting this assumption explicitly have been used by Sargent (1980) and Kydland and Prescott (1981). The effect however is theoreetically ambiguous. In the presence of adjustment costs, habit formation effects or accumulation of 'leisure capital' the sign can easily be positive.

The effects of changes in the other arguments of (11.2) can be analysed in a similar fashion. Both expected future wages and prices have uncertain effects. Increases in future wages have a negative income effect on current labour supply. The substitution effect depends on the sign of $U_{l_t l_{t+1}}$. If it is positive, the substitution effect is positive and leisure today and in the future are complements. In the case of an additively separable utility function $\partial w_t^* / \partial w_{t+1}^e$ is unambiguously negative.[13] This illustrates that past experience and future opportunities do not have symmetric effects, since past employment experience has no effect in this case. The difference arises essentially because of the income effects of future wage changes. Increases in expected future prices have a positive income effect on labour supply, and an ambiguous substitution effect depending on $U_{l_t c_{t+1}}$.

So far the theory has been developed for a single individual. People will in general differ in both their tastes and market opportunities as well as in their previous experience and asset accumulation. As a result there will exist a joint distribution of market and reservation wages. The aggregate participation rate L^s is then given by:

$$L^s = \iint_{w>w^*} g(w,w^*)dwdw^*. \qquad (11.3)$$

It is readily apparent that $\partial L^s / \partial w > 0$: an increase in wages available to all workers will unambiguously raise the participation rate. The so-called 'added worker' effect cannot exist in this model. Essentially, this is because at zero labour supply, increases in the wage do not change income. Income effects could be brought in if labour supply was modelled as the result of joint maximization by individuals within a family. They may also arise from changes in non-contemporaneous wages.

It follows from (11.3) that the participation rate is a function of the wage level and the determinants of the shadow wage. Recognizing that the labour supply relation is homogeneous of degree zero in wages and prices leads to the labour supply function:

$$L^s = f\left((1-l_{t+1}), \frac{w_t}{p_t}, \frac{w_{t+1}^e}{p_t(1+r)}, \frac{p_{t+1}^e}{p_t(1+r)}, \frac{A_t}{p_t}\right), \qquad (11.4)$$

where L^s is the function of the population in the labour force. For convenience we assume a logarithmic functional form. Equation (11.4) may then be rewritten as:

$$\ln L^s = \beta_0 + \beta_1 \ln (1-l_{t-1}) + \beta_2 \ln \left(\frac{w_t}{p_t}\right) + \beta_3 \ln \left(\frac{w_t+_1^e}{p_t(1+r)}\right)$$

$$+ \beta_4 \ln \left(\frac{p_{t+1}^e}{p_t(1+r)}\right) + \beta_5 \ln \frac{A_t}{p_t} \tag{11.5}$$

Equation (11.5) differs from the Lucas–Rapping formulation in that the term $(1-l_{t-1})$ is included, reflecting the assumed dependence of the demand for leisure on leisure enjoyed during the preceding period. While such a dependence would seem to be a clear property of the Lucas–Rapping model, it is lost in the translation into their estimating equation. The term $(1-l_{t-1})$ does appear in their equation but only as a result of a Koyck transformation. While they expect and obtain a positive impact of previous labour supply, it is clear from the above discussion that the effect is actually ambiguous. A strong form of the timing hypothesis would predict a negative effect of lagged labour supply (apart from its role as a distributed lag generator).

At this point, it is useful to consider the expected signs of $\beta_1, \ldots, \beta_5$. The signs depend on the relative importance of persistence and timing elements in fluctuations in labour supply. A key parameter is β_1, the elasticity of current labour supply with respect to past employment experience. Sufficiently large intertemporal substitution effects would insure that $\beta_1 < 0$ so that increases in experience reduce subsequent participation. On the other hand, persistence effects imply $\beta_1 > 0$ so that increases in employment experience raise the participation rate. The coefficient of β_2 is expected to be positive, as increases in comtemporaneous real wages raise the attractiveness of seeking work. The sign of β_3 depends on the relative size of timing and persistence effects. If timing elements predominate, β_3 will be negative as increases in expected wages cause labour supply to decline because of intertemporal substitution effects. In the context of a model like that of Lucas and Rapping, one would expect that $\beta_2 + \beta_3 \approx 0$, since the long-run wage elasticity of labour supply is expected to be small. If adjustment costs or capital accumulation effects cause labour supply decisions to have a permanent character, the sign of β_3 will be positive. The sign of β_4 is ambiguous while β_5 is expected to be negative.

Equation (11.5) as it stands is a labour supply curve. If the labour market were always in equilibrium, it could be estimated directly using the employment ratio (proportion of the population who are employed) as the dependent variable. If, however, the labour market does not always clear, the level of employment cannot be taken as a measure of desired labour supply. However, a measure of supply is provided by the labour force participation rate, the proportion of the population looking for work or working. This variable is the measure of labour supply used in this study. However, estimates using employment as the dependent variable are also discussed.

It is important to be clear about the issues involved in choosing between the employment and participation rate as dependent variables in equation (11.5). Lucas and Rapping take the position that an equation like (11.5) characterizes the level of employment, not the participation rate. On their hypothesis, workers who choose not to work because of a transitory decline in wages show up as unemployed and so are counted as labour force participants. Thus their argument implies that studying the labour force participation rate would obscure the important intertemporal substitution effects of wage changes. Although estimates of equation (11.5) using employment are presented below, we regard the Lucas–Rapping interpretation of the unemployment rate as problematic for several reasons. First, it provides no explanation for the fluctuations in the participation rate which account for a sizeable part of observed employment fluctuations. Second, unemployment is defined as inability to find work at prevailing wages. Individuals who are intertemporally substituting out of employment presumably know the prevailing wage, and do not desire work. They should therefore not report themselves as unemployed. Finally, our previous analysis (Clark and Summers, 1979) of individual unemployment experience suggests that the assumption of continuous labour market equilibrium is very problematic.

Once the possibility that the labour market may not clear is recognized, it is necessary to modify equation (11.5). When involuntary unemployment exists, the assumption that all who want them can get jobs at the prevailing wage is no longer appropriate. Individual decisions regarding labour supply will be affected by the knowledge that search costs are higher when unemployment is higher. Since the mean duration of a completed spell of employment in the United States is only about 20 months (Clark and Summers, 1979), relatively small changes in the duration of pre-employment search can have a large impact on the return to seeking employment. By increasing the duration of search as well as by reducing the pool of good jobs, and increasing the risk of layoff, unemployment discourages labour supply. We thus include the unemployment rate as an additional explanatory variable in some of our empirical work. In the next two sections we estimate alternative forms of (11.5) using both aggregate time-series and cross-section data for different demographic groups.

Time-series Evidence

This section describes the estimation of (11.5) using time-series data. Before the model can be estimated, it is necessary to develop operational measures of the variables. Both the proxy for previous employment experience and the measurement of expectations of inflation and the real wage require discussion. In equation (11.5) previous experience is represented simply by $(1-l_{t-1})$. This term is supposed to represent the entire past experience of a population group. Using simply the previous year's employment experience would be inappropriate since the logic of both the timing and persistence effects suggests current labour supply is conditioned by a longer history. We therefore follow the work of Houthakker and Taylor (1970) in developing a measure of the 'stock' of past employment. We assume that the labour supply of a cohort depends on a set of variables Z (such as those contained in (11.5)) and on its past employment experience. Past employment experience is assumed to be represented by:

$$E_t^* = \sum_{i=1}^{\infty} \lambda^{i-1} E_{t-1} = \frac{E_{t-1}}{1-\lambda L}, \qquad (11.6)$$

where L is the lag operator. Since participation is a function of this stock and the set of variables Z it is clear that:

$$PR_t = Z_t \beta + \beta_1 E_t^*, \qquad (11.7)$$

where PR_t is the participation rate. Using (11.6) the model can be expressed in terms of observables as:

$$PR_t = Z_t \beta - Z_{t-1} \lambda \beta + \lambda PR_{t-1} + \beta_1 E_{t-1}. \qquad (11.8)$$

Alternatively, as discussed in the previous section, the employment ratio could be taken as the dependent variable. Using equation (11.5) and (11.8), and appropriate measures for participation, employment and Z, the most general specification of our estimating equation can be written

$$PR_t = \beta_0 + \beta_1 E_{t-1} + \beta_2 W_t + \beta_{3t} W_f^e + \beta_{4t} P_f^e + \beta_5 t + \beta_6 UM_t + \lambda PR_{t-1}$$
$$-\lambda[\beta_2 W_{t-1} + \beta_{3_{t-1}} W_f^e + \beta_{4_{t-1}} P_f^e + \beta_5(t-1) + \beta_6 UM_{t-1}] + v_t, \qquad (11.9)$$

where t indicates times, W_t is the contemporaneous real wage, $_t W_f^e$ and $_t P_f^e$ are expected future discounted wages and prices, E_{t-1} is the ratio of employment to population in the previous period, UM_t is a measure of the unemployment rate and v_t is an error term in M.[14] The time trend has been included to reflect the possible influence of slowly changing determinants not captured by other included variables. In this formulation, the coefficient β_1 measures the persistence of labour supply, while λ reflects the lag in formation of the habit stock. The long-run impact of an increase in employment experience is $\beta_1/(1-\lambda)$. This may be interpreted in two different ways. It represents the increase in the participation rate at time t, if employment in all previous periods were raised by one unit. It also can be interpreted as the sum over all future periods of the increases in participation arising from a one-shot increase in employment.

Equation (11.6) gives us a way of measuring the employment stock and deriving the estimating equation in (11.9); the second issue which must be considered is the development of measures of expected wages and prices. Most standard econometric procedures seem inappropriate because theory suggests that labour supply should depend on the expected discounted value of wages and prices over a long horizon. Our procedure for modelling expectations begins with an estimate of a set of vector autoregressions relating wages, prices and real output.[15] These vector autoregressions are then simulated using data for each year in the sample to generate forecasts of wages and prices for the succeeding 5 years. These variables, $_t w^e_{t+1}$, are then adjusted to an after-tax basis and discounted back to year t, using year t's municipal bond rate.[16] They are then averaged to form proxies for $w^e_{t+1}/p_t(1+r)$ and $p^e_{t+1}/\dot{p}_t(1+r)$, which in their logarithmic form we have labelled $_t W^e_f$ and $_t P^e_f$, respectively.

This procedure is somewhat arbitrary in its choice of horizon and in the specification of the vector autoregressions. However, it seems to be the only computationally feasible way of handling the modelling of expectations which are more than one period ahead. Rational expectations techniques of the sort developed by McCallum (1976) are not applicable in the current example because of the quasi-differencing involved in moving to equation (11.8).

The data used in the actual estimation cover the period 1951–81. We have chosen to use annual data because timing and persistence effects are likely to be badly confounded with seasonal fluctuations in higher frequency data. Our measures of the participation rate and employment ratio are age-adjusted rates calculated as fixed weight averages of age-specific rates. This age-adjusted participation rate is used to avoid biases introduced by the changing age structure of the population.

In the results reported below, we have omitted assets from the estimating equation. Like others before us (e.g. Lucas and Rapping, 1969), we found assets to have no significant relationship to participation. This conclusion is based on an assets measure which includes the real value of household financial holdings, excluding equity. A variety of other assets measures which included equity, housing and social security wealth were tried with little change in the results.

Several econometric issues arise in the estimation of equation (11.9). First, the equation is highly non-linear in the parameters, necessitating non-linear estimation. Second, the error term v_t is likely to be serially correlated. Even if the error term in equation (11.7) relating participation to Z and E^* were not serially correlated, the transformation of E^* involved in deriving the estimating equation would induce moving average errors. Serial correlation in the error term is particularly serious in this case because both lagged participation and employment are included in the regression equation. Since there is no reason to suppose that the error in (11.8) follows a simple autoregressive scheme, the usual corrections (e.g. Cochrane–Orcutt) are not appropriate. We have chosen to estimate the equation using two-stage non-linear least squares, treating both lagged participation and employment as endogenous. The instrument list includes a time trend, a squared trend, real Federal government spending, the rate of money growth and the real *per capita* stock of non-residential capital, along with the included exogenous variables. In addition, to allow for simultaneity, the contemporaneous wage is treated as endogenous.

A third econometric difficulty is collinearity, which frequently precludes disentangling estimates of λ, which determines the mean lag of the 'past employment' effect, and β_1, the impact effect of changes in employment experience. Frequently, the estimated values of λ lie outside the range $0 \leqq \lambda \leqq 1$, and so the equations are not meaningful. Therefore, in many of the equations reported below, the value of λ is constrained to the a priori plausible value of 0.9. None of the qualitative conclusions were affected by the imposition of this constraint. In particular, all of the conclusions regarding the effects of transitory wage changes are wholly unaffected by the choice of λ.

Table 11.3 presents estimates of several variants of equation (11.9) using the log of the participation rate as the dependent variable. The results do not suggest that timing effects have an important role to play in explaining cyclical fluctuations. The estimated elasticity of labour supply with respect to a transitory wage change is always small and sometimes negative. Nor is there any clear evidence of a negative relationship between expected future wages and labour supply, as predicted by models which emphasize timing effects. No clear conclusions emerge about the effects of changes in the price of future consumption. It is noteworthy that the increases in the unemployment rate of mature men do appear to reduce the participation rate, as theory predicts.

The data provide weak support for the importance of persistence in explaining fluctuations in labour supply. It is not possible to interpret the estimated effect of employment experience in equations (3)–(5) of table 11.3 because the estimated value of λ lies outside its permissible range. In equation (8), where a time trend is not included, the estimated effect of the 'employment stock' variable is both substantively and statistically significant. However, when a time trend is included as in equations (6) and (7), the 'employment stock' coefficient remains

Table 11.3 *Timing and persistence effects in time-series participation equations*[a]

Equation	CONS	W	W*	P*	UM_t	TIME	E_{t-1}	λ	SEE	DW
1	4.975 (0.320)	−0.084 (0.100)	0.009 (0.039)	—	—	—	—	—	0.005	1.48
2	6.620 (0.815)	−0.052 (0.099)	−0.157 (0.122)	0.186 (0.125)	—	—	—	—	0.005	1.72
3	3.814 (0.060)	−0.186 (0.056)	−0.012 (0.041)	—	—	0.007 (0.001)	0.470 (0.234)	−0.501 (0.246)	0.009	1.125
4	3.777 (0.089)	−0.199 (0.060)	−0.030 (0.054)	—	−0.001 (0.003)	0.008 (0.002)	0.326 (0.293)	−0.352 (0.308)	0.008	0.920
5	4.232 (0.052)	0.219 (0.426)	−0.090 (0.454)	0.135 (0.459)	—	—	0.128 (0.444)	−0.127 (0.437)	0.016	0.377
6	0.297 (0.428)	−0.321 (0.179)	0.066 (0.058)	—	—	0.009 (0.005)	0.019 (0.110)	0.9[b]	0.006	1.898
7	0.301 (0.399)	−0.287 (0.181)	0.027 (0.062)	—	−0.002 (0.002)	0.009 (0.004)	0.018 (0.102)	0.9[b]	0.006	1.974
8	−0.584 (0.518)	−0.028 (0.162)	−0.194 (0.466)	0.310 (0.520)	—	—	0.243 (0.123)	0.9[b]	0.006	1.820

[a] Numbers in parentheses are standard errors.
[b] The parameter was set equal to the value indicated.

positive but becomes insignificant. Estimates using the employment–population ratio as a dependent variable are reported in table 11.4. The results are qualitatively similar to those obtained using the participation rate as a dependent variable. Here the evidence of persistence effects is very weak. Even when the time trend is omitted as in equation (6) of the table, the employment stock variable is statistically insignificant. Not surprisingly, the cyclical indicator, UM_t, enters the employment equations in a highly significant way.

The time-series evidence presented here suggests that transitory variations in the perceived real wage have little effect on the rate of labour force participation. We find no indication in the data of the strong intertemporal substitution effects which are the basis of classical macromodels. These findings on the effect of transitory wage changes are consistent with the positive impact of lagged employment found in table 11.3. While the quality of the evidence on lagged employment precludes strong conclusions, the results suggest that work may be habit-forming. Clearly, if experience in employment persists so that the decision to work is a relatively long-term commitment, it is not surprising that transitory wage changes have no discernible effect on labour supply.

These results conflict quite sharply with those of Hall (1980), who finds that the data support the intertemporal substitution hypothesis. Part of the conflict may lie in Hall's inclusion of fluctuations in hours per worker. The most serious problem, however, is Hall's measurement of the 'intertemporal substitution parameter'. He assumes that labour supply decisions are driven only by the price of future consumption in terms of today's labour. It is difficult to see what utility function would have this property in which the current price of consumption and future price of leisure are irrelevant. Our findings are consistent with the generally negative results obtained by Altonji (1982), and Mankiw et al. (1982) regarding the intertemporal substitution hypothesis.

Cross-section Evidence

The comparison of the relationships between labour market variables which are observed in time-series and cross-section data can shed light on the importance of timing and persistence effects. In particular, this section shows that recognizing the distinction between transitory and permanent effects embodied in the two hypotheses provides a framework for reconciling the large differences between cross-sectional and time-series estimates of the relationship between unemployment and participation rates. The conflict between these two types of evidence emerged in the early 1960s when several studies found large discouraged worker effects using decennial census data on local

Table 11.4 Timing and persistence effects in time-series employment equations[a]

Equation	CONS	W	W*	P*	UM_t	TIME	E_{t-1}	λ	SEE	DW
1	4.183 (0.041)	0.020 (0.114)	0.158 (0.101)	—	—	—	—	—	0.013	1.94
2	4.197 (0.090)	-0.184 (0.259)	0.434 (0.319)	-0.235 (0.319)	—	—	—	—	0.013	1.91
3	0.128 (2.167)	-0.215 (0.636)	-3.043 (1.966)	3.056 (2.010)	-0.028 (0.010)	0.042 (0.014)	-0.003 (0.497)	0.888 (0.084)	0.021	1.545
4	3.662 (0.387)	0.540 (0.613)	-0.808 (0.922)	0.950 (0.980)	—	0.005 (0.006)	0.261 (0.897)	-0.258 (0.955)	0.018	1.512
5	3.967 (0.021)	-0.051 (0.058)	0.034 (0.057)	-0.169 (0.118)	—	—	-4.121 (2.351)	4.154 (2.346)	0.012	1.801
6	-0.490 (0.994)	-0.564 (0.358)	0.508 (0.457)	-0.166 (0.552)	—	—	0.220 (0.239)	0.9[b]	0.016	2.022
7	0.265 (1.013)	-0.591 (0.422)	0.298 (0.138)	—	—	0.008 (0.011)	0.026 (0.259)	0.9[b]	0.015	2.033
8	1.260 (0.326)	-0.305 (0.096)	-0.009 (0.053)	—	-0.015 (0.001)	0.009 (0.002)	0.05 (0.085)	0.9[b]	0.006	1.490

[a] Numbers in parentheses are standard errors.
[b] Parameter has been set equal to value indicated.

participation and unemployment rates, while other studies found very small effects using time-series data (Long, 1958; Barth, 1968; Bowen and Finnegan, 1969).

Attempts to reconcile the divergent results have generally focused on possible biases in the cross-section evidence. In his often-cited review of the evidence Mincer (1966) conjectured that cross-section estimates were biased by omission of migration, seasonal differences across SMSAs in census timing and common errors in the rate of participation and unemployment which give rise to a spurious association. Mincer also noted but did not pursue the permanence of state unemployment differentials. Bowen and Finnegan (1969) have examined each of these possibilities and suggest that none can satisfactorily explain the difference between the two sets of estimates.[17] More recent attempts to resolve the anomaly (e.g. Fleisher and Rhodes, 1976) have also been unpersuasive.[18]

These results suggest that cross-section and time-series estimates cannot be reconciled by pointing to biases in the cross-section data. A potentially more fruitful approach is to recognize the fundamental differences between intertemporal and interspatial variations in unemployment. At any point in time in any labour market the rate of unemployment is composed of both a permanent and a transitory component. In cross-section data, most variation in unemployment is presumably due to variation in the permanent component across regions. This is in contrast to the aggregate time-series data where variation in the transitory component is likely to be dominant. Cast in these terms, the cross-section data provide estimates of the long-run or permanent effect of unemployment, while transitory effects are captured with time-series data.

At this point, it is important to be clear about the interpretation of the measured unemployment rate. In this section, we adopt the 'traditional' interpretation, which holds that the labour market does not clear and that the unemployment rate affects the attractiveness of seeking work. It is then meaningful to speak of the effect of changes in differences in unemployment rates on labour force participation rates. We prefer the traditional interpretation of the unemployment rate to that of Lucas and Rapping for several reasons. Most important, the substantial permanent component in the differences between local unemployment rates suggests that they are not consequences of transitory wage movement. In addition, the evidence that participation and unemployment rates are negatively correlated is difficult to account for in the classical view. Indeed, in its strong form, it lacks an explanation for fluctuations in the participation rate. Other results described below also incline us towards the 'traditional' interpretation of unemployment fluctuations.

In order to reconcile the time-series and cross-section estimates, it is necessary to examine the relationship between transitory and permanent effects, and to establish the conditions under which the permanent effect dominates. This is precisely the issue discussed in the third section which distinguishes the timing and persistence effects. There we found that persistence effects imply that employment in previous periods raises current participation. Short-run effects persist. If persistence effects predominate, the response of labour supply to permanent changes in demand should exceed the response to transitory changes. This prediction, which is borne out by the data, is not consistent with strong forms of the timing hypothesis, which imply that the response to transitory fluctuations should exceed the response to permanent changes.

It thus would seem that the predominance of persistence effects receives substantial support in the comparison of cross-section and time-series evidence. Similar support emerges from a comparison of transitory and permanent effects using cross-section data. Use of cross-section data provides a strong test of the relative importance of timing and perisistence effects since the two views of labour force dynamics have sharply different implications for the appropriate demand variable in cross-sectional equations. The timing view holds that the important determinant of participation is the deviation of demand from its normal level. When it is above its normal level, workers schedule themselves into the labour force, leaving when it falls below normal. The persistence view, on the other hand, implies that the normal level of demand is the appropriate variable since workers make labour supply decisions on a long-term basis.

The model embodied in this discussion can easily be made explicit. It is assumed that the level of demand may be represented by ER, the proportion of those desiring work who have it $(1-$the unemployment rate). We postulate that participation in region i, PR_i, depends on the permanent level of demand, ER_i^p, and the level of transitory demand, ER_i^t, defined as $(ER_i - ER_i^p)$. A simple characterization of the participation equation is given by

$$PR_i = f(ER_i^p, ER_i^t, Z_i) \qquad (11.10)$$

where Z_i is a vector of variables other than demand conditions which influence the participation rate.

As the discussion in the preceding paragraph makes clear, the persistence view predicts that $f_{ER_i^p}$ will be large while $f_{ER_i^t}$ is not important; the timing hypothesis has the opposite implication. The distinction between the two hypotheses may be drawn more sharply by considering their implications for a change in the normal rate of employment holding constant the current rate. It is apparent from equation (11.10) that

$$\frac{\partial PR_t}{\partial ER_t^p} = f_{ER_i^g} - f_{ER_i^t}. \tag{11.11}$$

The preceding discussion implies that this expression should be positive if persistence dominates and negative under the timing hypothesis. Intuitively, with current opportunities held constant, a decline in future opportunities will increase labour supplied by a worker who can easily substitute leisure across periods. On the other hand, it will make current employment less attractive to a worker for whom leisure is complementary across periods.

These implications of the timing and persistence hypotheses are clearly subject to empirical verification. To test the conditions laid out above we have estimated a basic labour supply model using the data from the 1970 US Census on participation and selected determinants by state. Time-series data (1966–74) on unemployment by state were taken from the *Manpower Report of the President*. These series are based on a combination of data on unemployment insurance, payrolls and, for some states, the monthly CPS. In addition to variables measuring the permanent and transitory effects of unemployment we have included measures of the permanent or expected real wage as well as structural and demographic variables which affect participation through the shadow wage. As a first approximation we assume that variation in nominal wages across states reflects primarily variation in the permanent component of real wages, so that the level of prices is excluded from the model.[19] For women the basic equation is:

$$\begin{aligned}
\ln PR_{ij} = {} & \alpha_1 + \alpha_2 \ln(WM)_i + \alpha_3 \ln(WW)_i + \alpha_4 EDW_i + \alpha_5 RW_i \\
& + \alpha_6 RBW_i + \alpha_7 URB_i + \alpha_8 MIGR_i + \alpha_9 C6_i + \alpha_{10} \ln(ER)^p_i \\
& + \alpha_{11} \ln(ER)^t_i + v_{ij},
\end{aligned} \tag{11.12}$$

where the variables are defined as follows:

PR_{ij} = participation rate of the jth demographic group in the ith state
WM = median earnings of men 18 and over
WW = median earnings of females 18 and over
EDW = median years of schooling – females 18 and over
RW = proportion of females in the population 16 and over
RBW = proportion of non-White females in the population 16 and over
URB = proportion of the population residing in Census urban areas
$MIGR$ = total net migration 1960–70 as a proportion of 1970 population
$C6$ = proportion of families with a child less than 6 living at home

ER=state aggregate employment rate
$\ln (ER)^p$=average of $\ln (ER)$ for 1966–74
$\ln (ER)^t=[\ln (ER)-\ln(ER)^p]$.

Letting EDM_i indicate median years of schooling of males 18 and over, and RBM, the proportion of non-White males in the population, the basic equation for the male group is:

$$\ln PR_{ij}=\beta_1+\beta_2\ln (WM)_i+\beta_3EDM_i+\beta_4RBM_i+\beta_5URB_i \\ +\beta_6MIGR_i+\beta_7\ln (ER)\,^p_i+\beta_8 \ln(ER)\,^t_i+u_{ij}. \tag{11.13}$$

The expected effects of the structural and demographic variables included in equations (11.12) and (11.13) have been dealt with at length in a variety of places and will receive only brief mention here. Education and degree of urbanization are expected to have a positive effect on participation through their effects on labour force attachment and the costs of transportation. Migration is expected to raise participation in the receiving areas and lower participation in states with net outflow. The proportion of Black men (women) in the population is included to control for well-known differences in participation behaviour between Blacks and Whites. The variable is expected to have a positive sign in the female equation, and a negative sign in the equation for males. The proportion of women in the population is included as a measure of potential competition among women; the expected sign is negative. The proportion of women with a child under 6 is expected to raise the shadow wage and thus to reduce participation. The expected sign of own-wage variables ($\ln WW_i$ in (11.12) and $\ln WM_i$ in (11.13)) is positive. Male earnings have been included in the female equation to allow for the effects of joint decision making in the family and are expected to reduce female participation. Female earnings on the other hand are specified to have no effect on male participation.

The differing implications of the timing and persistence views are captured in the coefficients of $\ln (ER)^p_1$ and in $\ln (ER)^t_i$. Using the female equation, under the timing hypothesis α_{11} is expected to be positive and to dominate α_{10}, so that $\alpha_{10}-\alpha_{11}<0$. The persistence hypothesis, on the other hand, implies that permanent effects are dominant so that $\alpha_{10}-\alpha_{11}>0$. In addition to the basic equations (11.12) and (11.13) we also have estimated a specification which allows no role for transitory effects so that $\alpha_{11}=\beta_8=0$.

Estimates of the basic model for both men and women are presented in table 11.5. The principal coefficients of interest, α_{10} and α_{11} (β_7 and β_8 for men) are presented in rows 9 and 10; for convenience we have computed the sum of the coefficients in row 11. The results provide clear support for the importance of persistence effects. The long-run effects of unemployment clearly dominate the transitory effects in virtually all demographic groups. The difference between the permanent and transitory components is less than zero in only three cases, and in no case is the negative coefficient significant. We find the strongest evidence of the persistence effects among women for whom the timing phenomenon was expected to be particularly relevant. In each of the female age groups, except women over 65, the transitory employment rate is totally insignificant, often entering with a negative sign. In contrast, the permanent effects are large and significant. For women 45–64, for example, the permanent effect (α_{10}) is 2.46, which implies that a decline in the permanent rate of unemployment from 0.06 to 0.05 would raise the participation rate by 2.46 per cent. The transitory effect for this group, on the other hand, is −3.15, clearly reflecting the dominance of the permanent employment rate which enters negatively in the deviation. The total effect of the permanent rate is thus 5.61. Similar positive effects are found for younger women as for women 45–64. Only among women over 65 does the timing hypothesis find any support and here the estimates are not particularly precise. The sum of the permanent and transitory effects is −0.10, which may be marginally important in determining the participation behaviour of women over the age of 65. A somewhat stronger finding for men over 65 leads to the paradoxical conclusion that the timing view, a construct based on life-cycle considerations, finds its support only among those nearing the end of their adult lives.

The results in rows 10 and 11 of table 11.5 clearly suggest that changes in the expected rate of unemployment strongly influence the participation decisions of most demographic groups. This conclusion is buttressed in row 12 of table 11.5, which presents estimates of the effect of unemployment assuming no transitory effects (i.e. $\alpha_{11}=0$). Among most demographic groups the expected rate of employment enters significantly with a relatively large positive coefficient. Differences in the size of the employment effect within and across demographic groups are consistent with the theoretical role of unemployment laid out in the third section. We find that unemployment is more important in those groups where employment durations are short. Thus within the male and female categories teenagers are more sensitive to variations in unemployment than are older persons. Similarly, within age groups, women tend to be more responsive than men. It should be noted, however, that the coefficients for the older adult men are far from trivial. We estimate that a 1 point decline in the long-term unemployment rate (0.06 to 0.05) leads to a 0.6 per cent increase in the participation of men 25–44, and a 1.3 per cent increase in the rate of participation of men 45–64.

The evidence on the relative importance of timing and persistence in the cross-section data relies on the use of the unemployment rate to capture market opportunities. We have already discussed some of our

Table 11.5 *Estimates of the basic cross-section model for men and women (standard errors in parentheses)*

	Male					Female				
	16-19	20-4	25-44	45-64	65+	16-19	20-4	25-44	45-64	65+
1 Male earnings (WM)	0.19 (0.13)	-0.03 (0.07)	0.06 (0.01)	0.17 (0.04)	0.31 (0.21)	0.42 (0.24)	-0.07 (0.11)	-0.39 (0.11)	-0.17 (0.16)	0.04 (0.24)
2 Female earnings (WW)	—	—	—	—	—	0.34 (0.20)	0.40 (0.09)	0.41 (0.09)	0.53 (0.13)	0.55 (0.20)
3 Education (EDM, EDW)	0.05 (0.04)	-0.0007 (0.02)	0.004 (0.005)	0.03 (0.01)	0.17 (0.07)	0.06 (0.08)	-0.01 (0.04)	0.03 (0.04)	0.06 (0.05)	0.21 (0.08)
4 Proportion female (RW)	—	—	—	—	—	2.28 (3.02)	1.65 (1.41)	-0.04 (1.38)	4.13 (1.99)	0.52 (2.93)
5 Proportion Black (RBW, RBM)	-0.44 (0.28)	0.02 (0.14)	-0.05 (0.03)	-0.16 (0.08)	0.53 (0.44)	-1.59 (0.52)	-0.30 (0.24)	0.41 (0.24)	-0.41 (0.34)	0.37 (0.50)
6 Urbanization (URB)	-0.0009 (0.001)	-0.0003 (0.0007)	-0.0004 (0.0001)	-0.0003 (0.0004)	-0.004 (0.002)	-0.0002 (0.002)	0.00003 (0.0009)	-0.0004 (0.0009)	-0.001 (0.001)	-0.005 (0.002)
7 Children under 6 (C6)	— (0.01)	— (0.005)	— (0.005)	— (0.007)	— (0.01)	0.008	0.004	0.004	0.01	0.02
8 Net migration (MIGR)	0.32 (0.11)	0.21 (0.06)	0.02 (0.01)	-0.05 (0.03)	-0.27 (0.18)	-0.08 (0.19)	0.006 (0.09)	0.23 (0.09)	-0.007 (0.12)	-0.33 (0.18)
9 Permanent employment rate (ER^p)	2.56 (1.09)	-0.38 (0.56)	0.63 (0.12)	1.33 (0.30)	3.29 (1.72)	5.97 (1.78)	2.96 (0.83)	2.46 (0.82)	2.31 (1.18)	2.17 (1.73)
10 Transitory employment rate (ER^t)	-3.26 (2.11)	-0.42 (1.08)	-0.05 (0.23)	0.12 (0.58)	4.62 (3.33)	0.85 (3.37)	-0.07 (1.57)	-3.15 (1.55)	-0.29 (2.22)	2.27 (3.27)
11 Full permanent effect (line 9–line 10)	5.82 (2.33)	0.04 (1.19)	0.68 (0.25)	1.21 (0.65)	-1.32 (3.68)	5.12 (3.82)	3.03 (1.78)	5.61 (1.75)	2.60 (2.52)	-0.10 (3.71)
12 Permanent employment rate (ER^p)[a]	2.64 (1.11)	0.37 (0.55)	0.63 (0.12)	1.33 (0.30)	3.18 (1.74)	5.97 (1.76)	2.96 (0.82)	2.45 (0.85)	2.31 (1.16)	2.17 (1.72)
R^2	0.52	0.26	0.65	0.74	0.33	0.71	0.67	0.76	0.60	0.60
SEE	0.09	0.04	0.009	0.02	0.14	0.12	0.06	0.06	0.08	0.12

[a] Line 12 reports the coefficient of ER^p when ER^t is excluded from the equation.

reasons for preferring this kind of interpretation in the third section. But there are two additional issues that need to be addressed. In the first place, classical models would call for the use of permanent and transitory real wages rather than unemployment rates as explanatory variables. The results of including real wages in time-series regressions have been discussed in the preceding section. We have made an attempt to gauge their effect in the cross-section analysis by calculating real wages by state. We used the BLS Standard of Living Estimates for 35 cities to construct state price indices; wages were based on data for manufacturing by state. Both permanent and transitory wage variations had only minor effects on state participation and employment rates. Therefore the unemployment rate has been used as a proxy for the attractiveness of entering and remaining in the labour force. The role of wages and prices in explaining cross-section differences in participation remains an important area for future research.

A second problem concerns the effect of omitted variables. Although we have included a number of structural characteristics of each state in the equation, there is always the possibility that omitted common third factors account for the observed correlations between unemployment and participation rates. We explored this issue by using other variables such as the employment–population ratio in place of the unemployment rate. This had little effect on the qualitative conclusions.

The analysis in this section has shown the predominance of the expected or natural level of demand in explaining participation differences across states. Except for those aged over 65, there is no evidence for the notion that transitory changes in opportunities play a significant role in decisions about participating in the labour force. These results suggest that a rise in expected opportunities, holding current opportunities constant, will call forth an increase in participation, a response consistent with the implications of persistence in labour supply. The notion that individuals schedule their labour supply according to variations in current opportunities finds little support in these data.

Conclusions

The results in this chapter suggest the importance of persistence in labour market decisions. A variety of types of evidence suggest that previous employment experience has an important effect on subsequent labour supply. This implies that labour supply decisions are not very responsive to transitory changes in employment opportunities. While no one of the tests presented in the chapter can be regarded as decisive, in conjunction they suggest that persistence elements are more important than timing elements in explaining fluctuations in either the number of persons employed or the number participating in the labour force. Our results leave open the possibility that timing elements are important in explaining cyclical fluctuations in average hours worked and in work effort.

Acceptance of these conclusions has important implications for both macroeconomic theory and policy. These results cast doubt on the medium-run relevance of the natural rate hypothesis. Because policy affects the level of employment in the short run, it has a long-run effect on the position of the labour supply schedule. Workers drawn into the labour force by cyclical upturns tend to remain even after the boom has ended. The converse is true for shocks which reduce employment. At this point, the quantitative importance of these effects is uncertain, although our interpretation of the evidence reported here suggests that they are quite important.

This chapter has only begun to touch on the implications of alternative life-cycle labour supply models for macroeconomic questions. Both the empirical and theoretical work described in this chapter could usefully be extended in several directions. It would be valuable to develop tests which can distinguish different aspects of persistence. In particular, the model developed here completely ignores the accumulation of human capital. The explicit inclusion of human capital in the model would provide a more satisfactory basis for rationalizing the observed persistence in labour supply, and would also suggest relationships between employment experience and subsequent wage levels. It would be valuable to extend the empirical work reported here by attempting direct estimation of utility function parameters using recently developed rational expectations techniques. Unsuccessful estimates of a relatively simple utility function which takes no account of persistence effects are presented in Mankiw et al. (1982). While these extensions would be valuable, it is unlikely that they would call into question the main conclusion reached here that a proper theory of labour supply must come to grips with the persistence of participation.

NOTES

Originally published in *Review of Economic Studies* 1982, XLIX, 825–44.

1 At the conference where this chapter was first presented we became aware of the important paper by Altonji (1982). His work provides a comprehensive set of econometric tests of what this chapter calls the timing hypothesis.

2 The most extensive empirical work is reported in Houthakker and Taylor (1970). Theoretical analysis is surveyed by Pollak (1978).

3 In a Keynesian framework, this may be interpreted as temporarily increasing aggregate demand, and increasing employment opportunities. In the context of a classical model, it can be thought of as an unexpected increase in the money stock, leading to a transitory increase in the perceived real wage. In

either case the expansionary policy is taken to be temporary in its direct effect.

4 For a recent statement of this argument, see Wachter (1977).

5 It is tempting but inaccurate to regard persistence effects as arguments in support of expansionary policy. If the economy is initially at an optimal Walrasian equilibrium, locking additional workers into employment is not an efficiency gain. Of course this conclusion does not hold if the 'natural rate' of unemployment is inefficiently high, as Phelps (1972) suggests is likely to be the case. If, as has been suggested, work is habit-forming, no clear basis exists for welfare judgments.

6 Such hysteresis effects in which the equilibrium level of employment is affected by the transition path have been discussed by Phelps (1972), but have, to our knowledge, received no empirical attention.

7 Milton Friedman, *Price Theory: A Provisional Text*, 1962, p. 200.

8 Ideally one ought to look at the participation of women of different ages rather than different cohorts. Thus, for example, the appropriate way to examine the impact of the War on 50-year-old women is to look at 46-year-olds in 1940 and 56-year-olds in 1950. Available data, however, precludes such an analysis.

9 This result was also obtained using employment instead of labour force participation as a measure of labour supply. It should be noted that the participation rates for married women have not been adjusted for differences in fertility. As others have noted, adjusting for fertility would accentuate the divergence between actual rates and extrapolation of 1930–40 trends (see Bowen and Finnegan, 1969, pp. 200–1). Fertility in 1940 was exceptionally low, while 1950 was part of the post-war baby boom. It may be that a fertility correction is inappropriate since fertility is jointly determined with labour supply.

10 It might be argued that the purportedly permanent shifts in participation induced by the Second World War experience actually reflect the very weak economy of 1940. In order to test this possibility, trends were estimated in 1930. This leads to even greater discrepancies between predicted and actual participation, both during and after the war. As a further check, we estimated trends using data for the whole 1890–1980 period. The results were qualitatively similar, although the estimated effects of the war on subsequent participation were significantly reduced. Of course, this procedure may be inappropriate because the war presumably affected post-war data.

11 *Monthly Labor Review*, May (1944).

12 Both in aggregate and within occupations, there was virtually no change in the ratio of male and female hourly and/or yearly earnings between 1939 and 1950. The data must be interpreted cautiously because of a plethora of selection effects.

13 Strictly speaking, all that is required is that (11.1) can be represented as $V_1(c_{t-1}, l_{t-1}) + V_2(c_t, l_t \ c_{t+1}, l_{t+1})$.

14 In the empirical work below, we use the unemployment rate for 35–44-year-old men. This avoids problems of demographic adjustment.

15 The estimates were performed using annual data for the period 1949–81. Two lags on each variable were included. Wages are measured using an index of compensation in the private business sector. Prices are measured using the consumption price deflator, and output is measured as real GNP.

16 The tax rate is the sum of the average marginal tax rate imposed on labour income, Federal income taxes, state and local taxes and Social Security taxes. The municipal bond rate is then used as a crude proxy for the other tax interest rate.

17 In the empirical work reported below, we control for migration so this difficulty does not arise. In results which are not reported, measures of demand were used other than the unemployment rate with very little effect on the results. The problem of seasonality in the census sampling is not dealt with.

18 Fleisher and Rhodes (1976) argue that the unemployment rate is properly treated as endogenous in participation equations. However, the instrumental variables they employ, such as the growth rate of employment, are probably at least as likely as unemployment to be correlated with the error term in the participation equation.

19 In the results reported below, earnings are used as a wage proxy. This creates an obvious upwards bias in the estimate of wage effects on labour supply.

REFERENCES

Altonji, J. 1982: The intertemporal substitution model of labor market fluctuations: An empirical analysis. *Review of Economic Studies*, 49.

Barth, P. 1968: Unemployment and labor force participation. *Southern Economic Journal*, 375–82.

Blinder, A. and Fischer, S. 1980: Inventories, rational expectations, and the business cycle. NBER Working Paper.

Bowen, W. and Finnegan, T. A. 1969: *The Economics of Labor Force Participation*. Princeton: Princeton University Press.

Chamberlain, G. 1978: The Use of Panel Data in Econometrics (unpublished).

Clark, K. B. and Summers, L. H. 1979: Labor market dynamics and unemployment: A reconsideration, *Brookings Papers on Economic Activity*, 13–61.

Fama, E. F. 1975: Short term interest rates as predictors of inflation, *American Economic Review*, 269–82.

Fischer, S. 1978: Long term contracts: Rational expectations and the optimal money supply rule. *Journal of Political Economy*, 111–205.

Fleisher, B. and Rhodes, G. 1976: Unemployment and the labor force participation of married men and women: A simultaneous model. *Review of Economics and Statistics*, 398–406.

Freeman, R. 1976: Individual mobility and union voice in the labor market. *American Economic Review*, 361–8.

Freeman, R. 1977: Quits, Separations, and Job Tenure: The Exit-voice Tradeoff (unpublished).

Friedman, M. 1962: *Price Theory: A Provisional Text* Aldine.

Ghez, G. and Becker, G. 1975: *The Allocation of Time and Goods Over the Life Cycle*. National Bureau of Economic Research.

Hall, R. E. 1973: The rigidity of wages and the persistence of unemployment. *Brookings Papers on Economic Activity*, 301–50.

Hall, R. E. 1980: Labor supply and aggregate fluctuations. *Carnegie Rochester Conference,* 12, 7–34.

Heckman, J. 1978: Statistical Models for Discrete Panel Data Developed and Applied to Test the Hypothesis of True State Dependence Against the Hypothesis of Spurious State Dependence (unpublished).

Houthakker, H. and Taylor, L. 1970: *Consumer Demand in the US Analysis and Projections.*

Kydland, F. and Prescott, E. 1981: Time to Build and Aggregate Fluctuations (mimeo).

Long, C. 1958: *The Labor Force Under Changing Income and Employment,* Princeton: Princeton University Press.

Lucas, R. E. 1973: International evidence on output-inflation tradeoffs, *American Economic Review,* 316–34.

Lucas, R. E. 1975: An equilibrium model of the business cycle. *Journal of Political Economy,* 1113–44.

Lucas, R. E. and Rapping, L. 1969: Real wages, employment, and inflation. *Journal of Political Economy,* 721–54.

Mankiw, N. G., Rotemberg, J. and Summers, L. H. 1982: Intertemporal Substitution in Macroeconomics (unpublished).

McCallum, B. 1976: Rational expectations and the estimation of economic models: An alternative procedure. *International Economic Review,* 484–90.

Medoff, J. L. 1979: Layoffs and alternatives under trade unions in US manufacturing. *American Economic Review,* 380–95.

Mincer, J. 1966: Labor force participation and unemployment: A review of recent evidence. In Gordon, R. A. (ed) *Prosperity and Unemployment,* New York: Wiley.

Okun, A. 1973: Upward mobility in a high pressure economy. *Brooking Papers on Economic Activity,* 1, 207–52.

Phelps, F. 1972: *Inflation Policy and Unemployment Theory.* New York.

Pollak, R. 1978: Endogenous tastes in demand and welfare analysis. *American Economic Review.*

Sargent, T. 1980: *Macroeconomic Theory.*

Thurow, L. C. 1976: *Generating Inequality.*

Wachter, M. 1977: Intermediate swings in labor force participation. *Brookings Paper on Economic Activity.* 2, 545–74.

Yatchew, A. 1977: Heterogeneity and State Dependence in Labor Supply (unpublished).

12

Testing for Multiple Natural Rates of Unemployment in the British Economy: A Preliminary Investigation

ALAN A. CARRUTH and ANDREW J. OSWALD

Introduction

There has been much recent research into the causes of unemployment. Economists from all over the world, and especially from the United States and Britain, have tried to explain the rise in unemployment rates which has occurred throughout the industrialized countries. Representative samples of this work can be found in Greenhalgh et al. (1983), Johnson and Layard (1986) and the 1986 Special Issue of *Economica*.

Although they differ in detail, these studies all start from the same methodological point. Each assumes that there is a single equilibrium rate of unemployment (Friedman's (1968) 'natural' rate) which, it is argued, has shifted over time from low levels in the 1950s. This view of the world is so deeply entrenched that until recently it was almost never seriously questioned in the modern literature.[1] Rather more casual observers of the debate on unemployment, however, have objected to the way last year's estimate of the equilibrium is so often revised upward in response to the current year's higher actual rate, and the latest move has been towards discussion of unemployment hysteresis.[2] Conventional wisdom, based on the idea of a single (if changing) unemployment equilibrium, is now in question.

The purpose of this chapter is to test the hypothesis that there is a unique natural rate of unemployment in the British economy. There are a number of reasons why this seems to be a worthwhile activity.

First, casual inspection of the data for Britain shows that unemployment was roughly stable in the second half of the 1970s, and also between 1982 and 1986, but changed dramatically (more than doubling) in the 2-year period between. Hence the data are consistent with the vague but intriguing idea that the British economy swiftly switched from one equilibrium to another. The debate has *assumed* that earlier equilibria no longer exist, but that is a belief produced by analytical habits of thought rather than by empirical proof.

Second, economic theory gives us no good reason to believe that general equilibrium systems produce unique equilibria. Models of competitive economies have been studied intensively, and Arrow and Hahn (1971) identify two sufficient conditions for uniqueness:

1 gross substitutability of goods;
2 diagonal dominance of the excess demand function.

Neither is an attractive assumption empirically. Slight relaxations of these have been found, but the consensus appears to be that non-uniqueness is, if anything, to be expected. General equilibrium analysis of imperfectly competitive systems is at a far more rudimentary stage. However, it is unlikely that uniqueness will occur more readily in such models. For non-cooperative Nash equilibria, for example, rather stringent conditions are required for uniqueness. The crucial one (Debreu, 1952; Friedman, 1977) is that there be a contraction mapping from the set of strategies into itself. This is a requirement for which there is usually no economic rationale.

Third, empirical analysis of unemployment and real wages is often based on highly aggregated data. Little is known about the extent of the aggregation bias thus produced, but if anything it seems likely to exacerbate the tenuousness of the assumption that there is a unique equilibrium.

Fourth, the existence of multiple equilibrium rates of unemployment would have profound implications for economic policy. Aggregate demand policy in such a world might be able to push the economy from one long-run equilibrium point to another. Under almost all kinds of multiple equilibria, therefore, governments would have to judge which equilibrium was most likely to maximize social welfare. There could be no presumption that the economy would move to the socially optimal outcome. Similar points have been made recently by Diamond (1982) and Pissarides (1985), who derive theoretical results which indicate the possibility of multiple equilibria in an economy with job search.

Fifth, one interpretation of Keynes (1936) is that there is no unique settling point for an economy. Empirical evidence for multiple equilibria could conceivably provide a form of empirical justification for Keynesian ideas.

There is no orthodox way to test for multiple equilibria. We adopted a method based upon the following economic intuition. Economists typically conceive of equilibrium geometrically, namely as the intersection of two curves. Multiple equilibria are then, on this view, points of multiple intersection (some of which may imply instability, as is well known). Hence, to try to estimate such equilibria, it seems natural to drop the assumption of monotonicity that is routinely made in almost all applied economics. In both of the models estimated below we develop two-equation systems and then estimate the equations (singly) using logarithmic polynomials in the key endogenous variables. Each model therefore consists of two highly non-linear equations, which, when combined, allows the solution to be checked for multiple equilibria. The methodology is in part formally equivalent to that used for the estimation of econometric models with varying parameters.[3]

The chapter's purpose is somewhat unconventional, so checks on the possibility of mis-specification are even more important than usual. Each of the estimated equations in the chapter is subjected to a number of diagnostic tests. One which, though not a model selection device, may be of particular interest to those who share Leamer's (1983) doubts about applied econometrics is the forecasting test reported later as a Chi^2 test. In the case of the labour demand model reported in table 12.1, for example, we estimate the model on 84 observations from 1957(1) to 1978(4), and then forecast ahead for the next 20 quarters up to the end of 1983(4). This is a severe test for a time-series model, because the forecast period saw immense changes in the British economy, and is in the spirit of the methodology advocated in, for example, Hendry (1980). As it turns out, our model tracks the data surprisingly well. It correctly forecasts four turning points and also the historically unprecedented decline in employment.

We also report diagnostic tests

1 for parameter stability across sub-sample time periods (a Chow test);
2 of autocorrelation of up to sixth order (a Lagrange multiplier test);
3 of whether the errors come from a Normal distribution;
4 for heteroscedasticity (one test from White, 1980, the other a test for non-constant error variances due to the squares of the regressors);
5 of instrument validity (a test from Sargan, 1964) where appropriate.

All the estimated equations attempt to encompass earlier work by allowing for non-monotonicity. Whenever other things were constant we chose that equation which had the lowest standard error. The empirical estimation was done using David Hendry's PC GIVE. In general our equations explain the quarterly data somewhat better than do Layard and Nickell (1986) and Smith and Holly (1985), but of course we have had the advantage of being able to build upon their work.

Another way to guard against the possibility of nonsense results is to impose only a little structure on the models. Hence the chapter does not make assumptions about the exact form of production or utility functions, nor about the precise nature of the bargaining solution which determines the real wage. The estimated equations ought to be of interest to those with rather different beliefs about labour markets, because in places they are close to reduced-form results. This approach seems to us to be the most natural one, given the present lack of real knowledge about economic systems, but it also means that we are forced to leave certain kinds of questions unanswered. Most structural parameters, for example, are not estimated here.

A final check on the models is made possible by the existence of necessary conditions for stability. These are rarely used in empirical work, because severe limitations are usually (unconsciously) placed on the degree of non-linearity of the functions. By dropping the assumption of monotonicity, however, it is possible to produce a much more demanding test of a theory's ability to explain the data. A good example in which wage reaction functions are estimated is encountered in a later section. Stability conditions require that these curves intersect in a particular way. This is a sharp test.

A Labour Demand Model

In this section we set out a conventional model of employment and wage determination. To allow comparison with earlier work it takes a form similar to that of Layard and Nickell (1985a, 1985b and 1986), Newell and Symons (1985) and Smith and Holly (1985). In one crucial respect, however, the empirical application differs from these. Rather than impose the assumption of log-linearity, and so of uniqueness of equilibrium, we test for that analytical structure.

We make the following assumptions.

A1. There is a single representative firm, which attempts to maximize profits, π, given by

$$\pi = R(n, k, \alpha, m, t_1, t_3) - wn - rk - p_m m - F, \qquad (12.1)$$

in which R is revenue, n is employment, k is capital, α is a vector of productivity and demand shift parameters, m is the quantity of imported inputs, t_1 is the tax rate on the firm's level of employment, t_3 is the indirect tax rate, r is the price of captial, p_m is the price of imported inputs and F is fixed costs.

A2. There is a single representative trade union, which attempts to maximize utility, V, given by

$$V = V(w,\ n,\ t_2,\ \rho),\qquad(12.2)$$

where w and n are again pay and the number of jobs, t_2 is the income tax rate and ρ is the unemployment benefit/wage replacement ratio.

A3. The union and firm together negotiate over the wage rate. The firm sets employment, capital and inputs unilaterally.

A4. There exists a bargaining function, B, which defines the wage rate. It is given by

$$w = \arg\max\ B(\pi,\ V,\ U,\ U^p,\ L,\ \rho,\ k,\ r,\ F),\qquad(12.3)$$

in which U is unemployment in the economy, U^p is exogenous union power, L is the labour force and the other variables are as defined earlier.

Assumptions A1 and A2 are fairly conventional. The model does not impose the assumption of a perfectly competitive product market, and it allows for three factor inputs. The assumption about the union utility function is sufficiently general to avoid most of the controversy which still exists in this field. However, the inclusion of employment is potentially undesirable, and in a sense A3 brushes past it. It is assumed here that there exists a labour demand function, which requires either:

1 that employment does not enter the utility function, V, or
2 that there is some impediment (such as a centralized union and a very large number of decentralized employers) to efficient bargaining over jobs.[4]

Assumption A4 is meant to allow for a range of different bargaining solutions. Bargaining strength is assumed to depend on the utility accruing to the firm and union during disputes and/or complete bargaining breakdown. The key variables are taken to be unemployment, the replacement ratio, the labour force size, fixed costs (including capital costs) and exogenous strength. The form of A4 means that it encompasses the Nash solution, which is the most common assumption in the literature (McDonald and Solow, 1981, *inter alia*).

When these assumptions are combined, we derive two equations. One is for the real wage rate and the other for employment. The first might be thought of as an inverse supply curve of labour, but we prefer to think of it as a bargaining wage equation. The second is a demand curve for labour. They can be written as

$$w^* = w^*(U,\ p_m,\ K,\ L,\ t_1,\ t_2,\ t_3,\ \alpha,\ r,\ F,\ \rho,\ U^p)\qquad(12.4)$$

$$n^*=n^*(w, \alpha, p_m, t_1, t_2, r). \tag{12.5}$$

As an empirical matter, moreover, the demand shift parameter must be represented by a proxy or proxies. We assume that

$$\alpha=\alpha(WT, AD, P^*/\bar{P}), \tag{12.6}$$

in which, following Layard and Nickell (1986), WT is deviations from world trade, AD is a measure of the fiscal deficit and $P^*/\bar{P}$ is international competitiveness.

Whether the labour demand and wage equations are monotonic is an empirical question. For the former, however, conventional price theory shows that under imperfect competition the marginal revenue product function can routinely have turning points. An alternative rationale is that there may be increasing returns to scale. Solow and Stiglitz (1968) also derive a labour demand function which is not monotonic.

Table 12.1 gives the results of estimating the labour demand curve (12.5), and table 12.3 the results for the wage equation (12.4). Theory gives no predictions about the appropriate lag structure, so that was decided by empirical experiment. Variables which were consistently insignificant have been discarded from the equations.

The labour demand curve in table 12.1 is highly non-linear in the real product wage rate (denoted W/P in the tables).[5] Layard and Nickell (1986) impose the assumption of log-linearity, but noticeably greater explanatory power is gained by entering also the square and the cube of the log of the real wage. Demand shift variables are very important and better determined than in Layard and Nickell (1986), who obtain t-statistics of 2.1 on the adjusted deficit (AD), 1.8 on the competitiveness term ($P^*/\bar{P}$) and 3.4 on the world trade (WT) variable. Their equivalent equation has a standard error of 0.0050. Our equation also has a noticeably lower coefficient on the lagged dependent variable, and so is less dominated by the dynamics.

We could find no effect from an employment variable lagged twice. By the standards of the early literature this is unconventional. Ashenfelter and Card (1982), for example, argue that employment series are generally AR(2).

The complicated difference term in world trade is a result of allowing the data to determine lag length. Unlike Layard and Nickell, we can reject the hypothesis that world trade, WT, a variable based on deviations from trend, has no effect in steady-state equilibrium. Our best such equation is given in table 12.2, which has a very slightly improved standard error over table 12.1, and includes the (weak) capital stock effect. The diagnostic tests are almost wholly encouraging. Normality is the exception, and that is the result of one outlier, in 1977(1), for which we have no good explanation. Our judgement, after

Table 12.1 *Labour demand equation with a polynomial in the real product wage*
(OLS estimation for 1957(1)–1983(4))

$\ln N_t =$ 0.81ln $N_{t-1}+$ 9.03ln$(W/P)_{t-1}-$ 2.05$(\ln W/P_{t-1})^2$
   (20.76)   (2.94)   (2.88)

   $+$ 0.15$(\ln W/P_{t-1})^3 +$ 0.31$AD_{t-1}+$ 0.028ln$(P^*/\bar{P})_{t-4}$
   (2.81)   (5.10)   (4.07)

   $+$ 0.029$WT_{t-1}+$ 0.034$[WT_t-0.5(WT_{t-3}+WT_{t-4})]+$ Seasonals$-$ 11.31
   (2.04)   (4.88)   (2.64)

s.e.$=0.00440$ $R^2=0.98$ RSS$=0.00186$

Forecast	Chi^2(20)/20$=$ 0.68
Chow test (sample split 1978(4))	$F(20, 76)=$ 0.47
Normality	Chi^2(2)$=$148.6
LM	$F(6, 90)=$ 1.67
Heteroscedasticity (squares of regressors)	$F(15, 80)=$ 1.06
Heteroscedasticity (White's)	$F(21, 79)=$ 0.82

---

t-values are in parentheses, full sample estimates are presented.
A full explanation of the data is given in the data appendix and in Layard and Nickell (1986).
The diagnostic test statistics' 5 per cent levels are not given. All test failures are discussed in the text of the chapter.
The poor Normality result is a consequence of an outlier in 1977(1).

much checking, is that there is some problem with the employment figure for 1977(1). The introduction of a dummy variable for the quarter solves the Normality problem, and has little effect elsewhere, but we prefer to present the equation as it is, so that the difficulty is out in the open. The model forecasts successfully: all four turning points, and the huge decline in British employment, are correctly predicted.

The short-run elasticity of labour demand in this model, at the mean, is -0.26. In the long run it is -1.24. Layard and Nickell (1986) obtain similar findings, but of course do not have a varying elasticity as employment and pay alter. They estimate the long-run elasticity at a constant -1.19.

What shape is the demand curve for labour? It turns out to be S-shaped, with turning points at the (log of the) wage rates $w=5.37$ and $w=3.73$. The curve has a point of inflection at $w=4.55$. Hence it is a monotonically decreasing function over the entire relevant range, because the real wage over the period varied from a minimum of 3.89 in

Table 12.2 *Labour demand equation with capital and a polynomial in the real product wage (OLS estimation for 1957(1)–1983(4))*

$\ln N_t = 0.79\ln N_{t-1} + 9.41\ln(W/P)_{t-1} - 2.13(\ln W/P_{t-1})^2$
      (19.52)   (3.07)   (3.00)

$+ 0.16(\ln W/P_{t-1})^3 + 0.33AD_{t-1} + 0.028\ln(P^*/\dot{P})_{t-4}$
   (2.92)   (5.30)   (4.02)

$+ 0.033WT_{t-1} + 0.035[WT_t - 0.5(WT_{t-3} + WT_{t-4})] + 0.019\ln K_{t-1}$
   (2.27)   (5.01)   (1.36)

$+$ seasonals $- 11.84$
          (2.77)

s.e. $= 0.00438$ $R^2 = 0.98$ RSS $= 0.00182$

Forecast	Chi^2(20)/20 = 0.64
Chow test (sample split 1978(4))	$F(20, 75) = 0.45$
Normality	Chi^2(2) = 143.7
LM	$F(6, 89) = 1.27$
Heteroscedasticity (squares of regressors)	$F(17, 77) = 1.06$
Heteroscedasticity (White's)	$F(21, 79) = 0.78$

t-values are in parentheses, full sample estimates are presented.

1956 to a maximum of 4.72 in 1983. Unless there are huge non-linearities in the wage equation, therefore, we can conclude that Britain has had a unique natural rate of unemployment during the period from the late 1950s. Figure 12.1 plots the labour demand function.

Although the adjusted government deficit (*AD*) is one of the independent variables, it is assumed here (following Layard and Nickell, 1986) that it is uniquely determined in equilibrium. Our own empirical checks, which are not reported, confirm uniqueness.[6] Hence this is apparently not a route to multiple equilibria.

Estimates of the real (product) wage equation are reported in tables 12.3, 12.4 and 12.5. Table 12.3 uses instrumental variable estimation; the other two are estimated by OLS. The term in $\ln P^e$ is a price expectations variable which, following Layard and Nickell (1986), was based on the fitted values of the equation

$\Delta \ln P_t = 0.0283\Delta\ln P_{t-1} + 0.6785\Delta\ln P_{t-2} + 0.3156\Delta\ln P_{t-3}$
     (0.29)   (7.5)   (3.5)

$- 0.0224\Delta\ln P_{t-4}$
  (0.24)

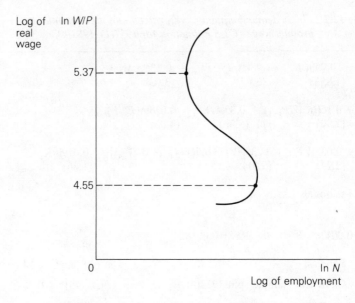

Figure 12.1 *The (steady-state) labour demand curve*

where p is a value added price index. The complete term $(\ln P^e - \ln P)$ is to capture price surprises and was instrumented using lagged values of the GDP deflator.

Despite extensive experiments we could find no evidence for (log) non-linearities in the wage equation. The data favour a log-linear form in the unemployment level and its change. The equation is similar to that in Layard and Nickell (1986), although our standard error is just over 0.018 compared to just over 0.020, and we have simpler dynamics. All the diagnostic checks are satisfactory, but the model fails to predict the size of the drop in real wages in 1980(1). The fit on certain occasions in the 1960s, and in the mid 1970s (possibly due to the incomes policies of 1976–7), is also less good than might ideally be hoped, and we have a suspicion that some influence – perhaps a profits variable – is missing. That is something we aim to improve upon.

Table 12.5 tests whether the short-run unemployment rate (*URS*), measuring those unemployed for less than 6 months, is a better market pressure variable than the aggregate rate *U*. It turns out to make no difference of consequence.

This completes the summary of the results from the chapter's first model. The principal conclusion is that, on the basis of this evidence, the British economy has been characterized by a unique natural rate of unemployment. Although the labour demand curve is S-shaped, the wage function is monotonic in unemployment, and during the period

Table 12.3 *Aggregate real product wage equation (IV estimation for 1957(1)–1983(4))*

$$\ln(W/P)_t = \underset{(2.12)}{0.70}(\ln P^e - \ln P)_t + \underset{(6.15)}{0.42}\ln(W/P)_{t-1} - \underset{(2.14)}{0.033}\Delta \ln U_t$$

$$- \underset{(3.70)}{0.030}\ln U_{t-1} - \underset{(3.05)}{0.08}\ln(P_m/\bar{P})_{t-1} + \underset{(3.57)}{0.27}\Delta \ln(P_m/\bar{P})_{t-2}$$

$$+ \underset{(7.45)}{0.502}\ln(K/L)_{t-1} + \underset{(4.00)}{0.84}\Delta t_{1t} + \underset{(5.59)}{0.0047}\text{Rho}_{t-1} - \underset{(1.67)}{0.003}\Delta\text{Rho}_{t-2}$$

$$+ \underset{(2.68)}{0.049}\ln(U^p)_{t-1} + \text{seasonals} + \underset{(8.14)}{4.12}$$

s.e.$=0.0183$ RSS$=0.0313$

Instrument validity	$\text{Chi}^2(1)/1=0.1$
Forecast	$\text{Chi}^2(20)/20=1.58$
Chow test (sample split 1978(4))	$F(20, 74)=1.29$
Normality	$\text{Chi}^2(2)=8.87$
LM	$F(6, 88)=0.71$
Heteroscedasticity (squares of regressors)	$F(24, 69)=1.05$
Heteroscedasticity (White's)	$F(27, 66)=0.61$

t-values are in parentheses, full sample estimates are presented.

under study the wage never left the band[7] successfully explained by the downward sloping segment of the labour demand function.

A Nash Equilibrium Model of Wage Interdependence

In this section we set out a rather different model of a unionized economy and again consider whether it might generate multiple equilibria. This way of thinking about the world is unconventional, but it accords closely with ideas about wage comparability which are stressed in the industrial relations literature, and it can be derived rigorously from models of union wage determination.

Consider a two-sector economy in which there are unions in both sectors. The optimal wage of the first union will depend on the wage obtained by the second, and vice versa. There are two particular

Table 12.4 *Aggregate real product wage equation (OLS estimation for 1957(1)–1983(4))*

$\ln(W/P)_t = 0.77(\ln P^e - \ln P)_t + 0.43\ln(W/P)_{t-1} - 0.033\Delta\ln U_t$
$\quad\;\;(5.58) \qquad\qquad\quad (6.30) \qquad\qquad (2.15)$

$\quad - 0.030\ln U_{t-1} - 0.08\ln(P_m/\bar{P})_{t-1} + 0.28\Delta\ln(P_m/\bar{P})_{t-2}$
$\quad\;\;\; (3.92) \qquad\quad (3.10) \qquad\qquad (4.45)$

$\quad + 0.502\ln(K/L)_{t-1} + 0.83\Delta t_{1t} + 0.0047\mathrm{Rho}_{t-1} - 0.003\Delta\mathrm{Rho}_{t-2}$
$\quad\;\;\; (7.46) \qquad\qquad (4.09) \qquad (5.61) \qquad\qquad (1.67)$

$\quad + 0.048\ln(U^p)_{t-1} + \text{seasonals} + 4.11$
$\quad\;\;\; (2.69) \qquad\qquad\qquad\qquad (8.17)$

s.e.$=0.0182$ RSS$=0.0312$

Forecast	$\mathrm{Chi}^2(20)/20 = 1.58$
Chow test (sample split 1978(4))	$F(20, 74) = 1.29$
Normality	$\mathrm{Chi}^2(2) = 11.78$
LM	$F(6, 88) = 0.80$
Heteroscedasticity (squares of regressors)	$F(24, 69) = 1.02$
Heteroscedasticity (White's)	$F(27, 66) = 0.62$

---

t−values are in parentheses, full sample estimates are presented.

channels for this interdependence. First, changes in the wage of one group will affect the demand for labour of the other. The form of the effect will be determined by whether the kinds of labour are substitutes or complements, by whether the goods they help to produce are substitutes or complements and by the importance of labour costs in the two sectors. Second, the wage of one union's members is likely to enter the utility function of the other union. This is often known colloquially as wage jealousy or concern for fair wage differentials. Wages depend – as any labour relations or industrial psychology textbook stresses – on what people elsewhere are being paid. Occasionally economists have preferred to close their eyes to such effects, but to do so requires that one ignores:

1 what one reads every week in the newspapers about wage negotiations and disputes,
2 the laboratory evidence gathered over decades by psychologists (see Adams, 1965; Adams and Rosenbaum, 1964; and Lawler 1968),

Table 12.5 *Aggregate real product wage equation: short-term unemployment case (OLS estimation for 1957(1)–1983(4))*

$$\ln(W/P)_t = 0.78(\ln P^e - \ln P)_t + 0.47\ln(W/P)_{t-1} - 0.025\Delta\ln(URS)_t$$
$$(5.47) (7.01) \phantom{0.47\ln(W/P)_{t-1} - } (1.94)$$

$$- 0.030\ln URS_{t-1} - 0.08\ln(P_m/\bar{P})_{t-1} + 0.26\Delta\ln(P_m/\bar{P})_{t-2}$$
$$(3.34) \phantom{\ln URS_{t-1} - }(2.98) \phantom{0.08\ln(P_m/\bar{P})_{t-1} + }(4.12)$$

$$+ 0.466\ln(K/L)_{t-1} + 0.87\Delta t_{1t} + 0.0046\mathrm{Rho}_{t-1} - 0.0035\Delta\mathrm{Rho}_{t-2}$$
$$(7.04) \phantom{0.466\ln(K/L)_{t-1} + }(4.22) \phantom{0.87\Delta t_{1t} + }(5.38) \phantom{0.0046\mathrm{Rho}_{t-1} - }(1.96)$$

$$+ 0.038\ln(U^p)_{t-1} + \text{seasonals} + 3.65$$
$$(2.18) \phantom{0.038\ln(U^p)_{t-1} + \text{seasonals} + }(7.77)$$

s.e.$=0.0186$ RSS$=0.0325$

Forecast	$\mathrm{Chi}^2(20)/20 = 1.40$
Chow test (sample split 1978(4))	$F(20, 74) = 1.18$
Normality	$\mathrm{Chi}^2(2) = 11.47$
LM	$F(6, 88) = 0.78$
Heteroscedasticity (squares of regressors)	$F(24, 69) = 0.87$
Heteroscedasticity (White's)	$F(27, 66) = 0.60$

t-values are in parentheses, full sample estimates are presented.

3 the industrial relations evidence documented in sources like Brown and Sisson (1975) and Willman (1982),
4 the sociology literature based upon Runciman (1972), and
5 the ideas promulgated by economists in other fields (for example, Becker, 1981; Collard, 1978; Hamermesh, 1975; and Oswald, 1983).

The model assumes that there are two sectors (manufacturing and non-manufacturing) and one union in each sector. Each sector or trade union sets its wage as a function of the other's wage. A non-cooperative Nash equilibrium exists where these wage rates are consistent. Geometrically this corresponds to the intersection of two wage reaction curves; topologically it is the fixed point of a mapping of wage space into itself. The theory of wage reaction functions is discussed in Rosen (1969, 1970), Oswald (1979, 1985), Jackman (1985) and Gylfason and Lindbeck (1984). Related theory and microeconomic tests are contained in Carruth and Oswald (1981, 1985, 1986a).

To try to maintain consistency with the first model we now sketch a bargaining framework into which wage – wage interdependence is introduced. The following assumptions are made.

A1. There are two sectors, 'manufacturing' and 'non-manufacturing'. Profits in the manufacturing sector depend on the same variables as in assumption A4 in the last section plus the selling price of non-manufacturing output, which is assumed to affect sales of the manufacturing sector's good. The equivalent is true for the non-manufacturing sector's profits.

A2. Define maximum profit functions, for the two sectors, as

$$\max \pi^m = \pi^m(\alpha^n, \alpha^m, w^n, w^m, t_1, t_2, r, p_m, F^n, F^m) \qquad (12.8)$$

$$\max \pi^n = \pi^n(\alpha^n, \alpha^m, w^n, w^m, t_1, t_2, r, p_m, F^n, F^m) \qquad (12.9)$$

where, in each sector, employment, capital and imports are chosen optimally. Manufacturing's maximum profit function, π^m, is defined on productivity and demand shift parameters α^n and α^m, wage rates w^n and w^m, taxes t_1 and t_2, cost of capital r, the price of imported goods, p_m and fixed cost levels F^n and F^m. It is assumed that t_1, t_2, r and p_m are common to both sectors.[8]

A3. Each sector has its own trade union. Their utility functions are

$$V^m = V^m(w^n, w^m, n^m, t_2, \rho) \qquad (12.10)$$

$$V^n = V^n(w^n, w^m, n^n, t_2, \rho) \qquad (12.11)$$

which are adapted versions of those in assumption 2 in the last section. The formulations allow for the possibility of wage jealousy.

A4. There exist bargaining functions, B^m and B^n, such that

$$w^i = \arg\max B^i(\pi^i, V^i, U, U^{pi}, L^i, \rho, k^i, r, F^i) \qquad (12.12)$$

where $i = m, n$. Once again, π is profit, V is union utility, U is unemployment, U^p is exogenous union power (see the appendix), L is the labour force, ρ is the unemployment benefit replacement ratio, k is capital, r is the price of capital and F is fixed costs. Davidson (1985) contains similar theory.

There are now two wage equations, and in equilibrium they must be consistent. When seen as a system (of two wage reaction functions) they may be written

$$w^m = \phi(w^n, U, p_m, K^m, L^m, t_1, t_2, t_3, \alpha^m, \alpha^n, r, F^m, \rho, U^{pm}) \qquad (12.13)$$

$$w^n = \psi(w^m, U, p_m, K^n, L^n, t_1, t_2, t_3, \alpha^m, \alpha^n, r, F^n, \rho, U^{pn}) \qquad (12.14)$$

The object, once again, is to check for non-linearities that are sufficient to generate multiple intersections. In this case, because prior beliefs suggest that both wage reaction curves should have positive derivatives, the existence of multiple equilibria does not here require that one function has a turning point.

The empirical estimates of the wage reaction functions are given in tables 12.6, 12.7, 12.8 and 12.9. Real (consumption) average earnings is used as the dependent variable. Tables 12.6 and 12.7 contain the results for manufacturing, using respectively the unemployment rate and

Table 12.6 *Manufacturing sector: real consumption wage reaction function (IV estimation for 1964(1)–1983(4))*

$$\ln WC_t^M = 0.47 \ln WC_{t-1}^M - 4.66 \ln WC_t^N + 0.56 (\ln WC_t^N)^2 + 0.025 \Delta_1 \ln U_{t-1}$$
$$ (4.65) \qquad\quad (3.35) \qquad\quad (3.59) \qquad\qquad (1.68)$$

$$- 0.00076 (\ln U_t)^3 - 0.26 t_{1t} + 0.42 \ln (K/L)_{t-1}^m$$
$$ (3.11) \qquad\qquad (3.00) \quad\; (3.44)$$

$$+ 0.20 \Delta_3 \ln (Q/E)_t^m - 0.08 \Delta_1 \ln (P_m/\bar{P})_t - 0.003 \Delta_1 \mathrm{Rho}_t$$
$$ (4.34) \qquad\qquad (1.51) \qquad\qquad (2.29)$$

$$-0.33 \Delta_1 \ln PC_t + \text{seasonals} + \quad 15.31$$
$$ (2.99) \qquad\qquad\qquad\qquad (3.72)$$

s.e.$=0.0101$ RSS$=0.00680$

Instrument validity	$\mathrm{Chi}^2(3)/3 = 2.69$
Forecast	$\mathrm{Chi}^2(20)/20 = 1.35$
Chow test (sample split 1978(4))	$F(20, 41) = 0.65$
Normality	$\mathrm{Chi}^2(2) = 0.59$
LM	$F(4, 63) = 1.32$
Heteroscedasticity (squares of regressors)	$F(21, 45) = 1.0$
Heteroscedasticity (White's)	$F(24, 42) = 1.47$

U is the aggregate unemployment rate. t-values are in parentheses, full sample estimates are presented.
Instruments were one and two lags on the short-term unemployment rate, the manufacturing wage and the non-manufacturing wage squared.

Table 12.7 *Manufacturing sector: real consumption wage reaction function (IV estimation for 1964(1)–1983(4)) (short-term unemployment case)*

$$\ln WC_t^M = 0.40 \ln WC_{t-1}^M - 4.12 \ln WC_t^N + 0.51 (\ln WC_t^N)^2 + 0.0327 \Delta_1 \ln URS_{t-1}$$
$$(3.71) \qquad (2.81) \qquad (3.10) \qquad (3.16)$$

$$- 0.00087 (\ln URS_t)^3 - 0.26_{t1} + 0.401 \ln(K/L)_{t-1}^m$$
$$(2.86) \qquad (3.06) \quad (3.02)$$

$$+ 0.19 \Delta_3 \ln(Q/E)_t^m - 0.10 \Delta_1 \ln(P_m/\bar{P})_t - 0.002 \Delta_1 Rho_t$$
$$(4.54) \qquad (2.05) \qquad (2.02)$$

$$- 0.43 \Delta_1 \ln PC_t + \text{seasonals} + 14.13$$
$$(3.87) \qquad\qquad (3.21)$$

s.e. $= 0.00953$ RSS $= 0.00608$

Instrument validity	$\text{Chi}^2(3)/3 = 0.43$
Forecast	$\text{Chi}^2(20)/20 = 0.95$
Chow test (sample split 1978(4))	$F(20, 41) = 0.88$
Normality	$\text{Chi}^2(2) = 0.76$
LM	$F(4, 63) = 0.82$
Heteroscedasticity (squares of regressors)	$F(21, 45) = 0.89$
Heteroscedasticity (White's)	$F(24, 42) = 0.38$

URS is the short-run unemployment rate. *t*-values are in parentheses, full sample estimates are presented.
Instruments were as in table 12.6 except that logs on the aggregate unemployment rate replace the short-term unemployment rate.

short-term unemployment rate. Tables 12.8 and 12.9 are the equivalent for the non-manufacturing sector. A fuller description of the data is given in the data appendix.

As the theory predicts, there is strong interdependence of wage rates. To check for multiple equilibria we tested in each case for up to a third-order logarithmic polynomial in the other sector's wage. The data favoured the quadratic forms reported here.[9]

The results largely speak for themselves, and are similar to those given earlier on aggregate wage behaviour. It makes relatively little difference whether total or short-term unemployment is used. The capital/labour force ratio is the dominant trend variable. In the manufacturing sector we identify as well an interesting productivity change effect ($\Delta Q/E$). Although, to maintain symmetry, we include an

Table 12.8 *Non-manufacturing sector: real consumption wage reaction function (IV estimation for 1964(1)–1983(4))*

$$\ln WC_t^N = 0.28 \ln WC_{t-2}^N + 4.91 \ln WC_t^m - 0.48 (\ln WC_t^m)^2 - 0.027 \ln U_{t-1}$$
$$(3.40) \qquad (4.01) \qquad (3.64) \qquad (2.73)$$

$$+0.29\Delta_1 \ln(Q/E)_{-1}^T - 0.25t_{1t} - 0.073 \ln(P_m/\bar{P})_{t-1}$$
$$(1.76) \qquad (1.64) \quad (2.56)$$

$$-0.11 \ln U_{t-3}^p + 0.37 \ln(K/L)_{t-1}^N + 0.004\Delta_1 \text{Rho}_{t-1}$$
$$(6.56) \qquad (3.06) \qquad (2.84)$$

$$+ 0.014 Q1_t + \text{seasonals} - 6.92$$
$$(3.80) \qquad\qquad (2.13)$$

s.e. = 0.0134   RSS = 0.012

Instrument validity	$\text{Chi}^2(4)/4 = 1.21$
Forecast*	$\text{Chi}^2(20)/20 = 3.64$
Chow test (sample split 1978(4))	$F(20, 41) = 0.71$
Normality	$\text{Chi}^2(2) = 0.44$
LM	$F(4, 63) = 0.54$
Heteroscedasticity (squares of regressors)	$F(20, 46) = 0.62$
Heteroscedasticity (White's)	$F(24, 42) = 0.79$
*Forecast	$\text{Chi}^2(16)/16 = 1.24$

t-values are in parentheses, full sample estimates are presented.
Instruments used were one and two lags on short-term unemployment, on the price of materials and fuel used in manufacturing relative to the unit value of world manufacturing exports, and one period lags on the endogenous wage variables.

aggregate effect in the non-manufacturing equations, it barely appears in that sector.

As is to be expected, there is a significant price shock term (ΔPC) in manufacturing, but (curiously) not in non-manufacturing.[10] In non-manufacturing the union power variable enters negatively, for which we have no explanation. Our judgement is that the non-manufacturing wage equations are the least satisfactory of those in this chapter. This is probably because of the heterogeneity within the sector and the consequent unreliability of the data.

Does this model produce evidence in favour of multiple equilibria? The manufacturing wage equation is a U-shaped function of the log of

Table 12.9 *Non-manufacturing sector: real consumption wage reaction function (IV estimation for 1964(1)–1983(4))*

$$\ln WC_t^N = \underset{(3.52)}{0.31\ln WC_{t-2}^N} + \underset{(4.54)}{5.32\ln WC_t^m} - \underset{(4.06)}{0.52(\ln WC_t^m)^2} - \underset{(1.43)}{0.04\ln URS_{t-1}}$$

$$+ \underset{(1.12)}{0.18\Delta_1\ln(Q/E)_{-1}^T} - \underset{(1.20)}{0.19t_{1t}} - \underset{(1.87)}{0.058\ln(P_m/\tilde{P})_{t-1}}$$

$$- \underset{(6.47)}{0.11\ln U_{t-3}^p} + \underset{(2.10)}{0.26\ln(K/L)_{t-1}^N} + \underset{(2.72)}{0.004\Delta_1\mathrm{Rho}_{t-1}}$$

$$+ \underset{(3.75)}{0.015Q1_t} + \text{seasonals} - \underset{(2.85)}{8.68}$$

s.e.$=0.0139$ RSS$=0.013$

Instrument validity	$\mathrm{Chi}^2(4)/4=2.61$
Forecast	$\mathrm{Chi}^2(20)/20=3.69$
Chow test (sample split 1978(4))	$F(20, 41)=0.79$
Normality	$\mathrm{Chi}^2(2)=1.38$
LM	$F(4, 63)=0.74$
Heteroscedasticity (squares of regressors)	$F(20, 46)=0.66$
Heteroscedasticity (White's)	$F(24, 42)=0.54$

t-values are in parentheses, full sample estimates are presented.
Instruments were as in table 12.8, except that aggregate unemployment replaced short-term unemployment.

Table 12.10 *Measures of wage–wage interdependence (Short- and long-run elasticities of wage i with respect to wage j)*

Dependent variable	Short-run elasticity	Long-run elasticity
Manufacturing wage	0.40	0.67
Non-manufacturing wage	0.64	0.90

These figures are calculated at the means (the elasticities are not constant), using the results of tables 12.7 and 12.8.
The elasticities were not constrained to be positive.

the non-manufacturing wage. It has a minimum where the latter equals 4.03, so over the relevant range the reaction function is upward sloping. The non-manufacturing wage reaction curve is an inverted U shape, with a maximum where the manufacturing wage equals 5.12, so over the relevant range this function too has a positive gradient. Figure 12.2 depicts the estimated equations.

These results again seem to offer support for the view that, over the period, Britain has had a unique equilibrium in the labour market. The observed band of real wages (minimum 4.17, maximum 4.70) is within the region characterized by the single intersection of positively sloped reaction curves. The significant (log) non-linearities play an important role empirically, but are not sufficient to generate multiple equilibria. Reassuringly, the equilibrium is stable, in the sense that the gradients of the reaction functions ensure that there is convergence of pay levels to their equilibrium values.

The estimated equations are somewhat different from those in Smith and Holly (1985). The find no effect from the non-manufacturing wage onto the manufacturing wage. However, as the authors acknowledge, their non-manufacturing pay equation exhibits autocorrelation and forecasts poorly. Nevertheless, it has the interesting feature that three lags on unemployment all matter empirically, which we could not find.

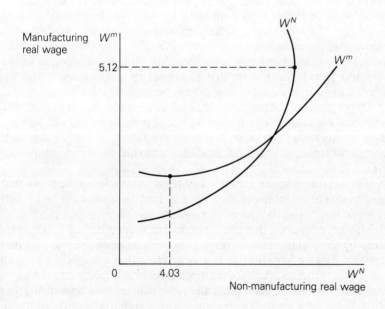

Figure 12.2 *The (steady-state) wage reaction functions*

Conclusion

The purpose of this chapter has been to test the hypothesis that Britain has a unique equilibrium (or natural) rate of unemployment. Economic theory indicates that non-uniqueness may occur, and the policy implications of such a possibility are profound, but as far as we know there is no published work which tests for the existence of multiple equilibria in an economy.

The results suggest that, over the post-war period covered by the data, the British economy has had a unique natural rate of unemployment. This was not the prior belief which stimulated our research (we suspected the opposite, and were unhappy with the literature's unconscious assumption of uniqueness), but the conclusions emerge in an apparently unambiguous way.

Are these findings really compelling? It is hard to be certain, but we have tried to enforce various checks.

1 Two quite different models have been tested. In the first, an aggregate labour demand function and an aggregate real wage equation are estimated. In the second, a two-sector Nash equilibrium model of wage reaction functions is used. Although we allow for the possibility of non-monotonicity (third- and fourth-order logarithmic polynomials were tried), in both cases the relevant equilibria are unique.

2 A number of diagnostic tests were done. We were especially surprised by the predictive power of the (S-shaped) labour demand curve. When estimated only on data up to 1978, the model – much shaped by Layard and Nickell (1986) – accurately predicts the behaviour of the economy from then to 1983. This is a severe test of any time-series model. Ours correctly forecasts four turning points in the data, and tracks the fall in Britain's level of employment. The literature's insistence on log-linearity may be undesirable.

3 Only general assumptions have been made in designing the theoretical equations. The results do not rest upon special production, utility or bargaining functions. It is difficult to think of any conventional theories which could not be modelled roughly in the form of our estimating equations.[11]

4 The equilibria in the estimated systems are stable (in the sense that the relevant curves intersect from the required direction). Although this is a weak test,[12] the data were in no sense forced to favour this form.

It may be, of course, that the economy is too complicated to be represented by small numbers of even highly non-linear equations, and that the techniques we have used here give answers that will one day be seen as seriously incorrect. Perhaps multiple equilibria actually do exist but it is necessary to have some radically new way of conceptualizing the notion.[13] Perhaps there is a continuum of equilibria. However, those who are unconvinced by the findings must suggest and perform an appropriate test. Our tentative judgement, at this stage, is that Britain has a unique natural rate of unemployment.

NOTES

An early version of this chapter was presented at the 1986 St Andrews conference on Unemployment Hysteresis, which was organized by Rod Cross. We owe a debt of gratitude to those who provided the data for this work. In true scientific spirit, Richard Layard, Steve Nickell, Peter Smith and Sean Holly kindly passed on to us the data sets used in Layard and Nickell (1986) and Smith and Holly (1985). The help of Andy Murfin was also invaluable, and Alex Bowen generously allowed us to use his data on the capital stock in the UK manufacturing sector. We are grateful to all these colleagues. For their helpful suggestions – over a number of years of discussion on this issue – we should also like to thank Steve Bazen, Olivier Blanchard, Charles Bean, Elias Dinenis, Richard Disney, Huw Dixon, Tim Jenkinson, Peter McGregor, Dennis Snower, David Stanton, Larry Summers and Steve Nickell. Just as the first draft of the chapter was being written, Chris Pissarides gave us a copy of Pissarides (1986), which also tests, though in a different way and on different data, for the existence of multiple equilibria. Our results are consistent with his.

1 There is, of course, an older Keynesian tradition which opposes it. See also Beckerman and Jenkinson (1986a and 1986b).
2 Where the equilibrium rate is a function of previous unemployment rates, perhaps, as in Hargreaves Heap (1980). Phelps (1972) is an early reference. Carruth and Oswald (1986) discuss related issues.
3 See, for example, Raj and Ullah (1981).
4 In fact the results are consistent with an efficient bargain model in which the contract curve has a negative gradient, but we have not explored this line.
5 We tested for up to a fourth-order polynomial and eventually settled on a third-order representation.
6 We tested for polynomials (in aggregate demand) in real wage and mark-up equations, but found nothing).
7 In this sense it could be argued that it may be going a little far to call the demand curve S-shaped.
8 Product prices are substituted out.
9 This is therefore a little different from the log-linear estimates in Smith and Holly (1985) and Dinenis (1986).
10 In this model we did not use a Layard-Nickell p^e variable.
11 This can only, of course, be a conjecture.
12 In the sense that it would accept incorrectly half the time.
13 There is no reason to believe that the world is best thought of using the mathematical concepts of functions and mappings. But it is hard to know what the alternative might be.

APPENDIX

Labour Market Model

We provide only a basic description of the data. For a full discussion of how the variables were assembled from published sources, see Layard and Nickell (1985a, 1985b, 1986).

N = employees in employment, males and females, Great Britain.

K = the capital stock, gross capital stock at 1975 replacement cost in £,000m. The quarterly data were interpolated using real investment data. The manufacturing capital stock data were calculated by Alex Bowen. We assumed $K - K^m = K^N$.

W/P = real product wage (an adjusted manual earnings variable).

AD = adjusted public sector deficit as a percentage of potential GDP.

$P^*/\bar{P}$ = a measure of competitiveness. p^* is the unit value index of world manufacturing exports from the UN *Monthly Digest of Statistics*. $\bar{P}$ is a gross output price index.

WT = the deviation of world trade from a quintic trend.

U = the male unemployment rate.

L = the labour force, and is defined by Log $L = U + $ Log N.

ρ = the unemployment benefit replacement ratio, Rho.

U^P = a measure of union power based on cross-section regressions of the union/non-union mark-up.

t_1 = employment tax borne by the firm, calculated from aggregate labour cost data.

t_2 = income tax rate, calculated as an average from aggregate data.

t_3 = indirect tax rate, calculated from aggregate data.

p_m = import price index for the UK.

p = value added price index.

Wage Reaction Function Model

These data were drawn from Smith and Holly (1985).

WC^M = real average consumption earnings in manufacturing.

WC^N = real average consumption earnings in non-manufacturing.

A full definition of these variables can be found in the LBS model manual.

The rest of the data used for the wage reaction functions were taken from the Layard and Nickell data set except for:

Q/E^m = Index of output per person employed, manufacturing industries, *Economic Trends*, 1986 annual supplement.

Q/E^T = Index of output per person employed, whole economy, *Economic Trends*, 1986 annual supplement.

PC = Consumer price index, *Economic Trends*, 1986 annual supplement.

REFERENCES

Adams, J.S. 1965: Inequity in social exchange. In Berkowitz, L. (ed.) *Advances in Experimental Social Psychology,* vol. 2. New York: Academic Press, 267–99.

Adams, J. S. and Rosenbaum, W. E. 1964: The relationship of worker productivity to cognitive dissonance about wage inequities. *Journal of Abnormal and Social Psychology,* 69, 19–25.

Arrow, K. J. and Hahn, F. H. 1971: *General Competitive Analysis.* Edinburgh: Oliver and Boyd.

Ashenfelter, O. and Card, D. 1982: Time series representations of economic variables and alternative models of the labour market. *Review of Economic Studies,* 49, 761–82.

Becker, G. S. 1981: Altruism in the family and selfishness in the market place. *Economica,* 48, 1–16.

Beckerman, W. and Jenkinson, T. 1986a: What stopped inflation? Unemployment or commodity prices? *Economic Journal,* 96, 39–54.

Beckerman, W. and Jenkinson, T. 1986b: Disaggregative Versus Aggregate Wage Equations. Oxford, mimeo.

Blackaby, F. T. 1978: The reform of the wage bargaining system. *National Institute Economic Review,* 85, 49–54.

Brown, W. A. and Sisson, K. 1975: The use of comparisons in workplace wage determination, *British Journal of Industrial Relations,* 13, 23–54.

Carruth, A. A. and Oswald, A. J. 1981: The determination of union and non-union wage rates. *European Economic Review,* 16, 285–302.

Carruth, A. A. and Oswald, A. J. 1985: Miners' wages in post-War Britain: An application of a model of trade union behaviour. *Economic Journal,* 95, 1003–20.

Carruth, A. A. and Oswald, A. J. 1986a: A test of a model of trade union behaviour: The coal and steel industries in Britain. *Oxford Bulletin of Economics and Statistics,* 48, 1–18.

Carruth, A. A. and Oswald, A. J. 1986b: On union preferences and labour market models: Insiders and outsiders. London School of Economics, Centre for Labour Economics, Working Paper No. 823.

Collard, D. 1978: *Altruism and the Economy.* New York: Oxford University Press.

Davidson, C. 1985: Multi-unit Bargaining in Oligopolistic Industries. Michigan State University, mimeo.

Debreu, G. 1952: A social equilibrium existence theorem. *Proceedings of the National Academy of Science,* 38, 886–93.

Diamond, P. A. 1982: Aggregate demand management in search equilibrium. *Journal of Political Economy,* 90, 881–94.

Dinenis, E. 1986: Wage Interdependence and the Persistence of Unemployment in an Economy. London School of Economics, Centre for Labour Economics, mimeo.

Friedman, J. W. 1977: *Oligopoly and the Theory of Games.* Amsterdam: North-Holland.

Friedman, M. 1968: The role of monetary policy. *American Economic Review.* 48, 1–17.

Greenhalgh, C. A., Layard, P. R. G. and Oswald, A. J. 1983: *The Causes of Unemployment*. Oxford: Oxford University Press.

Gylfason, T. and Lindbeck, A. 1984: Union rivalry and wages: An oligopolistic approach. *Economica*, 42, 420–37.

Hamermesh, D. S. 1975: Interdependence in the labour market. *Economica*, 42, 420–37.

Hargreaves Heap, S. P. 1980: Choosing the wrong natural rate: Accelerating inflation or decelerating employment and growth? *Economic Journal*, 90, 611–20.

Hendry, D. F. 1980: Econometrics – Alchemy or science? *Economica*, 47, 387–406.

Jackman, R. 1985: Counter-inflationary policy in a unionised economy with non-synchronised wage setting. *Scandinavian Journal of Economics*, 87, 357–78.

Johnson, G. E. and Layard, R. 1986: The natural rate of unemployment: Explanation and policy. In Ashenfelter, O. and Layard, R. (eds) *Handbook of Labor Economics*, Amsterdam: North-Holland.

Keynes, J. M. 1936: *The General Theory of Employment, Interest and Money*. New York: Harcourt Brace.

Lawler, E. E. 1968: Equity theory as a predictor of productivity and work quality. *Psychological Bulletin*, 70, 596–610.

Layard, R. and Nickell, S. J. 1985a: The causes of British unemployment. *National Institute Economic Review*. 111, 62–85.

Layard, R. and Nickell, S. J. 1985b: Unemployment, real wages and aggregate demand in Europe, Japan and US. *Journal of Monetary Economics*, Carnegie-Rochester Conference Series on Public Policy, No. 23, Supplement, Amsterdam: North-Holland.

Layard, R. and Nickell, S. J. 1986: Unemployment in Britain. *Economica*, Supplement, 53, S–121–S170.

Leamer, E. 1983: Let's take the con out of econometrics. *American Economic Review*, 73, 31–43.

McDonald, I. M. and Solow, R. M. 1981: Wage bargaining and employment. *American Economic Review*, 71, 896–908.

Newell, A. and Symons, J. 1985: Wages and Employment in the OECD Countries. London School of Economics, Centre for Labour Economics, Discussion Paper No. 219.

Oswald, A. J. 1979: Wage determination in an economy with many trade unions. *Oxford Economic Papers*, 31, 369–85.

Oswald, A. J. 1983: Altruism, jealousy and the theory of optimal non-linear taxation. *Journal of Public Economics*, 20, 77–88.

Oswald, A. J. 1985: A Theory of Incomes Policy. London School of Economics, Centre for Labour Economics, mimeo.

Phelps, E. S. 1972: *Inflation Policy and Unemployment Theory: The Cost-Benefit Approach to Monetary Planing*, New York: Norton.

Pissarides, C. A. 1985: Taxes, subsidies and equilibrium unemployment. *Review of Economic Studies*. 52, 121–34.

Pissarides, C. A. 1986: Unemployment and Vacancies in Britain: Facts, Theory and Policy. London School of Economics, Centre for Labour Economics, Working Paper No. 826.

Raj, B. and Ullah, A. 1981: *Econometrics: A Varying Coefficients Approach.* Croom Helm: London.

Rosen, S. 1969: Trade union power, threat effects and the extent of organisation. *Review of Economic Studies,* 36, 185–96.

Rosen, S. 1970: Unionism and the occupational wage structure in the United States. *International Economic Review,* 11, 269–86.

Runciman, W. G. 1972: *Relative Deprivation and Social Justice.* London: Routledge and Kegan Paul.

Sachs, J. D. 1986: High Unemployment in Europe: Diagnosis and Policy Implications. National Bureau of Economic Research, Working Paper No. 1830.

Sargan, J. 1964: Wages and prices in the UK. In Hart, P. E., Mills, G. and Whittaker, J. (eds) *Econometric Analaysis for National Economic Manning.* Macmillan: New York.

Smith, P. and Holly, S. 1985: Wage and Employment Determination in the UK. London Business School, Centre for Economic Forecasting, Discussion Paper No. 137.

Solow, R. M. and Stiglitz, J. E. 1968: Output, employment and wages in the short run. *Quarterly Journal of Economics,* 82, 537–60.

Symons, J. S. 1985: Relative prices and the demand for British manufacturing. *Economica.* 52, 37–50.

White, H. 1980: A heteroscedastic-consistent covariance matrix estimator and a direct test for heteroscedasticity. *Econometrica,* 48, 817–38.

Willman, P. 1982: *Fairness, Collective Bargaining, and Incomes Policy.* Oxford: Clarendon Press.

13

Why is Wage Inflation in Britain So High?

STEPHEN NICKELL

Introduction

One of the most puzzling features of the British economy over the last few years has been the persistence of a relatively high level of wage inflation despite record levels of unemployment. In the standard natural rate model, if unemployment is significantly above the natural rate, then we should observe falling rates of wage inflation. Since 1982, wage inflation has not fallen to any significant extent[1] yet male unemployment is now a staggering 10 percentage points higher than its 1979 level.[2] Must we then conclude that the natural rate of unemployment has risen by an equally staggering amount? Such evidence as we possess appears totally against this conclusion.[3] Therein lies our puzzle and it is the purpose of the chapter to take some tentative steps towards its resolution.

The fundamental question concerns the role played by the level of economic activity in the determination of inflationary pressure. The experience of the last few years has suggested that the *level* of activity has little impact in this regard and that only *changes* in the level have any significant effect. Unemployment rose dramatically in 1980–1 and inflation fell quite sharply, incidentally repeating the experience of 1975–7. However, as we have already noted, the persistence of the new higher level of unemployment seems to have had little effect. This is inconsistent with the standard natural rate story. As a consequence various explanations have been put forward, based loosely on the notion of hysteresis. In Phelps (1972), hysteresis is described in the following terms: 'The transition from one equilibrium to the other tends to have long lingering effects on the labour force, and these effects may be discernible in the equilibrium unemployment rate for a long time. The natural unemployment rate at any future date will depend upon the course of history in the interim.' The general idea, then, is that a rise in unemployment may, of itself, increase the 'natural' rate, at least for a considerable period, if not permanently.

In what follows, we investigate this idea in relation to the workings of the labour market in post-war Britain. In the next section we set up a simple model of wage and employment determination in order to provide a framework for the analysis. This is followed by a discussion of various models of wage behaviour focusing on the question of how the level of activity in the labour market may be expected to influence wages. In the third section we then look at the empirical evidence and present a model which appears to provide at least a partial explanation of events.

A Macroeconomic Framework

In order to analyse the implications of different theories of wage setting behaviour, we must provide some kind of macroeconomic framework.

That is the purpose of this section. The framework we use is very simple. In the long run, unemployment brings into equality (a) the 'feasible' real wage implied by the pricing behaviour of firms and (b) the 'target' real wage implied by the wage-setting behaviour of wage bargainers.

We begin with pricing behaviour. Firms may be thought of as setting value-added prices as a mark-up on wages, where the mark-up is modified, in the short run, by the level of activity in the product market and by price surprises. An increase in the former will tend to raise the mark-up, whereas a positive surprise will be associated with a fall in the mark-up. This latter result occurs because, for example, when inflation is increasing and prices and wages turn out higher than expected, profit margins tend to be squeezed both because wages are accelerating and because prices tend to be kept too low due to the underestimation of competitors' prices.[4]

On the wages side, firms and workers bargain about nominal wages as a mark-up on expected value-added prices, where this mark-up depends, in the short run, on the level of activity in the labour market, on real wages previously attained and on a series of wage pressure variables which we discuss later.

In the longer run the growth of the capital stock and technical progress will lead to productivity improvements, which will, on the one hand, lead firms to reduce their mark-up of prices on wages and, on the other hand, lead workers to bargain for a higher mark-up of wages on prices. In order for the price and wage equations to be 'self-contained' we may note that the (dynamic) production function (e.g. Okun's law) pins down the relationship between the level of activity in the output market (which affects pricing behaviour) and the level of activity in the labour market (which influences wage setting). This allows us to substitute out the level of output market activity from the price equation, thereby enabling us to write down a model where both prices and wages depend on the level of activity in the labour market.

Based on this description, we may write down the following model in log-linear form where we have kept the price equation deliberately simple (i.e. static).

$$\text{Price setting: } p-w=\alpha_0-\alpha_1(p-p^e)-\alpha_2 u-\alpha_3 x \qquad (13.1)$$

$$\text{Wage setting: } w-p^e=\beta_0'+\beta_1'(w-p)_{-1}-f'(u,u_{-1},\ldots)+\beta_3' x+z' \qquad (13.2)$$

where w=hourly labour cost, p=value-added prices, x=trend productivity, u=unemployment rate, z=wage pressure (includes the impact of unions, benefits, real wage resistence etc.) and all parameters are positive. In order to keep the price side simple we use the level of the unemployment rate as the appropriate indicator of labour market activity. On the wages side, however, the impact of activity on wages comes via the function f.

The wage-setting equation reduces to the expectations-augmented Phillips curve if $\beta_1'=1$. However, this restriction is both empirically unjustifiable[5] and theoretically without foundation, so we suppose it not to hold. Then, in order to simplify the theoretical discussion, it is convenient to work with the long-run solution to (13.2), so we set $(w-p)_{-1}=(w-p)-g$, where g is a constant growth rate. We thus obtain

$$w-p=\beta_0-\beta_1(p-p^e)-f(u,u_{-1},\ldots)+\beta_3 x+z \qquad (13.3)$$

where $\beta_0=(\beta_0'-\beta_1' g)/(1-\beta_1')$; $\beta_1=(1-\beta_1')^{-1}$; $f=f''/(1-\beta_1')$; $\beta_3'/(1-\beta_1')$; $z=z'/(1-\beta_1')$.

The great advantage of this model is that it enables us to determine the no-surprise ($p=p^e$) equilibrium values of unemployment and the real wage without recourse to any other parts of the macromodel. This has a cost, however, since it implicitly assumes that all the wage pressure variables, z, are exogenous. This will not be true in an open economy since wage pressure depends, in part, on the real price of imports which enters the wedge between the product wage ($w-p$) and the consumption wage, the latter being relevant to the employee side of the wage bargain. This difficulty can be dealt with at the expense of a good deal of space, and a full exposition may be found in Layard and Nickell (1986a) and the annex to Layard and Nickell (1986b).

The existence or otherwise of a no-surprise equilibrium (determined only by 'supply' factors) does not depend on this question so long as the real exchange rate is pinned down in the long run by a trade balance condition or something similar.

In order to see what this model reveals about the workings of the economy, we first eliminate the real wage between (13.1) and (13.3) to obtain

$$\alpha_2 u + f(u, u_{-1} \dots) = (\alpha_0 + \beta_0) - (\alpha_1 + \beta_1)(p - p^e) + (\beta_3 - \alpha_3)x + z. \quad (13.4)$$

This is the key equation since it reveals how unemployment is determined in the long run when price expectations are fulfilled ($p = p^e$) and, in the short run, how price surprises are associated with deviations from this long-run level. Two points are worth making. First, we assume that price surprises are associated with changes in the rate of inflation. When inflation is rising, then prices turn out to be higher than expected and vice versa. When inflation is completely stable, on the other hand, prices are accurately forecast and $p - p^e = 0$. So we suppose that

$$p - p^e = \gamma \Delta^2 p. \quad (13.5)$$

In reality, of course, we would expect there to be some dynamics in this equation but otherwise this appears to conform reasonably closely to the facts, at least in the recent past. Second, it is clear from (13.4) that unemployment in the long run is influenced by the wage pressure factors, z, and by trend productivity unless $\beta_3 - \alpha_3 = 0$. Suppose the latter restriction does not hold and that $\beta_3 - \alpha_3 > 0$, for example. This would imply that firms and workers were together taking more than 100 per cent of any increases in trend productivity. Such an outcome clearly generates increasing inflationary pressure which can only be neutralized by having permanently rising unemployment. Since this does not appear to have been the consequence of the last 200 years of economic growth, we might expect $\beta_3 - \alpha_3 = 0$ in the long run. This restriction typically appears to be consistent with the data (see Layard and Nickell, 1986a, for example). If we impose this restriction and utilize (13.5), then (13.4) becomes

$$\alpha_2 u + f(u, u_{-1}, \dots) = (\alpha_0 + \beta_0) - (\alpha_1 + \beta_1)\gamma\Delta^2 p + z. \quad (13.6)$$

When inflation is stable, unemployment is at the natural rate as determined by the wage pressure variables, z.[6] When unemployment deviates from the natural rate, this deviation is associated with a particular rate of increase or decrease in the rate of inflation. The form of this association depends crucially on the function $f(u, u_{-1}, \dots)$ which measures the impact of labour market activity on wage determination.

In order to see more clearly what is happening, we can present the equilibrium in terms of a diagram in real wage/unemployment space. In figure 13.1 we present the sort of picture which would emerge if

$f(u, u_{-1}, \ldots)$ was a simple linear function of current unemployment, that is

$$f(u, u_{-1}, \ldots) = \beta_2 u. \tag{13.7}$$

The price and wage equations are both drawn as relationships between the real wage and the level of unemployment, yielding a long-run natural rate of unemployment u^* given by

$$u^* = \frac{(\alpha_0 + \beta_0) + z}{\alpha_2 + \beta_2} \tag{13.8}$$

which is obtained by substituting (13.7) into (13.6) and setting $\Delta^2 p = 0$. If aggregate demand is reduced below the level required to sustain u^*, we move to a point such as A at unemployment $u > u^*$, which is consistent with price and wage setting because inflation is falling. It is clear that the rate at which inflation falls depends on the vertical distance BC since this distance is equal to $(\alpha_1 + \beta_1)\gamma|\Delta^2 p|$. The precise point which emerges depends on the relative sizes of α_1 and β_1. However, this is not our main concern. The key fact to note is that for any level of unemployment $u > u^*$, the reduction in inflation depends on the vertical distance between the price and wage lines at that level of u.

In the light of this framework, two particular aspects of the form of the $f(\cdot)$ function are important. These are its possible concavity and its dynamic structure. Taking concavity first, suppose that f has the form

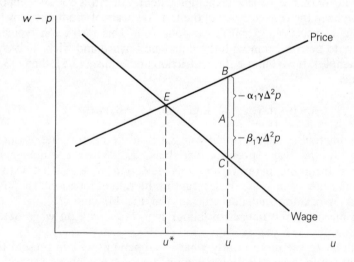

Figure 13.1 *Equilibrium unemployment in a wage/price model*

$$f(u,u_{-1}, \dots)=g(u), g'>0. g''<0. \tag{13.9}$$

How and why this might arise we leave until later although there are, in fact, good arguments in favour of this functional form. Let us simply concentrate on its implications. These are best shown diagrammatically. In figure 13.2 we present the wage–price lines based on (13.1) and (13.3) with (13.9) where it is important to recognize that the wage lines corresponding to different levels of wage pressure must have a constant *vertical* difference between them. The implications are clear-cut.

When wage pressure is low ($z=z_1$), we have equilibrium unemployment u_1^*. If unemployment is actually at $u_1>u_1^*$, then inflation falls at a rate proportional to B_1C_1. At a higher level of wage pressure, we have a higher natural rate u_2^* and when unemployment is at $u_2>u_2^*$, then inflation falls at a rate proportional to B_2C_2. However, it is clear from this diagram that when $u_1-u_2^*=u_2-u_2^*$ then $B_2C_2<B_1C_1$ because of the curvature of the wage line. Thus, the concave shape of f means that as the natural rate gets higher and higher, excess unemployment becomes less and less effective at reducing inflation.

Turning to the dynamic structure of f, suppose it has the form

$$f(u,u_{-1}, \dots)=\beta_2 u+\beta_{21}\Delta u \quad \beta_2,\beta_{21}>0. \tag{13.10}$$

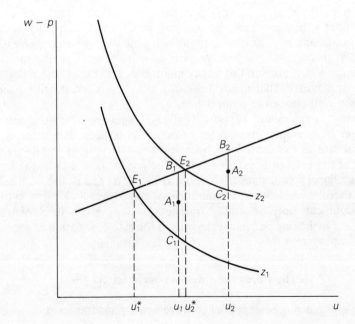

Figure 13.2 *The wage/price model with a concave unemployment effect on wages*

Again, the theory underlying this structure we may leave until later although the Δu term is often associated with a hysteresis effect. Using (13.10), the basic equation (13.6) may be written

$$(\alpha_2+\beta_2)u=(\alpha_0+\beta_0)-(\alpha_1+\beta_1)\gamma\Delta^2 p+z-\beta_{21}\Delta u. \tag{13.11}$$

So although the 'long-run' natural rate, u^*, is given by equation (13.8), when unemployment is falling ($\Delta u<0$), the effective natural rate appears to be somewhat higher since the term $-\beta_{21}\Delta u$ appears on the right-hand side. If we rearrange (13.11) and make use of (13.8) we obtain

$$\Delta^2 p=-\frac{[(\alpha_2+\beta_2)(u-u^*)+\beta_{21}\Delta u]}{(\alpha_1+\beta_1)\gamma}. \tag{13.12}$$

The equation makes the implications of this model quite clear. Even if u is greater than u^*, any attempt to bring down unemployment will generate an increase in inflation if

$$-\Delta u>\frac{\alpha_2+\beta_2}{\beta_{21}}(u-u^*). \tag{13.13}$$

So, for example, if $\alpha_2+\beta_2/\beta_{21}$ is 5, then even when unemployment is four points higher than the natural rate, an attempt to reduce unemployment at a rate of 1 point per year will generate increasing inflation throughout the four years it takes to reach equilibrium. The existence of Δu terms in the wage equation clearly makes the reduction of unemployment that much more difficult even when starting from a position well above the natural rate.

Finally, in this model, suppose $\beta_2=0$ and wages are influenced only by changes in unemployment. This in no sense implies that there is no natural rate as has sometimes been asserted. So long as there is some effect of the level of activity on pricing behaviour (i.e. $\alpha_2>0$), the long-run equilibrium continues to exist. Of course if α_2 and β_2 are both zero, then there is no long-run equilibrium and wage and price setting behaviour can only be made consistent, at any given level of wage pressure, by having perpetual changes in the rate of inflation or the rate of unemployment.

The Impact of Unemployment on Wages

Recalling that our basic model of wage setting has the form

$$w-p^e=-f(u,u_{-1},\dots)+\dots,$$

we have, in the previous section, seen the implications of both the shape and the dynamic structure of the $f(\cdot)$ function for the short- and long-run behaviour of the economy. In this section we discuss various factors which may influence the form of this function. In the original work of Phillips (1958) and Lipsey (1960), the wage/unemployment relationship was not thought of as linear. Indeed the concave shape which we have already mentioned was their preference and Lipsey presented an aggregation argument to justify this. The basic idea is very simple and is most easily described in a regional context with homogeneous labour. Suppose that wages are uniform across regions but that employment is determined within each local labour market as the minimum of the supply and demand within that market (see, for example, Muellbauer, 1978). Furthermore, assume that wages are influenced linearly by the excess demand for labour in the economy as a whole. Then we have the following kind of model. There are $i=1, \ldots, N$ markets with l_i^d, l_i^s being the demand for and supply of labour in each market. In market i,

$$l_i^d = l^d/N + \eta_i, \quad l_i^s = l^s/N + \epsilon_i \qquad (13.14)$$

where η_i, ϵ_i are zero mean random variables and l^d, l^s are the aggregate demands and supplies. Wages are then determined by an equation of the form

$$w - p^e = \beta_0 - \beta_2 z + \ldots \quad z = (l^s - l^d)/N \qquad (13.15)$$

z being the appropriate measure of excess supply. How does this relate to unemployment, U? Unemployment is given by the sum of the excess supplies of labour in those markets in excess supply. Thus we have

$$U = \sum_{\substack{\text{markets in} \\ \text{excess supply}}} (l_i^s - l_i^d) = \sum_{\substack{\text{markets in} \\ \text{excess supply}}} [z + (\epsilon_i - \eta_i)].$$

If we let $\epsilon_i - \eta_i = \theta_i$, then market i is in excess supply if $z + \theta_i > 0$. So we now have

$$U = \sum_{\theta_i > -z} (z + \theta_i). \qquad (13.16)$$

If N is large we may approximate this structure by a continuum of markets indexed by their value of θ. Suppose that θ has a density $g(\theta)$. Then we may write (13.16) as

$$U = \int_{-z}^{\infty} (\theta + z) g(\theta) d\theta \qquad (13.17)$$

which defines z as a function of U with the following properties:

$$\partial z/\partial U = 1/[1 - G(-z)] > 0, \quad G(x) = \int_{-z}^{x} g(\theta) \, d\theta \qquad (13.18a)$$

$$\partial z^2/\partial U^2 = -g(-z)/[1 - G(-z)]^3 < 0 \qquad (13.18b)$$

Thus (13.18a) indicates that z is increasing in unemployment and (13.18b) that it is a concave function of unemployment. So aggregation naturally leads to a concave relationship between the aggregate excess supply of labour and the level of unemployment.

More informal arguments tend to point in the same direction. For example, once the number of job seekers far outweighs the number of potential vacancies, it is not clear that further additions to the unemployed pool will have much impact on firms' wage-setting behaviour since they will have little difficulty in replacing natural wastage in any event. Generally, therefore, it should not surprise us to find that the extent of downward pressure on wages is a concave function of the level of unemployment.

We next turn to some more specific arguments concerning the composition of the pool of job seekers. The quotation from Phelps (1972) given in the introduction is, itself, quite suggestive. Implicit in it is the idea that the very act of becoming unemployed changes the individual concerned in a manner detrimental to his or her future labour market prospects. There may, for example, be a loss of human capital brought about by enforced inactivity. This is likely to be particularly marked if individuals remain unemployed for a long period. There is liable to be a general loosening of their attachment to the labour force as they simply get out of the habit of working, which may have two effects. On the one hand they may become less active in searching for work (see Jackman and Williams, 1985, for example, for positive evidence) and on the other hand they may become less desirable to employers. Both effects have the same implication since they reduce the effective excess supply of labour at any given level of unemployment. Since it is the effective excess supply of labour which influences wages, this analysis suggests that the impact of unemployment on wages will become attenuated as the proportion who have been without work for a considerable period increases. If true, it also has important dynamic implications. When unemployment falls, the proportion of long-term unemployed tends to rise initially since falls in unemployment have, historically, been brought about not only by an increased outflow but also by temporary reductions in the inflow. It is this latter effect which tends to generate a more than proportionate fall in the short-term unemployed. However, in the longer run, the proportion of long-term unemployed actually falls as the general level of unemployment declines. These dynamics imply just the kind of Δu effect on wages discussed in the previous section. Falling unemployment reduces the downward pressure on wages as the pool of job seekers then contains a higher proportion of those less easily assimilated into the ranks of the employed.

A further compositional hypothesis relates to the structure of unemployment not by duration but by region. Since wage bargaining is undertaken nationally in many sectors (e.g. the public sector) and companies (e.g. all the main motor manufacturers and ICI), there may be a tendency for wages to be most strongly influenced by labour market tightness in the most buoyant area of the country, namely the South-East. This indicates that downward pressure on wages will be stronger at any given level of unemployment, the higher is the share of unemployment in the South-East region.

Until now we have tended to look at wage-setting behaviour from the point of view of the employer. Unions are also concerned with the situation in the wider labour market, for their members may themselves become part of this market if they fail to retain their existing jobs. But unions will be concerned not only with the bleakness of the world outside but also with the probability of their members being ejected into it. Fear of job loss is thus a crucial factor. The extent of job loss depends, of course, on the degree to which the union presses for higher wages but it will also depend on how unfavourable is the demand curve which it faces. Reliable information on this may be quite hard to obtain since there will be a natural tendency to mistrust the employer on this question. A particularly relevant indicator may be the extent of recent job losses and this would suggest that wage behaviour may be influenced by the change in employment or the rate of inflow into unemployment as well as its level.

The notion that unions are concerned essentially with the employment prospects of their members and not with the wider labour market scene is the foundation of insider–outsider models exemplified, for example, by the work of Lindbeck and Snower (1985). The following model, due to Blanchard and Summers (1986), gives a flavour of the argument. Unions face a labour demand curve of the form

$$n=\lambda n_{-1}-(1-\lambda)b(w-p)+(1-\lambda)k+\epsilon \qquad (13.19)$$

n=log employment, k=log capital stock plus elements of technical progress and ϵ is a white noise error. Wages are set by unions at the start of the period and since they are primarily concerned with the employment of their own members, they choose wages so that

$$n^e=(1-a)n^*+an_{-1}. \quad 0\leqslant a\leqslant1. \qquad (13.20)$$

Thus they want expected employment (n^e) to be equal to some convex combination of last period's employment and some externally chosen level. Combining (13.19) and (13.20) reveals that wages must satisfy

$$w - p^e = \frac{1}{b(1-\lambda)} [(\lambda - a)n_{-1} - (1-a)n^* + (1-\lambda)k^e] \qquad (13.21)$$

where the e superscript refers to expectation. The key point about this model is that wages are only influenced by past *employment* and that the size of the labour force in relation to this is not relevant. Models of this kind suggest that it is what goes on inside firms that is important, not the world outside. Thus, for example, Gregory (1986) finds that for Australia, wage fluctuations are explained by fluctuations in hours worked within firms rather than by any wider measures of labour market slack.

To summarize, therefore, we have a wide variety of possible specifications of the way in which the level of activity in the labour market exerts downward pressure on wages. In particular we should investigate (a) the concavity of the unemployment effect on wages, (b) the role of compositional effects as modifiers of the basic unemployment effect, particularly those related to duration and region and (c) the importance of employment and other measures of activity within firms, changes in employment and inflow rates.

Results

In this section we present an empirical investigation based on the model described in the first section and the theoretical discussion of the second section. However, we do not estimate the two-equation model of the first section directly (equations (13.1) and (13.2)), but instead embed the wage equation in a three-equation model of the type estimated in Layard and Nickell (1985, 1986a). The remaining two equations are a price and an employment equation and these may be combined to generate the kind of price equation described in equation (13.1). The complete model and its theoretical underpinnings are discussed at length in Layard and Nickell (1986a) and its precise form is set out in the appendix for reference purposes. It contains a number of cross-equation restrictions arising from the production function and the kind of long-run neutrality assumption described in the first section with reference to trend productivity. These are also set out in the appendix. Here we shall simply report the wage equations bearing in mind that they are each based on 3SLS estimates of the complete model. Then for the one which we feel is the most satisfactory, we shall discuss its wider implications in the context of the whole model.

In table 13.1 we present a series of 11 wage equations. Their general form corresponds to that of equation (13.3) but a number of specific points must be noted. First, there is no price surprise term. The reason for its absence is that it proved very hard to find a satisfactory proxy for this unobserved variable. Many possibilities were considered but all proved unsatisfactory (insignificant or wrong signed). This problem does not arise in quarterly data (see Layard and Nickell, 1986a, table 14, for example) but with annual data it seems very difficult to overcome. As a consequence the price surprise term is relegated to the equation error. This does not cause serious problems because it should be close to white noise. However, it is liable to be correlated with current dated shocks, particularly on the demand side, and this explains both the plethora of variables within the equation which are treated as endogenous and the fact that no current dated instruments are used in estimation. Given this, we may safely claim to have obtained consistent estimates of all the relevant parameters despite the omission of the price surprise variable.

Second, the absence of the lagged dependent variable is merely a consequence of the fact that there is no evidence in these data that it belongs in the equation. When it is included, its coefficient is both numerically and statistically indistinguishable from zero. Third, the wage pressure variables, which are discussed at great length in Layard and Nickell (1985, 1986a), fall into two groups. Those which directly influence wages (mismatch, the replacement ratio and union power) and those which form part of the wedge between the real wage, namely hourly labour costs (w) deflated by value added prices (GDP deflator, p) and the consumption wage, namely post-tax hourly pay deflated by the retail price index. This wedge includes real import prices and three tax rates, the employers' labour tax rate, the income tax rate and the excise tax rate. The role of these wedge variables is to capture both short- and long-run real wage resistance. If any element of the wedge goes up, the real wage ($w-p$) will tend to rise if there is any attempt by workers to maintain their consumption wage. In fact, only two of the wedge variables are found to be relevant empirically.

Since these wage pressure terms are trying to capture a whole host of labour market effects on wages, some of which are probably very hard to quantify, we repeated the whole exercise replacing these terms by trend, trend^2, trend^3. The idea here is to check on the robustness of the unemployment effects, that is we try to guard against our finding in favour of a particular specification of these effects because they happen to fit the data exceptionally well in the presence of the particular combination of wage pressure variables we have been able to measure. In the lower part of table 13.1 we report the standard errors of these alternative trend specifications and their labour market activity coefficients in order to check whether any are notably out of line. Generally speaking, they tell much the same story.

Table 13.1 *Wage equations for Britain, 1956–83*

Dependent variable	\(w-p \)										
	1	2	3	4	5	6	7	8	9	10	11
Wage pressure variables											
Mismatch (MM)	0.067 (3.8)	0.042 (3.4)	0.068 (6.1)	0.041 (3.5)	0.043 (3.0)	0.0062 (0.3)	0.029 (1.2)	0.063 (6.1)	0.069 (6.1)	0.065 (6.4)	0.057 (5.4)
*Replacement ratio (ρ)	0.27 (2.8)	0.25 (2.7)	0.28 (2.7)	0.16 (1.2)	0.13 (0.9)	−0.021 (0.1)	−0.14 (0.7)	0.23 (2.3)	0.26 (2.3)	0.34 (3.0)	0.36 (3.6)
*Real import prices ($v \log Pm/\bar{P}$)	0.37 (1.9)	0.46 (3.3)	0.49 (3.1)	0.35 (1.8)	0.24 (1.1)	0.35 (1.1)	0.29 (0.9)	0.47 (3.1)	0.44 (2.4)	0.46 (2.7)	0.44 (3.1)
*$\Delta(v \log PM/\bar{P})$	0.37 (1.5)	0.45 (2.8)	0.29 (1.5)	0.51 (2.4)	0.28 (1.0)	0.31 (0.8)	0.10 (0.2)	0.40 (2.5)	0.29 (1.5)	0.31 (1.8)	0.34 (2.1)
*Union power (Up)	0.056 (1.3)	0.011 (0.4)	0.030 (1.1)	0.061 (2.2)	0.098 (2.4)	0.112 (1.7)	0.115 (1.9)	0.014 (0.6)	0.030 (1.1)	0.021 (0.8)	0.017 (0.7)
*Labour tax rate (t_1)	0.61 (2.3)	0.020 (0.1)	0.66 (3.8)	0.36 (1.7)	0.48 (1.7)	−0.53 (1.3)	−0.41 (1.2)	0.62 (3.8)	0.74 (3.6)	0.54 (2.5)	0.79 (4.6)
Constant	5.87 (4.3)	8.91 (0.4)	5.59 (6.3)	7.29 (7.1)	6.69 (4.7)	9.01 (3.9)	11.22 (6.9)	5.92 (7.2)	5.23 (5.2)	6.78 (5.0)	4.91 (5.6)
Trend productivity ($\log K/L$)	1.07	1.07	1.07	1.07	1.07	1.07	1.07	1.07	1.07	1.07	1.07
Labour market activity											
*$\log u$	−0.113 (5.2)	−0.084 (4.7)	−0.104 (7.8)	−0.067 (2.8)	−0.091 (5.2)			−0.0797 (4.6)	−0.107 (7.7)	−0.086 (5.7)	−0.118 (8.6)

Table 13.1 (*continued*)

Dependent variable	w−p										
	1	2	3	4	5	6	7	8	9	10	11
$\log u_{-1}$		0.042 (2.1)									
$\log u_{-2}$		−0.032 (1.4)									
$\log u_{-3}$		0.064 (3.8)									
*u	−0.378 (1.0)										
u_{-r}	0.803 (1.9)										
*Long-term proportion (u_{52}/u)			0.212 (3.7)					0.225 (4.0)	0.200 (3.1)	0.217 (4.1)	0.260 (4.7)
*South-East proportion (use/u)					−0.056 (1.1)				−0.0243 (0.7)		
Inflow rate (I_{-1})				−0.109 (0.01)				−0.0757 (1.3)			
Employment (n_{-1})						0.844 (2.7)				0.460 (2.2)	

Table 13.1 (continued)

Dependent variable	1	2	3	4	5	6	7	8	9	10	11
						$w-p$					
n_{-2}						-0.577 (1.2)				-0.522 (2.1)	-0.316 (2.1)
*Labour utilization (lu)							0.468 (1.5)				
s.e.	0.0125	0.0102	0.0114	0.0141	0.0142	0.0187	0.0212	0.0112	0.0116	0.0113	0.0103
DW	1.81	2.57	2.08	2.46	1.78	2.17	1.48	1.99	2.12	2.44	2.00
LM (autocorrelation λ^2 (2))	0.96	2.55	1.27	0.87	2.97	3.90	3.42	3.88	3.64	4.30	1.23
Parameter stability											
(a) Split 1970 χ^2	0.53 (χ^2_{10})	11.97 (χ^2_{11})	13.10 (χ^2_9)	6.69 (χ^2_9)	11.42 (χ^2_8)	10.67 (χ^2_8)	1.07 (χ^2_8)	8.58 (χ^2_8)	10.73 (χ^2_8)	9.48 (χ^2_{11})	6.81 (χ^2_{10})
(b) Split 1979 χ^2	6.55 (χ^2_4)	7.67 (χ^2_4)	5.96 (χ^2_4)	16.24 (χ^2_4)	54.9 (χ^2_3)	25.1 (χ^2_4)	5.13 (χ^2_4)	26.0 (χ^2_4)	56.62 (χ^2_3)	26.61 (χ^2_4)	43.59 (χ^2_4)
F	0.54 $F(4.14)$	0.87 $F(4.13)$	1.08 $F(4.15)$	1.79 $F(4.15)$	4.12 $F(3.15)$	2.25 $F(4.15)$	0.49 $F(4.16)$	1.19 $F(4.14)$	1.44 $F(3.14)$	3.05 $F(4.13)$	3.39 $F(4.14)$
s.e. equation replacing wage pressure by t, t^2, t^3	0.0127	0.0121	0.0122	0.0132	0.0134	0.018	0.0212	0.0118	0.0125	0.0119	0.0109
*log u	-0.126 (6.7)	-0.103 (4.1)	-0.0921 (6.3)	-0.100 (4.6)	-0.100 (3.2)			-0.0663 (2.6)	-0.0916 (6.0)	-0.0953 (3.4)	-0.0936 (7.0)

Table 13.1 (continued)

Dependent variable					$w-p$						
	1	2	3	4	5	6	7	8	9	10	11
log u_{-1}		0.0436 (1.7)									
log u_{-2}		−0.0421 (1.6)									
log u_{-3}		0.0457 (1.7)									
*u	0.583 (1.3)										
u_{-1}	0.309 (1.0)										
*Long-term proportion (u_{52}/u)			0.124 (1.8)					0.186 (2.2)	0.134 (1.8)	0.0512 (0.3)	0.223 (3.1)
*South-East proportion (*use*/u)					0.0063 (0.1)				0.033 (0.7)		
Inflow rate (I_{-1})				0.213 (0.3)				−0.872 (1.2)			
Employment (n_{-1})						0.669 (2.4)				−0.056 (0.1)	

Table 13.1 (continued)

Dependent variable							$w-p$				
	1	2	3	4	5	6	7	8	9	10	11
n_{-2}						−1.01 (3.3)				−0.187 (0.7)	
*Labour utilization (lu)							0.098 (0.3)				−0.438 (2.5)

Variables

MM = the absolute change in the proportion of employees in the production sector.
w = log (hourly earnings corrected for overtime plus hourly non-wage labour cost).
p = GDP deflator.
Pm = import prices. $\bar{P}$ = total final expenditure deflator at factor cost.
v = ratio of imports to GDP.
Up = log of union/non-union wage mark-up.
K = capital stock. L = labour force. u = male unemployment rate.
u_{52}/u = proportion of the unemployed with duration over 52 weeks.
use = unemployment rate in the South-East region.
I = inflow rate. n = log employment.
lu = labour utilization rate, which is related to overtime hours and is taken from Mendis and Muellbauer (1984).

All variables are discussed in the data appendix.

Asymptotic absolute t ratios in parentheses.

The parameter estimates are generated by non-linear 3 SLS (TSP 4.0) making use of the model described in the appendix. The autocorrelation and parameter stability statistics refer to single equation IV estimates of the same equation. Starred variables are treated as endogenous. Instruments are discussed in the appendix.

Turning now to the main point of the exercise, namely the labour market activity effects, equations (1) and (2) illustrate the effects of including various lags of the log and level of the (male) unemployment rate. It is clear from equation (1) that log u is a necessary component. This is consistent with our discussion of the concavity of the unemployment effects in the previous section. Equation (2) is rather a freak in the sense that it fits the data extremely well, having the smallest standard error of all the equations, yet we must confess to having discovered it by accident. Having a 3-year lag on unemployment is not something that would naturally spring to mind and the intention was only to go up to 2 years which generates a very poorly fitting model ($s.e. = 0.0185$). The third lag was, in fact, included by mistake and turned out to be the crucial term. The resulting equation then has a small negative level effect in the long run and a series of large negative rate of change effects. The theoretical foundation for the very long lags is not, however, entirely clear.

Models (3) and (5) incorporate composition effects and it is obvious that the duration effect dominates the regional effect. The regional effect (5) is particularly poor at forecasting the 1980s experience because, although wages have remained stubbornly high, South-East unemployment has risen relative to the average which should have led to increased downward pressure on wages. The duration effect, on the other hand, goes in the right direction because the proportion of long-term unemployed has risen sharply over the same period (from around 0.2 to 0.4) thereby reducing downward pressure on wages at any given level of unemployment. Model (4) reveals that the inflow rate is of little consequence so we move on to look at the *pure* insider/outsider models represented by (6) and (7). Here, only what goes on inside the firms is important, and it is clear that whether we use employment (6) or labour utilization[7](7) as our indicator of activity within the firm, the results are grossly inferior in terms of overall fit.

Leaving aside (2) for the moment, the model including a duration composition effect (3) is clearly dominant and so we proceed by incorporating additional effects into this model. Although the inflow effect (8) and the regional composition effect (9) are the right sign, they obviously add little to the model as well as weakening its ability to explain the 1980s, so these may be discarded. Models (10) and (11) are rather more interesting. Model (10) clearly indicates that the change in employment has an additional positive impact on wages over and above the other effects, suggesting that the past employment changes play some role in signalling to union bargainers that times are bad and that jobs are threatened. However, the improvement over model (3) is marginal and again the ability to forecast the 1980s is much weakened, suggesting a lack of robustness in the extra terms. Model (11) is a real puzzle since although it fits the data extremely well, the labour utilization term is significantly wrongly signed. Not surprisingly, therefore, the 1980s forecasting performance is extremely poor and so we simply discard the model.

Models (2) and (3) emerge as the most convincing models.[8] Since there is not much to choose between them, we select model (3) for the further analysis because it enables us to tell a coherent story. Writing it in the form of equation (13.3), we have

$$w-p=\beta_0-\beta_1(p-p^e)-0.104 \log u+0.212u52/u+1.07x+z \quad (13.22)$$

where trend productivity x is captured by the capital–labour force ratio K/L. Note that we were unable to estimate β_1 directly as we have already explained.

In table 13.2 we report the price and employment equations corresponding to wage model (3). The former has prices being influenced by activity in the output market (σ) and the latter generates the relationship between labour market activity and output market activity. In order to produce a dynamic version of the price-setting equation (13.3), we simply eliminate output market activity (σ) between the two equations and rearrange to obtain

$$p-w=(1-0.494)(\alpha_0-\alpha_1(p-p^e))+0.494(p-w)_{-1}$$

$$-0.349u+0.355u_{-1}-0.134u_{-2}+0.355\Delta 1$$

$$-0.123\Delta_2 1-(1-0.494)\ 1.07x, \quad (13.23)$$

Table 13.2 *Employment and price equations for Britain, 1956–83 (corresponding to wage equation (3), table 13.1)*

Dependent variable	$n-k$		$p-w$
Constant	3.09 (5.5)	Constant	−3.55 (3.5)
$n_{-1}-k$	1.02 (8.3)	$(p-w)_{-1}$	0.61 (6.3)
$n_{-2}-k$	−0.38 (2.8)	$*\Delta^2 w$	−0.31 (3.9)
$(w-p)_{-1}$	−0.34 (5.4)	$\Delta^2 w_{-1}$	−0.26 (3.8)
*Demand (σ)	0.089 (4.2)	$*\sigma$	0.031 (1.6)
s.e.	0.00781	s.e.	0.0159

$\sigma=\log (P^*/\bar{P})+9.02AD+0.793WT$. Otherwise see notes for table 13.1.

Variables: $n=\log$ employment; $k=\log$ capital stock; $P^*=$ unit value index of world manufacturing exports in pounds; $AD=$ adjusted budget deficit/potential GDP; $WT=$ deviation of world trade from trend, For other variables, see table 13.1.

where $u=l-n$ where l is log labour force, x is log K/L as before and the nominal inertia terms in the price equation, $\Delta^2 w$, $\Delta^2 w_{-1}$, have simply been represented by $\alpha_1(p-p^e)$. It will be observed that the long-run trend productivity effects are identical in (13.22) and (13.23), this having been imposed on the model.

In order to proceed further and to obtain an equation corresponding as closely as possible to equation (13.6), we first remove the lagged dependent variable[9] from (13.23) to obtain

$$p-w=\alpha_0-\alpha_1(p-p^e)-0.253u+0.075\Delta u-0.338\Delta^2 u$$

$$-1.07x+\text{small terms in } \Delta^3 u, \Delta l, \Delta x. \tag{13.24}$$

Thus the empirical equivalents to equations (13.1) and (13.3) are (13.24) and (13.22) respectively. The first point to note about the wage equation (13.22) is that an increase in the proportion of long-term unemployed, u_{52}/u, has exactly the same effect as an increase in wage pressure. Indeed, since this proportion has risen by 0.2 in the 1980s this corresponds to a permanent increase in wage pressure of around 4 per cent $(0.2\times0.212\simeq0.04)$ which has, of course, raised the effective natural rate of unemployment. However, it is obviously unsatisfactory to treat the duration composition of unemployment as exogenous when we know that it is intimately related to the level of unemployment itself. The following regression gives some idea of this relationship.

$$u52/u= 0.054+ 0.61(u52/u)_{-1}- 2.41u+ 5.58u_{-1}-2.18u_{-2} \tag{13.25}$$
$$\quad\quad (2.1)\quad (3.7)\quad\quad\quad (5.6)\quad (6.5)\quad\quad (2.4)$$

OLS estimation, 1956–83, s.e.$=0.023$, $\bar{R}^2=0.84$

This equation makes good sense. As unemployment rises, the long-term unemployed proportion falls initially since, historically, increases in unemployment come about because of temporary rises in the inflow. In the long run, however, the long-term proportion tends to rise with unemployment. If we remove the lagged dependent variable in (13.25) and substitute into (13.22), we have, after some manipulation

$$w-p=\beta_0-\beta_1(p-p^e)-0.104 \log u+0.532u-1.174\Delta u$$

$$-0.356\Delta^2 u+1.07x+z+\text{small terms in } \Delta^3 u. \tag{13.26}$$

So we have used the dynamic relationship between the long-term proportion and the level of unemployment in (13.25) to generate equation (13.26) where unemployment is the only relevant labour market activity variable. The positive impact of the long-term proportion in

(13.22) has generated a positive unemployment effect because of the long-run tendency for the long-term unemployed proportion to rise with unemployment. Furthermore we now have a large negative Δu effect arising from the fact that when unemployment is rising, the immediate effect is to reduce the long-term proportion and thus to increase the downward pressure on wages at any given *level* of unemployment. These additional terms illustrate the profound implications for the impact of unemployment on wages of the addition of the duration composition effect. So, for example, in the long run, higher unemployment will only tend to reduce wages up to the point where $\partial/\partial u(-0.104 \log u+0.532u)=0$, that is $u=19.45$ per cent. Further rises in unemployment beyond this point will, *in the longer term,* tend to raise wages as the duration composition effect outweighs the direct unemployment effect. Second, *in the short run,* increasing unemployment has a sharp negative impact on wages as the initial excess of short-term unemployed exerts considerable downward pressure on wage bargains.

In the context of the whole model, we can see what is happening by eliminating the real wage from the price equation (13.24) and the wage equation (13.26) to obtain

$$0.104 \log u-0.279u+1.10\Delta u+0.693\Delta^2 u=$$

$$(\alpha_0+\beta_0)-(\alpha_1+\beta_1)\gamma\Delta^2 p+z+\text{small terms in } \overset{3}{\Delta}u, \Delta l. \quad (13.27)$$

As in the first section of the chapter, we have replaced $p-p^e$ by $\gamma\Delta^2 p$ and have thereby obtained the empirical equivalent to equation (13.6). Following the analysis in the first section, we can use (13.27) (or the long-run solutions to (13.24) and (13.26)) and set $\Delta^2 p=\Delta u=\Delta^2 u=0$ to generate our long-run, natural rate equation as

$$0.104 \log u^*-0.279u^*=(\alpha_0+\beta_0)+z. \quad (13.28)$$

The inflation change equation corresponding to (13.12) is obtained by solving (13.27) for $\Delta^2 p$, giving

$$\Delta^2 p=-\left[\left(\frac{0.104}{\bar{u}}-0.279\right)(u-u^*)+1.104\Delta u\right]\Big/(\alpha_1+\beta_1)\gamma \quad (13.29)$$

where we have omitted $\Delta^2 u$, $\Delta^3 u$ terms for illustrative purposes and have expanded $\log u$ terms about $\bar{u}$.[10]

The natural rate equation (13.28) is derived from the long-run solution to the price equation (13.24) and the wage equation (13.26). These are illustrated in figure 13.3 which corresponds to figure 13.2. This figure demonstrates an important point. Even though increased unemploy-

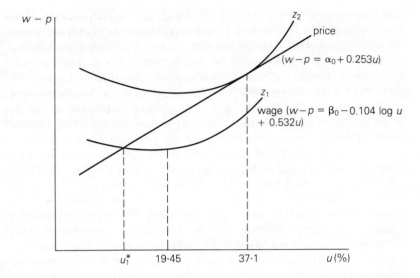

Figure 13.3 *Long-run wage and price functions and the natural rate*

ment no longer helps reduce wages when unemployment is higher than 19.45 per cent, there is no problem about the existence of the natural rate until wage pressure rises to the point where the natural rate reaches 37.1 per cent. Any further increase in wage pressure will then generate inflationary pressure which cannot be contained by more deflation.

If wage pressure is higher than z_2 in figure 13.3, no stable inflation equilibrium exists. This is, of course, a highly speculative result since one might expect some rather dramatic shifts in the structure of the economy before such a point is ever reached. However, the very possibility is of some interest.

More directly relevant to our present concerns are the implications of equation (13.29). In order to see these more clearly, we present a table of values of the expressions $(0.104/\bar{u} - 0.279)$ for different values of $\bar{u}$:

$\bar{u}$	$(0.104/\bar{u} - 0.279)$	$\bar{u}$	$(0.104/\bar{u} - 0.279)$
0.05	1.79	0.12	0.58
0.06	1.45	0.13	0.52
0.07	1.20	0.14	0.46
0.08	1.02	0.15	0.41
0.09	0.87	0.16	0.37
0.10	0.76	0.17	0.33
0.11	0.66	0.18	0.30

This illustrates, for example, that a one-point rise in unemployment from a baseline of 7 per cent (i.e. 1979 male unemployment) will cause inflation to slow down at four times the speed of the slowdown induced by similar rise in unemployment from a baseline of 17 per cent (i.e. 1985 male unemployment). However, this is a long-run effect. The Δu term in (13.29) reveals, for example, that if we start from the current baseline of 17 per cent male unemployment and assume that this is six points above the long-run natural rate, then any attempt to reduce unemployment to this level at a rate of more than two percentage points per year will actually generate increasing inflation from the start. Even if unemployment is reduced by one percentage point per year, inflation will start to rise well before the natural rate is attained. This arises because of the way in which the duration structure of unemployment changes when unemployment declines. Falls in unemployment lead initially to a sharp reduction in the short-term unemployed. This withdrawal of a considerable proportion of the most active and desirable workers from the unemployed pool generates an increase in wage pressure which only eases off when the duration structure returns to normal and the major reduction in unemployment has come from the long-term end of the spectrum.

As we have already noted, we are unable to estimate the impact of price surprises in the wage equation (i.e. the parameter β_1) and so we have, until now, presented our results without attaching any numbers to the parameters α_1, β_1 and γ. However, it seems worthwhile providing rough estimates of these numbers simply to give some idea of the orders of magnitude. In the price equation in table 13.2, we have estimates of nominal inertia generated by the terms in $\Delta^2 w$ and these yield a long-run estimate of $\alpha_1\gamma$ equal to 1.12 (the sum of the $\Delta^2 w$ coefficients in the price equation is -0.57 and we divide by $1-0.494$ to obtain the long-run effect (see equation (13.23)). Estimates of the nominal inertia effect in the wage equation can be obtained from the quarterly wage equation in table 14 of Layard and Nickell (1986).[11] This yields an estimate of $\beta_1\gamma$ equal to 0.36 and, as a consequence, we have the following total estimate

$$(\alpha_1+\beta_1)\gamma=1.48 \qquad (13.30)$$

which can be used to obtain the direct implications of equation (13.29). Given the current baseline of 17 per cent unemployment and assuming a natural rate of 11 per cent, then (13.29) and (13.30) indicate that (core) inflation should be falling at $0.33\times6/1.48=1.34$ per cent per annum. This rather small number illustrates again how even quite a large excess of unemployment above the natural rate has a relatively feeble impact on inflation once unemployment reaches a high level. Putting it more starkly, an additional 240,000 (1 per cent) on the dole queue will serve to reduce inflation by less than ¼ of a percentage point per annum, a rather miserable 'social reward' for so much additional hardship.

Finally, for comparison purposes, it is worth briefly considering the kind of result implied by the model (2) wage equation in table 13.1. The equation corresponding to (13.29) turns out to be

$$\Delta^2 p = -\left[\left(\frac{0.01}{\bar{u}}+0.253\right)(u-u^*)+\left(\frac{0.17}{\bar{u}}-0.075\right)\Delta u\right]\Big/(\alpha_1+\beta_1)\gamma$$

Although this has rather different implications at low baseline levels of unemployment, if we begin from a 17 per cent baseline, the implications are very similar. As before, if we assume that 17 per cent is six points above the long-run natural rate then a reduction of unemployment of two percentage points per year will again induce rising inflation from the start. So the implications for our present situation are much the same although this model provides us with no direct interpretation of this result.

To summarize, therefore, when we allow for the duration composition of unemployment, we are able to go some way towards understanding why, once unemployment reaches a high level, downward pressure on inflation appears weak even when we are a considerable distance above the natural rate. Furthermore we can explain why, in spite of this latter fact, any attempt to reduce unemployment at a significant rate may still lead to rising inflation.

Conclusions

In what has gone before, we have focused on the various ways in which the level of activity in the labour market influences wage setting. We have put forward a number of different theories and demonstrated their implications for unemployment and inflation in both the short and the long run. Our main purpose has been to shed some light on the question of why wage inflation in Britain does not appear to be falling rapidly in spite of the unprecedented levels of unemployment.

In our empirical section we have confronted a number of competing theories with the data and have tentatively concluded that changes in the duration composition of unemployment are of crucial importance in answering the above question. In particular we have found that an increase in the proportion of long-term unemployed strongly attenuates the downward pressure on wages exerted by any given level of unemployment. This arises because the long-term unemployed are less active in the labour market and are, in any event, less desirable to prospective employers. Given their somewhat marginal situation it is easy to understand why they have little impact on wage bargaining.[12]

When this fact is combined with the dynamic relationship between the duration composition and the unemployment level, we are able to go some way towards understanding our present difficulties on the unemployment/inflation front.

It must, however, be emphasized that this work is, of necessity, both tentative and preliminary. Any attempt to capture all the nuances of wage behaviour in the context of a simple, aggregate, annual model is bound to involve *heroic* simplifications and it would come as no surprise (at least to me) if our results turn out not to be highly robust. Nevertheless the evidence presented here indicates that these ideas are worth pursuing.

ACKNOWLEDGEMENT

Many of the ideas in this chapter have arisen as a result of endless hours of discussion with Richard Layard and they are thus as much his as mine. I am also grateful to Olivier Blanchard, Patrick Minford and Andrew Oswald for several stimulating discussions on the topics considered in what follows and to John Knight, Ken Mayhew, John Muellbauer and Nicholas Oulton for comments on an earlier draft. Finally I must thank Paul Kong and Andy Murfin for their most efficient assistance with this work.

NOTES

Originally published in *Oxford Bulletin of Economics and Statistics,* Vol. 49 No. 1, 1987.

1 Strictly speaking, we should talk about falling rates of 'core inflation', essentially wage inflation less productivity growth. The latter has not, however, risen since 1982, so the statement in the text is correct.

2 Throughout the chapter unemployment refers to male unemployment on the pre-1982 definition. Male unemployment is our preferred indicator since measured female unemployment in Britain is a partly unknown and highly variable proportion of its actual level.

3 Layard and Nickell (1985, 1986a) indicate that by 1983 the natural rate of unemployment was around 9–11 per cent. The evidence suggests that the key wage pressure variables underlying this estimate have, if anything, tended to move in a favourable direction since that time and there seem few reasons for believing that wage pressure has significantly increased in the last 3 years.

4 Any tendency to use elements of historic cost in the price-setting process will, of course, tend to exacerbate the squeeze on profits.

5 The paper by Grubb (1986) confirms this for all OECD countries. The results in Coe (1985) would appear to support the expectations-augmented Phillips curve formulation but the test is carried out in the absence of a term capturing the level of trend productivity (only its rate of change being included). Given that the key variable explaining the level of the real wage is omitted it is hardly surprising that the variable itself does not show up.

6 In theory, the model is unbalanced since we should include a set of price pressure variables in the price equation which would influence the price mark-up in the firm's sector. These price pressure variables would equally influence the natural rate and might, for example, include the degree of monopoly and the level of effective taxation. We have investigated the latter variable in Layard and Nickell (1986a) without conspicuous success but any investigation of the former must await conspicuous success but any investigation of the former must await the production of a reliable time series. There is definitely some scope for further research in this area.

7 Labour utilization is a non-linear but increasing function of overtime hours. Thus the higher is measured overtime, the more intensively labour is being utilized.

8 Time does not stand still and at the moment of going to press a number of further questions are being investigated. Despite the results reported in Carruth and Oswald and Gregory in the *Oxford Bulletin of Economics and Statistics*, 49(1), 1987, we have been unable to pin down any important independent role for profits in wage determination. On the other hand, John Muellbauer, using precisely the model structure defined here as well as the same data, has detected an important role for house prices in generating wage pressure, arising from either mobility or cost of living considerations. The unemployment effects are robust to this change although an additional negative term in $\Delta_3 \log u$ improves the explanatory power.

9 This is done by rewriting the model

$$(1-0.494B) (p-w)=\sum x_i \beta_i \text{ as} (p-w)=(1-0.494B)^{-1} \sum x_i \beta_i$$

where B is the lag operator and x represents the set of right-hand side variables. $(1-0.494B)^{-1}$ is then expanded as $1+0.494B+(0.494B)^2+(0.494B)^3+ \ldots$ and terms are collected together.

10 Note that by the mean value theorem,

$$0.104 (\log u-\log u^*)=\frac{0.104}{\bar{u}} (u-u^*)$$

where $\bar{u}$ lies between u and u^*.

11 In order to do this we use the regression in note (iv) of table 14 to compute the long-run relationship between $p-p^e$ and $\Delta^2 p$, noting that we must transform from quarterly to annual rates of change.

12 This interpretation reveals that what we have described is not so different from the insider–outsider model, the insiders are the employees and the short-term unemployed and the outsiders are the long-term unemployed.

APPENDIX

The complete model which is estimated is described at length in Layard and Nickell (1986a) and has the following form.

Employment

$$n=a_0+a_1 n_{-1}+a_2 n_{-2}+a_3(w-p)_{-1}+a_4\sigma+(1-a_1-a_2)k$$
$$\sigma=(p^*-\bar{p})+a_{41}AD+a_{42}WT.$$

Price setting

$$p-w=b_0+b_1(p-w)_{-1}+b_2\sigma+b_3(k-1)+b_4\Delta^2 w+b_5\Delta^2 w_{-1},$$

Wage setting

$$w-p=c_0+c_1 f(u,u_{-1},\ldots)+c_2(k-1)+c_3 v(p_m-\bar{p})$$
$$+c_4\Delta(v(p_m-\bar{p}))+c_5 MM+c_6\rho+c_7 Up+c_8 t_1.$$

Restrictions

$$b_3/(1-b_1)=(1-a_1-a_2)/a_3$$
$$c_2=-(1-a_1-a_2)/a_3.$$

$n=$log employment, $w=$log hourly labour cost, $p=$log GDP deflator, $k=$log capital stock, $p^*=$log unit value index of world manufacturing prices, $\bar{p}=$log total final expenditure deflator, $AD=$adjusted budget deficit/potential GDP, $WT=$deviations of log world trade from trend, $l=$labour force, $v=$share of imports in GDP, $p_m=$log import prices, $MM=$absolute change in the share of production employment in total, $\rho=$replacement ratio, $U_p=$union/non-union wage mark-up, $t_1=$employer's labour tax rate. The first restriction is implied by the fact that the first two equations are consistent with a constant returns production function and the second implies that $k-1$ does not influence the long-run natural rate (see Layard and Nickell, 1985).

The following variables are treated as endogenous: n, $w-p$, k, $k-1$, $p^*-\bar{p}$, AD, $\Delta^2 w$, $v(p_m-\bar{p})$, ρ, Up, t, plus all current unemployment and labour market activity variables included in $f(u,u_{-1},\ldots)$. Additional instruments are $v(p_m-\bar{p})_{-1}$, $(t_3)_{-1}$, ρ_{-1}, Up_{-1}, IPD plus lagged values of the unemployment and labour market activity variables included in $f(u,u_{-1},\ldots)$. t_3 is the excise tax rate and IPD is an incomes policy dummy taking the value 1 for 1976, 1977, zero otherwise.

DATA APPENDIX

Definitions and sources of the variables N, W, P, P^*, P_m, $\bar{P}$, K, L, AD, WT, v, MM, ρ, Up, t_1, t_3, u may be found in Layard and Nickell (1986a).

u_{52}/u (proportion of the unemployed with duration over 52 weeks) refers to the number of unemployed men who have been registered for more than 1 year divided by total male unemployment. Source: *D.E. Gazette*, various issues.

I (the rate of inflow of males to unemployment, GB) shows the number of new male benefit claimants during the course of the year. To obtain an inflow rate this series was divided by the number of male employees in employment. Source: Department of Employment and *D.E. Gazette,* table 2.1.

use (the male unemployment rate for the South-East) includes East Anglia in the South-East as data for each region separately are only available for 1965–83. For this period the individual region rates were weighted by the relative size of their male labour force to obtain an aggregate rate. Source: *D.E. Gazette,* table 2.3, 1.5; *British Labour Statistics Historical Abstract.*

lu (labour utilization rate) is based on a non-linear increasing function of overtime hours and is derived from production function estimates in Mendis and Muellbauer (1984). The actual series is defined by equation (11) of their paper and is based on the estimate given in equation (6).

REFERENCES

Blanchard, O. and Summers, L. 1986: Hysteresis and the European Unemployment Problem. April, mimeo.

Coe, D. T. 1985: Nominal wages, the NAIRU and wage flexibility. *OECD Economic Studies,* Autumn, 87–126.

Gregory, R. 1986: Wages policy and unemployment in Australia. *Economica* (Special Issue on Unemployment).

Grubb, D. 1986: Topics in the OECD Phillips curve. *Economic Journal,* March, 55–79.

Jackman, R. and Williams, C. 1985: Job Applications by Unemployed Men. London School of Economics, Centre for Labour Economics, Working paper No. 792.

Layard, R. and Nickell, S. 1985: The causes of British unemployment. *National Institute Economic Review,* February, 62–85.

Layard, R. and Nickell, S. 1986a: Unemployment in Britain. *Economica* (Special Issue on Unemployment), August.

Layard, R. and Nickell, S. 1986b: The Performance of the British Labour Market. London School of Economics, Centre for Labour Economics, DP No. 250.

Lindbeck, A. and Snower, D. 1985: Involuntary Unemployment as an Insider–Outsider Dilemma. Institute for International Economic Studies, University of Stockholm, Seminar Paper No. 282.

Lipsey, R. G. 1960: The relation between unemployment and the rate of change of money wage rates in the United Kingdom 1862–1957: A further analysis. *Economica,* 27, 1–31.

Mendis, L. and Muellbauer, J. 1984: British Manufacturing Productivity 1955–1983: Measurement Problems, Oil Shocks and Thatcher Effects. Centre for Economic Policy Research, DP No. 32.

Muellbauer, J. 1978: Macrotheory vs. Macroeconometrics: The Treatment of Disequailibrium in Macromodels. Birkbeck College, mimeo.

Phelps, E. S. 1972: *Inflation Policy and Unemployment Theory.* London: Macmillan.

Phillips, A. W. 1958: The relation between unemployment and the rate of change of money wage rates in the United Kingdom 1861–1957. *Economica,* 25, 283–99.

14
Hysteresis Effects in Aggregate Wage Equations
DAVID T. COE

Introduction: A Macroeconomic Puzzle

The major macroeconomic problem in many OECD countries is the high level of unemployment. To some extent, this is also a major puzzle for macroeconomic theory and policy. After the second oil price increase in 1979, macroeconomic policies in many OECD countries were initially non-accommodating, and then directed towards reducing inflation. There were large increases in unemployment, but by 1983 inflation had been substantially reduced from about 13 per cent in 1980 to almost 5 per cent for the OECD area (as measured by consumer prices). Since 1983, policies have been largely directed towards providing a stable macroeconomic framework. The OECD forecast made in the autumn of 1985, before the recent decline in oil prices, showed relatively stable inflation for the half-years from 1984(1) to 1987(1) with little or no decline in unemployment rates, which were expected to be stable at about 8.25 per cent.[1] Other forecasts, such as those of the European Community, also projected roughly stable inflation and unemployment.

Taken at face value, these results – relatively stable inflation after a period of steady macroeconomic policies and no major supply-side shocks – might suggest that the actual unemployment rate was not too different from the natural rate of unemployment. For the United States, this would indicate a natural rate of unemployment of about 7 per cent;[2] for Japan, Sweden and Norway, about 2 to 3 per cent; and less than 1 per cent for Switzerland. Given actual unemployment rates over the last decade or so, these estimates of the natural rate do not appear unreasonable for these countries.

But for much of Europe and Canada, this approach would suggest natural rates of unemployment of the order of 8 to 10 per cent (figure 14.1). These appear unreasonable given that actual rates of unemployment of this order of magnitude are themseleves post-war highs in most European countries. Moreover, it is difficult to identify any structural determinants of the natural rate which would have contributed to such a large increase. Indeed, recent developments in unemployment replacement ratios, minimum wages, non-wage labour costs, industrial relations legislation, the nature of labour contracts, the age/sex composition of the labour force, participation rates, labour mobility etc. indicate that for most countries there has either been little or no change in these factors since 1980. Where there has been some change, it has generally

Unemployment rates

High unemployment smaller European countries[b]

Germany, France United Kingdom, Italy

Australia and New Zealand

North America

Low unemployment smaller European countries[c]

Japan

60 62 64 66 68 70 72 74 76 78 80 82 84 86

[a] Country groupings are weighted averages, 1986 and 1987 are OECD forecasts.
[b] Belgium, Ireland, Netherlands, Portugal, Spain, Turkey.
[c] Austria, Denmark, Finland, Greece, Iceland, Luxembourg, Norway, Sweden, Switzerland.
Source: OECD

Figure 14.1 *Unemployment rates in the OECD*

been in the direction which would suggest a reduction in market imperfections which might be associated with structural unemployment. That is to say, looked at from the point of view of its structural determinants, it would seem that the natural rate should have remained roughly constant or possibly declined since 1980.

This apparent absence of strong disinflationary pressures in the presence of unemployment rates which appear to be far in excess of the natural rate would appear to be inconsistent with the decelerationist implication of the natural rate hypothesis. There are a number of possible explanations for this apparent inconsistency:

1 there may, in fact, still be strong disinflationary pressures arising from the labour market, but even after the large decline in oil prices in late 1985 and early 1986, most forecasts for the major European countries showed only a modest decline in inflation and relative stability in unemployment rates;
2 inflation may have stabilized because the unemployment rate was at the NAIRU, which may be different from the natural rate;[3]
3 the relevant equilibrating mechanisms which would drive the economy to the natural rate, in the absence of government policies directed to maintaining some 'unnatural' rate of unemployment, may be very weak and slow acting;
4 there may be a tendency for the natural rate to follow developments in the actual rate of unemployment.

The last possibility is the case of hysteresis in the natural rate. This chapter presents some preliminary empirical tests of hysteresis. In particular, explicit proxies for the natural rate of unemployment which have the property of hysteresis are tested in the context of an aggregate wage equation. Before presenting the empirical results, the following section briefly discusses the concept of the natural rate and hysteresis.

The Natural Rate of Unemployment and Hysteresis

The natural rate of unemployment, a concept which has enjoyed widespread acceptance among economic policy makers and academic economists alike, was defined by Friedman in 1968 in the following way:

> The 'natural rate of unemployment', in other words, is the level that would be ground out by the Walrasian system of general equilibrium equations, provided there is imbedded in them the actual structural characteristics of the labor and commodity markets, including market imperfections, stochastic variability in demands and supplies, the cost of

gathering information about job vacancies and labor availabilities, the costs of mobility, and so on.

The labour market is in equilibrium at the natural rate of unemployment, and hence there are no inflationary or disinflationary pressures emanating from the labour market. If the natural rate is determined by real structural features of the economy, and in the absence of money illusion, then there is no long-run trade-off between inflation and unemployment, i.e. the long-run Phillips curve is vertical. As is well known, this has strong implications for the conduct of macroeconomic policy; and the discussion of economic policy formulation in most OECD countries appears to be largely based on an acceptance of the implications of the natural rate hypothesis.

One of the reasons for the widespread acceptance of the natural rate hypothesis is that the accelerationist prediction appeared to be largely borne out by inflation developments in many countries in the late 1960s and the 1970s. The mirror image of the accelerationist hypothesis is that if unemployment is maintained above the natural rate, inflation will continuously decelerate. As noted above, this prediction appears to be at odds with the mid-1980s experience of a number of countries and poses a puzzle for macroeconomic theory and policy.

As stressed by Friedman, the natural rate is not constant but it is a function of the structural characteristics of the labour and commodity markets. The natural rate, unfortunately, is not directly observable and attempts to estimate the natural rate as a function of its structural determinants have not been particularly successful. This is not surprising given that we know very little about the properties of a complex general equilibrium system which would incorporate all the market imperfections, etc. noted by Friedman (cf. Tobin, 1972). The structural features of the economy which determine the natural rate, such as those noted above, are commonly thought to be relatively stable and largely independent of macroeconomic policy. But if some of the structural determinants of the natural rate are importantly affected by the actual disequilibrium path of the economy, the natural rate will be affected by macroeconomic policy and will have the property of hysteresis.

In spite of its recent popularity, the concept of hysteresis is certainly not new. Past policy discussions have included the possibility of the 'slow growth trap' or 'dashes for growth'. And at least some of the earliest proponents of the natural rate hypothesis were clearly aware of the potential importance of hysteresis:[4]

Further, the transforming effects of certain kinds of job experience upon people's habits and skills, and possibly too the *modus operandi* of the labor unions, suggest that a course of disequilibrium at a higher inflation rate would tend over time to reduce the equilibrium unemployment rate. The transition from one equilibrium to the other tends to have long-lingering effects on the labor force, and these effects may be discernible in the equilibrium unemployment rate for a long time. The natural unemployment rate at any future date will depend upon the course of history in the interim. Such a property is sometimes called *hysteresis*.

There are at least three structural features of the economy – determinants of the natural rate – which may be importantly affected by the actual path of the economy: the stock of human capital, the stock of physical capital and aspects related to wage bargaining.

Human and physical capital are conceptually similar in the sense that they are augmented by investment flows which can be expected to be related to macroeconomic developments. It is widely accepted that potential output is related to the size of the physical capital stock. The 'gap' measure conventionally used as the activity variable relevant to price developments is actual relative to potential output. Sustained periods of low growth and investment, by reducing potential output, may result in 'speed limits' – product-market bottlenecks – on a non-inflationary increase in the growth of real activity. This phenomenon has often been referred to as capital shortage unemployment.

The stock of human capital is related to such things as education and job experience. The latter is definitionally related to the course of actual employment because of the opportunities for learning-by-doing and on-the-job training. Work experience may also have salutary effects on important attitudinal aspects of the work ethic such as getting to work on time, being 'reliable', learning to work with other people etc. Prolonged unemployment may also lead to deterioration of skills and motivation for the job seeker. And the mere fact of being out of work for a long time may convey a negative signal about expected productivity to the employer, who may use duration of unemployment as a screening device.

The third structural feature of the labour market which may be importantly affected by macroeconomic developments has to do with wage bargaining. Recently, the distinction between insiders versus outsiders in the labour market has been stressed. This is somewhat broader than the distinction between union versus non-union, or between employed versus unemployed. For example, those unemployed for a short duration might reasonably be included in the insider group, whereas those unemployed for a long duration would presumably be included in the outsider group (Layard and Nickell, 1985). Chapter 15 in this volume and Lindbeck and Snower (1984) have developed formal models of insiders, who have an influence on the wage bargain, versus outsiders, who do not. Insiders are primarily interested in maximizing their real incomes and safeguarding their own employment and this leads to hysteresis in the natural rate. The basic intuition is that changes in employment are reflected in changes in the membership of the insider group who have sufficient market power to prevent real wages, and hence employment, from adjusting to ensure labour market equilibrium.[5]

To the extent that these macroeconomically sensitive determinants of the natural rate are important, they will result in hysteresis. The theoretical possibility of these effects, especially those associated with the stock of human and physical capital, might be considered to be largely uncontroversial. Their empirical importance, and hence the policy relevance of hysteresis in the natural rate, is less clear.

Tests for Hysteresis in the Natural Rate in Estimated Wage Equations

Estimates of aggregate nominal wage equations are reported in table 14.1. The specification of the equations is similar to those previously reported in Coe (1985); for the most part, the estimation results are also very similar although sample periods are sometimes different and for some countries data have been revised or changed. The equations generally perform well based on the standard criteria. The unemployment rate is specified to affect wage growth linearly except for Japan, Germany, Austria, the Netherlands and Spain. Inflation usually enters with a two- to three-semester lag, except in North America where the lags are somewhat longer, and the estimated coefficients on inflation are not significantly different from unity. Cyclical productivity growth, the relative growth of minimum wages and changes in the terms of trade enter the equations for some countries. These and other variables such as profits, wages and income taxes, lagged real wages etc., have also been tested in the equations reported in table 14.1.[6]

Hysteresis effects are tested by estimating the following variations on the wage equations reported in table 14.1:

$$w = a0 - a1.U + a2.U^* + \ldots \qquad (14.1)$$

$$w = a0 - a1(U - U^*) + \ldots \qquad (14.2)$$

where w is nominal wage growth, U is the unemployment rate and U^* is an explicit proxy for the natural rate. All other aspects of the equation specification are as reported in table 14.1. Because it may be difficult to distinguish empirically between non-linearity and hysteresis, a linear specification is also reported below for those countries with a non-linear specification in table 14.1.[7]

Data on long-term unemployment can be taken as a proxy for structural unemployment (figure 14.2).[8] The long-term unemployment rate (long-term unemployment as a percentage of the labour force) will

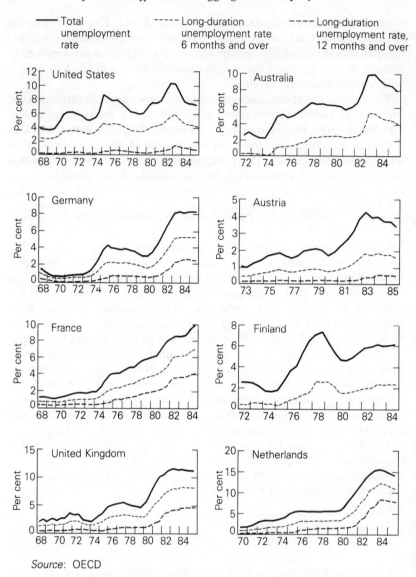

Source: OECD

Figure 14.2 *Unemployment rates by duration*

not be the same as the natural rate, which will also include normal search unemployment etc. A notable feature of recent unemployment developments has been the substantial, almost parallel, rise in long-term unemployment in many countries, especially in Europe. To the extent that the aggregate probability of finding a job decreases with the length of time without a job, the rise in long-term unemployment is indicative of the potential importance which macroeconomically sensitive human-capital effects could have on the equilibrium natural rate. Regression results reported in OECD (1983) indicate that long-term unemployment is itself related to actual and lagged unemployment developmens, i.e. long-term unemployment exhibits hysteresis.

An obvious hypothesis related to the insiders/outsiders distinction, is that the long-term unemployed are outsiders who exert little, if any, restraining influence on aggregate wage growth. In order to test this hypothesis, the wage equations have been estimated with the long-term unemployment rate added as an additional variable as in equation (14.1). Letting UL and US be the long- and short-term unemployment rates, respectively ($UL=U^*$ in equation (14.1)), and given that $U=UL+US$ (by construction), equation (14.1) can be equivalently written as

$$w=a0+(a2-a1)UL-a1.US+ \ldots \qquad (14.3)$$

If the long- and the short-term unemployed have the same impact on wage growth, then the relevant coefficients in (14.3) will be the same, i.e. the estimated coefficient $a2$ will be insignificantly different from zero. If the long-term unemployed have no impact on wage growth, as in the insiders/outsiders model, then the coefficient on UL in (14.3) would be zero, i.e. the estimated coefficient $a2$ will be equal to $a1$ but of opposite sign. This can be constrained to be the case by entering just the short-term unemployment rate (equation (14.2)). Tables 14.2 and 14.3 report regression results of equations (14.1) and (14.2) for alternative long-term intervals for those countries for which data are available. Table 14.2 reports only the estimated coefficients on the unemployment rate terms where all other aspects of the specification are as reported in table 14.1, except for a slightly shorter estimation period. Table 14.3 reports more fully on one of the equations from table 14.2.

For the United States, Germany, France and Australia, when U and U^* are entered separately (the 'unconstrained' results in table 14.2), the estimated coefficients on long-term unemployment (U^*) are incorrectly signed.[9] For the other countries the coefficients on U^* are positively signed and often of similar magnitude to the estimated coefficient on the total unemployment rate (U), especially for the United Kingdom. But in no case is the coefficient on U^* positive and significantly different from zero at the 10 per cent level. There is, however, a problem of multicollinearity; this is apparent in the graphs in figure 14.2 where alternative definitions of the long-term unemployment rate appear to be a relatively constant proportion of the total unemployment rate for some countries.[10] When the difference between the actual and the long-term unemployment rates is entered, the estimated coefficients are usually significantly different from zero and correctly signed.

Table 14.1 Aggregate wage equations[a]

	Constant	Unemployment rate			Inflation[b]	Productivity growth[c]	Other[a]	Dummy variables[e]			SEE	DW	$\bar{R}^2$
		U	$\ln U$	$1/U$									
United States 1964(II)–85(II)	2.646 (0.29)	−0.35 (0.08)			1.01 (0.15)			0.78 (0.18)	−0.56 (0.18)		0.34	1.15	0.87
	1.62 (0.25)	−0.29 (0.05)			0.91 (0.10)			0.64 (0.14)	−0.51 (0.12)	0.83 (0.13)	0.23	1.82	0.94
Japan 1970(I)–85(II)	−3.24 (0.87)			9.56 (2.08)	0.95 (0.15)			−4.40 (0.62)			1.21	1.93	0.89
Germany 1964(I)–84(II)	0.86 (0.81)		−0.62 (0.20)		0.91 (0.24)	0.64 (0.21)		3.90 (0.77)	1.32 (0.36)		1.01	2.39	0.71
France 1964(II)–84(II)	2.31 (0.27)	−0.33 (0.05)			1.09 (0.09)		0.10 (0.03)	1.74 (0.67)			0.64	1.78	0.87
United Kingdom 1964(I)–84(II)	2.28 (0.56)	−0.15 (0.07)			0.94 (0.10)			2.83 (1.53)	3.93 (0.60)		1.50	2.14	0.74
Italy 1971(II)–83(II)	5.58 (2.67)	−0.60 (0.31)			0.96 (0.21)			5.07 (1.54)			2.02	2.03	0.59
Canada 1966(II)–85(I)	4.77 (0.70)	−0.51 (0.10)			0.89 (0.18)			−4.87 (1.33)	−1.62 (0.79)		1.29	2.07	0.58
Australia 1970(II)–(II)	2.11 (2.55)	−0.39 (0.15)			1.14 (0.55)			5.81 (2.24)			1.94	1.99	0.66
Austria	2.66		−1.67		0.81		−0.79	3.50	3.10		1.02	2.38	0.73

971(II)–85(I)	(2.95)	(0.27)		(0.32)		(0.24)			
Netherlands 1971(II)–85(II)	3.48 (1.59)	−1.58 (0.50)	1.10 (0.23)			−2.04 (0.64)	0.87	2.08	0.87
Spain 1965(I)–84(I)	2.98 (1.76)	−1.61 (0.51)	0.99 (0.16)	0.82 (0.44)	0.09 (0.06)	−4.07 (1.23)	1.74	2.15	0.60

[a] The dependent variable is the growth of the wage rate as defined in the data appendix. All the equations are estimated by two-stage least squares on seasonally adjusted semi-annual data; per cent changes refer to semi-annual changes. The standard error of the estimate (SEE), the Durbin–Watson statistic (DW) and the adjusted proportion of explained variation ($\bar{R}^2$) are calculated using the actual values of the independent variables; $\bar{R}^2$ is based on the error sum of squares. Standard errors appear in parentheses below the coefficient estimates.

[b] Specified as current inflation (based on the personal consumption deflator) for Japan. For the United States separate two- and eight-semester moving averages with respective coefficients of 0.41 (standard error of 0.11) and 0.60 (0.19) for the first US equation and 0.31 (0.07) and 0.60 (0.13) in the second equation. For the other countries, inflation is specified as simple moving averages of current and past inflation of either two semesters (Germany, France, Australia, the Netherlands), three semesters (the United Kingdom, Austria, Finland), four semesters (Spain) or five semesters (Canada). For Italy, a two-semester weighted average is used with weights of 0.6 and 0.4.

[c] For Germany, productivity growth is specified as a two-period moving average. For Spain, it is a three-period moving average.

[d] The equations for France and Spain include the growth of the minimum wage relative to the lagged growth of aggregate wages. The difference between the growth of the private consumption deflator and the growth of the GDP deflator is included in the equation for Austria.

[e] Unless specified below, the dummy variables are equal to 1.0 in the following periods, and zero elsewhere. For the United States, the first is for 1970(II)–72(I), the second is 1 for 1973(II)–4(I) and −1 for 1974(II)–5(I); the second equation also includes a dummy variable for 1964(I)–83(I). For Japan, the dummy is seasonal starting as 1 then −1 for 1974(I)–5(II). For Germany, the first is for 1969(II)–70(I), the second is seasonal for 1971(I)–4(II). For France, the dummy is 1 in 1968(II) and −1 in 1969(I). For the United Kingdom, the first is for 1970(I), the second is for 1974(II)–5(I) and −1 for 1975(II)–7(II). For Italy, the dummy is for 1973(I)–3(II). For Canada, the first is for 1970(I), the second is for 1977(II)–8(II). For Australia, the dummy is for 1974(I)–4(II). For Austria, the first dummy is for 1971(I), the second is for 1973(II). For the Netherlands, the dummy is for 1980(II)–1(I). For Spain, the dummy is −1 in 1981(II) and 1 in 1981(II).

Table 14.2 *Estimated coefficients on the unemployment rate (U) and the long-term unemployment rate (U*)*ᵃ
(*indicates significant at the 10 per cent level)

		$U^*=\geq 3$ months			$U^*=\geq 6$ months			$U\geq 12$ months		
		Unconstrained			Unconstrained			Unconstrained		
		U	U^*	$U-U^*$	U	U^*	$U-U^*$	U	U^*	$U-U^*$
United States 1968(I)–85(II)		−0.16	−0.07	−0.65*	−0.21	−0.01	−0.39*	−0.21*	−0.22	−0.24*
Germanyᵇ 1968(I)–84(II)	L	0.75	−1.30	−1.32*	−0.25	−0.05	−0.74*	−0.30	−0.06	−0.40*
	NL	22.16*	−22.56	32.05*	8.43	−9.16	19.01*	0.24	−0.71	1.54*
France 1968(I)–84(II)		1.03	−1.49*	2.20*	0.40	−0.97	−1.14*	0.03	−0.77	−0.60*
United Kingdom 1968(I)–84(II)		−1.39	1.40	−1.31*	−1.34*	1.65	−0.68*	−0.58*	1.01	−0.33*
Austriaᵇ 1973(I)–85(I)	L				−2.52	4.11	−1.30*	−0.96*	2.70	−0.79*
	NL				−5.24	3.24	−0.80	−2.25*	0.41	−1.30
Australia 1972(I)–85(II)					1.41	−2.65	−0.66			
Finland 1972(I)–84(II)					−0.04*	1.42	−1.22*			
Netherlandsᵇ 1973(I)–85(II)	L	−0.53	0.45	−1.05*	−0.34	0.28	−0.48*	−0.20	0.14	−0.23*
	NL	2.47	−3.41	9.75*	−2.05	0.74	4.05	1.03	−1.06	2.21*

ᵃ Each line reports the estimated coefficients on the unemployment rate from two regressions for each definition of the long-term unemployment rate U^*. Unconstrained refers to a single regression where U and U^* are
entered separately; in the other equation $(U-U^*)$ is entered as a single variable. Except for the sample
period, each equation is specified analogously to those in table 14.1.

Table 14.3 reports in more detail equations from table 14.2 with the difference between the total and the long-term unemployment rate, i.e. the short-term unemployment rate $(U-U^*)$; and for comparison, equations comparable to those in table 14.1 estimated over the shorter period for which the long-term data are available. In general the equations with and without the long-term unemployment rate are quite comparable with little change in any of the summary statistics. Except for Finland and the Netherlands, the coefficient on inflation is closer to unity in the equations with the short-term unemployment rate, which is suggestive of a better specification. And for all countries, the coefficient on short-term unemployment $(U-U^*)$ is larger than the coefficient on the total unemployment rate, especially for the United Kingdom and the Netherlands. Thus, there is some evidence that the long-term unemployed exert a weaker influence on aggregate wage inflation.

The question of hysteresis can also be addressed by making explicit assumptions about a proxy for the natural rate. This is done below by emphasizing the degree of hysteresis, related to the speed with which the natural rate (U^*) is assumed to smoothly and monotonically adjust to the actual rate of unemployment, rather than the absolute presence or absence of hysteresis (Coe, 1985). At one extreme, the natural rate does not adjust at all, i.e. U^* is constant; at the other extreme, the natural rate completely adjusts to the actual unemployment rate in one period, i.e. $U^*(t)=U(t-1)$; in between, the natural rate adjusts to the actual unemployment rate with a smooth distributed lag, i.e. $U^*(t)=\sum ai.U(t-i)$ where the ai's sum to unity.

A specification with the change in the unemployment rate rather than the level of the unemployment rate is not unfamiliar.[11] It is, perhaps, somewhat unusual to characterize the change specification as an extreme form of hysteresis, but this is consistent with the insider–outsider hysteresis model developed in chapter 15. The change specification implies that there is only a transitory impact of changes in the unemployment rate on wage growth because the natural rate moves to the actual rate in the next period. Whether the total change takes place in one period, or is stretched out over a number of periods, the implication is that the restraining influence of unemployment on wage growth eventually completely disappears.

Table 14.4 reports the estimated coefficients on the unemployment rate and a proxy for the natural rate specified as lagged unemployment and as a 2- and a 4-year moving average of lagged actual unemployment. For the United States, Japan (the linear specification) and Italy the results in table 14.4 tend to suggest lagged negative effects from unemployment rather than hysteresis effects. But for the other countries there is evidence of hysteresis. This evidence is particularly strong for the United Kingdom and Finland, and perhaps also Germany, where the estimated coefficients on both U and U^* are often both significant, correctly signed and similar in magnitude.

Table 14.3 *Wage equations with the long-term unemployment rate[a]*
(standard errors in parentheses)

	Constant	Unemployment		Inflation	Productivity growth	Other[b]	SEE	DW	R^2
		U	U−U*						
Germany 1968(I)–84(II)	1.95* (1.09)	−0.29 (0.09)		0.69* (0.29)	0.62 (0.24)		1.00	2.75	0.74
	1.89 (1.07)		−0.40 (0.12)	0.77 (0.28)	0.62 (0.24)		1.00	2.81	0.74
France 1968(I)–(II)	3.28 (0.39)	−0.34 (0.05)		0.90 (0.10)		0.07 (0.03)	0.60	2.11	0.84
	3.26 (0.43)		−0.60 (0.09)	0.98 (0.12)		0.07 (0.04)	0.65	1.91	0.82
United Kingdom 1968(I)–84(II)	2.90 (0.80)	−0.19 (0.08)		0.89 (0.11)			1.48	2.12	0.75
	2.89 (0.77)		−1.31 (0.50)	0.97 (0.11)			1.46	2.20	0.76
	2.88 (0.76)		−0.68 (0.24)	0.94 (0.11)			1.45	2.21	0.76
Austria 1973(I)–85(I)	3.32 (1.28)	−0.71 (0.22)		0.68 (0.31)		−0.21 (0.51)	0.90	2.17	0.69
	3.24 (1.24)		−0.79 (0.24)	0.72 (0.31)		−0.25 (0.50)	0.90	2.26	0.69

Table 14.3 (continued)

| | Constant | Unemployment | | Inflation | Productivity growth | Other[b] | SEE | DW | $\bar{R}^2$ |
		U	U−U*						
Finland 1972(I)–84(II)	4.32 (5.36)	−0.63 (0.41)		0.74 (0.50)	0.77 (0.77)		1.85	2.63	0.57
	5.46 (4.82)		−1.22 (0.59)	0.72 (0.44)	0.68 (0.71)		1.83	2.98	0.58
Netherlands 1973(I)–85(II)	0.95 (1.14)	−0.13 (0.06)		1.25 (0.22)			0.79	1.77	0.88
	0.62 (0.96)		−0.48 (0.23)	1.43 (0.15)			0.81	1.79	0.88

[a] The first equation for each country is specified as in table 14.1, including unreported dummy variables, but over a shorter period. The unemployment rate enters linearly in all equations. The second equation is identical to the constrained equations reported in table 14.2. U^* is the greater than 12 months long-term unemployment rate, except for the United Kingdom where U^* is greater than 3 months in the second equation and greater than 6 months in the third equation, and Finland and the Netherlands where it is greater than 6 months.

[b] Relative growth of minimum wages for France and Spain, change in the terms of trade for Austria.

Table 14.4 *Estimated coefficients on the unemployment rate in alternative specifications of hysteresis[a] (equations specified as in table 14.1, except for the unemployment rate, * indicates significance at the 10 per cent level)*

| | | $U^*=U(-1)$ | | | $U^*=1/4\sum_{i=1}^{4}U(-i)$ | | | $U^*=1/8\sum_{i=1}^{8}U(-i)$ | | |
| | | Unconstrained | | | Unconstrained | | | Unconstrained | | |
		U	U^*	$U-U^*$	U	U^*	$U-U^*$	U	U^*	$U-U^*$
United States		-0.20*	-0.11	-0.07	-0.27*	-0.21*	-0.02	-0.24*	-0.19*	-0.01
Japan[b]	L	-1.11	-2.11	0.70	-1.64	-1.46	0.77	-1.87	-1.32	-0.72
	NL	3.52	7.27	-5.50	5.38	4.91	-6.18	5.50	4.87	-2.10
Germany	L	-0.94*	0.74	-1.04	-0.49*	0.33	-0.58*	-0.37*	0.25	-0.43*
	NL	-1.83*	1.19	-0.65	-1.26*	0.71	-1.02*	-1.02*	0.55	-1.00*
France		-0.54	0.21	-0.81	-0.47	0.14	-1.08*	-0.48	0.16	-1.41*
United Kingdom		-0.76*	0.64	-0.79*	-0.59*	0.52*	-0.64*	-0.39*	0.36	-0.42*
Italy		-0.01	-0.65	-0.16	0.76	-1.88*	0.05	1.12	-2.82*	-0.49
Canada		-0.68*	0.17	-0.11	-0.75*	0.28	-0.49*	-0.66*	0.24	-0.73*
Australia		-0.25	-0.13	0.30	-0.66	0.31	-0.22	-1.00*	0.77	-0.86
Austria[b]	L	-1.92*	1.36	-2.57*	-1.23*	0.77	-1.59*	-1.01*	0.70	-1.15*
	NL	-1.75	0.08	-3.71	-1.74	0.09	-3.36*	-1.62*	-0.11	-2.23*

Table 14.4 Continued

| | | $U^*=U(-1)$ | | | $U^*=1/4 \sum_{i=1}^{4} U(-i)$ | | | $U^*=1/8 \sum_{i=1}^{8} U(-i)$ | |
| | | Unconstrained | | | Unconstrained | | | Unconstrained | |
	U	U^*	$U-U^*$	U	U^*	$U-U^*$	U	U^*	$U-U^*$
Finland									
L	−1.95*	1.32*	−1.92*	−1.15*	0.84*	−1.08*	−1.01*	0.56*	−0.88*
NL	−6.30*	3.40	−6.45*	−5.10*	2.72*	−4.11*	−4.09*	3.79*	−3.98*
Netherlands[b]									
L	−0.19	0.02	−0.37	−0.21	0.07	−0.25*	−0.19	0.04	−0.22*
NL	−1.56	−0.01	−0.96	−2.22*	0.78	−2.16	−1.83*	0.42	−2.41*
Spain[b]									
L	−1.69*	1.61*	−2.14*	−0.86*	0.81	−1.03*	−0.59*	0.59	−0.59*
NL	−5.48*	3.96	−4.79	−2.36	0.81	−2.47	−1.48	−1.45	−3.51*

[a] Each line reports the estimated coefficients on the unemployment rate from six regressions, two for each definition of U^*. Unconstrained refers to a single regression where U and U^* are entered separately; in the other equation $(U-U^*)$ is entered as a single variable.

[b] L refers to a linear specification, NL refers to the non-linear logarithmic specification reported in table 14.1.

The estimation results reported in table 14.5 use the deviation of the 4-year moving average of the lagged unemployment rate from the actual. These equations can be directly compared to those in table 14.1. Based on the size of the standard error, the hysteresis specification is marginally better for the United Kingdom, Australia and Spain. For Finland, the size and significance of the inflation term and cyclical productivity is much improved with the hysteresis specification. For the other countries, the equations are roughly comparable to those in table 14.1.

Summary and Conclusions

This chapter has presented indirect evidence on hysteresis by explicitly incorporating hysteresis-type proxies for the natural rate into aggregate wage equations. The results using duration-specific unemployment rates suggest that for the European countries studied here, and particularly for the United Kingdom, the long-term unemployed may exert less influence on aggregate wage growth than do the short-term unemployed. These results are consistent with those reported in Layard and Nickell (1985). The results are also consistent with human capital arguments for hysteresis.

In the second test for hysteresis presented above, a proxy for the natural rate of unemployment was defined as a lagged moving average of the actual unemployment rate. These results suggest little evidence for hysteresis in the United States, Japan and Italy. The strongest evidence of hysteresis is for the United Kingdom, and perhaps Germany, Australia, Finland and Spain. For the other countries studied here, the data are not inconsistent with hysteresis effects as specified above, and certainly do not point to an absence of hysteresis effects. These results are consistent with those reported in chapter 15 for the United States and the major European countries.

Given that the natural rate is itself unobservable, it is not surprising that there is not strong evidence for hysteresis in the natural rate. It should be noted, however, that the phenomenon of hysteresis would only manifest itself after a long and sustained period of increasing (or decreasing) unemployment, i.e. hysteresis would have no implications for the natural rate during periods when fluctuations in actual unemployment were around an approximately stable average unemployment rate. Given that the large increases in unemployment rates have mostly occurred since 1980, it is not surprising that only recently has there been discussion about the potential empirical importance of hysteresis for Europe. This may also partly explain the absence of strong empirical evidence for hysteresis in some of the countries studied here.

Table 14.5 Wage equations with the natural rate specified as a moving average[a] (standard errors in parenthesis)

	Constant	Unemployment[b]		Inflation	Productivity growth	Other[c]	SEE	DW	$\bar{R}^2$
		$U-U^*$	$\ln(U/U^*)$						
Germany	-0.15 (0.72)		-1.00 (0.39)	1.12 (0.24)	0.89 (0.19)		1.03	2.26	0.70
France	2.09 (0.35)	-1.41 (0.29)		1.17 (0.13)		0.09 (0.04)	0.79	1.30	0.80
United Kingdom	1.89 (0.49)	-0.42 (0.17)		0.97 (0.10)			1.47	2.30	0.75
Canada	2.80 (0.62)	-0.73 (0.20)		0.57 (0.18)			1.45	1.68	0.48
Australia	1.63 (2.84)	-0.86 (0.54)		0.97 (0.70)			1.87	2.05	0.68
Austria	0.36 (0.94)		-2.23 (0.83)	1.32 (0.32)		-1.15 (0.43)	1.17	2.36	0.64
Finland	0.56 (1.48)	-0.88 (0.25)		1.05 (0.24)	0.61 (0.23)		1.75	2.44	0.61
Netherlands	-0.79 (0.54)		-2.41 (1.09)	1.74 (0.16)			1.01	1.72	0.82
Spain[d]	1.21 (1.59)	-0.59 (0.16)		1.01 (0.15)	0.87 (0.42)	0.09 (0.05)	1.69	2.13	0.63

a Except for the specification of the unemployment rate, these equations are specified exactly as in table 14.1, including unreported dummy variables.

b $U^* = 1/8 \sum_{i=1}^{8} U(-i)$.

c Relative growth of minimum wages for France and Spain, change in the terms of trade for Austria.

d The linear version with hysteresis gave better results than the non-linear specification used in table 14.1.

NOTES

I am grateful to John Martin and other colleagues in ESD for helpful discussions, and to Menahem Prywes and Clive Brooks for assistance and suggestions. The views expressed here do not represent those of either the OECD or its Member governments.

1 Cf. OECD *Economic Outlook* 38, December 1985. The aggregate figures, of course, mask diverse developments: in the four major European countries, for example, the decrease in inflation continued through 1985 and was expected to stabilize thereafter.

2 Mr Herbert Stein, former Chairman of the US Council of Economic Advisers, suggests the same estimate for the United States using the same reasoning, cf. 'Natural rate' of unemployment is a statistical trick, *The Wall Street Journal Europe*, 17.2.86.

3 The NAIRU is a disequilibrium concept which indicates what level of unemployment would be required to offset any inflationary or disinflationary pressures in the wage–price system. Thus the NAIRU might differ from the natural rate because of the large exchange-rate changes during the early 1980s, for example.

4 The quote is from the introduction to Phelps (1972, p. xxiii) who gave a clear statement of the natural rate hypothesis (Phelps, 1967) which predated Friedman's famous 1986 article. See also Tobin (1972), Hargreaves Heap (1980) and Buiter and Gersovitz (1981).

5 In this regard, it is interesting to note that in some major European countries collective bargaining agreements covering a potentially small number of workers are sometimes automatically extended by the government to a complete industry or group of associated industries. One potential effect of such a procedure would be to effectively reduce the size of the insider group in whose interest wages are bargained, while at the same time extending its influence over the wages of the outsider group. If the outsider group would have settled for lower wages, and presumably higher employment, the unemployment rate related to structural features of the economy will increase. This institutional feature is not important in the United States where, if anything, there appears to have been a decline in pattern bargaining.

6 See Coe (1985) for a more detailed discussion of alternative specifications, etc. The standard estimated Phillips curve implicitly assumes a stable natural rate which is subsumed in the constant. Changes in the natural rate should, therefore, be reflected in changes in the estimated constant terms. This has been tested for with discrete, one-time or sustained shifts in the estimated constants. The possibility of more or less continuous increases in the natural rate has also been tested for by including a time trend as a separate variable. As reported in the final note to table 14.1, there have been shifts in the constants of most of the estimated equations, usually for specific periods in the early 1970s. Only for the United States is there a sustained shift in the constant term (from 1983 (II) onwards). There is little evidence of a steady increase in the constant. A problem with these tests, of course, is that the constant includes things other than a stable natural rate, e.g. trend productivity growth or real wage aspirations, which may also be shifting, perhaps in opposite directions.

7 Linearity concerns the question of whether a given change in the unemployment rate from a low level has the same impact on wage growth as the same change from a high level of unemployment. Hysteresis concerns the question of whether the disequilibrium in the labour market implied by a given rate of unemployment will change over time because the natural rate is somehow related to the actual unemployment rate itself.

8 The annual data reported in OECD (1983) have been interpolated to half-yearly frequency using the aggregate unemployment rate as a reference.

9 The estimated coefficients in the non-linear specifications for the 3- and 6-month duration definition for Germany are very large, perhaps because the long-term unemployment rate was very low (less than 1 per cent) for much of the period.

10 This proportion is lower the longer is the definition of long-term unemployment. The estimated coefficients on $U-U^*$ (short-term unemployment) in table 14.2 would therefore tend to fall as the definition of long-term duration increases from greater than or equal to 3 months, to greater than or equal to 12 months.

11 A specification with both the level and the change in the unemployment rate implies loops around the Phillips curves à la Lipsey.

DATA APPENDIX

For all countries except the United States, Japan, Austria and Spain, the wage variable is constructed as the private sector National Accounts wage bill per dependent employee in the private sector. For the United States the wage variable is the adjusted hourly earnings index for production workers in the non-farm business sector. For Japan it is the index of total wages and salaries, including bonus payments, per regular worker. For Austria and Spain, it is the total national accounts wage bill per dependent employee.

Consumer prices are the implicit National Accounts deflator for private consumption expenditures; domestic output prices are the implicit GNP deflator. The unemployment rate, which is based on national definitions, is total unemployment as a percentage of the civilian labour force. Productivity is defined as real GDP divided by total employment.

Data sources are OECD, *National Accounts, Quarterly Labour Force Statistics* and *Main Economic Indicators* as well as individual country national accounts.

REFERENCES

Buiter, W. H. and Gersovitz, M. 1981: Issues in controllability and the theory of economic policy. *Journal of Public Economics,* February, 33–43.

Clark, P. K. 1986: The Cyclical Component of US Economic Activity. Stanford Business School Working Paper No. 875 (March).

Coe, D. T. 1985: Nominal wages, the NAIRU and wage flexibility. *OECD Economic Studies,* No. 5 (Autumn).

Friedman, M. 1968: The role of monetary policy. *American Economic Review,* March, 1–17.

Hargreaves Heap, S. P. 1980: Choosing the wrong 'natural' rate: Accelerating inflation or decelerating employment and growth? *Economic Journal,* September, 611–20.

Layard, R. and Nickell, S. 1985: The causes of British unemployment. *National Institute Economic Review,* February, 62–85.

Lindbeck, A. and Snower, D. J. 1984: Involuntary Unemployment as an Insider–Outsider Dilemma. Seminar Paper No. 282, Institute for International Economics, Stockholm.

OECD 1983: *Employment Outlook,* September.

OECD 1985: *Economic Outlook,* December.

Phelps, E. 1967: Phillips curves, expectations of inflation and optimal unemployment over time. *Economica,* August, 254–81.

Phelps, E. 1972: *Inflation Policy and Unemployment Theory.* London: Macmillan.

Solow, R. M. 1986: Unemployment: Getting the questions right. *Economica,* May, Supplement to No. 210, S23–S34.

Tobin, J. 1972: Inflation and unemployment. *American Economic Review,* March, 1–18.

15

Hysteresis and the European Unemployment Problem

OLIVIER J. BLANCHARD and
LAWRENCE H. SUMMERS

After 20 years of negligible unemployment, most of Western Europe has suffered since the early 1970s a protracted period of high and rising unemployment. In the United Kingdom unemployment peaked at 3.3 per cent over the 1945–70 period, but has risen almost continuously since 1970, and now stands at over 12 per cent. For the Common Market nations as a whole, the unemployment rate more than doubled between 1970 and 1980 and has again doubled since then. Few forecasts call for a significant decline in unemployment over the next several years, and none call for its return to levels close to those that prevailed in the 1950s and 1960s.

These events are not easily accounted for by conventional classical or Keynesian macroeconomic theories. Rigidities associated with fixed-length contracts, or the costs of adjusting prices or quantities are unlikely to be large enough to account for rising unemployment over periods of a decade or more. And intertemporal substitution in labour supply is surely not an important aspect of such a protracted downturn. The sustained upturn in European unemployment challenges the premise of most macroeconomic theories that there exists some 'natural' or 'non-accelerating inflation' rate of unemployment towards which the economy tends to gravitate and at which the level of inflation remains constant. The European experience compels consideration of alternative theories of 'hysteresis' which contemplate the possibility that increases in unemployment have a direct impact on the 'natural' rate of unemployment.

This chapter explores theoretically and empirically the idea of macroeconomic hysteresis – the substantial persistence of unemployment and the protracted effects of shocks on unemployment. Our particular motivation is the current European situation. We seek explanations for the pattern of high and rising unemployment that has prevailed in Europe since the mid-1970s and for the very different performance of the labour market in the United States and Europe, and we reach some tentative conclusions about the extent to which European unemployment problems can be solved by expansionary demand policies. The central hypothesis we put forward is that hysteresis resulting from membership considerations plays an important role in explaining the current European depression in particular and persistent high unemployment in general. The essential point is that there is a fundamental asymmetry in the wage-setting process between insiders who are employed and outsiders who want jobs. Outsiders are disenfranchized and wages are set with a view to insuring the jobs of insiders. Shocks which lead to reduced employment change the number of insiders and thereby change the subsequent equilibrium wage rate, giving rise to hysteresis. Membership considerations can therefore explain the general tendency of the equilibrium unemployment rate to follow the actual unemployment rate. A number of types of empirical evidence consistent with our hypothesis are adduced. The chapter is organized as follows.

The first section documents the dimensions of the current European depression. It documents, by looking at the movements in unemployment in the United States and United Kingdom over the past century, that high unemployment is in fact often quite persistent. It reviews standard explanations of the current European situation and finds them lacking. It then considers a number of mechanisms through which high persistence of unemployment could be generated.

The second section explores what we find to be the most promising of the possible mechanisms for generating hysteresis. It presents a formal model illustrating how temporary shocks can have a permanent effect on the level of employment in contexts where wages are set by employers who bargain with insiders. Persistence results in this setting because shocks change employment and membership in the group of insiders, thus influencing its subsequent bargaining strategy. We then discuss the role of unions and whether such effects can arise in non-union settings.

The third section examines the behaviour of post-war Europe in light of our theory of hysteresis. It presents direct evidence on the role of unions, on the behaviour of wages and employment and on the composition of unemployment. We find the European experience quite consistent with our model. Europe appears to have high hysteresis, much more so than the US. High unemployment in Europe and low unemployment in the US are well explained both by different sequences of shocks, especially in the 1980s, and by different propagation mechanisms, with Europe exhibiting more persistence than the US.

The fourth section returns to an issue which is of fundamental importance for policy. Granting that Europe has more hysteresis than the US, it is really due to unions or is hysteresis itself endogenous, being triggered by bad times? In an attempt to answer this question, the section compares Europe now to Europe earlier when unemployment was low, and compares the current European depression to the US Great Depression. This last comparison is especially important, given the ability of the US to decrease drastically unemployment in 1939 and 1940, mostly through aggregate demand.

The conclusion summarizes our beliefs and doubts, and draws the implications of our analysis for policy.

The Record of Persistent Unemployment

We start this section by documenting the dimensions of the current European depression. We then demonstrate that persistently high unemployment like that experienced in Europe at present is not historically unusual. Data for the past century suggest a surprisingly high degree of persistence in unemployment in both the United States and the United Kingdom. We argue that such persistence is not easily explained by standard natural rate theories and conclude that theories which allow for hysteresis, by which we mean a very high dependence of current unemployment on past unemployment,[1] are required to explain such persistence.

The European Depression

Table 15.1 presents some information on the evolution of unemployment in three major European countries as well as the US since the early 1960s. While European unemployment rates in the 1960s were substantially lower than those in the United States, unemployment rates in Europe today are substantially greater than current US unemployment rates. The unemployment rate in the United States has fluctuated considerably, rising from 4.8 to 8.3 per cent in the 1973–5 recession then declining to 5.8 per cent in 1979, then rising to 9.7 per cent in 1982 before declining to around 7.0 per cent today. In contrast, unemployment in Europe has risen seemingly inexorably since 1973. In France, the unemployment rate has increased in every single year since 1973, while it has declined only twice in Germany and the United Kingdom. The differences between the European countries and the United States are most pronounced after 1980. While the US unemployment rate is at roughly its 1980 level, the unemployment rate has approximately doubled in the three European countries. The rapid decline in US unemployment after 1982 contrasts sharply with the continuing increase in unemployment in Europe. The last line of the table gives forecasts of unemployment by the European Commission for 1986: they show little

Table 15.1 *European and US unemployment, 1961–1986*

	United States	United Kingdom	France	West Germany
1961–70	4.7	1.9	0.9	0.8
1971–5	6.1	2.8	2.6	1.8
1976–80	6.7	5.2	5.3	3.7
1980	7.1	6.0	6.4	3.4
1981	7.6	9.2	7.7	4.8
1982	9.7	10.6	8.7	6.9
1983	9.6	11.6	8.8	8.4
1984	7.5	11.8	9.9	8.4
1985	7.3	12.0	10.7	8.4
1986*	7.2	11.7	10.9	8.0

*Forecast
Source: Annual Economic Review, Commission of the European Communities, 1986

expected change. Longer run forecasts are very similar: baseline projections by the European Commission put unemployment for the EEC as a whole at 10.4 per cent in 1990, compared to 10.8 per cent in 1985.

Differences in unemployment rates actually understate the differences in the performance of American and European labour markets since the mid-1970s. Europe has suffered the concomitants of high unemployment – reduced labour force participation and involuntary reductions in hours – to a much greater extent than has the United States. Between 1975 and 1983, the labour force participation rate of men in the United States remained constant, while the corresponding rate in OECD Europe declined by 6 per cent. Average annual hours worked declined by 2.7 per cent in the United States between 1975 and 1982 compared with declines of 7.5 per cent in France and 8.1 per cent in Britain. Perhaps the most striking contrast of the labour market performances of Europe and the United States is the observation that between 1975 and 1985 employment increased by 25 per cent, or about 25 million jobs, in the United States while declining in absolute terms in Europe.

Unemployment Rates in the UK and the US over the last 100 Years

European unemployment has steadily increased and, pending an unexpected change in policy, is expected to remain at this new higher level for the foreseeable future. How unusual is such high and persistent unemployment? To answer this question, we now examine the behaviour of unemployment over the last 100 years in both the UK and the US.

Figures 15.1 and 15.2 plot unemployment for each of the two countries, for the period 1890–1985 for the UK, and 1892–1985 for the US.[2]

Estimation of an AR(1) process for the whole sample for each country gives:

$$\text{UK} : u=0.93\ u(-1)+e \ ; \ \sigma \ =2.1\%$$
$$(0.04)$$

$$\text{US} : u=0.90\ u(-1)+e \ ; \ \sigma \ =2.0\%.$$
$$(0.04)$$

In both cases, the degree of first-order serial correlation is high. Unemployment is indeed surprisingly persistent. It exhibits at best a weak tendency to return to its mean.

Examination of the two figures – as well as statistical work – suggests that the evolution of the unemployment rate over the past 100 years is however not well captured by any simple linear autoregressive representation. The degree of persistence as captured by the degree of first-order serial correlation reported above arises in large part from

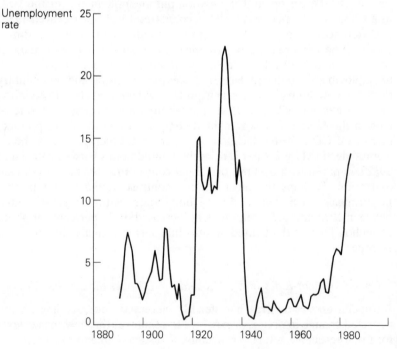

Figure 15.1 *UK unemployment rate*

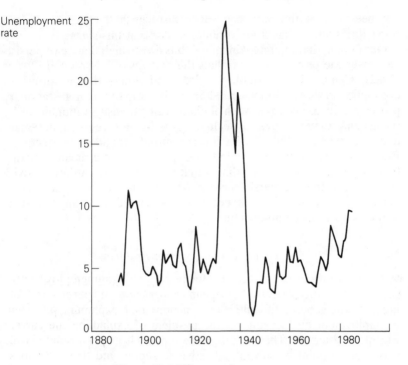

Figure 15.2 *US unemployment rate*

relatively infrequent changes in the level around which unemployment fluctuates. In the UK, when unemployment goes up between 1920 and 1940, it shows little tendency during that period to return to its pre-1920 level; it then returns to a low level during the Second World War, to stay there until the 1960s. The current episode, both past and forecast, is a second instance in which unemployment, after having sharply increased, stabilizes at a new, high level. The US experienced a sustained increase in unemployment from 1929 to 1939, only to see unemployment drop sharply during and after the war to a new, much lower, level. When the degree of persistence in unemployment is estimated separately for periods of high and low average unemployment, there is some weak evidence of greater persistence within periods of high average unemployment.

The time series studied in isolation give little indication as to the cause of the changes in the mean level, which account for much of the persistence in unemployment. They could be exogenous or instead be triggered by unemployment itself, with a few years of high unemployment triggering an increase in the mean level of unemployment, a few years of low unemployment triggering in turn a decrease in that level. In the absence of a tight specification of how this triggering occurs we do not believe that the data can easily distinguish between these two possibilities and we shall not attempt to do so at this stage.

Our finding that unemployment exhibits a very high degree of persistence over the past century parallels the findings of Nelson and Plosser (1982), Campbell and Mankiw (1985) and others that a variety of economic variables follow random walks or other non-stationary processes. In many cases such findings can be easily rationalized by recognizing that the level of technology is likely to be non-stationary and that other variables like the level of output depend on productivity. But the failure of unemployment to display more of a mean reverting tendency is troubling. It is unlikely that non-stationarity in productivity can account for the persistence of unemployment since the secular increase in productivity has not been associated with any trend or upwards drift in unemployment.

Diagnosing Unemployment Problems

What sort of theories can account for persistent high unemployment in general and the current European experience in particular? We highlight the general difficulties one encounters in explaining persistent unemployment by focusing on the problem of explaining the current European situation. The central puzzle it poses is its persistence. While it is easy to point to substantial, adverse supply and demand shocks since the early 1970s, we argue that our standard theories do not easily explain how they have had such enduring effects on the level of unemployment.[3]

Aggregate Demand There is little question that Europe has been affected by large adverse demand shocks, especially since 1980 (see for example Dornbusch et al., 1983). In the 1980s, Europe has to a large extent matched tight US monetary policy while at the same time engaging in a major and prolonged fiscal contraction (see Blanchard and Summers, 1984, for the UK, Germany and France; see Buiter, 1985, for a more detailed study of the UK fiscal policy).

But to the extent that aggregate demand shocks do not affect the equilibrium or natural rate of unemployment, one would expect sustained high unemployment to be associated with rapid declines in the rate of inflation. More generally, standard models of the effects of aggregate demand shocks would not predict that previous estimates of the relationship between inflation and unemployment would break down. There is substantial evidence however that this relation has broken down and that there has been a much smaller decline in inflation than would have been predicted by past relationships. Below we examine the relation between wage inflation and unemployment in detail. But the basic point that previous relations have broken down is evidenced in table 15.2 which gives the rates of inflation and unemployment in 1984 and 1985 for the United Kingdom, France and Germany. Despite the high rates of unemployment, there is no sign of disinflation, with the United Kingdom and Germany experiencing a small increase in inflation and France a small decrease. Econometric estimates of the rate of unemployment consistent with stable inflation show rapid increases since the mid-1970s. Layard et al. (1984), using crude time trends in a Phillips curve relation, find the unemployment rate consistent with steady inflation to have risen from 2.4 in 1967–70 to 9.2 in 1981–3 in Britain, from 1.3 to 6.2 in Germany and from 2.2 to 6.9 in France. Coe and Gagliardi (1985), also within the framework of the Phillips curve but using instead of a time trend a battery of potential determinants of equilibrium unemployment as right-hand side variables, obtain roughly similar results. Aggregate demand shocks have clearly played a role in explaining the increase in European unemployment; but they cannot be the whole story given the increase in the rate of unemployment consistent with steady inflation.

Aggregate Supply Aggregate supply explanations appear more promising if the goal is to explain an increase in equilibrium unemployment. This is indeed the approach followed by much of the recent research. Sachs (1979, 1983) and Bruno and Sachs (1985) have argued that unemployment in Europe is in large part the result of a combination of adverse supply shocks and real wage rigidity. The argument is that real wages do not adjust to clear the labour market so that adverse supply shocks which reduce the demand for labour at a given real wage create unemployment. This argument has two parts: real wage rigidity and the occurrence of adverse supply shocks. We starts by reviewing the evidence on the second.

Table 15.2 *Inflation and unemployment in the UK, France and Germany, 1984–1985*

	United Kingdom		France		Germany	
	π	U	π	U	π	U
1984	4.4	11.8	7.0	9.9	1.9	8.4
1985	5.5	12.0	5.7	10.7	2.1	8.4

π=Rate of change of GDP deflator.
U=Unemployment
Source: Annual Economic Review, Commission of the European Communities, 1986

Table 15.3 presents some information on the behaviour of various supply factors with a potential bearing on unemployment in the UK since 1960.[4]

A first candidate is *unemployment benefits*. Unemployment insurance may raise unemployment if it causes workers to search longer or less intensively for jobs, reducing the pressure that unemployment puts on wages. The second column of table 15.3 gives the average replacement ratio, that is the average ratio of after-tax unemployment benefits to earnings for different categories of workers; it shows no clear movement over time. This is not necessarily conclusive evidence against a role for unemployment benefits: one can easily envisage mechanisms through which increases in unemployment benefits lead to higher real wages, higher unemployment but little or no change in the replacement ratio.

Table 15.3 *Supply factors and UK unemployment*

Year	Unemployment Rate (%)[a]	Replacement rate (%)[b]	Mismatch index (%)[c]	Productivity growth (%)[d]	Change in tax wedge (%)[e]
1960	2.3	42	—	1.9	0.0
1965	2.3	48	41	2.8	1.0
1970	3.1	51	38	3.2	1.0
1975	4.7	49	43	2.7	0.8
1976	6.0	50	38	1.5	2.8
1977	6.4	51	35	1.7	1.9
1978	6.1	50	35	1.4	−0.9
1979	5.6	46	35	2.1	1.3
1980	6.9	45	37	1.5	1.3
1981	10.6	50	41	1.4	2.6
1982	12.8	54	37	1.1	1.0
1983	13.1	54	—	0.5	−1.8

[a] Standardized unemployment rate. *Source:* OECD.

[b] Weighted average of replacement rates relevant to families of different sizes. *Source:* Layard and Nickell (1985).

[c] Index constructed as $\sum | u_i - v_i |$ where u_i and v_i are the proportions of unemployment and vacancies in occupation i respectively. *Source:* Layard et al. (1984).

[d] Rate of change of total factor productivity growth, derived by assuming labour-augmenting technical change. The first four numbers refer to the change in the rate (at annual rate) over the previous 5 years. *Source:* Layard and Nickell (1985).

[e] The tax wedge is the sum of the employment tax rate levied on employers and of direct and indirect tax rates levied on employees. The first four numbers refer to the change in the rate (at annual rates) over the previous 5 years. *Source:* Layard and Nickell (1985).

Indeed, another way of reading the column is that it shows an increase in real unemployment benefits of roughly 30 per cent since 1970. Furthermore, it has been argued that the principal changes in unemployment insurance have occurred through changes in eligibility rules rather than benefit levels. Attempts to estimate the effect of unemployment benefits on unemployment have not been very successful (see Minford, 1982 and Nickell, 1984 for further discussion) and one is led to conclude that the increase in unemployment benefits probably does not account for a large portion of the increase in unemployment.

A second candidate explanation is *structural change*. The argument is that the need for large-scale reallocation of labour associated with structural change tends to increase unemployment. Often it is suggested that the energy shocks of the 1970s increased the rate of structural change and so led to higher unemployment. The adjustment to structural changes may be complicated by real wage ridigity. The fourth column of table 15.3 presents the index of 'mismatch' developed by Layard et al. (1984). The index tries to represent the degree of structural change in the economy by examining the extent to which unemployment and vacancies occur in the same sectors. The results in the table look at occupational mismatch, but results are largely similar when industrial and regional measures are used.[5] There is little evidence of an increase in the rate of structural change since the 1960s when the unemployment rate was consistently low.

Perhaps the most common supply-based explanations for persistent high unemployment involve factors which reduce labour productivity and/or drive a wedge between the cost of labour to firms and the wage workers receive. The fourth and fifth columns of the table give time series for *total factor productivity growth* and the change in the *tax wedge*.[6] It is clear from the table that there has been a substantial reduction in the rate of total factor productivity growth in the wake of the oil shocks. Over the years the total tax wedge has also risen substantially, by 30 per cent since 1960, by 10 per cent since 1970. While it is still true that the real after-tax wage consistent with full employment has risen fairly steadily, it has increased more slowly than it did in the first half of the post-war period.

The Problem with Aggregate Supply Explanations We have now documented the presence of adverse supply developments relative to what might have been expected in the early 1970s. But for these shocks to have a long-lasting effect on unemployment, there must be long-lasting real wage rigidity. If and when labour supply becomes inelastic, supply shocks are then reflected in real wages, not in unemployment. Individual labour supply is surely largely inelastic in the long run. As with aggregate demand explanations, we face the problem of explaining the mechanism that causes shocks to have long-lived effects.

Recent models of union behaviour (notably McDonald and Solow, 1981) have addressed this problem by showing that if wages are the result of bargaining between unions and firms, the result may be real wage rigidity, with shocks affecting employment only. There is however a fundamental difficulty with this line of argument. To take the model developed by McDonald and Solow, if real wages were truly rigid at a rate determined by the interaction of union preferences and firms' production technology, employment would steadily increase and unemployment steadily decrease through time. Annual productivity improvements due to technical change are equivalent to favourable supply shocks. As long as productivity increments and capital accumulation led to the demand curve for labour shifting outwards faster than the population grew, unemployment would decline. This appears counterfactual.[7] Even since the mid-1970s, the cumulative impact of productivity growth has almost certainly more than counterbalanced the adverse supply shocks that occurred.

To rescue this line of thought, it must be argued that real wages are rigid along some 'norm', which may increase over time. But this has two implications. The first is that the dynamic effects of supply shocks on employment then depend on the way the norm adjusts to actual productivity and this is left unexplained. The second and more important one here is that adverse supply shocks have an affect only as long as the norm has not adjusted to actual productivity. Thus, unless the norm never catches up with actual productivity, adverse supply shocks cannot affect unemployment permanently. It seems implausible that the current persistence of high unemployment can all be attributed to lags in learning about productivity. Both the United Kingdom and the United States have experienced enormous productivity gains without evident reduction in unemployment over the last century. High unemployment therefore cannot be blamed simply on poor productivity performance. It can only be attributed to *surprises* in productivity performance. But then it is hard to see how to explain protracted unemployment from lower productivity growth.

Where does this leave us? We have argued that there is plenty of evidence of adverse shocks, be it lower than expected productivity growth, increases in the price of oil or in the tax wedge in the 1970s or contractionary aggregate demand policies in the 1980s. But we have also argued that standard theories do not provide us with convincing explanations of how these shocks can have such a sustained effect on unemployment. Put differently, it is difficult to account for the apparent increase in the equilibrium rate of unemployment – or equivalently in the unemployment rate consistent with stable inflation – by pointing to these shocks. Borrowing from the business cycle terminology, it is not difficult to find evidence of negative impulses; the difficulty is in explaining the propagation mechanism. This leads us to look for mechanisms that can explain the propagation of adverse supply or demand shocks over long periods of time. These include the possibility that current unemployment depends directly and strongly on past unemployment.[8] We now consider various channels through which this may happen.

Theories of Hysteresis

Three types of explanation which loosely speaking might be referred to as the 'physical capital', 'human capital' and 'insider–outsider' stories can be adduced to explain why shocks which cause unemployment in a single period might have long-term effects.

The physical capital story simply holds that reductions in the capital stock associated with the reduced employment that accompanies adverse shocks reduce the subsequent demand for labour and so cause protracted unemployment. This argument is frequently made in the current European context where it is emphasized that, despite the very substantial increase in the unemployment rate that has occurred, capacity utilization is at fairly normal levels. For the EEC as a whole, capacity utilization has shown no trend since the mid-1970s. It currently stands at 81 per cent compared with 76 per cent in 1975, 83 per cent in 1979 and 76 per cent in 1983. It is then argued that the existing capital stock is simply inadequate to employ the current labour force.

We are somewhat skeptical of the argument that capital accumulation effects can account for high unemployment for two reasons. First, as long as there are some possibilities for substitution of labour for capital *ex-post*, reductions in the capital stock affect the demand for labour just like adverse supply shocks. As noted above, it is unlikely that an anticipated supply shock would have an important effect on the unemployment rate. Second, as we discuss in the fourth section, below, substantial disinvestment during the 1930s did not preclude the rapid recovery of employment associated with rearmament in a number of other countries. Nor did the very substantial reduction in the size of the civilian capital stock that occurred during the war prevent the attainment of full employment after the war in many countries.[9] The argument that reduced capital accumulation has an important effect on the level of unemployment is difficult to support with historical examples.

A second and perhaps more important mechanism works through 'human capital' broadly defined. Persuasive statements of the potentially important effects of unemployment on human capital accumulation and subsequent labour supply may be found in Phelps (1972) and Hargreaves Heap (1980).[10] Some suggestive empirical evidence may be found in Clark and Summers (1982). Essentially, the human capital argument holds that workers who are unemployed lose the opportunity to maintain and update their skills by working. Particularly for the long-term unemployed, the atrophy of skills may combine with disaffection from the labour force associated with the inability to find a job, to reduce the effective supply of labour. Early retirement may for example be a semi-irreversible decision. More generally, if for incentive or human capital reasons employers prefer workers with long horizons, it may be very difficult for middle-aged workers to find new jobs. A final point is that in a high unemployment environment, it will be difficult for reliable and able workers to signal their quality by holding jobs and being promoted. The resulting inefficiencies in sorting workers may reduce the overall demand for labour.

Beyond the adverse effects on labour supply generated by high unemployment, the benefits of a high-pressure economy are foregone. Clark and Summers (1982) demonstrate that in the United States at least the Second World War had a long-lasting effect in raising female labour force participation. Despite the baby boom, in 1950 the labour force participation of all female cohorts that were old enough to have worked during the war was significantly greater than would have been predicted on the basis of pre-war trends. The causal role of participation during the war is evidenced by the fact that the participation of very young women who could not have worked during the war was actually lower than would have been predicted on the basis of earlier trends. Similarly, research by Ellwood (1982) suggests that teenage unemployment may leave some 'permanent scars' on subsequent labour market performance. One channel through which this may occur is family composition. The superior labour market performance of married men with children has been noted many times. The effect of the Great Depression on fertility rates, both in the US and in Europe, has often been noted.

Gauging the quantitative importance of human capital mechanisms generating hysteresis if very difficult. Some of the arguments, early retirement for example, suggest that labour force participation should decline rather than that unemployment should increase in the aftermath of adverse shocks. Perhaps a more fundamental problem is that to the extent that there is some irreversibility associated with unemployment shocks, it becomes more difficult to explain why temporary shocks have such large short-run effects. If early retirement is forever, why should it be taken in response to a temporary downturn? Overall, while it seems likely that human capital mechanisms can explain some of the protracted response to shocks, it is doubtful that they are sufficient to account completely for the observed degree of persistence.

A third mechanism that can generate persistence and that we regard as the most promising relies on the distinction between 'insider' and 'outsider' workers, developed in a series of contributions by Lindbeck (see Lindbeck and Snower, 1985, for example) and used in an important paper by Gregory (1985) to explain the behaviour of the Australian economy. To take an extreme case, suppose that all wages are set by bargaining between employed workers – the 'insiders' – and firms, with outsiders playing no role in the bargaining process. Insiders are concerned with maintaining their jobs, not ensuring the employment of outsiders. This has two implications. First, in the absence of shocks, any level of employment of insiders is self-sustaining; insiders just set the wage so as to remain employed. Second and more importantly: in the presence of shocks, employment follows a process akin to a random walk; after an adverse shock for example, which reduces employment, some workers lose their insider status and the new smaller group of insiders sets the wage so as to maintain this new lower level of employment. Employment and unemployment show no tendency to return to their pre-shock value, but are instead determined by the history of shocks. This example is extreme but nevertheless suggestive. It suggests that, if wage bargaining is a prevalent feature of the labour market, the dynamic interactions between employment and the size of the group of insiders may generate substantial employment and unemployment persistence. This is the argument we explore in detail in the next section.

A Theory of Unemployment Persistence

This section develops a theory of unemployment persistence based on the distinction between insiders and outsiders. As the example sketched at the end of the previous section makes clear, the key assumption of such a theory is that of the relation between employment status and insider status. We can think of this key assumption as an assumption about *membership rules*, the rules which govern the relation between employment status and membership in the group of insiders. The possibility of persistent fluctuations in employment arises because changes in employment may change the group's membership and thereby alter its objective function.[11]

In the first part of this section, we develop a partial equilibrium model of bargaining between a group of insiders and a representative firm and characterize employment dynamics under alternative membership rules. (We use the term 'group' rather than the more natural 'union' to avoid pre-judging the issue of whether the membership considerations we stress are important only in settings where formal unions are present.) The second part of the section extends the analysis to a general equilibrium setting and shows how both nominal and real shocks can have permanent effects on unemployment. In the remaining part of the section, we consider mainly two issues; the first is that of the endogeneity of membership rules. The second is that of whether our analysis is indeed relevant only or mostly in explicit union settings.

A Model of Membership Rules and Employment Dynamics

To focus on the dynamic effects of membership rules on the decision of the group of insiders, the 'group' for short, we formalize the firm as entirely passive, as presenting a labour demand on which the group chooses its preferred outcome.[12] We start by characterizing employment and wages in a one-period model. In a one-period model, initial membership is given and membership rules are obviously irrelevant, but it is a useful intermediate step, which will allow us to contrast our later results with traditional ones which treat membership as exogenous. Throughout, we make no attempt at generality and use convenient functional forms and some approximations to retain analytical simplicity.

The One-period Model The group has initial membership n_0 (in logarithms, as are all variables in what follows, unless otherwise mentioned). It faces a labour demand function given by:

$$n = -cw + e \tag{15.1}$$

where n is employment, w is the real wage and e is a random technological shock, with mean Ee, uniformly distributed between $(Ee-a, Ee+a)$. The coefficient a captures the degree of uncertainty associated with labour demand. The group must decide on a wage w before it knows the realization of e. Given w and the realization of e, the firm then chooses labour according to the labour demand function. If n exceeds n_0, $n-n_o$, outsiders are hired. If n is less than n_o, n_o-n insiders are laid off. The probability of being laid off is the same for all insiders.

Before specifying the objective function of the group, we can derive, for given w and n_o, *the probability of being employed.* The probability of being employed for an insider is equal to 1 if $n > n_o$. For $n < n_o$, we approximate the probability (which is not in logarithm) of being employed for an insider by $1 - n_o + n$. This approximation will be good as long as n is not too much smaller than n_o. Under these assumptions, the probability p of being employed is given by (all derivations are in the appendix):

$$
\begin{aligned}
p &= 1 - (1/4a)(n_o + cw - Ee + a)^2 & \text{for } n_o + cw \geq Ee - a \\
  &= 1 & \text{for } n_o + cw \leq Ee - a.
\end{aligned} \tag{15.2}
$$

If even under the worst outcome, which is $e = Ee - a$ and thus $n = -cw + Ee - a$, n is larger than n_o, then the probability of employment is clearly equal to 1. Otherwise, the probability is an increasing function of expected productivity Ee, a decreasing function of initial membership n_o, and of the wage w. It is also a decreasing function of the degree of uncertainty a; the larger a, the lower the probability of being employed in bad times, while the probability remains equal to 1 in good times.

The second step is to derive the choice of w. This requires specifying the utility function of the group. The group maximizes the utility function of the representative group member, which we specify as:

$$U=p+bw.$$

Utility is linear in the probability of employment and the wage. This specification is not the most natural but it is however attractive for two reasons. The first reason is that, as will be seen below, it implies, together with the specification of probabilities given above, that the group exhibits the stochastic equivalent of inelastic labour supply: an increase in Ee is entirely reflected in an increase in real wages and leaves the probability of employment unchanged. We have argued in the previous section that this is a desirable feature of any model of wage determination given the absence of major trends in unemployment rates over long periods of time.[13] Note however that our assumption of stochastically inelastic labour supply is the opposite of that used by McDonald and Solow. Where they postulate a rigid real wage so that the labour supply curve is perfectly elastic, we postulate perfectly inelastic labour supply. The second reason is that it is analytically convenient.

Replacing p by its value from (15.2) and solving for the optimal wage w gives:

$$w^*=(1/c)\{-n_o+Ee+a[2(b/c)-1]\}.$$

Replacing in labour demand gives

$$n=n_o-a[2(b/c)-1]+(e-Ee).$$

Replacing w^* in equation (15.2) and rearranging gives the optimal probability:

$$p^*=1-a(b/c)^2.$$

Thus the wage depends negatively on initial membership. As by definition $E(e-Ee)=0$, whether expected employment exceeds membership depends on the sign of $a[2(b/c)-1]$ thus on whether b/c is less than 0.5 or not. The lower b, the more importance workers attach to employment protection as opposed to the wage; the higher c, the smaller the wage reduction required to increase expected employment. If b/c is less than 0.5, workers set a wage low enough to imply expected net hirings of outsiders by the firm. Note, as mentioned above, the optimal probability of being employed depends neither on the initial membership nor on expected productivity.[14]

Until now, the analysis has been rather conventional. Given the initial membership, insiders choose a wage. This wage and the realization of a disturbance determine employment. But when we go from this one-period model to a dynamic one, there may well be a relation between employment this period and next period's membership. This relation will depend on the form of membership rules. We now examine how this affects employment dynamics.

We first define *membership rules*. We can think of various membership rules as being indexed by m. Those workers who have been working in the firm for the last m periods belong to the group and are insiders. Workers who have been laid off for more than m periods lose membership,[15] that is, become outsiders. There are two extreme cases: the first is the case where m is equal to infinity, so that the initial membership never changes. The second is the case where $m=1$ so that membership always coincides with current employment. The extreme cases highlight the effects of alternative membership rules so we consider them before turning to the more difficult intermediate case.

The Case of a Constant Membership (m=infinity) Let us denote by n_i beginning of period i membership, and by n_i realized employment in period i. In the present case, membership is equal to n_o forever. So, each period, if n_i exceeds n_o, all members work; if n_i is less than n_o, the probability of being employed is given for each member by (approximately) $1-n_o+n_i$. We assume that the one-period utility function of a worker is given, as above, by (p_i+bw_i) and that the workers' discount factor is equal to θ. Thus the utility of a member as of time zero is given by:

$$U_o = E_o \sum_{i=0}^{\infty} \theta^i (p_i+bw_i) \text{ where } \theta \text{ is less than 1.}$$

We assume for the moment that the shocks affecting labour demand are uncorrelated over time, or more precisely that e_i is *iid*, uniform on $(-a, +a)$. (We shall return below to the case of serially correlated shocks.) Then by the analysis of the previous section, the probability of being employed in period i, conditional on w_i is given by (using the fact that $Ee_i=0$):

$$p_i = 1 \qquad \text{for } n_o+cw_i \geq -a$$

$$= 1-(1/4a)(n_o+c\ w_i+a)^2 \text{ for } n_o+cw_i \leq -a.$$

Given that employment outcomes do not affect future membership, and given the assumption that shocks are white noise, the problem faced by members is the same every period, and thus its solution is the same as that derived above:

$$w^*_i=(1/c)(-n_o+a[2(b/c)-1] \text{ and}$$

$$n_i =n_o-a[2(b/c)-1]+e_i. \tag{15.3}$$

In response to white noise shocks, employment will also be white noise. Whether employment is on average larger or smaller than membership depends on whether (b/c) is smaller or larger than 0.5. If the insiders want strong employment protection, they will choose a wage so that, on average, employment exceeds membership and the firm has a cushion of outsiders who are laid off first in the case of adverse shocks.

It is easy to see that the result that employment is white noise will continue to hold regardless of the stochastic process followed by e. As shown above, our assumptions ensure that labour supply is stochastically inelastic. Changes in the expected value of e affect real wages but do not affect the level of employment. Only the deviation of e from its expected value affects the level of employment. By the properties of rational expectations, the unexpected component of e must be serially uncorrelated.

The Case Where Membership Equals Employment (m=1) We now go the opposite extreme, in which membership comes and goes with employment. In this case membership at time i is simply given by employment at time $i-1$: $n_i=n_{i-i}$. If the group kept the same decision rule as in equation (15.3) but applied it to n_i rather than to n_o, equation (15.3) would become:

$$n_i=n_{i-1}-a[2(b/c)-1]+e_i. \tag{15.3a}$$

Thus, employment would follow a random walk, with drift. Optimal wage behaviour (15.3a) under the assumption that membership equals beginning of period employment is however not given by (15.3a). Unlike the behaviour implied by (15.3a) current members should recognize their inability to commit future memberships to wage policies. The subsequent policies of the group will depend on its then current membership. This changes fundamentally the character of the maximization problem. The group membership, when taking wage decisions today, knows that wage decisions will be taken next period by a membership which will in general be different from that of today. This implies in particular that if an insider is laid off, he becomes an outsider and thus considerably decreases his chances of keeping employment with the firm; this presumably leads him to choose a lower wage than in the previous case, where being laid off did not affect his future chances of being hired.[16]

The formal solution to this problem is treated in the appendix. Even with the simplifying assumptions we have made so far, the problem is intractable unless we further simplify by linearizing the group's intertemporal objective function. Let w' be the wage around which the objective function is linearized and let the shocks to labour demand be white noise. The solution to the maximization problem is then:

$$w^*_i = (1/c)\{-n_{i-1} + a[2(b/c)(1/(1+b\theta w'))]\}$$
$$n_i = n_{i-1} - a\{2(b/c)[1/(1+b\theta w')] - 1\} + e. \tag{15.4}$$

The probability of employment for a member is a constant and is given by:

$$p^*_i = 1 - a\{(b/c)[1/(1+b\theta w')]\}^2.$$

Thus, under this membership rule, employment follows a random walk with drift. For a given labour force, there is unemployment hysteresis. Uncorrelated shocks to labour demand affect current employment, and through employment, membership and future expected employment. The drift is positive if (b/c) is less than $(1+b\theta w')/2$, if workers care sufficiently about the probability of employment as compared to the wage. In such a case, although they do not care about the unemployed, they will set the wage each period so as to have the firm hire on average new employees. For a given membership, the wage is always set lower than in the $m=$infinity case and thus the probability of employment is set higher; this is because being laid off implies a loss of membership and imposes a much larger cost than before.

This analysis can again easily be extended to the case where labour demand shocks are serially correlated. The results remain the same; employment continues to follow a random walk. This is a consequence of our maintained assumption that expected changes in labour demand have no effect on the level of employment.

The Intermediate Case (m between 1 and infinity) The intermediate case where workers remain insiders for some time after losing their jobs and where newly hired workers eventually but not immediately become insiders raises an additional conceptual problem. There will no longer be unanimity among insiders. Those who have already experienced some unemployment, or those who have been working in the firm for a short period of time, for example, will favour more cautious wage-setting policies than those who have not. A theory of behaviour in the face of conflict between members is beyond our grasp.[17] A plausible conjecture is that allowing for values of m between 1 and ∞ leads to wage-setting policies that are less cautious than in the $m=\infty$ case but more cautious than in the $m=1$ case.

More importantly, rules corresponding to m between 1 and ∞ are likely to generate unemployment behaviour such as that shown in figures 15.1 and 15.2, namely infrequent but sustained changes in the level of unemployment. Short sequences of unexpected shocks of the same sign have little effect on membership and thus on mean employment. In the case of adverse shocks, insiders are not laid off long enough to lose insider status; in the case of favourable shocks, outsiders do not stay long enough to acquire membership. But long – and infrequent – sequences of shocks of the same sign have a large effect on membership and may lead to large effects on the mean level of employment. The length of the shock necessary to cause a permanent change in employment depends on the membership rules. In general there is no reason why these rules have to be symmetric. The length of time after which an unemployed worker becomes an outsider need not equal the length of time until a new worker becomes an insider. Hence favourable and unfavourable shocks may persist to differing extents.

The results of this section have been derived under very specific assumptions, from fixed membership rules to the assumption that the firm was passive and that outsiders played no role, direct or indirect, in the negotiation process. We must return to these assumptions. Before we do so however, we first show how the model of this section can be used to generate permanent effects on aggregate employment of both nominal and real shocks.

Persistent Effects of Nominal and Real Disturbances on Unemployment

We now assume that there are many firms in the economy, each dealing with its own group of insider workers. We further assume that wages are set in nominal terms, so that nominal disturbances can affect employment. We then characterize the effects of nominal and real disturbances on employment and real wages.

The Derived Demand for Labour Facing each Group The economy is composed of many firms indexed by j, each selling a product which is an imperfect substitute for all others, but being otherwise identical. The demand facing firm j is given by:

$$y_j = -k(p_j - p) + (m - p), \; k > 1.$$

All variables are in logarithms and all constants are ignored for notational simplicity. The variables y_j and p_j denote the output and the nominal price charged by firm j respectively, m and p denote nominal money and the price level. Demand for the firm's output depends on the relative price as well as on aggregate real money balances. The restriction on k is needed to obtain an interior maximum for profit maximization.

Each firm operates under constant returns to scale; the relation between output and employment is given by $y_j=n_j$. If w_j is the wage that firm j pays its workers, constant returns and constant elasticity of the demand for goods imply that prices are given by $p_j=w_j-e$, where e is a random technological shock, which is assumed common to all firms.[18]

Each firm j faces a group of insiders with the same objective function as above, which chooses a nominal wage and lets the firm determine employment. Given the relation between p_j and w_j, we can think of each group j as choosing w_j subject to the demand function:

$$n_j=k(w_j-e-p)+(m-p). \tag{15.5}$$

The Choice of the Wage and Employment We now characterize the decisions of each group j at time zero (and for the moment we do not introduce the time index explicitly). We assume each group to operate under the membership rule $m=1$, so that at time zero, membership in group j is given by $n_j(-1)$. The group now chooses a nominal rather than a real wage, based on its expectations of the price level, Ep, nominal money, Em, and the expected value of the technological shock, Ee, which all enter the derived demand for labour. As we have shown earlier, given such a demand function and its objective function, it chooses a wage so that the expected level of employment is equal to its membership plus a constant term. Ignoring again the constant, this implies:

$$k(w_j-Ee-Ep)+(Em-Ep)=n_j(-1) \tag{15.6}$$

which defines implicitly w_j as a function of $n_j(-1)$, Em, Ep and Ee.

To solve for w_j, we must solve for the value of Ep. We do so under the assumption of rational expectations. As all firms and groups are the same, and are all affected by the same aggregate nominal shock, all groups have the same membership: $n_j(-1)=n(-1)$. Furthermore all nominal prices are the same and equal to the price level, so that the first term in equation (15.6) is equal to zero. Thus, from equation (15.6)

$$Ep=Em-n(-1), \text{ and}$$

$$w_j=Ee+Em-n(-1).$$

The expected price level depends on expected nominal money and negatively on membership. The nominal wage in turn depends positively on expected nominal money and the expected technological shock, and negatively on membership. Replacing w_j and Ep by their values in (15.5) and aggregating over j gives the equation characterizing the dynamic behaviour of aggregate employment:

$$n=n(-1)+(m-Em)+(e-Ee)$$

or, if we reintroduce the time index i,

$$n_i=n_{i-1}+(m_i-Em_i)+(e_i-Ee_i). \tag{15.7}$$

Shocks, Employment and Wages From equation (15.7) only unexpected shocks affect employment. In the case of real shocks, this comes as before from the assumption of inelastic labour supply, which implies that each group sets wages so as to leave employment unaffected by anticipated real shocks. In the case of nominal shocks, the result is the same as in other nominal contract models (Fischer, 1977) and the intuition is straightforward. Workers set a nominal wage which, in view of expected aggregate demand, will maintain last period's level of employment. Firms simply mark-up over this nominal wage. Unexpectedly low aggregate demand leads to unexpected decreases in output and employment, with no changes in nominal wages (by assumption) and in prices (because of constant returns).[19]

These unexpected nominal and real shocks, unlike other contract models, have however permanent effects on employment. This is the result of our assumptions about membership rules. Once employment has decreased, it remains, in the absence of other shocks, permanently at the lower level. A sequence of unexpected contractions in aggregate demand increases equilibrium unemployment permanently. If we assumed that m, the membership rule, was greater than 1, we would again obtain the result that while short sequences of adverse shocks had no effect on equilibrium unemployment, a long sequence of such shocks would increase equilibrium unemployment permanently.

While the implications for employment are straightforward, the model implies that there is no simple relation between employment and real wages. Consider in particular the effects of nominal shocks. By our assumption of constant returns to scale and constant elasticity of demand, they leave the mark-up of prices over wages unaffected. Equivalently, they leave the real wage unaffected. Thus, a sequence of adverse nominal disturbances will decrease employment, with no effect on the real wage. This lack of a simple relation between real wages and employment comes from our assumptions of monopolistic competition and constant returns, not from our assumptions about insiders and outsiders. As our focus is on the dynamic effects of membership rules, we do not explore the relation between real wages and employment further. But it is an important caveat to the line of research which has focused on the role of real wages in 'explaining' high European unemployment. In the model constructed here, it is quite possible to have sustained high unemployment without high real wages. It is also possible for expansionary policies to raise employment without altering real wages.

The Endogeneity of Membership Rules

In the rest of this section, we return to the original model and examine various extensions. Here, we focus on the determination of the membership rules.

We have shown that the time-series evolution of employment depends critically on the nature of these rules. To the extent that insider status is closely linked with employment, substantial persistence is likely to result. If membership does not change or changes relatively little when employment changes, employment is likely to be much less persistent.

It is clear that at any point in time the currently employed would find it optimal to commit the group to maximizing their interests indefinitely, while ignoring the welfare of those currently laid off. That is, they would like to apply the rule $m=1$ this period and $m=\infty$ hereafter. But this means that if the currently employed are those who decide about membership, the only time-consistent rule is $m=1$, which is always the best current period rule for the currently employed. The issue is therefore whether the group can precommit itself, or more accurately whether the currently employed can commit the group to take care of their interests in the future whether or not they are still employed by the firm.

Achieving the $m=\infty$ solution is probably not feasible. But it seems plausible that the group will be able to commit itself to at least some extent. The factor limiting the commitment will be the degree of divergence between the original membership and the group of employed workers in some subsequent period. Where the divergence is too great, current employees will wrest control of the group from those controlling it in the interests of some group of past workers. The extent to which groups can commit themselves is probably greatest where demand shocks are small so that level and composition of employment change relatively little from period to period.

This suggests that m will depend on the distribution of the shocks. If shocks have large variance, m may have to be close to 1 to avoid large differences between membership and the employed. Or m may instead be a function of the realization of the shocks. A sequence of large positive or negative unexpected shocks may lead to the takeover of the group by the then current employees. When a large fraction of the original labour force is on layoff, the incentive for the workers still employed to ignore them and thus not take the pay cut required to get them back may be strong. This is much less likely in the face of small shocks. Changes in the vlaue of m associated with major shocks provide another possible explanation for coincidence of persistent and high unemployment.

Our model thus suggests two alternative explanations for the empirical observation that unemployment remains at high levels for long periods of time. First, for a given fixed value of m greater than 1 but less than infinity, a sequence of adverse shocks will lead to a change in membership and therefore alter the level of employment permanently. Second, in bad times currently employed workers are more likely to take over and disenfranchize the unemployed, thus reducing the value of m and increasing persistence. The two differ in their implications for the process for unemployment at high levels. In the first, after the level change, the process for unemployment will have a higher mean but the same degree of persistence around the new mean as it had before. In the second case, unemployment will not only be higher but exhibit more persistence.

Limitations and Extensions of the Model

In developing our analysis, we have made a number of simplifying assumptions regarding functional forms and the structure of bargaining between workers and firms. The question arises of how sensitive our results are to these assumptions. We have also carefully avoided using the term 'union' to refer to the group of insiders. But it is clear that 'union' would often have sounded more appropriate and the issue arises of whether our analysis is actually relevant in non-union contexts. We now discuss these issues informally.

Other Bargaining Structures It is well known that even in a one-period model, it is in general inefficient to let the firm choose employment unilaterally given the wage (see for example Oswald, 1985). In our multi-period model, the assumption that the firm chooses employment according to its short-run profit-maximizing labour demand is even more questionable. Even if bargaining takes the form of the union setting a wage and allowing the firm to control the level of employment, firms will not choose to operate on their short-run labour demand curves. Through its employment decision, the firm can affect future membership (unless $m = \infty$). By employing more workers this period, it can increase membership next period and thus lower the expected cost of labour. This will lead the firm to choose a level of employment higher than that implied by short-run profit maximization. We suspect that taking account of this consideration would not substantially alter our analysis of employment dynamics. Rather, it would simply shift each period's labour demand curve outwards.

Another important possibility would be for the firm to introduce two-tier systems, where newly hired workers get lower wages than those hired previously. Under such systems, insiders should have no reluctance to let firms hire more workers, and employment should increase until new hirees are paid their reservation wage. The general reluctance of unions to accept such arrangements, especially in Europe, suggests that a central issue is that of what happens over time to those hired at lower wages. Unions do not encourage two-tier arrangements at least in part because of the fear that second tier workers will come to control the wage-setting process. Indeed the rarity of two-tier arrangements is strong evidence for the relevance of the membership considerations stressed here. Without some such consideration, it is difficult to see why unions do not always favour such systems as a way of maximizing the rents that they can capture.

Going back to the setting of the wage, if we allow the wage not to be set unilaterally by the insiders but to be determined by bargaining between insiders and the firm, wages will depend both on the utility of insiders and on the value of the firm, the present discounted value of profits. Profit is a decreasing funtion of the wage. Thus, the larger is the weight of the firm in bargaining, the lower is the wage, and thus the higher the average level of employment. The implications for employment persistence depend on the weight of the firm in bargaining when the wage is far from the reservation level of workers. If the firm is relatively more powerful when the wage is much above the reservation wage, then the wage will tend to decrease when it is high and employment will tend to return to a higher level. Whether or not this happens depends on the structure of bargaining between insiders and the firm.

The specific utility function we have used for insiders is also important for our results. Its main implication, which we have argued is a desirable one, is that the probability of employment chosen by the group is invariant to the size of the group of insiders, or to the level of productivity. If instead an increase in membership, given productivity, led the group to choose both a lower wage and a lower probability of employment – which we can think of as the stochastic equivalent of elastic labour supply – employment would depend on both the anticipated and unanticipated components of productivity and may show less persistence. Even under the rule $m=1$, an unanticipated increase in employment would, if the increase in productivity was temporary, lead to the choice of a lower wage and a lower probability of employment in the following period, implying an expected return to the initial level of employment over time. The same effects would also arise if as unemployment became larger and being unemployed became more costly, the group chose a higher probability of employment, leading to an expected increase in employment over time.

Groups or Unions? Is our analysis still relevant when workers are not formally organized in unions, when for example wages are simply set unilaterally by the firm?

The work of Lindbeck and Snower (1985) suggests that even in the absence of formal unions current workers have some leverage *vis-à-vis* firms. And Slichter (1950) provides confirming empirical evidence suggesting that even before unions were economically important, wages tended to be high in industries with relatively inelastic labour demand.

In many non-union settings, current incumbent workers and prospective workers cannot be regarded symmetrically. The requirement of cooperation among workers and the collective knowledge possessed by incumbent workers make their position very different from that of prospective new workers. This leads us to suspect that the membership considerations we have stressed are at least somewhat applicable even in non-union contexts. The potential applicability of our analysis to non-union settings may be argued informally as follows. Imagine a firm facing a collection of insider workers. The firm must choose a wage and an employment level. It cannot credibly threaten to lay off all its workers and replace them, except at very high cost, because of the specialized expertise of its labour force. On the other hand, the firm cannot credibly threaten to replace workers individually with lower wage workers because the remainder of the labour force will not tolerate the hiring of 'scabs'. Under these conditions, wages and expected employment will be set in some way to divide the surplus resulting from a continued relationship between workers and firms. Workers will in general be able to extract some surplus even when they are unorganized. If firms make an 'inadequate' wage offer, they can refuse to work. As long as they have some specific capital, it will be preferable for management to make another higher offer rather than lay the worker off.

If agreements are renegotiated only periodically and firms are permitted to vary employment in the interim, shocks will in general influence the level of employment. Even without a formal model of the bargaining process between workers and firms, it seems reasonable to expect that a reduction in the number of incumbent workers will lead to the setting of a higher wage and a lower level of expected employment. Thus persistence in employment, though not necessarily as much as with unions, may result even in that case. Note that this also may help explain what goes on in the non-union sector of economies with large unions.

This argument is clearly tentative. But we conclude from it that, while the effects we have described are more likely to be present when there are explicit unions, they many also arise in settings in which insider–outsider considerations are important.

The Presence of a Non-union Sector We finally consider how our conclusions must be modified if part of the labour market is neither unionized nor subject to insider–outsider considerations.

The simplest analysis of a setting with a competitive sector would hold that there was no involuntary unemployment. Wages in the non-union sector would fall to the point where all those workers ejected from the union sector could find employment.[20] There are at least three reasons why even granting the existence of a competitive sector, this analysis is suspect. First, competitive firms may be reluctant to lower wages because of the fear of being unionized after they have alienated their current labour force. Second, unemployment benefits may be sufficiently high that the market clearing wage in the non-union sector is below some workers' reservation wage. In one sense their unemployment is voluntary since jobs are available. In another sense the unemployment is involuntary since the unemployed may envy workers with the same skill in the union sector. The general consideration is that when there are wage differentials across jobs, the concept of involuntary unemployment becomes elusive (see Bulow and Summers, 1986, for an elaboration of that theme). Third, unemployment may occur even with a competitive sector if remaining unemployed is in some sense useful – or thought to be useful by workers – in getting a union job. This may occur if substantial search effort or queuing is required or alternatively if accepting a low-quality job sends a bad signal to employers. This unemployment is related to that of Harris and Todaro (1970) where workers must migrate to urban areas to have a chance at high-wage urban jobs.

There is a more fundamental point regarding the inability of a non-union sector to prevent unemployment. As Weitzman (1982) argues persuasively, there are strong reasons to believe that most economic activity involves fixed costs and monopolistic competition. Imagine a monopolistically competitive economy with fixed costs of production and constant marginal costs where there is intitially no involuntary unemployment. Suppose that an adverse demand shock reduces the demand for goods in this economy but that nominal wages remain constant in all existing firms. Then employment and output will fall as will the profitability of existing firms. Will it pay new firms to enter the market and hire the unemployed at low wages? It may not because unlike incumbent firms, new firms must cover fixed as well as variable costs. Particularly in settings where labour costs do not represent a large fraction of sales, entry may not be able to ensure the employment of the unemployed.[21] These considerations may enhance the power of unions because they reduce the incentive to start up new non-union firms.

Empirical Evidence on Hysteresis Theories

Having developed a formal theory of hysteresis, we now examine whether the model is consistent with the observed patterns of persistently increasing unemployment in Europe and whether it can illuminate the very different behaviour of unemployment in Europe and the United States in the recent past. We start by giving direct, institutional evidence on the strength of unions in Europe. We then estimate wage and employment equations implied by our model, for both the Europe and the US. We finally examine patterns of labour market turnover, in the UK and the US.

The Role of Unions in Europe

The Size of the Union Sector Our model suggests that, even if hysteresis may arise in non-union contexts, it is probably more likely to arise the stronger and the larger the union sector. Thus, we start by reviewing the role of unions in Europe; we limit, as before, our investigation to the UK, France and Germany.[22]

Membership figures indicate a union density of approximately 45 per cent for the UK, 20 per cent in France and 38 per cent for Germany. But these figures give very limited information as to the strength of unions. A better indicator is union coverage, that is of the proportion of workers covered by some form of collective bargaining. For the UK, coverage is of approximately 70 per cent for manual workers, and of 55 per cent for non-manual workers. For France and Germany, the proportion of all workers covered exceeds 80 per cent. But even coverage numbers are misleading. To understand why, one must be given some institutional background.

On the surface, the three countries appear to be very different. In France there are three main national unions. In Germany, there are only industry unions. In the UK, there is a maze of craft and industry unions. But the structure of bargaining is in fact quite similar and can be described as follows: in all three countries, most of the formal bargaining is done at the industry level. But, in all three countries, wages are determined much more at the company or plant level.

In the UK, industry bargaining sets rates, which are usually floors that have little effect on actual wages. Until the Employment Act of 1980, there was scope for extension, i.e. for provisions to extend the terms of the agreement to the whole sector. These provisions were eliminated in 1980. Since the mid-1960s, there has been an increase in the amount of bargaining, both formal and informal, at the plant level, between shop stewards and employers. Given that plant/company bargaining is the really important level of bargaining, it is relevant to look at how many workers are covered by both industry and plant/company level bargaining. In 1978, the number of workers covered by at least a company agreement was 33 per cent for all industries and 47.7 per cent for manufacturing. Given the importance of informal bargaining, these figures understate the importance of unions in setting wages.

In France, the '*Conventions collectives*' which are usually but not always at the industry level direct most of the formal bargaining. These agreements are signed between a 'representative' union and a 'representative' employer and apply even if not all unions sign (which is frequently the case). Subject to some minor conditions, they can be extended to all firms in the industry, by decision of the Minister of Labour. As in the UK however, the importance of industry agreements with respect to wages should not be exaggerated. They usually set floors, which do not appear, either directly or indirectly, to have a large effect on actual wages. As in the UK, a growing portion of the bargaining takes place at the company level, although often in haphazard fashion. Until 1982, wages were largely determined unilaterally by firms, or in response to complaints of union representatives in the plant, with little bargaining or even consultation; local strikes were however a standard instrument used by unions to achieve a better deal. Since 1982, there has been a change in the law (Lois Auroux) which requires annual bargaining at the company level on pay and other matters. The result has been a drastic increase in the number of company-level agreements.

In Germany, most of the formal bargaining again takes place at the industry level. Agreements can be extended – to either firms in the same industry or to non-union workers in firms which sign the agreements – by the state or federal Minister of Labour if (a) half of the employees of the sector are employed by firms which have signed the agreement and (b) extension is approved by both unions and employers who have signed.[23] But, as in the other two countries, bargaining is increasingly taking place at the company level and there is general agreement that pay is very largely determined at the company level.

To conclude, it is difficult to give an exact estimate of the 'union sector' in these countries. To the extent that much bargaining over wages in fact takes place at the company level, union coverage numbers, which are based on both company- and industry-level bargaining, probably overstate the number of workers for whom the wage is determined as a result of bargaining between unions and employers. Even with this adjustment, the size of the union sector still remains high, much higher than in the US. Also, if we believe that the more disaggregated the level of bargaining the less likely it is to take into account the interests of the unemployed as a whole, then these countries are good candidates for hysteresis in the union sector.[24]

An alternative approach is to ask the question: can a firm be non-union? Can a firm become non-union? In the UK, the answer is yes: a firm can be or can become non-union. There is nothing in the law which prevents it. There are some well-known examples of non-union firms, most often subsidiaries of US companies (Kodak). There are very few examples of firms going non-union.[25] In France and Germany, extension agreements put some constraints on firms in a given sector. There are non-union firms in both countries. In France, these are nearly exclusively small firms. In France furthermore, various requirements are imposed on firms with more than 50 employees. In particular they must allow for the presence of *delegues du personnel* who are union representatives within the firm. All national unions have a right to be represented. Since 1978, firms must also allow for the presence of a *section syndicale d'entreprise*, for the presence of the union inside the firm. Together, these facts suggest that it is difficult to be or go non-union in these countries.

Finally, there is the question of how different the non-union sector is from the union sector. A study by Kaufman (1984) of the competitive sector in the UK finds relatively little difference in wage behaviour across the two sectors. Together with the arguments given in the previous section, this suggests that the size of the formal union sector may not be a major determinant of the extent of hysteresis. We shall return to this question in the next section.

Membership Rules Membership rules determining who the union represents at each point in time, play an important role in our analysis. The empirical evidence on actual membership rules is fairly clear: workers have the right to join unions if they want to. Workers who are laid off can remain in the union although they often lose the right to vote; this may happen either because of formal restrictions, or because voting takes place inside the plant. But this tells us little about the question of in whose interest the union actually acts. A study of the unemployed and the unions in the UK (Barker et al., 1984) gives some information. It finds that, while laid off workers are officially encouraged to remain in the union and have their union fees waived, they do not, for the most part, see reasons to stay in the union.[26] This provides support for the idea that the union cares mostly about the currently employed.

Wage and Employment Equations

Theory We now derive, and then estimate later, the wage and employment equations associated with an expanded version of the model of the previous section. There are two extensions. First we allow for a dynamic specification of labour demand; the reason for introducing it will be clear below. Second, we specify explicitly an alternative hypothesis to that of hysteresis.

We thus specify labour demand as:[27]

$$n = s\, n_{-1} - (1-s)b(w-p) + e. \tag{15.8}$$

Following the analysis of the previous section, we assume that the union acts to set expected employment according to the relation:

$$En = (1-a)n^* + an_{-1}. \tag{15.9}$$

The case where $a=1$ corresponds to the case where $m=1$ in the preceding section and there is hysteresis; the case where $a=0$ corresponds to the case where the union's policy is independent of history and so there is no hysteresis. Clearly, intermediate outcomes are also possible.[28]

Finally, let the wage which satisfies (15.8) and (15.9) be denoted by w^*. We assume the actual wage to be given by:

$$w = w^* + u,$$

where the disturbance term u is assumed to be white noise, uncorrelated with w^*, and reflects factors outside the model. Combining this assumption with equations (15.8) and (15.9) yields a wage and an employment equation:

$$w = Ep + [1/b(1-s)][-(1-a)n^* + (s-a)n_{-1} + Ee] + u \tag{15.10}$$

$$n = (1-a)n^* + a\, n_{-1} + [e - Ee + (1-s)b(p-Ep-u)]. \tag{15.11}$$

The wage equation holds that the wage of the union is a decreasing function of n^*. When the union is larger, it is more cautious in setting wages. The impact of n_{-1} is ambiguous. A larger value of n_{-1} raises the size of the group in whose interest the union is maximizing but it also increases labour demand.

The employment equation on the other hand implies that employment follows a first-order process. The degree of persistence depends only on a, not at all on s. Unexpected movements in employment are due to price and productivity surprises, and deviations of wages from target. Equation (15.11) can be estimated by OLS. This is however not the case for equation (15.10): expected productivity is likely to be correlated with past productivity and thus with past employment. Therefore we now derive the reduced form wage equation. To do so requires an assumption about the process followed by e: we assume that e follows a random walk.[29] Lagging (15.8) and substituting it in (15.11) yields:

$$w - w_{-1} = k + (Ep - p_{-1}) + [1/b(1-s)][(1+s-a)n_{-1} - s\, n_{-2}] + u, \qquad (15.12)$$

where $k \equiv -[1/b(1-s)](1-a)n^*$.

This equation can be estimated by OLS. It gives the rate of wage inflation as a function of expected price inflation, and employment lagged once and twice. It is worth examining it further.

Consider first the case where there are no costs of adjustment in labour demand. In this case the relation gives a relation between expected real wage growth and lagged employment only. If $a=1$, then expected wage growth does not depend on employment but if $a<1$, it does: after an unexpected decline in productivity, which leads to lower employment, the remaining workers accept a cut in real wages only to the extent that they care about the workers who have been laid off.

If there are costs of adjustment to employment, then expected real wage growth depends on employment lagged both once and twice. If $a=0$, then the ratio of employment lagged twice to employment lagged once cannot exceed 1/2 (in absolute value). But as a increases, the ratio tends to 1. If $a=1$, the ratio equals unity: expected real wage growth depends on the change rather than on the level of employment.

Note that we cannot identify a and s separately from estimation of the wage equation. But a must be positive if we find the ratio described above to be larger than 1/2. Furthermore, a can be directly obtained from the employment equation.

While we have derived the wage equation (15.12) from a rather specific theory of union behaviour, it can be motivated in other ways. Following the logic of the monopolistic competitive model in the preceding section just as we have followed the logic of the competitive model gives rise to an equation for wage inflation parallelling (15.12). Much more generally, equation (15.12) is very close to a standard Phillips curve which allows for a rate of change effect, *à la* Lipsey. The only real difference is the presence of employment rather than unemployment on the right-hand side. We now turn to estimation of the wage and employment equations.

Results The results of estimation of the wage equations for the UK, France, Germany and the US, for the period 1953 to 1984 are reported in tables 15.4 and 15.5.

Table 15.4 *Wage equations, 1953–1984*

Country	π_{t-1}	$\log E_t$	$\log E_{t-1}$	$\log E_{t-2}$	Time $\times 100$	θ	DW	R^2
Germany								
(1)	0.6*	—	0.92	−0.80		0.07	1.99	0.54
			(4.0)	(−4.2)		(0.3)		
(2)	0.6*	—	0.71	−0.57	−0.12	0.04	2.03	0.59
			(2.4)	(−2.2)	(1.5)	(0.2)		
(3)	0.6*	1.12	−0.89			−0.10	2.00	0.74
		(9.6)	(−8.9)			(−0.5)		
(4)	0.6*	(0.96)	−0.74		−0.07	−0.13	2.01	0.76
		(6.2)	(−5.1)		(−1.5)	(−0.7)		
United Kingdom								
(5)	0.75*	—	0.67	−0.76	—	0.25	2.01	0.23
			(2.6)	(−2.5)		(1.5)		
(6)	0.75*	—	0.86	−0.84	0.19	0.09	1.97	0.31
			(3.2)	(−2.8)	(1.9)	(0.5)		
(7)	0.75*	0.13	−0.08	—	—	0.21	1.83	0.07
		(0.4)	(−0.2)			(1.0)		
(8)	0.75*	0.34	−0.19	—	0.20	0.16	1.84	0.15
		(1.0)	(−0.5)		(1.5)	(0.7)		
France								
(9)	0.8*	—	0.58	−0.39	—	—	2.03	0.12
			(1.5)	(−0.9)				
(10)	0.8*	—	0.61	−0.42	0.00	−0.05	1.92	0.13
			(1.2)	(−0.7)	(0.0)	(−0.2)		
(11)	0.8*	0.97	−0.74	—	—	—	2.04	0.29
		(2.9)	(−2.1)					
(12)	0.8*	1.28	−1.16	—	0.12	—	2.09	0.33
		(3.1)	(−2.1)		(1.2)			
United States								
(13)	0.7*	—	−0.07	0.00		0.54	2.03	0.26
			(−0.8)	(0.0)		(2.2)		
(14)	0.7*	—	−0.07	0.00	0.00	0.54	2.02	0.26
			(−0.8)	(0.0)	(0.0)	(2.2)		
(15)	0.7*	0.24	−0.25	—	—	0.48	1.98	0.49
		(4.6)	(−4.8)			(2.5)		
(16)	0.7*	0.28	−0.16	—	−0.13	0.34	1.99	0.63
		(5.9)	(−3.3)		(−3.9)	(1.7)		

$\dot{w}$: rate of change of average hourly earnings in manufacturing.
π : rate of change of the consumer price index.
E : manufacturing employment.
t-statistics in parentheses.
All equations for Europe are run with a first-order autocorrelation correction.
All equations for the US are run with a first-order moving average correction.
*Coefficient from a regression of π on $\pi(-1)$ for each country for the sample period.
Source. OECD data bank, extended back to 1950 by D. Grubb. See Grubb (1984)

Table 15.5 *Wage equation residuals, 1953–1984*

Year	Germany	United Kingdom	France	United States
1980	−1.91	1.7	1.6	−1.2
1981	−0.32	−4.1	1.4	−0.8
1982	−0.75	3.9	−0.0	−0.1
1983	0.57	−2.7	0.1	−0.9
1984	−0.44	1.1	−1.5	0.3
	σ=1.87	σ=3.2	σ=3.9	σ=1.5

Residuals from equations (3), (5), (11) and (15) in table 15.4.

In table 15.4, four alternative specifications of the wage equation are estimated for each country. Because the appropriate timing is unclear with annual data, we estimate the equations using alternatively contemporaneous and once-lagged employment, and once- and twice-lagged employment.[30] We also estimate each equation with and without a time trend; many researchers have captured the shift of the Phillips curve by a time trend, that is by an increase over time unrelated to the history of unemployment and it is interesting to see what happens to our specification when a time trend is allowed. This gives us the four alternative specifications. Finally, we use for expected inflation the forecast of inflation obtained from estimation of an AR(1) process for inflation over the sample period and constrain the coefficient on expected inflation (which is therefore equal to a constant plus a scalar times lagged inflation) to equal unity.

In table 15.6, we perform the same set of estimations, but using unemployment rather than employment as a right-hand-side variable. We do this because unemployment is the variable used in standard Phillips curve specifications. Some theories of hysteresis, such as the idea that the long-term unemployed exert less pressure on wages than those recently laid off, also suggest that unemployment is more appropriate than employment in the Phillips curve.

Tables 15.7 and 15.8 give the results of estimation of the employment and unemployment processes for each country for the period 1953 to 1984. Here again, while our theory has implications only for employment, we think it is useful to report also results for unemployment as well.

The results are fairly clear cut and indicate that there are substantial differences between the European countries and the United States. Starting with the wage equations, one can draw the following conclusions:

Table 15.6 *Wage equations, 1953–1984*

Country	π_{t-1}	U_t	U_{t-1}	U_{t-2}	Time $\times 100$	ρ	DW	R^2
Germany								
(1)	0.6*	—	-2.86	2.62	—	0.30	1.97	0.57
			(-4.3)	(3.8)		(1.6)		
(2)	0.6*	—	-2.41	2.12	-0.08	0.27	1.94	0.59
			(-3.0)	(2.6)	(-1.1)	(1.4)		
(3)	0.6*	-2.39	1.68	—	—	0.06	1.99	0.50
		(-4.0)	(2.6)			(0.3)		
(4)	0.6*	-1.60	0.95	—	-0.10	0.08	2.00	0.54
		(-2.1)	(1.2)		(-1.5)	(0.4)		
United Kingdom								
(5)	0.75*	—	-2.31	2.58	—	0.04	2.02	0.33
			(-3.6)	(3.4)		(0.2)		
(6)	0.75*	—	-2.57	2.46	0.14	(-0.03)	2.02	0.37
			(-4.0)	(3.3)	(1.4)	-0.2		
(7)	0.75*	-0.96	0.78	—	—	0.22	1.83	0.12
		(-1.0)	(0.7)			(1.0)		
(8)	0.75*	-1.43	0.62	—	0.28	0.13	1.85	0.25
		(-2.0)	(0.8)		(2.4)	(0.6)		
France								
(9)	0.8*	—	-1.42	1.35	—	0.07	1.93	0.03
			(-0.7)	(0.6)		(0.4)		
(10)	0.8*	—	-3.01	2.10	0.25	-0.10	1.86	0.15
			(-1.3)	(0.9)	(2.1)	(-0.5)		
(11)	0.8*	-3.57	3.78	—	—	0.13	1.99	0.14
		(-1.97)	(1.8)			(0.7)		
(12)	0.8*	-4.97	4.12	—	0.33	-0.10	1.91	0.33
		(-2.9)	(2.2)		(3.0)	(0.5)		
United States								
(13)	0.7*	—	-0.07	-0.06	—	0.40		
			(-0.2)	(-0.1)		(1.3)		
(14)	0.7*	—	0.11	0.07	-0.07	0.47	2.01	0.24
			(0.3)	(0.2)	(-1.7)	(1.6)		
(15)	0.7*	-1.02	0.47	—	—	0.41	1.99	0.62
		(-6.0)	(2.9)			(2.2)		
(16)	0.7*	-1.05	0.43	—	0.02	0.42	1.99	0.63
		(-5.8)	(2.4)		(0.06)	(2.2)		

See table 15.4 for notes.

U: standardized unemployment rate.

Source. OECD and Grubb (1984)

Table 15.7 *Employment processes, 1953–1984*

Country	ρ	θ	$\frac{\alpha}{\times 100}$	R^2
Germany				
	0.76	1.00	—	0.96
	(22.3)	(5.3)	—	
	0.86	0.78	-1.9×10^{-2}	0.97
	(26.7)	(3.9)	(0.0)	
United Kingdom				
	1.07	0.54	—	0.96
	(23.3)	(2.6)	—	
	0.95	0.41	−0.20	0.94
	(16.3)	(2.0)	(−3.8)	
France				
	0.94	0.81	—	0.94
	(19.5)	(3.0)	—	
	1.08	0.48	−0.13	0.94
	(19.5)	(2.5)	(−4.0)	
United States				
	0.82	0.07	—	0.72
	(7.5)	(0.3)	—	
	0.34	0.46	0.40	0.77
	(1.5)	(1.6)	(2.5)	

Results of estimation of:
$\log E = \rho \log E(-1) + \alpha(\text{TIME}) + \epsilon + \epsilon\theta(-1)$.
E: manufacturing employment.

1 Virtually all specifications for Germany, France and the United Kingdom in tables 15.4 and 15.6 suggest a substantial degree of hysteresis.

Let us denote by R the absolute value of the ratio of the coefficient on lagged employment–unemployment to the coefficient on contemporaneous employment–unemployment (or of the coefficient on employment–unemployment lagged twice to the coefficient on employment lagged once as the case may be). As we have seen, under strict hysteresis ($a=1$) this ratio should be equal to unity. R is indeed close to unity for nearly all specifications; it is not affected by the inclusion of a time trend, or by the use of employment versus unemployment. There is little difference across countries: R is higher in the UK, sometimes exceeding unity. It is closer on average to 0.85 for Germany and France.[31]

Table 15.8 *Unemployment processes, 1953–1984*

Country	ρ	θ	α $\times 100$	R^2
Germany				
	0.92	0.65	—	0.91
	(14.8)	(3.4)	—	
	0.94	0.39	0.06	0.93
	(17.5)	(1.9)	(5.0)	
United Kingdom				
	1.02	0.77	—	0.95
	(20.9)	(3.9)	—	
	0.81	0.82	0.09	0.96
	(9.9)	(3.9)	(3.5)	
France				
	1.12	−0.06	—	0.97
	(32.7)	(−0.3)	—	
	1.04	−0.22	0.02	0.97
	(18.2)	(−1.1)	(1.4)	
United States				
	0.72	0.06	—	0.58
	(4.5)	(0.2)	—	
	0.36	0.31	0.07	0.63
	(1.4)	(0.9)	(1.9)	

Results of estimation of:
$U = \rho U(-1) + \alpha(TIME) + \epsilon + \theta \epsilon(-1)$.
U: standardized unemployment.

The time trend itself contributes little. If the increase in unemployment was due to an autonomous increase in the natural rate over time, the coefficient on the time trend should be positive. Only in the UK when employment is used, and in the UK and France when unemployment is used, is the time trend positive and either significant or marginally significant. Even then, its quantitative contribution is small. In the case in which it is largest and most significant (equation (12) for France in table 15.6), it only explains a 1.5 per cent increase in the unemployment rate consistent with a given level of expected real wage growth over the sample period. Further evidence that the apparent increase in the natural rate through time is a consequence of rising unemployment and not autonomous comes from the absence of substantial serial correlation in our estimated Phillips curves. An upward drift in the constant term would manifest itself in the form of serial correlation.

A final piece of evidence is given in table 15.5 which reports the residuals associated with the best fitting equations from 15.4, not including a time trend, for each country, for 1980 to 1984. There is little evidence of significant prediction errors in recent years. This is in sharp contrast to the performance of wage equations which do not allow lagged employment to enter.

2 In contrast to the results for Europe, the results for the United States provide evidence of much less hysteresis. There is evidence of a significant effect of either lagged employment or lagged unemployment. But, with the exception of one specification using employment, the value of R for the US is smaller than for Europe, being in most cases around 0.5. There is also no evidence in favour of a time trend in the wage equation.

3 A comparison of the results of estimation in tables 15.4 and 15.6 does not give a clear answer as to whether employment or unemployment belongs in the wage equation. Using R^2's gives a draw, with employment doing better for France, unemployment doing better for the UK. We have also run regressions including current and lagged values of both unemployment and employment – or equivalently, employment and the labour force. They give the same ambiguous answer, with the labour force being significant in the UK, but not in France or Germany. We see the UK results however as presenting a problem for our model.

The employment and unemployment equations reported in tables 15.7 and 15.8 confirm to a large extent the conclusions from the wage equations. Both unemployment and employment are more persistent in Europe than in the US. In particular, the process generating unemployment appears non-stationary in all three European countries, whether or not a time trend is included in the regressions. The US process is instead stationary. The data however strongly suggest that an ARMA(1,1), rather than the AR(1) process implied by our theory, is needed to fit the employment and unemployment processes of all four countries. This may reflect a difference between the length of a period in the model and annual frequency of observation used in the estimation.

Patterns of Labour Market Turnover

A central element in our theory of hysteresis is the lack of concern of employed workers for the unemployed. It is the fear of job loss for current workers and not the outstanding labour market pool that restrains wage demands. Indeed the formal model explains why firms hire at all only assuming that wages which are set low enough to ensure the jobs of current workers will sometimes make it profitable for firms to hire new workers. While this is clearly an oversimplification, the point remains that insider–outsider or union models of the type we have considered are really theories of why the unemployed are not hired, not theories of why lay-offs take place. This suggests the utility of looking at data on labour market turnover. A finding of high turnover with many workers having short spells of unemployment and then being rehired would tend to cast doubt on the relevance of insider–outsider formulations, while a finding that the rate of flow into and out of employment was relatively low but that the unemployed remained out of work for a very long time would tend to support these theories.

Table 15.9 presents some evidence on the rate of flow into unemployment in the United States and United Kingdom since the mid-1970s. The flow is measured as the number of persons becoming unemployed over a 3-month period. For the United States, this is estimated as the number of unemployed reporting durations of less than 14 weeks. For Britain it is the number of unemployment registrants over a 3-month period.

Two conclusions emerge clearly from the table. First, despite the much higher rate of unemployment in the United Kingdom than in the United States, the rate of flow into unemployment is actually lower

Table 15.9 *Patterns of inflow to unemployment*

	United States		Great Britain
Year	Number unemployed less than 14 weeks as a % of employment	$\dfrac{14\times unemployed}{employment\times average\ duration\ (weeks)}\times 100$	Quarterly inflow as a % of employment[a]
1970	4.4	8.4	3.3
1971	4.8	7.8	3.6
1972	4.5	6.9	3.6
1973	4.2	7.2	2.9
1974	4.8	8.5	3.2
1975	6.3	9.2	4.2
1976	5.7	7.4	4.9
1977	5.5	7.5	4.7
1978	5.0	7.6	4.5
1979	5.0	8.0	4.2
1980	5.8	9.0	4.9
1981	6.0	8.4	5.2
1982	7.2	9.6	5.5
1983	6.5	7.4	5.6
1984	5.5	6.2	

[a]Average of quarterly values.

there. The implication is that the unemployment problem is not one of an excessive rate of job loss but of an insufficient rate of hiring of the unemployed. The second striking feature of the data is that the rate of flow into unemployment in Britain has increased surprisingly little as unemployment has soared. Between 1970 and 1984, when the rate of unemployment in Britian rose more than 300 per cent, the rate of flow into unemployment rose by only about 75 per cent. This pattern of rising unemployment with only a modest increase in the rate of inflow appears more pronounced in British than American labour markets. In the United States, the inflow rate has accounted for a significant part of the increase in unemployment during recession periods. For example, between 1979 and 1982, unemployment increased by 67 per cent and the inflow rate rose by 44 per cent.

The OECD (1985) summarizes the fragmentary information available on labour market turnover for other European nations. The data in general parallel our findings for Britain – suggesting relatively modest increases in the rate of flow into unemployment starting from a very low base. They do suggest however that the composition of the newly unemployed has changed over time as the unemployment rate has increased. Lay-off rates have increased while quit rates have declined.

Given the magnitude of the increases in European unemployment rates and the relatively small increases in flow rates, it is inevitable that unemployment durations have increased substantially. Table 15.10

Table 15.10 *The importance of long-term unemployment*

	United States		United Kingdom		FR of Germany		France	
	1980	1984	1980	1984	1980	1984	1980	1984
Unemployment rate	7.2	7.5	6.5	12.7	3.4	8.1	6.6	10.0
Average duration of unemployment for adult men currently unemployed	3.6	5.8	12.2	19.4	8.6	12.6	12.6	14.4
Per cent contribution to adult male unemployment of those unemployed at least–								
6 months	50	72	91	96	85	92	92	93
12 months	15	39	74	87	59	75	75	80
18 months	4	18	57	76	38	58	58	64
24 months	1	8	41	65	23	43	43	56

Source: Based on authors' calculation

presents some information on the increasing imporance of long-term unemployment in Europe. Along with information on the average duration of unemployment, it presents estimates of the fraction of all unemployment due to persons whose complete spells will exceed various threshold lengths.[31] The table demonstrates that at the same level of unemployment, long-term unemployment is much more important in Europe. In 1980, when the American unemployment rate was 7.2 per cent, only an estimated 15 per cent of all unemployment was due to persons out of work for more than a year. The corresponding percentages were 74 per cent, 59 per cent and 75 per cent in the United Kingdom, Germany and France even though the unemployment rates were lower. The table also demonstrates that long-term unemployment has increased in importance as overall unemployment rates have risen in Europe. Indeed, the increase in duration of unemployment is almost proportional to the increase in unemployment.

Summary In this section, we have shown that unions play an important role in Europe and that the behaviour of European unemployment is consistent with our hypothesis about hysteresis. It is obviously tempting to conclude that unions are at the root of the European problem. But the temptation must be strongly resisted. First, even if unions create hysteresis, they just create a channel for persistence, which implies that both favourable and adverse shocks will have long-lasting effects. The sequence of unfavourable shocks, at least some of which are the consequence of policy, may equally well be said to be the cause of persistent high unemployment. Second, it is as yet unclear whether the cause of hysteresis in Europe is unions or the sequence of adverse shocks which has caused high unemployment. We consider this issue in the next section.

Is Eurosclerosis Really the Problem?

The previous section has shown that our model of persistent unemployment may explain important aspects of the current European depression and the very different behaviour of European and American labour markets. The evidence presented so far leaves open a crucial question however. Is the presence of hysteresis in European unemployment a consequence of the heavily regulated and unionized character of European labour markets? Alternatively, is hysteresis the result of a sequence of adverse shocks to employment? The case that major structural reforms are needed if full employment in Europe is to be restored depends on an affirmative answer to the first question, while the case for expansionary macroeconomic policies is more compelling if the second question can be given a positive answer.

Resolving whether the source of hysteresis lies ultimately in European institutions or in the sequence of adverse shocks that have buffetted European economies requires comparisons of the current situation with situations where only one of these elements is present. Comparison with the United States at present cannot resolve the issue because the American economy lacks institutions like those in Europe and has not suffered a sequence of contractionary aggregate demand shocks like those experienced by Europe in the 1980s. But we are able to make two comparisons which can shed some light on the sources of hysteresis. The first is a comparison of the behaviour of European labour markets in the recent period with their behaviour over the 1953–68 period. Broadly speaking, labour market institutions were similar in the two periods but the pattern of shocks was very different.[33] The second comparison is between the current European depression and the US depression of the 1930s. At the time of the US depression, unions were weak, social programmes and labour market regulations were a small factor and there were few if any important adverse supply shocks. The US depression may also shed light on the role of expansionary policies in alleviating persistent high unemployment. We consider these comparisons in turn.

European Labour Markets Before the Current Depression

The previous section has examined the persistence of unemployment and the behaviour of wages in Europe since the early 1950s. This long interval contains the current depression period and the period of unparallelled prosperity of the 1950s and 1960s. We examine the extent to which hysteresis is a product of bad times by considering labour market behaviour separately over each of the two periods. Table 15.11 presents estimates of the stochastic process followed by unemployment separately for the 1952–68 and 1969–84 periods.[34] The degree of persistence in unemployment in Europe is much higher in the latter period when unemployment was high. Similar but somewhat less dramatic results are obtained using employment rather than unemployment. For the earlier sample period, unemployment appears to be more persistent in the United States than in the United Kingdom or France. These results tend to suggest that hysteresis is a feature of bad times rather than a consequence of the structure of European labour markets.

Table 15.12 presents estimates of wage-change equations paralleling those reported in table 15.6, but now for the 1953–67 period. Taken together the results suggest somewhat less hysteresis in the 1953–67 period than is present over the whole sample period, with the difference being pronounced in the United Kingdom where the ratio R, which was close to one for the full sample is now close to 0.5. However, the results for the 1953–67 period like those for the entire period suggest a greater degree of hysteresis in Europe than in the United States. The fact that persistence is present in the early period in Europe to a greater degree

Table 15.11 *The persistence of unemployment in good and bad times*

Country	ρ	θ	s.e. regression
France			
1952–68	0.41	0.81	0.3
	(1.1)	(1.8)	
1968–84	1.11	−0.48	0.4
	(5.0)	(1.4)	
Germany			
1952–68	0.86	0.22	0.5
	(12.3)	(0.9)	
1968–84	1.07	0.51	0.8
	(5.1)	(1.4)	
United Kingdom			
1952–68	0.01	0.97	0.5
	(0.0)	(2.5)	
1968–84	1.0	0.99	0.9
	(27.6)	(3.8)	
United States			
1952–68	0.75	−0.37	1.0
	(1.6)	(−0.7)	
1968–84	0.59	0.50	1.1
	(1.7)	(1.1)	

The results represent estimates of the ARMA (1,1) process for the unemployment rate.

than in the United States but that it becomes increasingly important as the unemployment rate increases makes it difficult to draw any firm conclusion about its causes.

On balance, evidence on the changing behaviour of European labour markets suggests that bad times as well as unions account for findings of hysteresis. But this evidence is not sufficiently powerful to permit a judgement about their relative importance.

A Tale of Two Depressions

Salient features of many discussions of the current European depression include pessimistic forecasts that unemployment will never return to earlier levels, concern that reduced investment and lower capital stocks have made it impossible to employ the entire labour force, and fears that expansionary policies will lead directly into inflation with little or no favourable impact on output or employment. These pessimistic views

Table 15.12 *Wage change equations, 1953–1967*

Country	π_{t-1}	U_{t-1}	U_{t-2}	Time $\times 100$	ρ	DW	R^2
Germany							
(1)	0.6*	−6.48	5.86	—	−0.14	1.91	0.55
		(−3.7)	(3.7)		(−0.4)		
(2)	0.6*	−6.25	4.53	−0.60	−0.14	2.07	0.60
		(−3.6)	(2.2)	(−1.1)	(−0.4)		
United Kingdom							
(3)	0.75*	−2.91	1.89	—	−0.00	1.71	0.50
		(−3.2)	(2.0)		(0.0)		
(4)	0.75*	−3.49	1.74	0.16	−0.17	1.71	0.57
		(−3.8)	(1.9)	(1.4)	(−0.5)		
France							
(5)	0.9*	−6.11	4.53	—	−0.47	2.18	0.61
		(−3.8)	(2.8)		(−1.8)		
(6)	0.9*	−6.25	4.12	−0.06	−0.50	2.19	0.62
		(−3.8)	(2.3)	(−0.5)	(−1.9)		
United States							
(7)	0.7*	−1.23	0.37	—	0.73	2.05	0.66
		(−5.2)	(1.7)				
(8)	0.7*	−1.25	0.57	−0.17	−0.04	1.90	0.86
		(−7.0)	(3.2)	(−4.2)	(−0.1)		

are premised on the conviction that structural problems are central to high unemployment in Europe, and that the causes of persistent high unemployment go beyond a sequence of adverse shocks. Yet the American depression of the 1930s was ended by the expansion in aggregate demand associated with rearmament. Unemployment recovered to pre-depression levels. Recovery was not inhibited by an insufficient capital stock or by the overly rapid adjustment of wages and prices. Are this experience and the current European experience sufficiently comparable to permit the inference that hysteresis arises from a sequence of adverse shocks rather than from structural problems in the labour market? Or do major differences in the character of the American and European depressions render the American experience irrelevant for thinking about current European problems?

We begin by briefly reviewing the record of the American economy over the 1925–45 period. A number of basic economic statistics are presented in table 15.13. The outstanding feature of the period is of course the dramatic upsurge in unemployment that began in 1929. Unemployment rose from levels comparable to those experienced in

Europe in the late 1960s and early 1970s to 25 per cent in 1933 and remained above 14 per cent until 1940. As in Europe today employment actually declined over a 10-year period despite a rapidly increasing population. Beginning in late 1939 with the declaration of war in Europe, unemployment began to decline rapidly as rearmament stimulated the economy. The benefits of increased defence spending spilled over widely into the rest of the economy. While there were only 822,000 men in the Army in November of 1940 and 2.1 million a year later, non-agricultural employment increased by 16 per cent or 6 million persons between 1939 and 1941. Production of a variety of non-defence goods increased rapidly. Mitchell (1947) reports that between 1939 and 1941 automobile sales rose by 35 per cent, refrigerators by 69 per cent and washing machines by 63 per cent. Overall industrial production rose by 20 per cent.

These rapid improvements in economic performance were unexpected. Indeed in the wake of the 1937 recession many observers had despaired of any eventual return to full employment. Paul Samuelson

Table 15.13 *The American economy, 1925–1945*

Year	U	$\dot{w}$ (all workers)	$\dot{P}$(CPI)	Index of productivity	Non-residential capital (1958$)
1925	3.2	0.9	4.0	92.6	211.0
1926	1.8	1.5	0.0	95.0	218.7
1927	3.3	3.2	−6.0	95.4	223.9
1928	4.2	0.3	−1.0	96.1	229.3
1929	3.2	3.5	−1.0	100.0	236.6
1930	8.9	−0.6	−3.0	97.0	238.8
1931	16.3	−5.0	−8.3	98.5	233.5
1932	24.1	−8.9	−9.0	95.4	222.8
1933	25.2	−5.8	−5.0	93.2	212.2
1934	22.0	12.0	2.6	103.3	203.9
1935	20.3	2.3	2.6	106.7	198.3
1936	17.0	1.9	1.2	111.3	197.0
1937	14.3	5.9	3.7	110.4	198.4
1938	19.1	1.8	−2.4	113.5	194.5
1939	17.2	1.2	−1.2	117.6	192.2
1940	14.6	2.4	1.2	122.2	193.6
1941	9.9	9.7	4.9	124.2	198.3
1942	4.7	26.9	10.5	123.3	193.5
1943	1.9	10.6	6.3	124.6	186.5
1944	1.2	7.8	2.0	134.4	183.0
1945	1.9	9.0	1.9	142.0	185.5

Source: Baily (1983) and *Historical Statistics*

noted in 1944 that 'in the years just prior to 1939 there were noticeable signs of dwindling interest in the problem of unemployment which took the form of ostrich-like attempts to think away the very fact of unemployment by recourse to bad arithmetic and doubtful statistical techniques. And even among economists there was increased emphasis on the recovery of production and income to 1929 levels.' Such pessimism was pervasive even among those charged with alleviating the situation. Harry Hopkins, a liberal confidante of Roosevelt, wrote in 1937 that 'it is reasonable to expect a probable minimum of 4 to 5 million unemployed even in future prosperity periods' (Leuchtenburg, 1963: 263). Similar sentiments were echoed by others including LaGuardia who concluded that the situation had passed from being an emergency to being the new norm.

Similar pessimism is often expressed in Europe today. The pessimism reflects the view that unlike the US depression's persistent unemployment, persistent unemployment in Europe is caused by structural problems, not merely the residue of adverse shocks. Giersch has coined and popularized the word 'eurosclerosis' to denote these structural problems. Is there some important difference between the two situations which suggests that rapid expansionary policies would fail in Europe today even where they succeeded so spectacularly in the United States in 1940? There are surprisingly many similarities between the two experiences. The failure of inflation and real wages to recede more rapidly is an often noticed aspect of the current European experience. Indeed, it is this observation that drives conclusions that problems are structural and that the equilibrium rate of unemployment has increased. In the latter half of the depression, a similar pattern appears in the United States. Between 1936 and 1940 unemployment fluctuated around a very high mean but there was essentially no deceleration in inflation and real wages rose by about 10 per cent, close to the normal rate of productivity growth. Prior to the 1930s, periods of steady inflation had had much lower average unemployment rates.

Just as unemployment in Europe is highly persistent today, it appeared highly persistent during the American depression. The autocorrelation of unemployment was 0.874 in the United States over the 1919–41 period. To examine further the issue of hysteresis during the depression, table 15.14 presents some estimated wage equations for the 1920–41 period. The war years are omitted because of the influence of controls. The results dramatically suggest hysteresis parallelling that found in Europe today. When only contemporaneous employment or unemployment are entered into the equation, it is insignificant, but the change in employment or unemployment is strongly associated with changes in the rate of wage inflation.[35] These results are robust to a variety of ways of treating expected inflation. While parallelling our results for present-day Europe, these results differ from our results

Table 15.14 *Wage equations and the American depression*

	U_t	U_{t-1}	$logE_t$	$logE_{t-1}$	π_{t-1}	R^2	DW
(1)	−0.06	—	—	—	0.22	0.0	1.71
	(0.2)				(0.8)		
(2)	−1.13	1.26	—	—	0.50	0.29	2.13
	(2.9)	(3.2)			(2.1)		
(3)	—	—	0.67	—	0.24	0.03	1.75
			(0.50)		(0.9)		
(4)	—	—	2.71	−2.72	0.38	0.36	1.99
			(0.74)	(3.2)	(1.7)		

The dependent variable is the rate of wage inflation. Data drawn from *Historical Statistics of the United States.*

using American data for the post-war period. This may be taken as evidence that hysteresis is a phenomenon associated with bad times rather than with particular labour market institutions.

In considering contemporary European labour markets, we laid considerable stress on the importance of long-term unemployment emphasizing that turnover rates were if anything lower in Europe than in the United States. Tables 15.15 and 15.16, drawn from Woytinsky (1942), present some of the limited evidence available on patterns of labour market turnover during the American depression. Again, the results parallel Europe today. There is little evidence of an increase in the flow rate into unemployment, though quits decline and lay-offs increase. As in Europe today the duration of unemployment appears to have increased substantially. Woytinsky reports evidence from a 1937 Philadelphia survey which found that 61.7 per cent of unemployed adult men had been out of work for more than a year. More generally, he concludes that the depression era saw the emergence of a new group of hard-core unemployed. Patterns in labour market turnover do not appear to provide a basis for distinguishing European labour markets and American labour markets during the depression.

Hysteresis appears to be an important feature of the American depression. Earlier in the chapter, we have suggested three possible sources of hysteresis. Of these, physical capital accumulation appears an unlikely culprit. As table 15.13 demonstrates, the real value of the non-residential capital stock actually declined between 1929 and 1939. This reduction did not represent an important bar to full employment during or after the war when demand for goods was strong. This makes us somewhat skeptical of claims that insufficient capital is holding up a European recovery. However, it should be noted that Mitchell (1947) claims that capacity utilization rates were very low prior to the 1939

Table 15.15 *Labour market turnover and the American depression (median monthly rates per 100 workers)*

Year	Accessions	Separations			
		Total	Quits	Discharges	Lay-offs
1919	10.1	7.5	5.8	1.1	0.6
1920	10.1	10.3	8.4	1.1	0.8
1921	2.7	4.4	2.2	0.4	1.8
1922	8.0	5.3	4.2	0.7	0.4
1923	9.0	7.5	6.2	1.0	0.3
1924	3.3	3.8	2.7	0.5	0.6
1925	5.2	4.0	3.1	0.5	0.4
1926	4.6	3.9	2.9	0.5	0.5
1927	3.3	3.3	2.1	0.5	0.7
1928	3.7	3.1	2.2	0.4	0.5
1929	4.4	3.8	2.7	0.5	0.6

Source: Monthly Labour Review, July 1929, pp. 64, 65; February 1931, p. 105

expansion. This is not true in Europe today. There is some evidence of human capital hysteresis in labour force participation. The labour force participation rate of men over 65 dropped from 54 to 42 per cent between the 1930 and 1940 censuses.[36] This is considerably more rapid than its trend rate of decline. Between 1920 and 1930, it fell by only 1 per cent, and it remained essentially constant between 1940 and 1950. It seems unlikely however that this could have much effect on unemployment. Indeed to the extent that marginal workers were induced to drop out of the labour force, bad times might have reduced subsequent unemployment.

This leaves our insider–outsider story of wage setting. Beyond documenting the importance of hysteresis, and confirming its implications for wage equations, it is difficult to test the story directly. But the judgement of Leuchtenburg (1963) is perhaps revealing, 'By Roosevelt's second term, as it seemed the country might never wholly recover, the burden of the unemployed had become too exhausting a moral and economic weight to carry. Those who drew income from other sources could hardly help but feel that the Depression had been a judgement which divided the saved from the unsaved. Increasingly, the jobless seemed not merely worthless mendicants but a menacing Lumpenproletariat.' While Leuchtenburg is referring primarily to public attitudes toward the unemployed, similar private attitudes are the driving force behind the hysteresis mechanism we have stressed.

Table 15.16 *Extent of labour turnover from 1930–1940, by years (average monthly rates per 100 workers)*

Year	Accessions	Separations			
		Total	Quits	Discharges	Lay-offs
Median rates					
1929	4.4	3.8	2.7	0.5	0.6
1930	1.6	2.4	1.1	0.2	1.2
Weighted average rates					
1930	3.1	5.0	1.6	0.4	3.0
1931	3.1	4.1	1.0	0.2	2.9
1932	3.4	4.3	0.7	0.2	3.4
1933	5.4	3.8	0.9	0.2	2.7
1934	4.7	4.1	0.9	0.2	3.0
1935	4.2	3.6	0.9	0.2	2.5
1936	4.3	3.4	1.1	0.2	2.1
1937	3.5	4.4	1.2	0.2	3.0
1938	3.8	4.1	0.6	0.1	3.4
1939	4.1	3.1	0.8	0.1	2.2
1940	4.4	3.35	1.0	0.15	2.2

*Including miscellaneous separations because of death, retirement on pension, etc., reported separately since January 1940.
Source: Monthly Labor Review, 1930 to 1941. For a summary of labour turnover from 1931 to 1939, see *ibid.*, September 1940, pp. 696–704.

The finding of so many parallels between the current European depression and the American depression suggests to us that hysteresis in Europe may be more the result of a long sequence of adverse shocks than the result of structural problems. Perhaps most telling is the observation that the apparent natural rate of unemployment drifted upwards following the actual unemployment rate during the American depression just as it has in Europe. Given the absence of structural explanations for this drift, the inference that it resulted from high past unemployment seems compelling. So too, the high apparent European natural rate of unemployment may be the result of hysteresis arising in the aftermath of a sequence of adverse shocks. As we discuss below, this implies that expansionary macroeconomic policies may well work in reducing unemployment in Europe.

Conclusions

Periods of persistently high unemployment are not uncommon events in a broad historical context. Yet standard macroeconomic theories have a difficult time accounting for them. We have argued that they can only be understood in terms of theories of hysteresis that make long-run equilibrium depend on history. And we have argued that membership effects may well be important sources of hysteresis. Such effects appear to be an important source of persistence in unemployment in Europe today.

High unemployment is not however always persistent. A crucial issue is identifying the circumstances under which persistence is likely to arise. The main issue is that of whether hysteresis is the result of specific labour market structures, of the presence of unions in particular, or whether it is itself the result of adverse shocks, which by increasing unemployment, trigger the insider–outsider dynamics we have discussed in the chapter. Our tentative conclusion, from the historical record, is that membership effects become important in bad times and are not crucially dependent on the presence of unions. We have not provided however a fully satisfactory theory of membership effects in non-union settings.

Our theory permits a broad brush account of the increase in unemployment in Europe since the early 1970s. In the 1970s, European economies were hit with surprises in the form of rising oil prices, the productivity slowdown, and rapid increases in tax rates. With wages rigid in the short run each of these types of shocks created unemployment. Because of the membership considerations stressed here, the decrease in employment was validated by higher wage demands. As a result, by the end of the 1970s the equilibrium level of unemployment had increased substantially. In the 1980s, the European economies, unlike the US economy, experienced a series of adverse aggregate demand shocks as European monetary policies followed US policies, but fiscal policies turned contractionary. This led to further unemployment which was then validated by wage demands by those who remained employed. At this point, unemployment will remain high even if there are no more adverse shocks, because of the power of insider workers to set wages.

Our argument is that Europe has experienced a sequence of adverse shocks since the early 1970s, each of which had a fairly permanent effect on the level of employment. Current high unemployment can equally be blamed on a propagation mechanism which leads the adverse shocks of the past to have a lasting impact, or on the shocks themselves. Unlike simple Keynesian explanations for the European depression which stress only aggregate demand, our theory explains increases in the apparent natural rate of unemployment. Unlike some classical explanations for European unemployment which deny any role for demand management policies, our theory explains how aggregate demand can have protracted effects even in the absence of any long-lasting nominal rigidities.

This view of the European unemployment problem has a number of fairly direct policy implications. A first policy implication of our analysis is the desirability of using measures to 'enfranchize' as many workers as possible. If work-sharing programmes cause more workers to be employed and therefore represented in wage-setting decisions, they may lead to reduced wage demands and increased employment. Profit-sharing plans such as those proposed by Weitzman (1985) may also raise employment by making it possible for employers to reduce the cost of labour by increasing hires. On the other hand they would increase unions' resistance to hiring new workers and might thereby increase membership problems. An obvious alternative policy is measures to reduce the power of unions and thereby allow outsider workers to have a larger impact on wage bargains. Our findings regarding the US depression where unions were probably not of great importance lead us to be somewhat skeptical of the efficacy of such measures. Certainly it does not yet appear that efforts to reduce the power of unions in the United Kingdom have borne macroeconomic fruit.

Our model suggests that shocks, positive or negative, are in a sense self-validating. If employment changes, wage-setting practices adapt to the new level of employment. This means that positive shocks contrived through demand management policies can reduce unemployment regardless of the source of the shocks which caused it. Even if unemployment initially originated from adverse productivity shocks, expansionary policies, if they succeed in raising the level of employment, will yield permanent benefits. Symmetrically, even if most of the increase in unemployment in the 1980s is due to demand, the large decrease in the price of oil may well decrease it permanently. At the same time the model suggests that only policies or shocks which are in some sense surprises will be efficacious. This means that it may be difficult to increase employment a great deal with expansionary policies. The crucial question becomes the length of time over which expansionary policies can 'surprise' wage setters. To whatever extent they can, very long-lasting benefits will be derived.

Do the many parallels between the American and European depressions imply that a major expansion in aggregate demand would create the same miracles in Europe as it did in the United States? Unfortunately comparison of the two depressions cannot lead to a very definite answer. While it does dispose of the idea that the apparent increase in the natural rate of unemployment means that demand expansion cannot possibly succeed, and the idea of real wage growth must be restrained if expansion is to take place, an important problem remains. The likelihood of achieving a surprise for a protracted period through inflationary policies may well have been much greater in the United States after a decade including a major deflation than it is in Europe today after a decade of stagflation. On the other hand, the very political infeasibility of expansion in Europe suggests its possible efficacy. Certainly the protracted high unemployment caused by the deflationary policies of the recent past stands as a testament to the potent effects of macroeconomic policies.

NOTES

We have benefitted from the hospitality of the Centre for Labour Economics at the LSE. Richard Layard has been especially generous in helping us in a variety of ways. We thank David Grubb, John Martin and Andrew Newell for providing us with data, and Michael Burda, Robert Waldman, Changyong Rhee and Fernando Ramos for research assistance. We thank Stanley Fischer, David Metcalf, Steven Nickell, James Poterba and Andrew Shleifer and participants in the NBER macro conference at which this chapter was presented for useful discussions and comments. The chapter was originally published in National Bureau of Economic Research, *Macroeconomics Annual 1986,* ed. Stanley Fischer, MIT. Press, 1986.

1 Formally, a dynamic system is said to exhibit hysteresis if it has at least one eigenvalue equal to zero (unity, if specified in discrete time). In such a case, the steady state of the system will depend on the history of the shocks affecting the system. Thus, we should say that unemployment exhibits hysteresis when current unemployment depends on past values with coefficients summing to 1. We shall instead use 'hysteresis' more loosely to refer to the case where the degree of dependence on the past is very high, where the sum of coefficients is close but not necessarily equal to 1.

2 For the United States we made use of the revised unemployment rates calculated by Romer (1986) for the 1890–1929 period.

3 This part relies heavily on the empirical work presented for individual European countries at the Chelwood Gate Conference on Unemployment, to be published in *Economica,* 1986. The reader is refered to individual country papers for further evidence.

4 We focus on the UK because detailed data are more easily available. Available data for France and Germany tell a very similar story.

5 The mismatch index by industry goes up however in 1981 and 1982 – which are the last 2 years for which it has been computed.

6 Let a be the rate of growth of productivity and θ be the change in the tax wedge. Then the rate of growth of the after-tax real wage consistent with a given capital–labour ratio is approximately given by $a-\theta$.

7 When a time trend is added to the AR(1) specification of unemployment estimated above, its coefficient is both small and insignificant, for both countries.

8 This is also the direction of research recently followed by Sachs (1985) to explain European unemployment.

9 Unemployment remainded high – around 10 per cent – in Italy until 1960 approximately, but other factors are thought to be at work in that case.

10 Drazen (1979) constructs a related model, based on learning by doing, which also generates hysteresis. Hall (1976) explores the possibility that unemployment has long-lasting effects on productivity, and its implications for economic policy.

11 The issue of membership and membership rules is clearly closely related to the issue of union size and union membership in the union literature. See Faber (1984, section 6) for a survey. This literature has not however focused on the dynamic implications of membership rules.

12 Formalizing the firm as passive allows us to concentrate on the effects of alternative membership rules on the decisions of the group of insiders. Allowing for wage bargaining between the firm and insiders as well as for some control of employment *ex post* by insiders introduces additional issues which we shall discuss later.

13 The assumption of stochastically inelastic labour supply maintained here is not realistic for a single firm. It is best to think of the firm under consideration as a representative firm, facing the same shocks as other firms.

14 Because we use a long-linear approximation to define p, p^* as defined can be negative. But the approximation is only acceptable for p close to 1, that is for values of $a(b/c)^2$ not too large.

15 We may also think of assymetric rules where it takes m_1 periods to acquire membership, and m_2 periods to lose it. We shall briefly return to their likely implications later.

16 There is another effect which works in the opposite direction. Choosing a high real wage leads to lower employment, thus lower membership and higher expected real wages in the future. This effect however turns out to be dominated by that emphasized in the text.

17 Farber (1984) reviews the research on union behaviour when members have different seniority status, and thus conflicting interests.

18 Thus, we assume implicitly that the technological shock affects costs, but not the relation between output and employment. This is the case for example if output is produced with a labour and a non-labour input, according to a Leontief technology, and the technological shock reflects changes in the relative price in the non-labour input. A change in productivity growth would instead affect both the relation between output and employment, and between prices and wages. Allowing the technological shock to affect the relation between output and employment in the model is straightforward but introduces ambiguities in the effects of supply shocks on employment which are not central to our argument.

19 Like in other contracting models, staggering of wage decisions across unions would lead to effects of even anticipated nominal shocks. See Taylor (1979).

20 There is some evidence that this has actually occurred in Britain. Despite the legal changes which have decreased the legal power of unions since the mid-1970s, the size of the union wage differential appears to have risen sharply in recent years.

21 Consider a simple example. Suppose restaurant wages were rigid, and a big decline in the demand for restaurant meals took place so there were unemployed chefs. Would it pay to open a new restaurant with a low paid

chef? Probably not if fixed costs were high. These considerations may have something to do with why in bad times employment growth may be concentrated in small establishments.

22 Given that this chapter is written for an American audience, we do not review the role of unions in the US in any detail. As will be clear from our description of Europe, unions in the US play a much more limited role than in Europe.

23 Actual extensions are rare but the threat of extension is considered to be very effective in making all firms respect the content of these agreements.

24 In future research, it would be valuable to study Japanese labour market institutions with a view to evaluation of the theories of persistent unemployment put forward here. There are a number of similarities between Japanese and European institutions including the importance of company-level bargaining. There may however be important differences as well, particularly in the attitude of Japanese unions towards outsiders.

25 Two recent cases have been in the news; that of British Petroleum which has gone non-union for some of its shipping operations, and that of Rupert Murdoch, who has in effect gone to a more accommodating union.

26 The reason why unions encourage the unemployed to remain in the union appears to be due in part to their desire to increase membership figures, and through these, their role in the national union movement.

27 Allowing labour demand to depend on current and expected real wages, as it should under costs of adjustment, would complicate our task here.

28 Note that a between 0 and 1 does not correspond exactly to m between 1 and infinity. As we have argued before, m between 1 and ∞ leads to a more complex, non-linear, specification.

29 This is a plausible and convenient assumption. Suppose we assumed instead that productivity was the sum of a linear function of observable variables and a stationary or borderline stationary process, say an AR(1) process with coefficient ρ. The wage equation would then differ from that in the text in two ways. The first would be the presence of lagged real wages, with coefficient $\rho - 1$. The second would be the presence of the ρ first differences of the observable variables affecting productivity. We have explored these more general specifications empirically for the UK and found our simple wage equation not to be misleading.

30 Because our wage data refer to manufacturing wages, we use manufacturing employment as the employment variable in the results reported here. Very similar results were obtained using total employment.

31 All these findings are quite robust. The value of R is substantively the same if, following the argument of the previous note, the lagged real wage, current and lagged values of the capital–labour ratio, the price of oil and a proxy for productivity growth (when available) are added to the regressions. The results are also robust to changes in the coefficient on lagged inflation, say within 0.2 of the values used in the table.

32 The motivation for calculations of this type is laid out in Clark and Summers (1979). In performing the calculations, we have assumed that the exit rate from unemployment is not duration dependent. If more realistically, we allowed for it to decline, the estimated concentration of unemployment in long spells would show up even more clearly.

33 Some of the institutional rigidities of European labour markets date however from social policies introduced in the 1960s and 1970s.
34 It is clear that with such short samples, and such a drastic increase in unemployment in the second subsample, estimation cannot be very precise.
35 A similar finding is emphasized by Gordon and Wilcox (1981) who also provide evidence that it holds for Europe during the depression period. Gordon (1983) emphasizes the importance of the rate of change effect in the Phillips curve during the depression period in both the US and the UK but finds the level effect to be dominant outside of this interval.
36 This drop-off may reflect the effects of the introduction of Social Security to some extent. The programme was sufficiently small in 1940 that this is unlikely to be the whole story. Moreover, the timing of its introduction surely had something to do with the fact of the depression.

APPENDIX

Derivation of the probability of being employed

For a given realization of e, thus for a given $n=-cw+e$, the probability of employment is given by:

If $n \geq n_o$, or equivalently for $e \geq n_o + cw$, then $p=1$.
If $n \leq n_o$, or equivalently for $e \leq n_o + cw$, then $p=N/N_o \div 1 - n_o + n$.

This implies that, for an arbitrary distribution of e, with density function $f(e)$, and support $(e^- e^+)$, the probability is given by:

$$p = \int_{e_-}^{n_o+cw} (1-n_o-cw+e)f(e)de + \int_{n_o+cw}^{e^+} 1 \, f(e)de.$$

If, as assumed in the text, e is uniform on $(Ee-a, Ee+a)$, p becomes:

$$p = (1/2a)\{[(1-n_o-cw+e/2)e]_{Ee-a}^{n_o+cw} + (Ee+a-n_o-cw)\}$$

$$= 1 \qquad\qquad\qquad \text{for } n_o+cw \leq Ee-a$$

$$= 1-(1/4a)(n_o+cw-Ee+a)^2 \text{ for } n_o+cw \geq Ee-a.$$

Derivation of the solution in the case when $m=1$

We first derive the objective function maximized by the union at any point in time.

We assume that, if laid off, the probability of being rehired by the firm is equal to zero. As in the text, we assume that the utility of being unemployed is equal to zero. Let p_i be, as in the text, the probability of being employed at time

i for a member of the union at time i. Then, given the membership rule that membership depends on employment in the previous period, the probability for a union member at time zero to still be a union member in period i is given by $E_o(p_o p_i \ldots p_{i-1})$. Thus, the utility of the union member as of period 0 is given by:

$$U_o = E_o[(p_o + bw_o) + \theta p_o(p_1 + bw_1) + \theta^2 p_o p_1(pU + bw_2) + \ldots]$$

or, in recursive form, by:

$$U_o = p_o + bw_o + p_o E_o(\theta U_1).$$

Even under the assumption that the shocks are independently distributed through time, the random variables within the expectation operator above are not in general independent, making the maximization problem intractable. Thus, we solve instead the problem associated with the objective function linearized around some p', w'. This linearized objective function is given by the following recursion:

$$V_o = (A + dp_o + bw_o) + \theta p' E_o V_1$$

where $A = -\theta p'(p' + bw')/'1 - \theta p')$ and
$\qquad d = 1 + \theta(p' + bw')(1 + \theta p' + \theta'^2 + \ldots)$
$\qquad = (1 + b\theta w')/(1 - \theta p')$.

The weight put on the probability of being employed, p_o, is now higher than in the previous case. This is because p_o affects not only today's outcome but the probability of union membership and employment in the future.

We now derive the solution to the maximization using the linearized objective function. Under the assumption that shocks to labour demand are independent and uniformly distributed on $(-a, +a)$, the solution to the linearized maximization problem is derived as follows:

We first guess that the maximized value V_o is of the form

$$V_o = \alpha - \beta n_{-1} \qquad (a.1)$$

With coefficients α and β to be determined. We then solve for optimal p_o and w_o given α and β, and finally solve for α and β.

If $V_o = \alpha - \beta n_{-1}$, then $E_o V_1 = \alpha - \beta E_o n_o = \alpha^+ \beta c w_o$. Replacing in the recursive form which characterizes U_o gives:

$$V_o = (A + \theta p' \alpha) + (b + \theta p' \beta c) w_o + dp_o. \qquad (a.2)$$

The probability p_o is given by:

$$p_o = 1 - (1/4a)(n_o + cw_o + a)^2.$$

Replacing p_o in (a.2) and solving for optimal w_o gives:

$$w_o=(1/c)[-n_o-a+2a(b+\theta p'\beta c)/dc].\tag{a.3}$$

This in turn gives:

$$p_o=1-a[(b+\theta p'\beta c)/dc]^2.\tag{a.4}$$

This gives us w_o and p_o as functions of structural parameters and of α and β. We now solve for the values of α and β. Replacing w_o and p_o in (a.2) and comparing (a.2) and (a.1) gives the values of α and β. The value of α is of no interest here. The value of β is given by:

$$\beta=(b/c)/(1-\theta p').$$

REFERENCES

Barker, A., Lewis, P. and McCann, M. 1984: Trades unions and the organisation of the unemployed. *British Journal of Industrial Relations*, 3, 391–404.

Blanchard, O. and Summers, L. 1984: Perspectives on high world real interest rates. *Brookings Papers on Economic Activity*, 2, 273–334.

Bruno, M. and Sachs, J. 1985: *The Economics of Worldwide Stagflation*. Oxford: Basil Blackwell.

Buiter, W. 1985: A guide to public sector debt and deficits. *Economic Policy*, 1, November, 13–60.

Bulow, J. and Summers, L. 1986: A theory of dual labor markets with application to industrial policy, discrimination and Keynesian unemployment. *Journal of Labor Economics* (forthcoming).

Campbell, J. and Mankiw, G. 1985: Are Output Fluctuations Transitory? Harvard, mimeo.

Clark, K. and Summers, L. 1979: Labor market dynamics and unemployment: A reconsideration. *Brookings Papers on Economic Activity*, 1, 13–60.

Clark, K. and Summers, L. 1982: Labour force participation: Timing and persistence. *Review of Economic Studies*, 49 (159), 825–44.

Coe, D. and Gagliardi, F. 1985: Nominal Wage Determination in ten OECD Countries. OECD Economics and Statistics Department Working Paper 19, March.

Dornbusch, R. et al. 1983: Macroeconomic Prospects and Policies of the European Community. Center for European Policy Studies Discussion Paper 1, Bruxelles. Reprinted in Blanchard, O., Dornbusch, R. and Layard, R. (eds) 1986: *Restoring Europe's Prosperity*. Cambridge, MA: MIT Press, 1–32.

Drazen, A. 1979: On permanent effects of transitory phenomena in a simple growth model. *Economics Letters*, 3, 25–30.

Ellwood, D. 1982: Teenage unemployment: permanent scars or temporary blemishes? In Freeman, R. and Wise, D. (eds) *The Youth Labor Market Problem: Its Nature, Causes and Consequences*. Chicago: Chicago Press–NBER.

Farber, H. 1984: The Analysis of Union Behaviour. MIT working paper 355, November.

Fischer, S. 1977: Long term contracts, rational expectations, and the optimal money supply rule. *Journal of Political Economy,* 85 (1), February, 191–205.

Gordon, R. 1983: A century of evidence on wage and price stickiness in the United States, the United Kingdom and Japan. In Tobin, J. (ed.) *Macroeconomics, Prices and Quantities.* Brookings Institution, 85–120.

Gordon, R. and Wilcox, J. 1981: Monetarist interpretations of the Great Depression, an evaluation and a critique. In Brunner, K. (ed.) *The Great Depression Revisited.* Martinus Nijhoff, 49–207.

Gregory, R. 1985: Wages Policy and Unemployment in Australia. Presented at the Chelwood Gate Conference on Unemployment, Chelwood Gate.

Grubb, D. 1984: The OECD Data Set. LSE Centre for Labour Economics working paper 615.

Hall, R. 1976: The Phillips curve and macroeconomic policy. *Carnegie Rochester Conference on Economic Policy,* 1, 127–48.

Hargreaves Heap, S. P. 1980: Choosing the wrong natural rate, accelerating inflation or decelerating unemployment and growth. *Economic Journal,* 90, September, 611–20.

Harris, J. and Todaro, M. 1970: Migration, unemployment and development: A two sector analysis. *American Economic Review,* 60 (1), 126–43.

Kaufman, R. 1984: On Britain's competitive sector. *British Journal of Industrial Relations,* March.

Layard, R. and Nickell, S. 1985: Unemployment in Britain. Presented at the Chelwood Gate Conference on Unemployment.

Layard, R., Nickell, S. and Jackman, R. 1984: On Vacancies. LSE Centre for Labour Economics Discussion paper 165, August.

Layard, R. et al. 1981: Europe: The case for unsustainable growth. Center for European Policy Studies, 8/9, May. Reprinted in Blanchard, O., Dornbusch, R. and Layard, R. (eds) 1986: *Restoring Europe's Prosperity,* Cambridge, MA: MIT Press, 33–94.

Leuchtenburg, W. 1963: *Franklin D. Roosevelt and the New Deal.* New York: Harper and Row.

Lindbeck A. and Snower, D. 1985: Wage Setting, Unemployment and Insider–Outsider Relations. Institute for International Economic Studies, Stockholm, WP 344, December.

McDonald, I. and Solow, R. 1981: Wage bargaining and unemployment. *American Economic Review,* 71 (5), 896–908.

Minford, P. 1982: *Unemployment: Cause and Cure.* Oxford: Martin Robertson.

Mitchell, B. 1947: *Depression Decade: From New Era Through New Deal,* New York: Holt, Rinehart.

Nelson, R. and Plosser, C. 1982: Trends and random walks in economic time series: Some evidence and implications. *Journal of Monetary Economics,* 10, 139–62.

Nickell, S. 1984: A Review of 'Unemployment: Cause and Cure' by Patrick Minford and David Davies, Michael Peel and Alison Prague. Discussion Paper 185, Centre for Labour Economics, London School of Economics.

OECD, *Employment Outlook,* 1984.

Oswald, A. 1985: The economic theory of trade unions: An introductory survey. *Scandinavian Journal of Economics* (forthcoming).

Phelps, E. 1972: *Inflation Policy and Unemployment Theory*. New York: Norton.

Romer, C. 1986: Spurious volatility in historical unemployment data. *Journal of Political Economy*, 94 (1), 1–37.

Sachs, J. 1979: Wages, profits and macroeconomic adjustment: A comparative study. *Brookings Papers on Economic Activity*, 2, 269–319.

Sachs, J. 1983: Real wages and unemployment in the OECD countries. *Brookings Papers on Economic Activity*, 1, 255–89.

Sachs, J. 1985: High Unemployment in Europe. Harvard, mimeo.

Samuelson, P. 1966: *The Collected Scientific Papers of Paul A. Samuelson*, Vol II. Cambridge, MA: MIT Press.

Slichter, S. 1950: Notes on the structure of wages. *Review of Economics and Statistics*, 31, 283–8.

Taylor, J. 1979: Staggered wage setting in a macro model. *American Economic Review*, 69 (2), 108–13.

Weitzman, M. 1982: Increasing returns and the foundations of unemployment theory. *Economic Journal*, 92, 787–804.

Weitzman, M. 1985: *The Share Economy*. Cambridge, MA: Harvard University Press.

Woytinsky, W. S. 1942: *Three Aspects of Labor Dynamics*. Washington, DC: Social Science Research Council.

16

The NAIRU: Statistical Fact or Theoretical Straitjacket?

T. J. JENKINSON

Introduction

In recent years much attention has focused, in both theoretical models and macroeconomic debates, on the concept of the non-accelerating inflation rate of unemployment, or NAIRU. According to the proponents of this concept, the level of the NAIRU is an important structural parameter of an economy.[1] Some would even interpret the NAIRU as a target variable, since the theory suggests that deviations of the actual unemployment rate from the NAIRU in the long term can only be achieved by sacrificing control over the inflation rate. In this chapter the empirical estimates of NAIRUs for a number of OECD countries are considered, and found in general to be highly misleading and statistically ill-defined. This confirms the evidence presented using cross-country data in Beckerman and Jenkinson (1986).

The equilibrium predictions of NAIRU models are then examined and the existence of the theoretical equilibrium tested on the time-series data for the UK. The results suggest that the theoretical restrictions imposed on the models in general are not supported by the data. An alternative model is then presented in which demand factors are allowed a role in the determination of the equilibrium rate of unemployment. Given that estimates of NAIRUs can form the basis of important macroeconomic policy design, these results suggest that the whole concept of the NAIRU should be viewed with great suspicion.

NAIRU Models

A popular and simple method by which the NAIRU for an economy can, in principle, be calculated is via a simple structural wage equation of the form:

$$\Delta W_t = \alpha \Delta W_{t-1} + \beta (\Delta P - \Delta W)_{t-1} + \gamma U_t + \delta, \qquad (16.1)$$

where W represents nominal wages, P the price level and U the rate of unemployment. This is simply an error correction model in which the nominal wage responds to unemployment and, with a lag, to changes in the level of the real wage. Since the theory defines the 'equilibrium' rate of unemployment in terms of changes in the rate of wage inflation, the restriction that $\alpha = 1$ is imposed so that the dependent variable becomes the acceleration of wages. In addition, many widely used estimates include one or more time trend terms, which are generally supported by the assertion that the equilibrium level of unemployment has been rising over time.

This may be considered to be a rather weak straw man, but many such estimates are produced which are often used to justify far-reaching economic policies. For example, Jackman et al. (1984) claim that, 'The greatest blow to textbook Keynesianism of the 1950s and 1960s was the advent of the idea of the natural rate of unemployment. We accept this idea on the basis of innumerable augmented Phillips Curves . . . '. The validity of such claims is examined below.

Many NAIRU estimates have been produced using this basic methodology over the past few years, and it would be impossible to examine the empirical basis of all such models. But rather more public attention than usual was given to one particular set of results contained in a report to the Centre for European Policy Studies (CEPS).[2] In this report the case for expansionary policies to be adopted in the member countries of the European Community was based to a large extent on the excess of the actual unemployment rates in these countries over the authors' estimates of the NAIRUs for the countries in question. In order for the notion of the NAIRU to have any real economic content, at least in this very simple model, it is necessary that wage inflation and unemployment are linked in a well-defined and robust way. This would be quite contrary to the results presented in Beckerman and Jenkinson (1986) and, indeed, a number of other recent papers.[3]

The actual wage equation estimated in the CEPS paper is given in equation (16.2). The dependent variable in this model is clearly the acceleration of wages, which is postulated to depend upon lagged real wage growth, the unemployment rate and two time trend terms.

$$\Delta^2 W_t = \beta (\Delta P - \Delta W)_{t-1} + \gamma U_t + \eta t + \nu t^2 + \delta. \qquad (16.2)$$

One rather obvious objection to this equation (aside from the rather liberal use of time trends) is that current prices play no explanatory role in the determination of wages. If workers are concerned, in wage negotiations, with changes in their *real* wages then the rate of price inflation, as well as the level of their real wages in the previous period, should be important. In order to meet this criticism, without proposing an alternative but completely unrelated model, we estimate the more general model given in equation (16.3).

$$\Delta^2 W_t = \varphi \Delta^2 P_t + \beta \, (\Delta P - \Delta W)_{t-1} + \gamma U_t + \eta t + \nu t^2 + \delta. \qquad (16.3)$$

The point of such an exercise is to *encompass* the CEPS model, that is, to propose an alternative model that not only fits the 'facts' of the data more accurately, but also can explain why the CEPS results occurred.[4] This is achieved with considerable success by equation (16.3), the results for which are shown in table 16.1. It is in no way claimed that the wage equations estimated below for the individual EEC countries are the best possible[5] but simply that they are an improvement on the basic CEPS NAIRU estimates.

The results reported in table 16.1 show that in five of the seven countries included, the effect of unemployment on wage dynamics is not statistically significant at conventional significance levels. In three cases the estimated coefficient is even positive. Indeed, even in the cases of Denmark and Belgium, where the unemployment rate is significant, the results depend upon the inclusion of the squared trend term, which most people would view as a rather vigorous massaging of the data-generating process.

The average standard error for the model reported in table 16.1 is 1.1 per cent, compared with 2.94 per cent for the regressions reported in the CEPS report. Hence it is possible not only to fit the 'facts' of the data more precisely, but also to explain why previous NAIRU estimates occurred.

Does Demand Influence 'Equilibrium' Unemployment?

One of the most contentious elements of natural rate theories is that aggregate demand does not affect the attainable equilibrium rate of unemployment, but simply determines where the economy is in the short run relative to that equilibrium. In other words, in the long run there is not only a unique natural level of employment but also a corresponding natural level of demand. In the short run, however, there can be higher employment than at the NAIRU, but only if we are prepared to accept increasing inflation. The NAIRU itself is determined independently of demand factors: running the economy at a low level of demand since the early 1980s has not affected the attainable rate of unemployment.

There are numerous objections to such a theoretical model. There is nothing in theory that dictates that the natural rate of unemployment should be unique, especially in an open economy, and government fiscal

Table 16.1 *A model of wages for EEC countries, 1963–1983*

Country	$\Delta^2 P$	$(\Delta P - \Delta W)$	U	t	t^2	γ
UK	0.73	1.30	0.16	0.49	−2.89	−0.01
	(1.44)	(3.84)	(0.30)	(1.31)	(1.14)	(0.38)
	%s.e.=1.76		DW=2.02		$\chi^2(3)$=4.04	
Italy	1.05	1.01	−0.28	0.44	−2.14	0.02
	(2.81)	(3.22)	(0.21)	(1.53)	(1.49)	(0.34)
	%s.e.=1.59		DW=2.13		$\chi^2(3)$=1.61	
Denmark	0.10	0.85	−0.63	0.13	−0.14	0.03
	(0.32)	(3.88)	(2.44)	(0.83)	(0.15)	(2.64)
	%s.e.=0.79		DW=2.22		$\chi^2(3)$=6.60	
France	0.64	1.30	−0.92	0.39	−0.56	0.02
	(2.32)	(3.21)	(1.09)	(2.58)	(0.46)	(1.61)
	%s.e.=0.60		DW=1.96		$\chi^2(3)$=2.58	
Holland	1.74	1.20	0.38	0.21	−2.56	0.02
	(2.32)	(3.20)	(1.47)	(0.82)	(1.52)	(1.46)
	%s.e.=1.20		DW=2.15		$\chi^2(3)$=3.32	
Belgium	0.71	0.83	−1.21	−0.23	3.70	0.05
	(3.08)	(5.64)	(4.06)	(1.71)	(2.80)	(4.47)
	%s.e.=0.38		DW=2.87		$\chi^2(3)$=9.81	
Germany	1.51	0.67	0.29	0.11	−1.12	0.01
	(1.81)	(2.22)	(0.57)	(0.63)	(1.04)	(0.75)
	%s.e.=0.75		DW=1.50		$\chi^2(3)$=14.35	

t-statistics appear in parentheses, %s.e. is the percentage standard error of the equations, DW is the Durbin–Watson statistic and the χ^2 statistic is a test for the validity of the instruments used. Unemployment and $\Delta^2 P$ are treated as endogenous variables, and the method of estimation was therefore two-stage least squares. Additional instruments used were the current and lagged 'world' price level, and the current and lagged 'world' rate of unemployment.[6]

policy may be able to influence the equilibrium we attain, perhaps via changing expectations. More persuasive, perhaps, is the fact that if the economy is 'disinflated' for a number of years, then one response to falling real demand in the goods markets, especially in the face of downwardly inflexible wages, is to scrap productive capacity. Plant closures and company liquidations are not quickly reversible, even if fiscal and monetary policy were to change. In this sense the level of demand would influence in a direct way the attainable equilibrium of the economy, not simply the position of the economy relative to the natural rate.[7]

If in addition the labour market is segmented into insiders and outsiders, an increase in the level of unemployment brought about by falling demand will not be easily or quickly reversible. As workers are laid off, and so become 'outsiders', their impact on wage negotiations becomes exceedingly weak. This type of market failure can lead to a ratchet effect in unemployment in response to very low levels of real demand. Rather than view the continual rise in estimated NAIRUs since the mid-1970s as a problem on the supply side of the economy, then, many factors suggest that demand has had a direct effect on the attainable rate of unemployment, which, of course, would have strong policy implications.

In this section we apply recently developed econometric techniques to examine the theoretical implications of NAIRU models. Rather than estimate dynamic wage equations – the approach of the previous section – an alternative line of analysis would be to test directly the existence of the equilibrium relationship implied by NAIRU theories. Perhaps the leading example of recent developments in this area is the work of Layard and Nickell (1986). In their paper the causes of British unemployment are examined within the context of a NAIRU model. Unlike many earlier models, price taking is not imposed and a variety of wage-setting procedures are explored. This allows a role for aggregate demand in both the price and labour demand equations, although demand is, of course, *assumed* only to influence the position of the economy relative to the NAIRU in the short run. From a three-equation structural model, a reduced form natural rate equation is derived, which accounts for post-war unemployment growth in the UK in terms of the exogenous variables of the model. To be precise, the natural rate U^* has the following functional form:[8]

$$U^* = f(MM, \rho, P_m, UP, T_L) \qquad (16.4)$$

where MM is an index of labour mismatch, ρ is the benefit replacement ratio, P_m is the real price of imports, UP is a measure of union power as captured by the union/non-union mark-up and T_L is employers' labour taxes.[9] This equilibrium relationship is imposed by the theory, the coefficients being estimated from structural equations, many of which ' . . . are not determined with any degree of precision'.[10] An alternative method of estimating the long-run parameters of the equilibrium model, which in addition allows the important question of existence to be examined, is to use the theory of cointegration introduced[11] by Granger (1983), and used in practical applications by, for example, Jenkinson (1986a) and Hall (1986).

The basic idea behind the notion of cointegration is that most economic time series are non-stationary, and require differencing to induce stationarity. In other words, an autoregressive integrated moving average (ARIMA) representation of most economic time series will have orders of integration greater than zero; a series x_t which is integrated of order b is denoted $x_t = I(b)$. However, if over a long period of time linear combinations of individually non-stationary time series are stationary, then the evolutionary behaviour of those series is linked in an important way over time. Following this approach, equilibrium is treated as a statistical property of the time series, whose putative existence can, and should, be tested. This is especially the case when important theoretical restrictions are imposed on the empirical model, upon whose validity all results are conditional.

Details of cointegration methods and statistical properties[12] of the estimators may be found in Granger (1983). The procedure is to estimate the long-run parameters of the relationship, in this case given by equation (16.4), and observe the behaviour of the residuals. The long-run parameters may be consistently estimated by running a simple *static* OLS regression, with all variables measured in levels.[13] The residuals then include all the dynamics of the data-generation process, and the hypothesis we can test is whether these residuals move in a systematic way towards the estimated equilibrium. This can be performed by testing the null hypothesis that the residuals follow a random walk, in which case this would imply that any value of unemployment could be observed with finite probability. In addition, if the short-run behaviour of the economy relative to the theoretical equilibrium is random, then we may infer that the data do not support the existence of such an equilibrium relationship.

The first stage in such an analysis is to determine the order of integration of the individual time series. This can be performed in various ways, but the two testing procedures that appear most powerful are those suggesting by Sargan and Bhargava (1983) and Dickey and Fuller (1981). The former approach amounts to running a regression of each variable on a constant and testing the null hypothesis that the residuals follow a random walk. That is, for each series x_t, the null hypothesis is that the value of ρ in equation (16.5) is unity. If we cannot reject this hypothesis the series would appear to be generated by a simple random walk, and hence would not be a stationary series.

$$x_t = \text{constant} + \epsilon_t$$
$$\epsilon_t = \rho \epsilon_{t-1} + v_t \qquad v_t \sim \text{IN}(0, \sigma^2). \tag{16.5}$$

The standard Durbin–Watson (DW) test can be used in this case, and Sargan and Bhargava present the appropriate critical bands for the test under the null hypothesis that the residuals are generated by a random walk.[14] This test can be shown to be the uniformly most powerful invariant test against the alternative hypothesis that the errors are being generated by a stationary first-order Markov process. If this hypothesis cannot be rejected the next step is to repeat the test on differenced data until the hypothesis that the residuals are generated by a random walk can be rejected.

Following the Dickey–Fuller procedure, the regression (16.6) is estimated for each series x_t,

$$\Delta x_t = \alpha x_{t-1} + \mu_t \qquad (16.6)$$

and the significance of α tested using adapted t-tables. If x_t was not being generated by a random walk, but rather by a stationary Markov process, we would expect the value of α to be negative and statistically significant. The distribution of the t-statistic is non-standard in this case because under the null of $\alpha = 0$ the x_t series would be non-stationary. Dickey and Fuller (1981) provide the appropriate t-tables for this case. This approach has the advantage that higher order autoregressions can be allowed for in the residuals. For example, with the quarterly data used below we allow for a fourth-order autoregressive process, that is:

$$\Delta x_t = \alpha_o x_{t-1} + \sum_{i=1}^{4} \alpha_i \Delta x_{t-i} + \zeta_t. \qquad (16.7)$$

This test has been called the augmented Dickey–Fuller test (ADF). The null hypothesis is still that there is a unit root in the data-generation process for x_t, which would imply non-stationarity. If non-stationarity cannot be rejected from (16.7), the data are differenced and the procedure repeated until non-stationarity is rejected. The results in table 16.2 give the values of the test statistics for the null hypothesis that the series are individually I(0). In order to avoid statistical incomparabilities the data and definitions are the same as those used by Layard and Nickell (1986)[15], and are quarterly for the UK over the period 1954–83. The critical value for the DW test, for one variable, at the 5 per cent level, is around 0.259, and for the ADF test on the t-statistics the 5 per cent critical value is around 3.1. Using the DW test, only mismatch appears to a stationary series, although using the ADF test, the null hypothesis of non-stationarity is not quite rejected at the 5 per cent level. For the moment we will suspend judgement on mismatch, and assume it is not I(0). In fact, it plays such a minimal role in the models below that it is eventually excluded. All the other series certainly appear to be non-stationary in the levels.

Table 16.2 *Testing whether NAIRU variables are I(0)*

Variable	DW	ADF^a
Unemployment	0.016	0.004 (0.37)
MM	0.463	−0.114 (2.26)
ρ	0.051	0.002 (1.06)
P_m	0.123	−0.002 (0.91)
UP	0.038	−0.006 (1.60)
T_L	0.028	0.001 (2.51)
Number of observations	112	107

[a] The coefficient on α_0 is reported for the ADF test, along with its associated t-statistic in parentheses.

The next stage then is to first-difference the data and repeat the testing procedure. These results are presented in table 16.3. In this case the tests on all the individual series easily reject non-stationarity (in first differences) and hence the NAIRU time series appear integrated to order unity, or I(1).[16] Now it is possible to search for a linear combination of the (individually non-stationary) levels of the NAIRU series, to test for the existence of the equilibrium relationship imposed by the theory on the data. This requires searching for a cointegrating vector, which is typically performed by running a simple OLS regression on the levels of the variables. This cointegrating regression should produce the long-run parameters of the NAIRU relationship, if such a relationship exists. The results are presented in table 16.4. The important result is that both the cointegrating regression Durbin–Watson statistic (CRDW) and the ADF test strongly reject the existence of any NAIRU-type relationship in the data for the UK. This is equally true when annual data are used.[17] t-statistics are not reported as these will be badly biased, but both mismatch and import prices are not even signed as we would expect a priori. The CRDW statistic indicates that there is a large autoregressive component in the residuals. Indeed this is confirmed by the LM test for first-order autocorrelation in the residuals which has a value, in the form of an F-test with (1,105) degrees of freedom, of 973 and an estimated autocorrelation coefficient of 0.995. Not surprisingly, then, the value of the CRDW statistic falls well below the lower bound of the DW tables constructed by Sargan and Bhargava (1983), under the null hypothesis that the residuals follow a random walk. The equilibrium relationship constructed from theory does not,

Table 16.3 *Testing whether NAIRU variables are I(1)*

Variable	DW	ADF
Unemployment	1.18	−0.40 (3.26)
MM	1.97	−1.17 (6.18)
ρ	1.52	−0.82 (4.41)
P_m	2.07	−0.97 (5.18)
UP	1.21	−0.88 (5.17)
T_L	2.65	−1.41 (4.44)
Number of observations	111	106

Table 16.4 *A NAIRU model of unemployment (dependent variable: unemployment)*

Variable	Parameter estimate
MM	−0.420
ρ	0.001
P_m	−0.014
UP	0.038
T_L	0.343
Constant	−1.452
Time period	1956(I)−1983(IV)
CRDW	0.091
ADF	−0.07 (1.87)

therefore, appear to be supported by the data. In this case the concept of the NAIRU, with its strong implications for economic policy, may be highly misleading.

Following the above discussion, an important question is whether demand factors directly affect the attainable rate of unemployment. The problem of how to measure demand has been the subject of much debate, but Layard and Nickell offer one of the more sophisticated attempts. They define their demand shift variable, σ, as a weighted average of the adjusted budget deficit (AD) normalized on potential GDP, the level of competitiveness (Comp) and the deviations of world trade from a quintic trend, where the weights are derived from their estimated coefficients in the labour demand equation. We also use the first two variables, the latter being of rather dubious merit, and investigate whether demand factors influence the equilibrium rate of unemployment in the economy. The procedure is identical to that followed above, but now we include AD and Comp as additional explanatory factors in the estimated equilibrium unemployment relationship (both appear to be integrated of order unity). The results are presented in table 16.5, where both mismatch and labour taxes have been eliminated, since their impact was trivial. The results are quite striking. The value of the CRDW statistic has increased considerably and now exceeds the lower bound of the test constructed under the null hypothesis of random walk residuals (5 per cent lower bound: 0.247). In addition the ADF test indicates a significant negative test statistic, well above the 5 per cent critical value. Whilst the exact critical value of the CRDW test is itself a function of the data (and requires the Imhof routine to be calculated exactly) the existence of our estimated equilibrium relationship is at the very least not denied by the data.

Both demand factors have an important role to play and enter into the equilibrium relationship in such a way that running the economy at a low level of demand over a number of years will tend to result in a higher equilibrium rate of unemployment. However, the role of government is not simply restricted to working on supply-side factors such as reducing trade unions' power in wage negotiations, or reducing the ratio of supplementary benefits to wages. The level of demand now has an important impact on the equilibrium the economy attains. Recent theoretical macroeconomics, associated for example with Hahn and Solow (1986), has suggested that there may exist a number of

Table 16.5 *Does demand influence equilibrium unemployment? (dependent variable: unemployment)*

Variable	Parameter estimate
ρ	0.003
P_m	0.245
UP	0.043
AD	−1.037
Comp	−0.235
Constant	−0.270
Time period	1956(I) − 1983(IV)
CRDW	0.334
ADF	−0.26 (3.53)

possible equilibria which the economy could arrive at, and that government fiscal and monetary policy can influence which equilibrium is actually attained. The results presented here could be interpreted as support for this contention.

Conclusions

The 'natural rate hypothesis', or the 'NAIRU', is one of the most important theoretical straitjackets that has been imposed upon economic models and policies. By assuming that government fiscal and monetary policies do not influence the long-run equilibrium of the economy, their role is reduced to one of minimizing short-run deviations of the economy from the NAIRU. In this chapter the equations that have been used to estimate the NAIRU for various countries have been re-estimated in a rather less restrictive form, and indicate that statistically well-defined relationships between unemployment and the acceleration of prices are hard to find, and that the results produced to date should certainly not be used as the justification for far-reaching economic policies.

A rather different approach was then followed to test the validity of the theoretical restrictions imposed by NAIRU models on the data. The question of the existence of the sort of equilibrium relationship derived from NAIRU models was strongly questioned, and an alternative model proposed in which the attainable level of unemployment itself was a function of fiscal and monetary policies. The interpretation of the NAIRU as some structural parameter of the economy, whose value can only be influenced by concerted supply-side measures, is therefore challenged. The rise in the attainable level of unemployment in the UK since the early 1980s has not been as a result simply of adverse supply-side factors, but has been a direct result of national and international restrictions on demand.

NOTES

I have benefitted greatly from discussions with Chris Allsopp, Wilfred Beckerman, Rod Cross, Steve Nickell and Andrew Oswald. Errors and omissions are my own.

1 It was once remarked that to propose that the natural rate was a key structural parameter of the economy was like observing that the Boston Celtics basketball team won on a Wednesday and then claiming that Wednesday was their *natural day*.

2 Basevi et al. 1983: 'Europe: The case for unsustainable growth.'

3 See for example Ashenfelter and Card (1982) or Geary and Kennan (1983) who cannot reject the null hypothesis of independence between real wages and unemployment for 12 OECD countries.

4 For an exposition of the encompassing approach in econometrics see Mizon (1984).

5 Indeed, by excluding some of the time trends in equation (16.3) not only can the residual variance be reduced, for some countries, but also the results become easier to interpret.

6 World prices and unemployment are calculated as the average of the Consumer Price Index and of the unemployment rate over 12 major industrialized countries, but, for each country in table 16.1, excluding the values for the country in question.

7 For an interesting exposition of the non-uniqueness of the NAIRU in open economies, see Carlin and Soskice (1985).

8 It should be noted that the Layard and Nickell model is essentially non-linear, with both the unemployment rate and the log of the unemployment rate appearing. In what follows, a model of the NAIRU is tested and estimated which is a log-linear function of supply-side variables. This is presumably the sort of reduced form relationship which most people associate with NAIRU.

9 In addition an incomes policy dummy is included, which we ignore for the reasons that should become clear.

10 Layard and Nickell (1986 : p.61).

11 Important developments have since been made by, amongst others, Stock (1984) and Granger and Engle (1985).

12 The most important properties being that, if cointegration holds, biases in the parameter estimates will be of the order $(1/T)$, where T is the sample size, and that the estimates will be super-consistent in the sense that they will converge to their true value at a faster rate than normal OLS estimates, i.e. order $(1/T)$ rather than the normal $\sqrt{(1/t)}$.

13 This is only strictly the case when all variables are integrated of order unity – which is the case for the natural rate theory we examine in this chapter. If the order of integration exceeds unity differenced series may be included.

14 The standard Durbin–Watson tables are, of course, constructed to test the null hypothesis that the residuals are generated independently.

15 The data were kindly supplied to me by Alan Carruth, in a form suitable for use with PC-GIVE.

16 The power of these tests of orders of integration do, however, become rather poor against certain autoregressive alternatives. For a cautionary note, see Jenkinson (1986b).

17 Details available from the author on request.

REFERENCES

Ashenfelter, O. and Card, D. 1982: Time series representations of economic variables and alternative models of the labour market. *Review of Economic Studies,* XLIX.

Basevi, G., Blanchard, O. Buiter, W. Dornbusch, R. and Layard, R. 1983: Europe: The case for unsustainable growth. *Centre for European Policy Studies Papers,* 8/9, and appendices.

Beckerman, W. and Jenkinson, T. J. 1986: What stopped the inflation? Unemployment or commodity prices? *Economic Journal,* March.

Carlin, W. and Soskice, D. 1985: Real Wages, Unemployment, International Competitiveness and Inflation: A Framework for Analysing Open and Closed Economies. Institute of Economics and Statistics, Oxford University, mimeo.

Dickey, D. A. and Fuller, W. A. 1981: The likelihood ratio statistic for autoregressive time series with a unit root. *Econometrica,* 49.

Geary, P. T. and Keenan, J. 1982: The employment–real wage relationship: An international study. *Journal of Political Economy,* 90.

Granger, C. W. J. 1983: Co-integrated Variables and Error Correcting Models. University of California, San Diego, mimeo.

Granger, C. W. J. and Engle, R. F. 1985: Dynamic Model Specification with Equilibrium Constraints: Co-integration and Error Correction. University of California, San Diego, mimeo.

Hahn, F. H. and Solow, R. 1986: Is wage flexibility a good thing? In Beckerman, W. (ed.) *Wage Flexibility, Unemployment and Economic Policy,* Duckworth, London.

Hall, S. G. 1986: An application of the Granger and Engle Two Step Estimation Procedure to UK Aggregate Wage Data. NIESR Discussion Paper.

Jackman, R., Layard, R. and Pissarides, C. 1984: Policies for Reducing the Natural Rate of Unemployment. LSE Centre for Labour Economics Discussion Paper, 199.

Jenkinson, T. J. 1986a: Testing neoclassical theories of labour demand: An application of cointegration techniques. *Oxford Bulletin of Economics and Statistics,* August.

Jenkinson, T. J. 1986b: A Note on Alternative Tests for Cointegration when Individual Time Series are Highly Autoregressive, rather than Non-Stationary. Merton College, Oxford, mimeo.

Layard, R. and Nickell, S. J. 1986: Unemployment in Britain. Centre for Labour Economics Discussion Paper, 240.

Mizon, G. 1984: The encompassing approach in econometrics. In Hendry, D. and Wallis, K. (eds) *Econometrics and Quantative Economics,* Basil Blackwell, Oxford.

Sargan, J. D. and Bhargava, A. 1983: Testing residuals from least squares regression for being generated by the gaussian random walk. *Econometrica,* 51.

Stock, J. H. 1984: Asymptotic Properties of Least Squares Estimators of Co-integrating Vectors. Harvard University, mimeo.

17

The NAIRU: Some Theory and Statistical Facts

STEPHEN NICKELL

The view that there is an upper limit to the level of activity in the economy beyond which there is a danger of increasing inflation appears to be a contentious one. This is particularly true if the level of unemployment associated with this level of activity is called the natural rate or the NAIRU. The former term is, of course, somewhat invidious since it seems to imply that it is beyond the wit of people to influence it, a view which is clearly nonsense and to which no one would subscribe. However, it is true that the natural rate is, more or less by definition, independent of government fiscal policy to the extent that this affects the level of activity. Again, it is obvious that fiscal policy, to the extent that it directly influences wage or price behaviour, via tax or benefit changes for example, could influence the natural rate and this would be true even in a perfectly competitve Walrasian economy.

Tim Jenkinson, in the third section of his contribution to this volume (chapter 16), goes beyond this and after a few theoretical remarks on the status of the NAIRU as a useful concept, presents two statistical facts based on the empirical model set out in Layard and Nickell (1985, 1986). First, he shows that the unemployment rate, u, is not cointe-grated[1] with the 'supply-side' variables which Layard and Nickell use to explain long-run trends in unemployment; and second, he shows that the level of unemployment is cointegrated with some of these supply-side variables augmented by some of the demand-side variables used by Layard and Nickell. He then interprets these facts as casting some doubt on the usefulness of the NAIRU concept as it is usually interpreted.

My purpose in this short chapter is to provide an interpretation of his results which differs in emphasis from that given by Jenkinson. Since it is, at least in my view, impossible to provide any interpretation of such results without the help of a theoretical framework, I shall begin by presenting such a framework and then look at the results in this context.

A Theoretical Framework

We begin with the technology of the economy which we write as

$$y-k=a_0+a_1(n-k) \tag{17.1}$$

where y=output (value added), k=capital stock, n=employment and lower case letters refer to logs. It is also convenient to define $\bar{y}$, the potential output of the economy, by

$$\bar{y}-k=a_0+a_1(l-k) \tag{17.2}$$

where l=labour force. We take l, k as given throughout this exercise since we are fundamentally concerned with the ability of the economy to utilize available resources. Real demand in the economy, y^d, can be measured in terms of deviations from $\bar{y}$ and we thus define real demand relative to potential output, σ^d, by the expression

$$y^d=\sigma^d+\bar{y}. \tag{17.3}$$

We also suppose that real demand is equal to output and hence

$$y^d-k=a_0+a_1(n-k). \tag{17.4}$$

So far we have not introduced any behavioural relationships, but it is worth noting that the production side of the economy can be summarized by

$$\sigma^d=-a_1u \tag{17.5}$$

where $u=l-n$, the unemployment rate. This follows from (17.2), (17.3) and (17.4).

Turning now to the demand side, this we write as a reduced form

$$\sigma^d=\sigma(x_f,x_m,y^*) \tag{17.6}$$

$$c=c(x_f,x_m,y^*) \tag{17.7}$$

where c=price competitiveness, x_f=fiscal policy, x_m=monetary policy, y^*=world economic activity, the latter three variables being exogenous.[2] It is also convenient to write the expression for the level of competitiveness consistent with trade balance, c_{tb}, as

$$c_{tb}=B(\sigma^d+\bar{y},z_c) \; , \; B_1>0 \; , \; B_2<0 \tag{17.8}$$

where z_c refers to exogenous factors tending to improve the trade balance such as North Sea oil.

The supply side consists of two equations reflecting price-setting behaviour by firms and wage-setting behaviour in the labour market. These are discussed at some length in my other contribution to this volume so they are simply stated here as

$$p-w=\alpha_0-\alpha_1\Delta^2p+\alpha_2'\sigma^d-\alpha_3 x \qquad (17.9)$$

$$w-p=\beta_0-\beta_1\Delta^2p-f(u,\Delta u)+\alpha_3 x+z. \qquad (17.10)$$

p=value added prices, w=hourly labour cost, Δ^2p=rate of change of inflation, x=trend productivity, z=factors inducing wage pressure.

A few points are worth noting. First, rising inflation is associated with a fall in the price mark-up on wages as firms tend to under price because costs are rising faster than expected. On the other hand it tends to squeeze real wages as prices turn out higher than was expected when wages are set. Second, trend productivity is taken as given and is related to k and l. Third, z includes a set of exogenous factors, z_1, and the level of competitiveness, c, the latter arising from the possibility of real wage resistance (improved competitiveness raises import prices and hence increases retail prices relative to p). Fourth, increases in trend productivity reduce the price mark-up on wages since unit labour costs fall at fixed wage rates. We assume that this effect is the same as the impact on wages (the coefficient is the same in both equations) thereby asserting that, in the long run, trend productivity growth does not lead to persistent inflationary pressure arising from a combined desire by firms and workers to have more than 100 per cent of the incremental output. This does not rule out the possibility that, when productivity growth fails, desired real wage growth on the part of workers adjusts only slowly to the new situation. These effects are included in z but are assumed not to last for ever. Fifth, the function f is non-decreasing in u and Δu and is likely to be concave in the former. These affects arise for a variety of reasons (e.g. insider–outsider models, hysteresis, etc.) which are described at length in my other chapter.

If we make use of (17.5), the price equation may be rewritten as

$$p-w=\alpha_0-\alpha_1\Delta^2p-\alpha_2' a_1u-\alpha_3x \qquad (17.11)$$

and the remarks on the elements of wage pressure, z, imply that (17.10) can be written as

$$w-p=\beta_0-\beta_1\Delta^2p-f(u,\Delta u)+\alpha_3x+z_1+\alpha_4c, \qquad (17.12)$$

z_1 being exogenous wage pressure variables.

Two notions of the long-run equilibrium of the economy may now be described. The first is that consistent with stable inflation given competitiveness, c. For fixed competitiveness, equations (17.11) and (17.12) reveal the real wage and level of unemployment at stable inflation simply by setting $\Delta^2 p=0$, $\Delta u=0$. Equation (17.5) then reveals the level of demand associated with this level of unemployment and the demand equations (17.6) and (17.7) tell us the fiscal and monetary policies which will produce this level of demand and the given level of competitiveness at the existing level of world activity. The empirical work by Jenkinson looks at this notion of equilibrium in the sense that competitiveness is implicitly included in the supply-side variables used in his equations via the real price of imports. However, as Carlin and Soskice (1985) (quoted approvingly by Jenkinson) and incidentally, Layard and Nickell (1986) make clear, this is obviously not a suitable notion of long-run equilibrium since demand and competitiveness can be manipulated independently by appropriate mixes of monetary and fiscal policy. Thus the government can reduce unemployment at stable inflation simply by ensuring the appropriate rise in demand is accompanied by a reduction in competitiveness (via an exchange rate appreciation) which reduces wage pressure. This is precisely the policy followed by the United States government in 1983–4 and is the type of 'non-uniqueness' of the NAIRU referred to in note 7 of chapter 16. Such manipulation cannot, however, be sustained indefinitely because of the chronic trade deficit which it induces.

The real NAIRU concept in an open economy must clearly refer to the equilibrium at stable inflation consistent with trade balance. In the context of our model, this may be obtained by setting $\Delta^2 p=0$, $\Delta u=0$ and $c=c_{tb}$. Equations (17.5), (17.8), (17.11) and (17.12) now reveal the level of unemployment, real wages, demand and competiveness at this equilibrium and the demand equations (17.6) and (17.7) simply tell us the monetary and fiscal policies necessary to bring it about. This equilibrium is therefore independent of monetary and fiscal policies *except* insofar as they influence the wage pressure and trade balance factors, z_1 and z_c.

Before going on to discuss some statistical results, three further points are worth noting. First, this equilibrium is perfectly well defined even if unemployment has no impact on wages whatever $[f(u,\Delta u)=0]$. Second, there are innumerable ways in which monetary and fiscal policies can influence z_c and z_1 in both the short and the long run and thereby influence the attainable equilibrium of the economy. Relevant factors might include the mix of direct and indirect taxation, inflation taxes, the tax rate on North Sea oil profits, the level of unemployment benefits and any impact on trend productivity growth, although the latter will not have a permanent effect. Third, the dynamic effects of unemployment on wages are crucial in determining the short-run unemployment–inflation tradeoff, as my other contribution in this volume makes clear.

The Statistical Facts

On the basis of this framework, we can now see precisely how unemployment might be related, in the long run, to both demand- and supply-side variables. There are two relevant equations here. Equation (17.5) tells us that

$$u = -\sigma^d/a_1. \tag{17.13}$$

Thus via the production function, we must expect the level of unemployment to be cointegrated with demand-side factors only. This is a purely technological relationship and would hold in any economy. Its existence tells us nothing about how the economy behaves, whether or not there is a NAIRU or indeed anything whatever about the functioning of the economy. It is pure identity theory. Just to check that Layard and Nickell have included enough demand factors in their model, we report in table 17.1 a test of cointegration between unemployment and the Layard and Nickell demand factors and we see that the hypothesis of no cointegration is indeed rejected using the CRDW test described in Jenkinson's chapter.

In order to retain consistency with Jenkinson's empirical analysis, we now turn to the equilibrium level of unemployment conditional on competitiveness. Solving (17.11) and (17.12), and setting $\Delta^2 p = \Delta u = 0$ gives

$$f(u^*,0) + \alpha'_2 a_1 u^* = \alpha_0 + \beta_0 + z_1 + \alpha_4 c. \tag{17.14}$$

Table 17.1 *The cointegration of unemployment with demand-side variables*

Dependent variable	u
Independent variables	
AD	−0.857
Comp	−0.217
WT	−0.361
Constant	−0.0469
Time period	1954–83 (annual observations)
CRDW	0.79
(5% lower bound 0.65)	

AD=adjusted deficit/potential GDP, Comp=competitiveness, WT=deviation of world trade from trend. These variables are described in detail in Layard and Nickell (1986), data appendix.

In the simplest versions of the Layard and Nickell model, $f(u^*,0)=\log u^*$ which captures the concavity of the f function, a vital feature as Layard and Nickell make clear. In the Layard and Nickell model, this is the dominant factor on the left-hand side of (17.14) and so we may expect $\log u$ to be cointegrated with the supply-side factors. In table 17.2 we report the relevant cointegration test in column 2 and for comparison purposes we present the same test using u instead of $\log u$ in column 1. The supply-side variables here are identical to those used in Jenkinson, table 16.4. We find, as expected, that the hypothesis of no cointegration is not rejected in the case of u but is rejected in the case of $\log u$. This is precisely what we expect from the Layard and Nickell model and confirms the Jenkinson result in the former case. Indeed, it is worth noting that if $\log u$ and the supply-side variables are cointegrated then it is unlikely (although not impossible) that u would be cointegrated with them, given that u and $\log u$ are, themselves, not cointegrated.

So what are we to make of the Jenkinson cointegration tests? He finds that u is cointegrated with a selection of demand- and supply-side variables (see Jenkinson, table 16.5). Given our results, this is hardly surprising but is not very informative about the nature of the economy. He also finds that u is not cointegrated with supply-side variables as I do in table 17.2. He remarks in note 9 that the Layard and Nickell model is essentially non-linear (i.e. f is concave) but concludes that most people apparently associate the NAIRU with a linear relationship between u and the supply-side variables. Since a glance at the original papers by Phillips (1958) and Lipsey (1960) reveals that the Phillips curve is, indeed, curved,[3] it is not clear why most people should take this view. In any event, the fact is that there are good theoretical reasons why the

Table 17.2 *The cointegration of unemployment with supply-side variables*

Dependent variable	u	$\log u$
Independent variables		
MM	0.026	0.335
ρ	0.0023	0.0274
Pm	0.497	2.32
UP	0.0317	0.420
TL	0.0982	6.46
Constant	−0.479	−29.06
Time period	1954–83	1954–83
CRDW	0.40	1.03
(5% Lower Bound 0.65)		

Variables are as defined in chapter 16

relationship is non-linear and so it is in practice. Hence the cointegration between log u and the supply-side variables.

To conclude, therefore, the cointegration properties of the data are perfectly consistent with the NAIRU view of the British economy as formulated in the first part of this chapter and in the model described in Layard and Nickell (1985, 1986).

NOTES

This chapter was prompted by the third section of the preceding chapter by Tim Jenkinson.

1 Jenkinson provides an explanation of this term so I shall not elaborate here.

2 The complete demand side in the case of floating exchange rates with perfect capital mobility may be written

$$\text{IS: } \sigma^d = \sigma_0 + \sigma_1 x_f - \sigma_2(r - \dot{p}^{\,e}) + \sigma_3 c + \sigma_4 y^*$$

$$\text{LM: } m - p = l_0 - l_1 r + l_2(\sigma^d + \bar{y}).$$

Uncovered interest parity: $r = r^* + \dot{e}^e$.

Definition: $\qquad\qquad c = e + p^* - p$

where r=nominal interest rate, $\dot{p}^{\,e}$=expected inflation rate, m=money stock, e=exchange rate, r^*=foreign nominal interest rate, p^*=foreign price level and $\dot{e}^{\,e}$=expected exchange rate depreciation.

To close the model we may specify expected depreciation as

$$\dot{e}^e = \dot{p}^f - \dot{p}^{*e} - \sigma(c - c^*)$$

where c^* is the long-run 'expected' equilibrium level of competitivness. The latter three equations can be used to derive

$$\text{IS: } \sigma^d = \sigma_0 + \sigma_1 x_f - \sigma_2 R^* + (\sigma_2\delta + \sigma_3)c - \sigma_2\delta c^* + \sigma_4 y^*$$

$$\text{LM: } m - p = l_0 - l_1(\dot{p}^f + R^* - \delta(c - c^*)) + l_2(\sigma + \bar{y})$$

where $R^* = r^* - \dot{p}^{*e}$, the foreign real interest rate. If we let $m - p$ be represented by x_m, monetary policy, and suppose that $\dot{p}^f, c^*$ are functions of monetary and fiscal policy as well as other exogenous factors, we can solve out for the reduced forms (17.6) and (17.7). Various exogenous factors such as R^* have been omitted for convenience.

Finally, it is worth noting that other demand-side assumptions can be made without changing the basic format. Thus, under fixed exchange rates, for example, e can be taken as the exogenous monetary policy instrument with m now endogenous.

3 Lipsey (1960), indeed provides an elegant theoretical justification for this curvature.

REFERENCES

Carlin, W. and Soskice, D. 1985: Real Wages, Unemployment, International Competitiveness and Inflation; A Framework for Analysing Open and Closed Economies. Institute of Economics and Statistics, Oxford University, mimeo.

Layard, R. and Nickell, S. 1985: The causes of British unemployment. *National Institute Economic Review,* February, 62–85.

Layard, R. and Nickell, S. 1986: Unemployment in Britain. *Economica,* Unemployment issue, August.

Lipsey, R. G. 1960: The relation between unemployment and the rate of change of money wage rates in the United Kingdom 1862–1957: A further analysis. *Economica,* 27, 1–31.

Phillips, A. W. 1958: The relation between unemployment and the rate of change of money wage rates in the United Kingdom 1861–1957. *Economica,* 25, 283–99.

Part VI

Panel Discussion: The Implications of Hysteresis Effects for Unemployment Policy

18

Hysteresis: Some Policy Implications

DAVID STANTON

1 If I am to attempt to draw out the policy implications of this stimulating conference I will need to set out, as a preamble, what I think are the main points relevant to policy. I am also going to limit what I say to the UK.

2 *Reflation.* I have heard nothing at this conference that would support Government-initiated reflation as a means of reducing unemployment. The stark fact of earnings growing at over 7 per cent p.a. when inflation has fallen to 3 per cent p.a. or less overrides any attempt to argue that unemployment is so high because of insufficient demand. I might say, in parenthesis, that despite our good fortune in having papers and speakers from abroad there has been little attention paid to the contrast between Britain and nearly all the other OECD economies; Britain has had low inflation and high real wage growth: others have had wages and price growth falling.

3 *NAIRU.* There was an almost universal willingness to accept the Layard/Nickell model as a means of asking whether NAIRU had increased in recent years. In some trivial sense it has – wage inflation continues in the UK at over 7 per cent despite a level of unemployment well in excess of 3 million. None of the Layard/Nickell measured traditional determinants of NAIRU – union power, tax wedge and mismatch as measured by their index – have changed so as to increase NAIRU in the 1980s: union power however measured cannot be stronger now; the tax wedge has declined and policies have aimed to increase competition in product markets and hence labour markets.

4 I would therefore conclude that there is no major new policy initiative that can be drawn from the papers and discussion on NAIRU and its determinants as usually defined. A general vote for supply-friendly policies doing more to encourage responsiveness is probably consistent with the focus of this conference but I doubt if anyone could be more specific.

5 *Long-term unemployed.* An important theme in several papers and in discussion has been the role of the long-term unemployed. We have been presented with evidence that it is the short-term unemployed and not the long-term unemployed who exert downward pressure on wages. The explanation for this evidence, and consequently policy, can be divided into two groups.

6 First, there is the employer-based explanation illustrated by the flower analogy. If there is a surplus of labour, employers will often use length of unemployment as an initial sift: in a flower shop, given the chance of buying today's rather than yesterday's flowers, everyone buys today's. I think it is fair to say we have had no clear micro evidence for this theory and only a little evidence on whether employers are rational to choose the shortest durations. Suggestions that human capital depreciates during long periods of unemployment were made but many of us were doubtful.

7 Other interpretations suggest the long-term unemployed do not affect wages because they have 'withdrawn' themselves from the labour market, become discouraged job seekers and there are some microeconomic cross-section data to support this.

8 Olivier Blanchard and Dennis Snower focused our attention on insiders and outsiders as an explanation of the general problem and in particular an explanation of the long-term unemployed who are seen as a growing pool of outsiders. Attractive though this analysis is I find it says little about how to translate the explanation into action.

Existing Policies

9 It may help to focus discussion if, in the light of this short and limited summary of what I have heard at this conference, I examined existing British employment policies to see how the relate to our current knowledge of the labour market. Without needing to reach a consensus on the current level of NAIRU we can begin by asking whether policies are tending to reduce NAIRU.

10 *Training and mismatch.* The Youth Training Scheme (YTS), the initiatives in Schools (TVEI) and Higher Education (the Switch to Engineering) are designed to produce a labour force better equipped to deal with changing technology. The YTS also has contributed to a relative pay structure that shows signs of reflecting market pressures in this sector of the labour market. In the language of this conference, it has helped to turn 'outsiders' into 'insiders'; it has helped to ensure that concentrations of unemployment among the young do not affect pay increases and has therefore put downward pressure on NAIRU.

11 Training policies are especially relevant if you doubt the finding that mismatch in the UK has not risen since 1979. I would go further and

ask if some of the empirical findings about the long-term unemployed are not really findings about mismatch. In 1980/1 there was a major structural change in the pattern of demand for employment. Employment in manufacturing, especially vehicles, engineering and metals, fell very heavily. The people who lost these jobs have formed a shadow that has now worked its way into those unemployed for 5 years or more. The geographic concentration of these unemployed people, their work experience and skill, all suggest mismatch rather than discouraged workers. The real challenge to those designing policies is how to translate chronic pockets of unemployed people, who used to work in manufacturing, into an active part of the labour supply.

12 *Community Programme and LTU*. The focus of this conference on the long-term unemployed is reflected in specific employment measures. The Community Programme at a cost of £1 billion is expressly designed to provide activity for this group: to keep alive the habit of working; to prevent the unemployed from withdrawing from the labour market. But there are other measures also. First there is a new scheme called Restart which gives every long-term unemployed person a special interview to review what is available and suitable to his or her needs. Another new scheme called Jobstart pays £20 per week for 1 year to the long-term unemployed who accept lower paid jobs.

13 *Other policies*. Turning to other aspects of NAIRU, policy has brought changes which will have tended to reduce rather than increase it: the abolition of the earnings-related supplement to unemployment benefit will have reduced the average replacement rate; recent changes in National Insurance contributions and the abolition of the surcharge will also have lowered non-wage costs and hence lowered NAIRU. No one could give a precise measure of changes in union power or how various factors have affected it. But there must be general assent that it is lower in this decade than it was in the 1970s.

14 I do not want to end with bureaucratic complacency. But I do want the discussion to focus on new ideas and not ignore the existing package which I have argued is consistent with the broad thrust of analysis we have heard here in St Andrews.

NOTE

The views expressed here are personal ones, and do not necessarily reflect those of the Employment Market Research Unit, or the Department of Employment.

19

Hysteresis Effects and Unemployment

CHARLES ADAMS

In structuring my comments, I want to focus on two issues. The first concerns the various reasons for why there might be hysteresis effects in unemployment rates and the second, the implications which hysteresis effects might have for economic policy. In the process, I will use the idea of hysteresis to refer loosely to the possibility that a period of unemployment might essentially validate itself, in the sense that it might give rise to adjustments that preclude a rapid return to high employment conditions. In this sense, I take the focus on hysteresis effects as part of a broader attempt to understand the reasons for persistence in unemployment rates, particularly as regards the recent European experience.

The conference covered three major reasons why there might be hysteresis in unemployment rates. In broad terms, these were as follows. In the first place, a period of unemployment might lead to a stock of human capital below what it would otherwise have been, either as a result of a loss of previously acquired skills on the part of the unemployed or because of a failure to acquire skills on the part of the unemployed or because of a failure to acquire new ones. Secondly, a period of unemployment, and the weak demand that accompanies it, might lead to underinvestment in physical capital, giving rise to insufficient physical capital to allow a rapid return to high employment conditions. Finally, those who become unemployed might lack an effective mechanism to offer their labour to the marketplace when those who are employed manage to monopolize the wage-setting process.

There did not appear to be agreement as to the importance of each of these factors in giving rise to hysteresis effects. The lack of agreement appeared to be based both on a lack of empirical evidence on certain aspects of the unemployment situation and on differing views as to ways in which markets functioned. A number of participants expressed doubt as to whether losses of human capital could in themselves represent a significant reason for the persistence of unemployment, for two reasons. In the first place, unemployment generally falls predominantly among those in unskilled occupations, for whom any losses of skills are presumably relatively small. Under these conditions, only modest retraining is required to compensate for any loss of skills. Secondly, wages can always adjust to offset the consequences for employment of skill losses. Against these somewhat optimistic assessments, however, it has been suggested that the human capital losses implied by unemployment might be less tangible than generally assumed, and that they might be more difficult to offset by way of wage adjustments. The losses might include deteriorations in the work ethic and in the ability to discipline oneself for regular employment, and they might give rise to a permanent pool of unemployable individuals.

The potential for shortages of physical capital to explain the persistence of unemployment was also questioned. A number of participants pointed to the existence, in general, of some unused capacity and/or to the potential for *ex post* labour–capital substitution. It appeared to be widely believed that physical capital shortages were not an important element in the persistence of unemployment or a barrier to a return to high employment conditions. Of course, to the extent that physical capital did become scarce the returns to investment would be expected to rise, which would tend to induce an increase in the supply of capital. A self-correcting mechanism would therefore be at work, if incipient shortages of capital did emerge.

A considerable amount of attention was paid to the significance of insider–outsider models of wage determination as a means of understanding persistence in unemployment rates. The insider–outsider framework adopted by Blanchard and Summers is particularly useful in this context. In the Blanchard–Summers framework, any shock that leads to a rise in unemployment may be accompanied by long-lived unemployment, if those who remain employed (insiders) manage to prevent a downward adjustment in wages. The precise dynamics of unemployment depend on a number of considerations and, in particular, on the nature of membership rules among the employed.

The insider–outsider framework depends importantly on insiders having some degree of monopoly power. Their ability to set wages depends on employers being unable to bargain directly with the unemployed, and on the inability of new firms to be established to employ outsiders. The monopoly-type power of insiders is based ultimately therefore on constraints on wage bargaining between employers and outsiders and/or costs or regulations that limit the creation of new firms. Blanchard and Summers note the importance of these kinds of constraints but they do not note what seems to be an important implication, namely that the persistence of unemployment is likely to reflect conditions in a number of markets, and not just the market for labour. The structure of financial markets will be important because it will influence the terms and conditions under which finance can be obtained to set up new firms. Conditions in goods markets will be important in so far as they influence the incentives of employers to try to negotiate directly with the unemployed, and as far as they influence the possibility of new firm entry.

Having outlined some of the factors that have been mentioned as possible sources of hysteresis in unemployment rates, let me express a reservation. It is that several papers did not pay enough attention to the significance of price flexibility for the question of unemployment persistence. That is to say, they did not pay enough attention to the failure of prices to adjust to clear markets as being a basic source of persistence in unemployment, but instead emphasized considerations such as skill losses. In the process, one can loose sight of the fact that losses in skills etc. may not in themselves be sufficient to explain hysteresis in unemployment rates. One usually requires, in addition, that wages can not adjust to offset those losses, but if this is the case then the failure of wages to adjust becomes an important part of the problem. Alternatively, in a situation, for example, in which real wages are inflexible one is likely to experience persistent unemployment in response to any real decline in the demand for labour, even if there are no losses of human capital. Had more attention been paid to the role of price adjustment, it would have been possible to examine the implications of losses of human capital for the amount of wage adjustment necessary to return to high employment, and the possible role of hysteresis effects in making for an increasingly difficult adjustment problem.

In the absence of agreement on the significance of the various factors discussed for generating persistence in unemployment rates, it is difficult to arrive at concrete policy conclusions. In thinking about what some of the policy implications of the papers presented might be, it seems useful however to focus separately on long- and short-term issues, and to recognize that one is ultimately dealing with a failure of prices to adjust to clear markets when attempting to explain the persistence of unemployment.

In the longer term, the possibility of hysteresis effects clearly raises important issues in the area of micro or structural policies. While it is possible to conceive of solutions to deal with any immediate unemployment problem, for example, retraining schemes to overcome shortages of human capital, these can at best be partial solutions. Ideally, any longer term solution must lie in identifying the sources of hysteresis and in undertaking structural reforms that will increase the flexibility of prices in response to them. In this context, all of the explanations for hysteresis discussed at the conference involved some particular market failure and longer term structural policies can be directed at these failures. It has been recognized for some time, of course, that a number of European markets have been hampered by structural rigidities. Many European governments have accordingly undertaken measures to improve the efficiency of markets, particularly those for labour. The papers at the conference seem to confirm this emphasis on structural policies, at least in a longer term context, and will hopefully serve to focus attention on those rigidities that are of importance in giving rise to slow adjustment. The kinds of lessons that can be drawn from the insider–outsider framework can serve as an example here. To the extent that an insider–outsider problem is at least part of the reason for the persistence of European unemployment, structural policies need to be aimed at increasing the influence of the unemployed on wage setting. Such policies can be directed at, for example, closed shop practices, at the influence of trade unions on wage setting and at reducing barriers to setting up new firms.

In the shorter term, concerns about the extraordinarily high levels of unemployment in Europe necessarily raise questions about the desirability of demand inflation. Since restrictive demand management policies in the early 1980s may have contributed to the current levels or European unemployment, an easing of such policies might contribute now to a lowering of unemployment. The attractiveness of demand reflation will of course depend, in general, on a broad range of considerations including the extent to which weak demand is viewed as having been a major contributor to Europe's unemployment problem. As regards the potential for reflation to contribute to a lowering of unemployment, it seems clear that the returns here will depend on what are believed to be the sources of persistence in unemployment. In situations in which hysteresis is caused by losses of human or physical capital, with a failure of prices to adjust, the returns may not be very high. Surprise reflations might confront a rather steep aggregate supply curve, with large effects on prices and little or no effect on output or employment. Alternatively, to the extent that surprise reflations did lower real wages, they might have to be very large in order to bring about the declines in real wages necessary to offset previous losses of human and physical capital. In the insider–outsider type situation, there are no inherent capacity constraints to expansion. In this case, the constraints are related solely to whether surprise reflations can bring about a decline in real wage growth and hence enfranchize the unemployed. It is not clear, however, as to how governments could engineer such reflations, while at the same time retaining credibility for their anti-inflationary policies.

Against these somewhat pessimistic assessments of the potential for reflation to lower unemployment when there are hysteresis effects, there are some grounds for short-term optimism as regards the unemployment position in Europe. In particular, several of the negative shocks of the last few years have begun to reverse themselves: progress in reducing fiscal deficits and inflation is being reflected in less contractionary macroeconomic policies in Europe; the appreciation of the European currencies against the US dollar is allowing a given rate of consumption wage growth to translate into a lower growth of product wages; and the recent declines in oil prices are presumably imparting a significant stimulus to demand and supply. Nonetheless, it seems likely that sustained reductions in unemployment will also require improvements in the functioning of markets, with a view to increasing the flexibility of factor prices in response to disturbances to both demand and supply.

NOTE

The views expressed are those of the author and do not necessarily represent the views of the International Monetary Fund.

20

Hysteresis in Output and Employment: A Comment

MARCUS H. MILLER

It has been argued that, in the absence of overlapping wage contracts, there is little essential difference between Keynesian and Classical approaches to the determination of output and prices if expectations are formed 'rationally', see for example Parkin and Bade (1982), chapters 27 and 28. In this 'New' Keynesian analysis money wages are rigid in the short run, so output varies more in response to unanticipated shocks to demand than in 'New' Classical models where wages are flexible: but in either case output and employment fluctuate around a high employment equilibrium. We are indebted to Blanchard and Summers for their elegant demonstration of how rational expectations may be combined with a plausible account of wage setting in a segmented labour market to generate *persistent* responses to temporary shocks.

In this brief expository comment aggregate demand and supply schedules are used first to bring out the stark contrast between the now conventional New Keynesian and New Classical accounts, and the 'hysteresis' which comes from giving insiders sole influence on wage setting; and second, to illustrate how this hysteresis ensures that fiscal and monetary policies have 'orthodox' Keynesian results – but only if they come as a surprise! It is noted, however, how giving influence to outsiders can remove the hysteresis and replace it with sluggish adjustment.

In recent econometric work, Layard and Nickell have made the important discovery that *some* outsiders (the long term unemployed) cease to exert an influence on wage setting. There is, of course, the possibility of hysteresis arising from this source: but not if, as Layard and Nickell argue, there is an equilibrium relationship between the long term unemployed and total unemployment.

Three Accounts of the Effect of Adverse Demand Shocks

The comparison is easily seen by reference to figure 20.1 which displays aggregate demand and supply schedules in the upper panel and labour market outcomes in the lower panel. (All variables are measured in logs, but the axes are scaled so as to make output and employment commensurate.) Associated with the expected aggregate demand schedule D^e are shown the two short run aggregate supply schedules. The New Keynesian variant $S_k(\bar{w})$ is simply the marginal cost of producing output where money wages are fixed so as to generate full employment when the price level is at p^e. Should demand differ from what was anticipated so that $p \neq p^e$, this will affect the *real* wage, but not the money wage. If, for example, there is an adverse demand shock so that demand is as shown by D_A, then the outcome will be at point A_k. The forecast error $\varepsilon_k = p^e - p_k$ will, given money wage rigidity, show up as a change in the real wage (raising it from equilibrium $\bar{w} - p^e$ to $\bar{w} - p_k$ as shown in lower panel).

The New Classical supply curve $S_c(p^e)$ is less elastic as the cost of labour responds even in the short run. Adverse demand shocks will have less of an impact on employment and output as money wages respond as well as prices. The short run equilibrium at A_c found when the forecast error $\varepsilon_c = p^e - p_c$ corresponds to the gap between the "full information" demand and supply of labour schedules shown in the lower panel. Given an inelastic supply of labour, the fall of money wages, shown as δw_c, will offset to a large extent the real wage consequences of such forecasting errors.

While the short run supply responses differ in this way, the response to the demand shock will be identical in the longer run. If, for example, D_A was expected to persist, then both supply curves would promptly shift to point F as money wages were adjusted to match the new forecast of the price level to be expected at full employment levels of output and employment.

Compare this with the random walk possibility suggested by Blanchard and Summers. In that case, from the same starting position at E, the short run outcome would be that shown by the New Keynesian supply schedule. But were the lower level of the aggregate demand schedule correctly expected to persist, so would the low level of employment: if the criterion in setting the money wage is simply that it ensures the continued employment of those currently in jobs, then there is no need to adjust the money wage. Thus equilibrium would remain at A_k, indicating a permanent output and employment response to a temporary error of forecast.

Were demand to suffer adverse shock, of course, the story would be repeated with the new equilibrium shifting to a point such as B_k (while under New Classical assumptions, taking account of the adjustment of

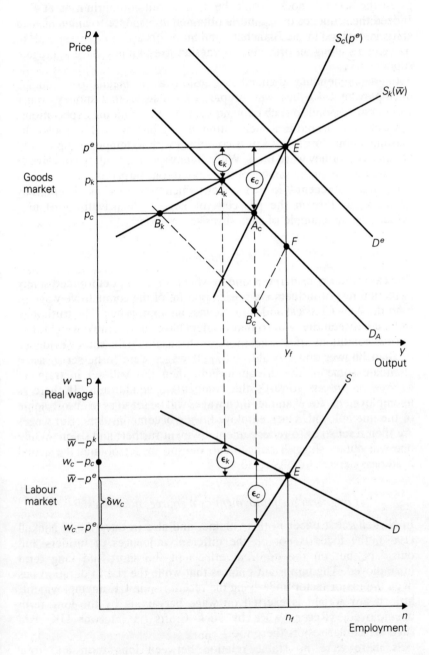

Figure 20.1 *The effects of adverse demand shocks compared*

price expectations and of the flexibility of money wages, the outcome, given the second shock, would be a short run equilibrium as at B_c). Indeed the sequence of equilibria obtained in response to *unanticipated* shifts in demand in the Blanchard and Summers account corresponds to movements along an orthodox Keynesian fixed-money-wage aggregate supply curve!

In recommending demand expansion as a means of reducing unemployment Keynes was prepared to assume that money wages would not respond to such demand stimuli. With rational expectations, however, it turns out that such a stimulus will only work if it "fools" the existing labour force – or if it is combined with a (temporary) policy of "fixing" the money wage level. While it may seem difficult to conceive of a policy of demand management based on surprises, it has been suggested that recent UK fiscal policy (which "conceals" fiscal deficits by setting against them the proceeds of large scale privatisation) may actually be an example of such surprise reflation!

A qualification

The case so far considered is one in which wages are determined solely in the interest of insiders – a polar opposite of the competitive wage of both the New Classical and New Keynesian approaches. The truth may well lie between the two, so that insiders have considerable weight, but outside conditions affect wages too: see for example the survey evidence of Blanchflower and Oswald (1987). If wages were to be set so as to eliminate some of the disequilibrium, then this will set in train an *adjustment process* towards the competitive equilibrium. If there is unemployment, for example, then wages will be set so as to absorb some of the unemployed. Once employed, they become insiders. But wages are then reset so as to reduce unemployment further; and so on. While one will obtain sluggish adjustment, one no longer obtains the actual hysteresis depicted in figure 20.1.

Long term unemployment as a source of hysteresis?

In Nickell's first paper in this volume, and also in Layard and Nickell (1987), the focus is not on the different influences of insiders and outsiders, but on the different effects of the short and long term unemployed. The important point is that while the rise in duration has been the major factor underlying the recent rise in UK unemployment, little if any weight is exerted on wage bargaining by the long term unemployed. (Recent work by Nick Crafts on interwar UK data suggests similar results there too.)

If there were no stable relation between long term and total unemployment, then there would be the possibility of hysteresis in this case too: adverse shocks could throw people out of the labour market never to return. What Layard and Nickell argue, however, is that there *is* a stable relation between the long term unemployed and total unemployment (roughly 1:5), so that the concept of a 'natural' rate of unemployment remains applicable.

Conclusion

The papers presented address important distinctions between insiders and outsiders, and between long term and short term unemployed. Whether the evidence points to actual hysteresis coming from either of these sources in the UK is not yet resolved. At the very least, however, these accounts emphasise the importance of market segmentation and of those factors which sustain it.

REFERENCES

Blanchflower, D. L. and Oswald, A. J. 1987: Internal and External Influences upon pay settlements: New Survey evidence, *L.S.E. Centre for Labour Economics Discussion Paper, No. 275*, LSE, March.

Layard, R. and Nickell, S. 1987: The Performance of the British Labour Market, *L.S.E. Centre for Labour Economics Discussion Paper No. 249*, forthcoming in R. Dornbusch and R. Layard (eds)., *The Performance of the British Economy*, Oxford University Press.

Parkin, M. and Bade, R. 1982: *Modern Macroeconomics*, Oxford: Philip Allan.

21

Hysteresis and Unemployment Policy: The Case for Activism

PETER G. McGREGOR

The presence of hysteresis effects in any economy considerably strengthens the case for policy activism, both in terms of supply and of demand management policies. This seems to me to be the major policy implication of the conference, although it is not one that was always immediately apparent from the various written contributions, nor from the ensuing debate. The subsequent comments accordingly attempt to provide a rationale for this optimistic, and possibly somewhat idiosyncratic, interpretation of the role for policy within economies exhibiting hysteresis.

The contributions to this volume generally imply that hysteresis effects arise out of some form of labour market segmentation. Such models naturally afford greater potential scope for policy activism than neoclassical 'natural rate' models in which 'the' aggregate labour market is regarded as an integrated whole. However, the wide variety of properties of the hysteresis models elucidated here appears to imply that any inquiry into the policy implications of hysteresis per se is misconceived: these are dependent on the precise definition of hysteresis, on its source and on the structural model into which hysteresis is incorporated. Furthermore, the technical manifestations of hysteresis also vary across models, encompassing multiple equilibria of a continuous or discrete nature (e.g. chapters 9 and 12, this volume), irreversibilities, and instability of equilibria (Cross, 1987). Nevertheless, some general policy implications do emerge, as the ensuing discussion, organized around sources of hysteresis, seeks to establish.

Consider, first, the insider–outsider models of Blanchard and Summers, and Lindbeck and Snower contained in this volume. Insiders determine wages with a view to establishing a desired relation between wage levels and insider employment levels. Outsiders' status in the labour market is of no concern to insiders and they have no power to influence wages or employment. The precise implications of the approach depend, of course, on the 'membership rules' which define the two groups, but some general comments on appropriate policy responses are possible.

First, at the micro/structural level, higher employment and lower unemployment are achievable for any given inflation rate through policies which increase the market power of outsiders relative to insiders. Policies directed at reducing non-wage labour costs, such as employment and training subsidies, reduce the rent-raising capability of insiders and would (under reasonable membership rules) increase the comparative power of outsiders. Other sources of insider power relate to their ability to cooperate with or harass new employees with impunity and to vary their own productivity within certain limits so as to influence overall efficiency (Lindbeck and Snower, 1986). Legislation or improved firm monitoring devices offer little scope for significant inroads here. Competition from new entrants who would employ outsiders might be effective, but would, of course, require governmental financial encouragement in imperfectly competitive industries.

Whilst the insider–outsider distinction need not be confined to unionized firms, this is the context in which the comparative power of insiders is likely to be particularly marked: collective action considerably enhances the power and range of weapons at insiders' disposal. However, anti-union legislation on these grounds neglects the possible positive role of unions elsewhere, and in any case may be regarded as ill-advised when the product market structure is, by assumption, far removed from the perfectly competitive ideal.

Extension of the insider–outsider framework to accommodate a more encompassing view of segmentation promises a profitable link-up with dual labour market theories and recent notions of the 'core' and 'peripheral' workforce, which may prove capable of explaining other features of recent European labour market experience such as the growth in the use of contractual labour and part-time (predominantly female) employment.

At the macroeconomic level the power of outsiders relative to insiders would be increased by the adoption of flexible prices and incomes policies since these restrict insiders' wage increases, although the feasibility of such policies which do not frustrate microeconomic processes has yet to be established. Similarly, successful demand management policies would enhance the power of outsiders relative to insiders. The comparative pressimism of the Blanchard and Summers chapter on this latter point reflects the 'only surprises matter' structure of their model, familiar from the New Classical Macroeconomics literature, although hysteresis effects introduce a handle through which policy shocks exert a permanent influence on economic activity. This structure ensures the ineffectiveness of systematic demand management policies since these become part of the private sector's information set and thus are rendered incapable of generating surprises under Muth-rational expectations. Under alternative, and arguably more relevant, expectation formation schemes for evaluating short-run macro-policy, systematic expansionary policies would have sustained beneficial effects on real activity.

Whilst it is particularly interesting and instructive to build hysteresis effects into macroeconomic contexts which are known to be otherwise inimical to policy activism, there can be no presumption that this necessarily informs us about the real world. Insider–outsider relations could be incorporated into a range of alternative structural models with radically different results (although, admittedly, this may amount to introducing additional hysteresis effects into systems which already exhibit hysteresis properties).

The sources of hysteresis emphasized by other contributions all focus on the possible effects of unemployment experience on labour market behaviour. One variant of this asserts a deterioration in human capital through the 'deskilling' effects of prolonged unemployment. Another view, analysed in some depth by Tötsch, emphasizes the impact of the duration of unemployment on employability through the signal this conveys to employers' screening devices rather than through actual changes in productivity. A further link with segmented labour market theory is reflected in the notion that workers' 'tastes' for leisure *vis-à-vis* work may be endogenous with respect to unemployment duration. Each of these arguments implies a degree of stratification of the labour market with respect to the duration of unemployment, and implies that there exists the possibility of improving the unemployment situation with no deterioration in inflation if appropriate micro/structural policies are pursued.

If deskilling is an important phenomenon, then schemes directed at 'reskilling' the longer term unemployed, through some combination of retraining and work experience programmes, would be appropriate. There is also a reasonable prospect that such schemes would at least improve the signal conveyed to potential employers by participants, but this depends on the existence of convincing public sector programmes. If changing 'tastes' are important, there is no reason to suppose that such changes are irreversible, so that retraining and work experience may ultimately meet with some success even in this case. In fact the current 'Restart' programme can be interpreted in this light, but this and existing retraining/work experience schemes appear to be of a rather minor scale in relation to the overall size of the current problem in the UK (since over 40 per cent of the unemployed have now been so for in excess of 1 year). Also, an employment subsidy for the long-term unemployed could be implemented at little cost if it was related to unemployment benefit levels.

However, structural or supply-side policies merely create the potential for improved output and employment especially in the face of wage inflexibilities (of whatever form). The macroeconomic policy stance must be right if this potential is to be realized. In any case, models with this type of segmentation do appear to allow the possibility of some role for conventional demand management policy as Price's chapter suggests (even within the context of an entirely 'flex-price' model). The externality implied by the unemployment–worker quality link also implies the desirability of an employment subsidy.

Whilst Price's chapter is concerned with comparative statics, much of Nickell's first contribution is concerned with the dynamics of unemployment – wage–price interaction in a framework which allows for hysteresis effects. The model ultimately selected has apparently pessimistic implications for the effectiveness of expansionary policies, even when these are implemented at a position in which unemployment lies above its natural rate. Falls in unemployment initially reduce the level of short-term unemployment significantly, and thereby exert a marked upward pressure on wage inflation.

A number of points are worth noting in this context, however. First, the result relates only to the dynamics of adjustment: a temporary inflation increase is to be traded off against a steady-state output gain. Secondly, the temporary inflation cost can be minimized by conducting policy in a gradualist manner. Thirdly, and perhaps least realistically, the relation could be influenced by other policies, notably those directed at wage and price moderation. Finally, and most importantly, the relationship is applicable to changes in unemployment of 'typical' form. Policy makers are not, though, confined to effect changes by means of general demand expansion of the sort which would be expected to activate this 'typical' reaction. Specifically, demand expansion can be directed at the long-term unemployed (at least in the first round of the multiplier process). Such a 'targeted demand expansion' would minimize the inflation cost, particularly if combined with an employment subsidy to, and prior reskilling of, the long-term unemployed.

All of the models developed in this volume incorporate aspects of imperfect competition, but in the interesting chapter by Dixon this becomes the focal point of analysis. The supply and demand management policy implications are, however (under some circumstances at least) similar to those we have identified with other hysteresis models.

Before proceeding to consider the empirical evidence, however, it may be worth noting that hysteresis notions, albeit under other names, are by no means confined to the labour market or to the body of literature considered here. For example, post-Keynesian cumulative causation models, and emphasis on the concept of 'real time', can be alternatively expressed in hysteresis terms.

Naturally, the policy implications of models which exhibit hysteresis only become of practical relevance if such effects exert a quantitatively significant influence in practice. The content of this volume constitutes a major contribution to our knowledge of this issue, although not surprisingly some controversy remains. Thus the chapters by Coe and by Nickell suggest that hysteresis effects, operating through unemployment duration, exert a significant influence on wage determination at least in the UK, and Budd, Levine and Smith present evidence of similar effects in the $U–V$ relation. Some supporting evidence for the insider–outsider approach is found by Blanchard and Summers and accounts of the composition of UK unemployment stocks and flows by Creigh and by Hughes and Hutchinson are consistent with the presence of hysteresis. However, whilst Jenkinson presents evidence in support of the existence of multiple equilibria in the UK, Carruth and Oswald could detect no trace of multiple equilibria in the sense of non-unique intersections of demand and supply curves in real wage space. Clearly, considerable scope remains for further empirical work devoted to discriminating carefully among conventional structural models and those incorporating hysteresis effects.

In conclusion, such evidence of hysteresis effects as currently exists, given the present level and composition of unemployment in the UK, seems to merit at least cautious experimentation with an appropriate combination of supply and (targeted) demand management policies of the type suggested by the contributions to this volume.

ACKNOWLEDGEMENT

The author acknowledges the financial support of the ESRC.

REFERENCES

Cross, R. 1987: Hysteresis and instability in the natural rate of unemployment. *Scandinavian Journal of Economics,* 89 (1).
Lindbeck, A. and Snower, D. J. 1986: Wage setting, unemployment and insider–outsider relations. *American Economic Review,* 76 (2), 235–9.

Index of Authors

Index by Geoffrey C. Jones

Index of Subjects

Index by Geoffrey C. Jones